CONTENTS

CHAPTER 3
Video Editing: The Invisible Art 46

CHAPTER 4
Shooting Video in the Field 61

Television Field Production and Reporting

A Guide to Visual Storytelling

Sixth Edition

Fred Shook
Professor Emeritus
Colorado State University

John Larson
Network Correspondent,
Producer and Video Journalist

John DeTarsio
DeTarsio Productions, Inc.

Routledge
Taylor & Francis Group
LONDON AND NEW YORK

First published 2013, 2009, 2005, 2000 by Pearson Education, Inc.

Published 2016 by Routledge
2 Park Square, Milton Park, Abingdon, Oxon OX14 4RN
711 Third Avenue, New York, NY 10017, USA

Routledge is an imprint of the Taylor & Francis Group, an informa business

Credits and acknowledgments borrowed from other sources and reproduced, with permission, in this
textbook appear on page 341.

ISBN: 9780205111589 (pbk)

Cover Designer: Suzanne Behnke

Library of Congress Cataloging-in-Publication Data

Shook, Frederick.
    Television field field production and reporting / Fred Shook, John Larson, John DeTarsio.—6th ed.
        p. cm.
    Includes bibliographical references and index.
    ISBN 978-0-205-11158-9
    1. Television broadcasting of news.   2. Television—Production and direction.
    I. Larson, John, 1953-   II. DeTarsio, John.   III. Title.
PN4784.T4S53 2011
070.1—dc23   2011051038

Employ your time in improving yourself by other men's writings,
so that you shall gain easily what others have labored hard for.
—Socrates

*The National Press Photographers Association recommends
this book for both beginning students in the field of news photography
and for advanced educational training. Professionals who have been in
the business for years will find the pages to be a wonderful refresher
course and the thoughtful reader will see that this book not only
teaches, but makes us think ... no matter what our
level of expertise.*

—NPPA

CHAPTER 5
Writing with Light 82

CHAPTER 6
The Sound Track 104

CHAPTER 7
The Video Interview 126

CHAPTER 8
Video Script Formats 140

PREFACE

NEW TO THIS EDITION

Every year, audiences for traditional newspapers and television news decline, even as alternative media employ print and television's unique strengths to attract and hold today's fickle, impatient audiences. What are those strengths? The very ones *Television Field Production and Reporting: A Guide to Visual Storytelling* emphasizes in the sixth edition, as it has throughout its more than twenty-five years on the market: the use of images, silences, sounds, actions, and behaviors to show people to people, and to capture and communicate a sense of experience. The perspective widens in this edition to reflect, through practitioners' eyes, how to achieve those same goals while working in the field alone, as a self-contained visual reporter and storyteller.

This is the newest edition of a book that addresses what you need to know and master to become a visual storyteller, even when you must do it all alone – report, shoot, write, and edit. It has served as the harbinger and interpreter of how best to communicate with video for a quarter century, with each successive edition highlighting the best, most up-to-date practices and new technologies—not only for the medium at hand, but also for the audiences that coalesce around that medium. Some of the features of the sixth edition include:

- An all-new chapter, "Video Journalism: Storytelling On Your Own," by network correspondent and producer John Larson, offers insights on "backpack" journalism. He reports and produces stories for PBS Need to Know, and is a former Dateline NBC correspondent. Larson also has become an international "backpack" or Video Journalist (VJ) since he joined this book's previous edition as a co-author. In his latest chapter, he offers new, experience-based insights that will help visual storytellers — beginners and professionals alike—improve how they shoot, write, edit, deliver, and reshape visual stories for digital media.
- Far-reaching revisions throughout, including significant contributions by co-author John DeTarsio, network freelance photojournalist, who explains how one person can use the camera, microphone, video editing, and lighting as storytelling instruments to create compelling and memorable stories. He also describes how he works with story subjects to capture their most telling insights, actions, and behaviors.
- Important updates regarding "The Digital Millennium Copyright Act" (Chapter 14), which affect anyone who records and/or disseminates digital media content, whether in private, on television, the web, via social networking sites, or in commercial venues.
- This sixth edition features all color photographs and adds many new photographs that portray the Video Journalist and reporting teams at work. All photos reflect and illuminate contemporary storytelling practices and dissemination technologies.

▪ A revised chapter on shooting in the field (Chapter 4) that includes new tips on pre-planning, composition, camera movements, and effective use of the zoom.

▪ A revised chapter on improving your storytelling ability (Chapter 12) teaches you how to involve the camera in your reporting and emphasizes the importance of letting your audience experience a story as you did.

Television Field Production and Reporting: A Guide to Visual Storytelling is more than a book; it is three lifetimes of insights and approaches that the authors will share with you herein. Together, they have invested more than a century to learn what you can absorb in just a few weeks. Even better, you can learn from this book for years to come by using it as a professional reference. Simply knowing or being aware of something differs from deeply understanding, renewing, and applying that knowledge as circumstances change.

You will learn from this book proven ways to achieve excellence in your own reporting and storytelling, even as technology changes. You will discover how to become more innovative and creative, and how to take that extra moment to think and plan stories no one else sees, even while covering the same events and topics. That's a formidable head start on your competitors, who may someday compete against you for the same jobs you want, but without the knowledge or commitment to make themselves or their work unique. The authors will help you begin your journey toward that goal in the pages to come.

Finally, you are buying a work that will help you navigate the evolving world of solo or "backpack" journalism, in which the visual reporter and storyteller does it all – reporting, shooting, writing, editing.

This book is dedicated to helping you become one of a kind—a visual storyteller rather than simply a photographer or reporter. Anyone with a camera is a photographer; anyone with a microphone can be a reporter. Today it may seem as if everyone has a video camera, and everyone's shooting video and reporting stories. Relatively few among those multitudes, however, will ever become accomplished visual storytellers.

You will need additional skills and digital "languages" if you intend to make visual storytelling and reporting your professional career. At its simplest level, you will have to master two ways of communicating: one is with pictures, and the other is with sound, including the spoken word. Although it may sound easy, it's not.

Your images must sparkle with articulate meaning; your lighting must mimic the Renaissance mastery of light and shadow on a digital canvas; storytelling sound must become the other half of the image, because we "see" with our ears; your writing must incorporate not only the spoken word, deftly told, but all the tools of visual media. Storytelling is a learned art in a world where only excellence, originality, and interesting, relevant content will attract and hold the attention of viewers who patronize tomorrow's digital screens.

Your mastery of the visual languages in digital media and a commitment to excellence will help ensure a long, profitable, and rewarding career.

ACKNOWLEDGMENTS

The following individuals and institutions deserve recognition for their contributions to this undertaking:

The National Press Photographers Association (NPPA) for its sponsorship of the annual Television News-Video Workshop at the University of Oklahoma. This workshop is internationally recognized for its achievements in illuminating the art of effective visual storytelling. The distinguished professionals who serve as faculty and give this workshop its direction initiated many concepts that appear in this book.

NBC News national correspondent Bob Dotson is a close friend of the authors. His reporting has long been a hallmark on *NBC Today* and the *NBC Nightly News*. Chapter 1 of this book, "Telling the Visual Story," reflects a close study of Dotson's work and reporting philosophies and is a product of interviews and correspondence conducted with him for more than two decades.

Grateful recognition also is extended to photojournalists Ernie Leyba, and the late Bob Brandon, both of Denver; KUSA-TV: Patti Dennis, news director, Eric Kehe, director of photography, and photojournalist Manny Sotello; KCNC-TV: chief photographer Bob Burke, and the station's former helicopter reporter Luan Akin; and to all KUSA and KCNC staff and private citizens who appear in photographs throughout the book.

Other contributors include the following reviewers:

Kenneth Fischer, University of Oklahoma
Peggy Elliot, University of South Carolina Aiken
Joe Sampson, Miami University Ohio
Jeffrey Guterman, University of Pittsburgh at Bradford
Peter Galameau, West Virginia Wesleyan College

To these individuals and to those whose contributions are recognized elsewhere, the authors extend most grateful appreciation.

Fred Shook's professional experience encompasses television reporting, production, writing, photojournalism, and video editing. He has taught and worked nationally and internationally as a television producer, consultant, writer, director, and editor for commercial television, corporations, and government agencies. Shook is a National Television Academy Silver Circle Member for significant contributions to television over at least 25 years. He received a Rocky Mountain Emmy Nomination for writing, and the National Press Photographers Association's Robin F. Garland "Outstanding National Educator" award. He also is a recipient of the National Press Photographers Association's J. Winton Lemen National Fellowship Award for his contributions to television photojournalism. He has written *The Process of Electronic News Gathering; Television News Writing: Captivating an Audience;* and *Television Field Production and Reporting, ed. 1-4*, and lead author on *ed. 5-6*.

Network correspondent *John Larson* is recognized as one of the country's best storytelling reporters in investigative, breaking, and feature news reporting. Larson reports and produces stories for PBS *Need to Know*, and is a former *Dateline NBC* correspondent. He also serves as a reporting and storytelling consultant, and works internationally as a Video Journalist who does it all. His creativity and powerful writing have made him a sought-after speaker, teacher, and motivator at workshops and newsrooms across the country. His many regional and national awards include four DuPont Columbia awards, two Peabody awards, and 22 Emmys. Larson's accolades include National Emmys for Investigative Reporting of the Louisiana Police and Breaking Reporting coverage of the Houston floods. Most notably, Larson is a four-time recipient of the prestigious Alfred I. duPont-Columbia Baton Award, the equivalent of television's Pulitzer Prize for his investigation of the insurance industry, which became one of the most honored works of journalism in broadcast history; for an expose on racial profiling; and for his work with other NBC reporters covering Hurricane Katrina. Before he joined *Dateline NBC* as a correspondent, Larson spent eight years at KOMO-TV in Seattle, Washington, where he won 16 regional Emmy awards for his reporting.

John DeTarsio has worked for five news stations as a photographer, editor, and on-air reporter. At KNSD 7/39 San Diego, he became Executive Producer of Creative Development, before becoming a freelance network photographer and consultant. Today he works for all the television networks and their magazine programs, including *CBS News 48 Hours, CBS News 60 Minutes, ABC News 20/20, and Dateline NBC*, as well as for network reality shows. DeTarsio Productions' clients include *"Extreme Makeover, Home Edition," "Access Hollywood," "EXTRA," "The Today Show,"* and CBS Sports. As a consultant (www.DeTarsioProductionsInc.com), he works with national and international television photographers, editors, reporters, and managers, sharing his passion for visual storytelling. His awards include NPPA National Photographer of the Year, the national Iris Award, six national NPPA awards, and 46 regional Emmys. In addition to twenty-eight San Diego Press Club Awards and nine Golden Mic Awards, he also has received more than fifty regional NPPA Awards.

INTRODUCTION

Digital media that provide sound and moving images accomplish two things better than most other media. They show people to people, and they can capture and communicate a sense of experience. People have always invested in media that introduce them to interesting people, and give them a sense of "being there." Print- and audio-only media seldom come as close.

This book is a blueprint full of tested, contemporary concepts to help you achieve excellence in visual storytelling and reporting. It can help you prepare for opportunities only vaguely imagined now, and help you decide what further academic or professional areas to pursue in coming years. This book can help you prepare for a meaningful career, or shift directions in an existing career. It can help you think smart and work smart in the field, and help you create reports and stories that surpass those of even your most formidable competitors.

The following chapters thus emphasize how to tell compelling visual stories on specific digital media platforms. As you work with digital media, you may discover they function primarily as ways to *gather*, *process* and *disseminate* content. That leaves room in this book, and for you, to place greater emphasis on visual storytelling and writing for the eye and ear, than upon technology—but with a caveat. Mastering that technology on many platforms gives you ever greater creative latitude as you plan, originate, gather, package and disseminate information using various media formats. Professionals who have failed to keep up with changing times and job demands now face uncertain futures.

This edition reflects the proven ideas and tested wisdom of some of the best in the business–including contemporary video and television professionals who have learned to play every instrument in the orchestra. They can do it all–report, write, shoot, and edit video on various digital media platforms. Everyday, such professionals help viewers learn much about the larger world and themselves through stories about others.

Countless such pros once practiced their art and craft as a single discipline– whether as video editor, writer, correspondent, photojournalist, lighting specialist, or audio engineer.

Today they may perform all those tasks and more as video reporters and storytellers who work on their own to research, field produce, report, write scripts and web copy, update stories, set up lights, shoot video, record audio, edit video and audio, and present or record information vocally and for live shots and on-camera standups. As you will discover a bit further along, one such person does all this *and* anchors the news in the country's 53rd largest city, and had to build more shelves in his home to hold all his awards.

How good could such stories be, you might wonder, given all that's expected of these folks? But routinely, their stories equal and often outshine the work of larger, more expensive, and cumbersome crews. Video reporters and storytellers with passion and dedication consistently produce interesting, memorable, award-winning stories.

NEW TITLES FOR NEW JOB DESCRIPTIONS

Visual storytellers and reporters go by various titles in different regions and at different shops. This edition uses the following terms interchangeably throughout to identify anyone who reports, writes, shoots, and edits video reports and stories, whether for news, the web, or any other platform or field of employment. Please think of the terms as applying interchangeably to identify anyone who gathers, writes, shoots, and edits visual stories *alone*.

All-platform journalist
Backpack journalist
Backpack reporter
Electronic journalist
Electronic reporter
Multi-platform journalist
Multi-platform reporter
One-person band
Solo journalist
Solo video reporter
Video journalist
Video reporter
Video journalist
Visual storyteller

Titles aside, these visual reporters and storytellers work in many nations, both in news and fields beyond journalism. You can follow their representative work and activities in more than 100 countries at www.vjmovement.com. Sometimes, their assignments take them to other countries. They work for corporations; government entities; public institutions; military branches; public relations, advertising and marketing firms; and even as freelancers.

If you work outside journalism, be assured that every technique, approach and philosophy applies to you, as well, and to all visual storytellers whose job is to "do it all" by themselves, regardless of the profession, industry, or institution in which they work.

Should you be employed in a more traditional setting where it's commonplace to work in crews of two or even a half-dozen, this book provides the same valuable, up-to-date information that has made it the standard reference for professional visual storytellers and students around the world for more than a quarter century.

HOW TO RENEW OR JUMPSTART YOUR CAREER

Many pros spend years to learn and adopt the same storytelling philosophies, methods, and practices that you will discover in this book. You'll find such information valuable, whether you're just starting out, or already a pro who must keep up-to-date by learning new insights and evolving skills in visual storytelling. Countless other individuals may one day benefit further from the information herein, provided you choose to learn and apply it in your own professional work—and perhaps to someday "pass it on" as you guide others coming along behind you.

HOW TO EXCEL IN MULTIPLE CAPACITIES

The book also offers guidance on finding a starting point from which you can master each discipline progressively as a writer, reporter, videographer, editor and visual storyteller on various digital media platforms. You can gain proficiency in all these areas, just as thousands of others before you, by emphasizing whatever you do best and most enjoy doing, and then developing other skills along the way. Often, persistence separates winners from losers.

You also will discover approaches that can help you move your work from "good enough" to "good," and even beyond "good" to "outstanding." That's really what continued employment, job satisfaction, and professional growth are all about.

ANTICIPATE KEY INTERVIEW QUESTIONS

Where are you headed in life? A television executive from a large television ownership group sometimes challenges university journalism and mass communication students to contemplate their intended careers by considering "The Way It Was, The Way It Is, and The Way Will Be." He asks students if they're prepared to enter the professional world, posing the same questions he asks job applicants.[1]

- Why should I hire you?
- What do you want to be doing five years from now? When you're 40? What do you need to be doing now to achieve those goals?
- What makes you and your work different than the 50 others who want this job?
- What makes your storytelling style so unique that no one else can easily imitate it?
- What can you do better than anyone else who is already on our staff?
- Are you skilled enough to work with our marketing and promotion experts?
- How can you and the skills you've developed help this organization achieve greater profitability?
- You could be working in many non-broadcast careers that require broadcast knowledge and skills—using television to educate citizens in developing countries, for example, or bringing quality television to newspaper web sites. Why journalism? (or) the field you've chosen?
- We always like to hire professionals with obvious passion for their jobs. Tell me about your passions.
- I've read your resume and viewed some of your video stories. Tell me how well those materials represent your most important aptitudes and character traits.
- If all the stations in town look alike, what can you add to help make certain viewers choose our station?
- You know yourself better than anyone. How would you conduct yourself, both on the job and off, to always represent this organization in a good light? How will you dress? How will you act and behave in public when you're off duty— whether in small ways or large, both negative and positive?

NOTE

1. Based on proprietary information by the lead author, in affiliation with NuFuture.TV.

Telling the Visual Story

I'm sometimes asked what story I'd most like to do, what fire
burns in my gut? That story is the dullest one of which you can
think (the making of the Interstate Commerce Commission budget
comes to mind), and the fire in my gut is to look and listen for the
small things that will bring it to life.

—*Ray Farkas, Off Center Productions*

Reporters report. Writers write. They attend events. Observe. Tell us what happened.
If you subscribe to such conventional wisdom, your work will forever imitate what
everyone else is doing. Odd as it may sound, the most powerful visual storytellers
often stop reporting and writing, stand back, and serve as producers in helping their story
subjects tell the story.

Imagine for a moment that you have been assigned to cover a city council meeting.
Other journalists from around town are there, taking notes, recording city council members'
comments, listening to citizens make statements. It's journalism with a capital J. Except that
it isn't storytelling. That's because a meeting is never the thing that happened.

Let's assume city council is deciding whether to apply for federal matching funds to help
local minority businesses. Sounds like a clickable or turn-the-page story? How will you make
this story interesting? Should you make it interesting? Isn't it up to you to provide just the
facts? Isn't it your audiences' job to understand? Not if you wish to have a satisfying career
or wish to compete against other writers, reporters, and storytellers who labor to make their
work as interesting, visual, and understandable as possible.

Let's return to city council, this time visualizing an audience of one in our mind, an
approach that the Poynter Institute's Roy Peter Clark advocates. When he is struggling to make
something clear, he says he fantasizes a conversation with his mother: "If she asked me, 'What
did you learn at city council today?'" he says he would not respond: "The city council agreed
by a one-vote margin Friday to apply for federal matching funds to permit them to support a
project to aid small minority-owned businesses by giving them lower interest loans." He says,

"I might be more inclined to say, 'Well, Ma, minority business people are struggling, and the city council thinks it's found a way to help them out.'"[1]

Note how Clark converts the central character from "The City Council" to the more powerful and accessible "minority business people." Now we have real people, noninstitutional representatives, who can tell us their story from a people perspective.

If we also tell the story from their viewpoint, or even an observer's viewpoint, we can show their struggles, the forces that make it difficult to earn a living in the community, how they've tried to survive, and why they're failing.

We can still report the city council story, for it too is important. Once audiences understand why the story matters, then we can cover city council and cast the council meeting itself as a story element: the story outcome that remains unknown until council takes its vote.

THROUGH STORIES WE SHARE HUMAN EXPERIENCE AND UNDERSTANDING

We sometimes live inside stories. Sometimes they live inside us. Stories help us understand ourselves, and to grow in self-knowledge beyond personal experience. Stories also help us understand what all humans share in common, whether as children, parents, lovers, relatives, workers, senior citizens, or in belonging to similar cultures or religions, in which we embrace common values and codes of conduct. Through voyagers and explorers, past and present, we learn about places and people we may never visit. And in the end, most humans ponder what it all means and what happens when it ends.

Visual media help viewers feel they're part of the action, essentially experiencing the events on screen (Figure 1.1). The most compelling stories contain a beginning, middle, and unknown ending, the same format in which we experience our own lives and other real-life events. We've been telling stories this way since the first hunters gathered at night to relate the day's happenings: "We began our hunt before sunrise . . ." proceeding next to the story's middle where one or more characters struggle against an opposing force to achieve a goal, and on to the ending when the audience learns how things turned out.

Along the way, the best stories address larger issues. From them we gain deeper understandings—perhaps the value of patience and persistence, the futility of hunting in the dark, or what lethal dangers a hunter must confront to feed the clan. The story's narrative structure commonly begins with someone in pursuit of a difficult goal and follows a narrative timeline through to the ending.

"Amazingly, the same neurons fire whether we do something or watch someone else do the same thing, and both summon similar feelings," writes author Diane Ackerman. "Learning from our own mishaps isn't as safe as learning from someone else's, which helps us decipher the world of intentions. . . . The brain evolved clever ways to spy or eavesdrop on risk, to fathom another's joy or pain quickly, as detailed sensations, without resorting to words. *We feel what we see, we experience others as self.* (Emphasis added)."[2] Further understanding of this phenomenon comes from memory expert James McGaugh, a renowned neurobiology professor at the University of California Irvine. Dr. McGaugh says that when we experience something, positive or negative, our bodies release adrenalin, searing those memories into our brains more strongly.[3]

FIGURE 1.1

Photography captures tactile impressions of the environment that give viewers a vicarious sense of experience.

THE DIFFERENCES BETWEEN VISUAL STORIES AND REPORTS

Visual stories reveal someone's goals and actions as they unfold sequentially, *along a timeline*. They use moving images and sound to mimic how viewers experience the world in their personal lives.

Reports commonly emphasize just the facts. They may show people in interviews, walking here and there, and sometimes doing interesting things. In the end and with exceptions, however, they highlight facts and information more than they use video and field audio to help communicate a sense of experience or to introduce interesting people to viewers. Structure also differs. Reports may even begin with the story's outcome: "Five mastodon hunters suffered grave injuries early this morning . . ."

If you equate powerful visual storytelling with mere feature reporting, abandon such prejudices now. Images and sounds are different tools than words on paper or even words spoken aloud. Typically, print informs or reports first to the *intellect*. Visual stories commonly report first to the *heart*.

HEART. EMOTION. DEMEANOR

In turn, the emotional reactions that viewers experience help them understand the story's significance. Consider how emotion lends significance to events and situations in your own life: your favorite NFL team just won its eighth consecutive game and you *hope* today's injuries won't derail the team; unemployment is high and you're *afraid* you soon may lose your job; you're *excited* because you just found a job, received a raise, or won the lottery; you're *annoyed* by all the political ads on TV; you feel *intimidated* by that menacing dog next door; you feel *sad* and *angry* because your stock portfolio just lost half its value.

"Facts exist independently, outside people. Seven inches of rain in a night is a fact, so long as you merely see an item about it in the paper," observed author and scriptwriter Dwight Swain. "Let it wash through your living room and ruin two thousand dollars' worth of furnishings, and it takes on true meaning and significance for you. For significance, remember, starts within the individual, in feeling."[4] Clearly, the same thing happens to viewers when stories or situations elicit honest human emotions. Sometimes, the best writing may occur when your images help viewers feel as if those seven inches of rain are washing through their own living rooms.

During four years as the editor of *Life* magazine, Thomas Griffith, later a *Time* columnist, says he learned the different effect of words and pictures. "I concluded that *Time* was about meaning and *Life* about feeling, and that both were valid paths to take," says Griffith. "That gave me a clue to television's influence. I no longer scorn the way even sophisticated voters, while they might sigh for a sober debate over the issues, get as much from a candidate's demeanor as they do from his words."[5]

Note how Griffith differentiates between journalism's traditional currency— *meaning*—and what many journalists struggle to eliminate from their reports (e.g., *feeling*) on grounds that emotion biases meaning. But whenever audiences don't know why certain information matters, or find it dull or too complex, the best approach may be to package the information as a visual story. Stories that show how issues and events affect people draw viewers to the screen, because they help make information more interesting and accessible. They show how situations affect people.

Authors Tom Peters and Robert Waterman make similar observations in their book, *In Search of Excellence:*

> Moments that touch or surprise writers often go unreported in the storytelling process. Sometimes, writers strip feelings and emotions from their stories on grounds such elements are unjustifiable in objective reporting. But stories that don't touch feelings often wash over audiences and fade quickly from memory. The fact that we not only experience the world, but respond to it with honest, human emotions, gives meaning to life.[6]

WORDS VS. IMAGES

We cannot always trust words literally, especially in our role as journalists, corporate or other public communicators. Listen for a moment to the respective comments about the value of words versus images from individuals who have influenced many generations of Americans, past and present. Collectively, their perspectives may help you reflect on what words and images do, do best, and perhaps cannot do.

About Words—In Their Words

Most news is made up of what happens in men's minds, in what comes out of their mouths. And how do you put that in pictures?
Edward R. Murrow, CBS News

Movies are about making mental things physical.
John Carpenter, film director, composer, and screenwriter

Whatever is said hides what cannot be said.
Robert McKee, author and scriptwriter

Words don't tell you what people are thinking. Rarely do we use words to really tell. We use words to sell people or to convince people or to make them admire us. It's all disguise. It's all hidden—a secret language.
Robert Altman, film director ■

PLACING THE HUMAN PERSPECTIVE IN PERSPECTIVE

"What can television do that can't be conveyed—at least not nearly as well—in any other medium?" asked Ray Farkas, the noted network producer and visual storyteller, who once directed a documentary about his own brain operation. "How about touch and feel and context and character? Not the all-network aerial of the flood, but the terror of water creeping in under the doorjamb."[7]

In television journalism, one camp honors the word as the most legitimate, and sometimes the *only* acceptable form of information. For generations, these journalists have been told their job is to gather facts and write sentences.

They also have been taught the "product" they produce is information. "[Journalism] is a craft based on one premise only, and that's information, bringing information to the public," says Jim Lehrer, a partner on the original "MacNeil/Lehrer NewsHour." "We are an instrument of information and that is *all we* are."[8]

Adherents of this camp speak typically about "telling" the audience the news, even when they refer to stories on television. "[BBC radio correspondents during World War II] had a power different from TV journalists of today because they dealt in words only. Nothing distracted the listener's attention from their voices and the words they spoke," observed Robert MacNeil of the original "MacNeil/Lehrer NewsHour." "All the authority was in the word. It wasn't that it was beautiful or poetic language or anything else. It was just that the word was everything."[9]

THE VALUE OF PICTORIAL NARRATIVE

A second camp of writers understands the word's value, but they also have learned to see and think in images, in sounds, and as storytellers rather than electronic stenographers. These writers use digital media to communicate pictorial narrative and to package and produce sounds and images that tell stories far more profoundly than words alone. They tell and show not only what happened, but also let viewers watch and take part in the action, as those things happened.

Often, they plan the pictures first, before the words. "It is a better way. But it's tougher for a reporter; it makes you work harder and think more," says journalist Linda Ellerbee, who discovered the technique early in her television career. "It makes you write to the pictures and with the pictures, letting the pictures tell the story. Don't misunderstand. This technique works only when the pictures *do* tell the story."[10] (Figure 1.2 shows a photojournalist at work.)

At first, the pictures-first approach may seem alien, especially to those who have always thought of writing as putting words on paper and who think only words carry editorial content and meaning. But in this approach, no longer are the words always written first, then illustrated almost as an afterthought with semi-appropriate, semi-literate video or sound.

"Pictures are different than words. They are not illustrations of words. They are a different dimension of information," said Reuven Frank, then senior executive producer at NBC News. "Pictures are as different from words as smells are from sounds, but all four of those are kinds of information. Nor are they the only kinds. All the five senses inform."[11]

Frank believed that because words go mostly to the intellect, while pictures go more to the heart and emotions,

FIGURE 1.2

The photojournalist is a visual storyteller, separate and distinct from photographers who think of their job as merely to take pictures.

the best pictures from an airline crash, for example, might be a woman's stocking hanging from a tree, or a doll with a broken face, or waiting relatives, or perhaps the close-up shot of a wedding ring on a victim's hand. "These, in their way, can tell you more than someone saying in 'words' how many died, more than a newspaper report; more even than body bags being carried down a hill," said Frank.[12]

Linda Ellerbee worked with Frank during her tenure at NBC. "Reuven believed that television was a narrative medium, and that understanding if any, came out of the story, not from describing the story or explaining the story," she said. "We were to tell the story, that's all."[13]

SILENCE AS A WRITING TOOL

Silence can be just as powerful as sound, and more eloquent than words. Some of the most compelling World War II newsreel footage of atom bombs falling on Hiroshima and Nagasaki occurs when the music stops and silence takes over the screen. Nothing else competes for the mind's attention against the images of devastation.

Night after night, television viewers imitate the behavior of film audiences who seem to watch most closely when the screen goes silent, even for a few seconds now and then, to let a moment play out without distraction. "Very early . . . I discovered that viewers are more attentive to silent sequences than they are to dialogue scenes," writes filmmaker Edward Dmytryk. "When the screen talk[s], so d[oes] the viewer. Silent scenes command attention.[14] But still today, too few video journalists consciously build silence into their reports.

THE SILENT LANGUAGES OF THE SENSES

"In real life, many of our vocabularies are wordless and silent. The raised eyebrow, the downcast eye, the wink, the turned cheek, the hesitation, the grimace, the blush, the stance, the choice of clothes, the scratch of an index finger against a person's back, all these are silent languages, a common, taken-for granted, and quite ordinary part of life," writes author Shannon Brownlee.[15] But seldom do informational media take much advantage of these silent languages.

Just as audio serves to draw audiences into the environment of a real-life event, listeners and viewers become more deeply and more tangibly involved if you allow them to see, and feel, and smell, and touch, and taste that moment. When you write to the senses, you draw viewers into your story in an almost physical way, and your work becomes a little better and more competitive. "Writing to address the five senses reaches out and brings you into the scene and touches your senses," says author James D. Mitchell. "If they're seeing, feeling, tasting, then they're involved in it."[16]

Writers generally have less trouble describing the visual sense than other physical sensations such as smell and taste. But the best video writers make addressing any of the senses sound easy. NBC national correspondent Bob Dotson, for example, portrayed Mississippi paddle boats as great floating wedding cakes; he talked of a teapot bubbling over an open fire; the night wind that flipped the page in an old man's hymnal; he caricatured a Texas wildflower enthusiast as having a face that could sell Marlboros; and he described an old Indian woman as thin as a dying moon.[17]

Often, in such writing, lyrical imagery emerges. It will be up to you whether you write, "It was a clear day and the wind wasn't blowing," or whether you write, "The day dawned as still and clear as if the sky intended to hold its breath."[18] Sometimes, the best writers help us see what we could not see ourselves, even standing next to them.

WRITING FACE-TO-FACE CONVERSATIONS

When you think about it, visual storytelling and film-making share much in common. But early television journalism took more of its cues from print and radio journalism, and in the beginning favored the written word spoken aloud, while treating images as an afterthought. Many early-broadcasts literally were the written word spoken aloud. A photo once displayed in the lobby at WFAA-TV, Dallas, even showed a person reading a newspaper into the microphone.[19]

Too often, today's scripts still echo old ways. When you write for video you are writing to show things and speak to people, not read to them. That means you must write conversationally, the way you speak. "Viewers are used to two things: reading the written language and hearing the spoken language. But [listeners and] viewers are not used to hearing reporters speaking the written language, yet that's the standard too often encountered in broadcast journalism," observed James Bamber, a television reporter with Société Radio-Canada, the Canadian Broadcasting Corporation's French television service.[20]

KMGH anchor Mike Landess advises, "Your writing should be so conversational you could read it to your mother over the telephone, and she won't know you're reading it."[21] In some respects, writing for video is like talking on the telephone to a respected friend, although you can never see or hear your audience responding. ■

PUTTING IT ALL TOGETHER

In media that contain moving images and sound, we are always writing with one instrument or another—camera, microphone, sound, silence, actions and behaviors, video editing, and the spoken word. But in the end, all those instruments come down to this: *In video media you can only communicate in two ways; one way is with images, the other is with sound.*

How might television journalism have developed in the late 1940s, had filmmakers handled its inception, rather than print and radio journalists? How might sounds from the natural environment have played a larger role from the start, at the hands of those who already had discovered that we "see" with our ears, and that all the senses inform?

Such ongoing differences guarantee that not all journalism, every journalist, or every digital medium, can achieve their utmost potential should visual reporters and storytellers employ only techniques and approaches most applicable to print media, in which words can dominate and sometimes overwhelm the visual story.

CULTURE IMPACTS PERCEPTION

Cultural influences also affect how we define and practice storytelling and reporting. For centuries, the spoken word, and later the printed word, helped us keep records and articulate everything from the banal to the abstract. Before the fine arts—such as music, painting, sculpture and theater—and before film, television, video, and the Internet, we conferred meaning upon things that existed outside ourselves by assigning them a word. Even now we may not appreciate the voices that still whisper to us from the past, whether as brushstrokes on canvas, or as a Pharaoh's likeness frozen 3,000 years ago in sculpted stone.

Today, words remain a vital communication tool. But leading still photographers and videographers have proven the still and moving images' worth as well. Powerful stills capture an exact and representative moment in time, often an insight or meaning that would have gone unnoticed in the photographer's absence. Yet a mere 50 years ago, photographers still lobbied for greater acceptance of "visual literacy" in journalism and

HOW HUMANS COMMUNICATE

We exchange knowledge each time we communicate. Frequently, we communicate a point of view or help make people aware of an issue. We might inform them to take a necessary action or give them a sense of what it was like to experience an event or situation. We might motivate them to buy, vote, or change their behavior. We might warn them, deceive them, or even entertain them.

We might use words both spoken or printed, still photographs or moving images, sounds of warning or affection, line drawings, audio, a color (red for stop, green for go), body language, a symbol, a line, or even a pyramid-shaped pile of rocks, but always we communicate.

Even sound blasting from a train or ship's whistle assumes the meaning we assign it, telling us, "Ten minutes until all passengers must be aboard!" Different symbols—words—might carry the same meaning if a train conductor were to shout into a megaphone, "All aboard in 10 minutes!"

In truth, there is no such thing as a neutral transaction. Humans cannot *not* communicate. This is true from the moment we begin to move within the womb and—for such folks as physicists, scientists, philosophers, musicians, actors, artists, authors, and filmmakers—even after we die, until our influence and works fade from all human consciousness and records. ■

the arts—the idea that images alone could convey meaning, even abstract concepts, and that viewers could "read" and acquire valuable insights and "experience" from wordless images. Today, we regard such ideas as self-evident.

Realizing video's great powers, never be afraid to show people and the consequences they experience, even in hard news, legal, education, and investigative stories. Most events and issues affect or involve people, and interesting people involve viewers. People who can be seen doing interesting things in your stories help viewers relate to important information or issues they might otherwise ignore. Not everything you create must be in story form. A half-hour newscast might not require more than one or two stories, with the remaining time devoted to short on-camera readers and straight video reports. Corporate video might achieve the corporation's goals with a traditional, fact-based format. But, if your audiences might not realize why crucial stories matter, or would better understand them with more context and perspective, video storytelling can take your work to unparalleled heights.

HOW TO PLAN THE VISUAL STORY

Visual stories take form the same way any other story originates, with a summary statement that identifies the story to be told. This summary statement is sometimes called the **focus statement**. You may also encounter the term *story commitment*. Terminology aside, the process is as simple as summing up the story in your mind before you start to shoot. Defining the story focus with discipline forces the video reporter not just to identify the story, but also to identify what is most important and interesting about that story. It embodies the centuries-old concepts of theme, story line, premise, and the reporter's point of view.

The focus is a simple, vivid, declarative sentence expressing the heart, the soul of the story, as it will be on air.[22] It is the "takeaway," the main idea or insight the audience will remember about your story. But until *you* know the story yourself, it will be difficult to tell it to anyone else. "If you can't express your idea for a story on a 3 × 5 card, in one sentence, you don't understand the story," in the words of television journalist Shellie Karabell.[23]

Sometimes reporters and photojournalists say, "My focus—or **commitment**—is to show the demonstration..." or whatever story they happen to be covering, but defining the story's focus goes beyond merely showing the subject. The story itself remains unidentified until it can be stated as a complete sentence: "The economics of farming affect all Americans." Focus statements help define the story's essence. Until you've defined the story firmly in your mind, you can't tell it to anyone else. Simple as the idea sounds, it is often overlooked.

THE BEST STORIES CONVEY A SENSE OF PROGRESSION

As a storyteller, remember to search for elements that will help your story develop or progress. Something is happening. Somebody is trying to accomplish something. Somebody is going somewhere. Somebody is involved in something. Often, the most compelling stories address the story subject's struggle to attain something important or valuable. Jack Bickham, author of the book, *Apple Dumpling Gang*, and other works, said every good story involves a strong central character engaged in the quest for a goal against opposition.[24]

If you can process the story in your mind, identify what the story subject wants to achieve (and why), and make sense of the story visually, you're on the road to reporting stories people want to watch.

The process requires an ability to notice real-life happening as it happens, an ability to find something interesting in it, and an ability to use images and sound to capture and transmit that experience to a viewing audience. In the hands of those who possess such skills, video ranks among the most powerful media in the world.

FIND IMAGES THAT CONVEY A CLEAR STORY FOCUS

A telling distinction separates photographers and **photojournalists**. "Anyone with a camera is a photographer," says Larry Hatteberg, a KAKE-TV video journalist who has been telling award-winning stories with his camera for most of his career (Figure 1.3). "My mother is a photographer; my grandmother is a photographer," says Hatteberg, "but no one is a photojournalist until they learn how to tell the visual story."[25]

Whether you work alone, in a crew, or even with just one other person, Hatteberg's definition of the photojournalist extends to everyone involved. "In television," says Hatteberg, "everyone's contribution is coequal."[26] Still, some video photographers have never tried to tell a visual story before they become solo journalists, and not all video reporters have learned to think of themselves as visual storytellers, even though their final product is built around—and upon—images.

To achieve excellence in visual storytelling, video journalists typically decrease their on-screen presence. "Telling" the audience is lecturing. "Showing" the audience is teaching. "Letting the audience experience the moment" is visual storytelling. Wise reporters know they are never the story or even the "star" of the story. They work instead to step back and produce other people's reality. They work to sell the people in their story and then let the people themselves sell the story. They may still appear on screen in a standup and during an interview, but seldom more, in stories less than two minutes in length. Obviously, exceptions will occur.

At first, this approach may feel foreign, even awkward, to reporters whose job is, after all, to report the news. Reporters know better than anyone that their name is on the end result. When a story shines, they receive most of the credit. When it fails, they receive most of the blame. Some reporters may also equate fame and

---

FIGURE 1.3

Anchor/reporter Larry Hatteberg has done it all, and still does it all, in his more than 40 years in television. He began at KAKE-TV in 1963 and never left despite network job offers for his ability to communicate visually, letting his subjects tell their stories. He has received more than 100 local, state, and national awards for news photography and reporting and is Kansas's most honored journalist.

Copyright © 2012 Larry Hatteberg

fortune with their frequency of on-camera appearances, and at personality-driven shops this may be true, although rare. "If people remember your stories, they'll more likely remember your name," says NBC's Bob Dotson.[27]

WRITE THE PICTURES FIRST

The strongest television news stories result when you *write the pictures first*. This advice requires that you think first about the left side of the script (the video instructions) before thinking about the words that will be in the report. In the field, look first for pictures that will tell your story. Search for sounds (and sound bites) that will add impact, emotion, and meaning to your reporting. Write words as necessary to interpret and explain what the pictures can't say (see Figure 1.4).

REPORTORIAL EDITING

This approach, known as **reportorial editing,** is the process of previsualizing the story, including the pictures, the sounds, the words, and even the visual and audio transitions needed to move the final edited story forward with logical structure and continuity. In essence, reportorial

FIGURE 1.4

In television news, words serve as blue-prints to help guide the pictures and sounds that make up television's content.

FIGURE 1.5

The video editor is a vital team member who influences the reporting process, from inception to finished story.

editing is the field search for the building blocks of visual communication, the equivalent of a mind's-eye **storyboard** that begins to take shape even before you arrive on location. Note that converting from two-person teams to solo journalists leaves the video journalist fewer opportunities to talk over the story with anyone, and less time to call sources while on tight deadlines or while en route to cover breaking news.[28] In such scenarios, two heads are better than one. But even working alone, you can think ahead to identify at least a rough story focus, think of images that might prove your main points, and at times leave yourself a voice mail about potential words, voice-over script, images, and sounds that might give you a head-start when you write the story, or go live at the scene.

WORKING AS PART OF A TEAM

Whenever you work with a crew, reportorial editing links all disciplines in the partnership among reporter, producer, photographer, and editor. There is no "partnership," no "team effort," until all members of the crew begin to see the story in their mind's eye along common lines.

Normally, such harmony of vision is impossible until all members of the reporting team, including the editor (Figure 1.5), begin to share their ideas, their visions, and their perceptions of the story. Such communication is rare, and without some effort on everyone's part, it cannot happen.

Perhaps the best approach is this: Talk out your ideas and negotiate them with one another. Talk to the assignment editor or manager. And the minute you get in the car with the photographer or reporter, start talking again. Ask yourself and one another, "What is the story we're about to cover, and what do we want out of it?"

Often reporters may not even use the pictures they bring home to show viewers what happened. They use the pictures to illustrate their scripts, which are first written, then later "wallpapered" with available video. Slide shows, not compelling video, commonly result.

PROVE THE STORY'S FOCUS VISUALLY

Once the story has been assigned and researched and the story's focus identified, you or your team can proceed to prove the focus visually. Perhaps your assignment is to report about a new school district policy that requires teachers who suspect child abuse to notify police within twenty-four hours.

If you state your focus as "School officials have adopted a get-tough policy toward child abusers," you have charted a very specific course in the way you'll cover this story. If your focus is "Abused children have a new friend in the public schools," then the story may concentrate more on the teacher's role in helping protect children and veer away from officials who speak about putting child abusers where they belong.

If your subject is a routine warehouse fire, you may identify the focus by the statement as, "This is a big fire." Your "visual proof," just as your words, will then follow naturally. **Visual proof** is one or more shots that illustrate a main point or help convey the overall story focus. If your focus is "Firefighting is long days of boredom, followed by moments of sheer terror," then your visual proof will change accordingly. If, in the same story, your focus had been "This fire offered a study of the firefighter's ability to endure searing heat and freezing cold," your visual emphasis would have been different still.

Imagine the pictures and main points that would result if your story focus involved the high sugar content, and potential health dangers, of your community's top-selling soft drink. Now imagine how the pictures and main points of your story would change if your story focus were to address that soft drink's emerging popularity as a status symbol in developing countries. Clearly, your focus statement drives not only the story you tell but also the pictures you bring back from the field.

THE FOCUS MAY CHANGE

Sometimes, through prior research, you can adequately identify the story's essence and state its focus before you enter the field. At other times, the real story can't be nailed down until after you arrive at the scene. You may discover, contrary to the assignment editor's best-educated conjecture, "This is not a big fire, but it's giving firefighters practice for the next big one." Or you may determine "Tighter security could have prevented this fire," or you may watch even the most valid focus change before your eyes as the story develops (a firefighter becomes trapped inside the warehouse and rescue efforts fail).

The essential responsibility is to be ready to change your focus if the story changes or was improperly identified at the start. Any story suffers when a producer, reporter, or photojournalist imposes a preconceived focus on it, and the damage will be instantly apparent to the audience. Just as obviously, any story suffers when a focus is absent.

LOOK FOR A STORY FOCUS IN SPOT-NEWS EVENTS

There is a story in every event you cover, even when you are under a tight deadline and the story is not under your control. This often happens with **spot-news** stories or hard news events that are generally unpredictable. Assume that you have just received word of a fire in the central downtown area. You jump in the van and within minutes arrive at the scene. At this point, you may not know what's going on, whether anyone is hurt, or even what caused the fire. You spend lots of time shooting the smoke going up, the walls falling down, and perhaps you capture a moment or two of drama as fire victims are rescued. But you commit an unpardonable professional error if you return home without having asked yourself, regardless of whether you are the photographer or the reporter, "What is the story?"

TELL YOUR STORY THROUGH PEOPLE

Try to tell your stories through strong central characters engaged in compelling action that is visual or picturesque. So often, reporters try to tell the story themselves, using authority figures—the mayor, the fire chief, the sociology professor—to explain what ordinary people enact every day in far more compelling ways. The sociologist can tell you that suburban neighbors live in isolation, relatively anonymous to one another, but so can one of the neighbors. Simply ask her if she knows her next-door neighbor's name. When she scrunches up her shoulders, hesitates, then says sheepishly, "I don't," her information is just as valid and far more visually interesting and memorable. Why do we need the mayor to tell us the earthquake scene is a frightening mess when area residents can take us into their homes and show us the damage themselves?

Sometimes you will need authority figures in your stories, but strive to include everyday people as well. Such people can help sell your story, so your job is to "sell" them by bringing them to life on viewers' screens.

Storytellers are far less compelling when they tell audiences the story after it takes place, rather than couch it as a story unfolding in the present moment.[29] Strong central characters let viewers live someone else's life for a moment and experience the story as it unfolds. Viewers become more powerfully engaged and may remember the story far longer.

STRONG NATURAL SOUND HELPS TELL THE STORY

Night after night, television viewers sit and watch a half hour of news, then can't remember what they saw because they have been told what happened—not allowed to experience something of the event themselves. "The television reporter's contract with the audience lasts for about fifteen to twenty seconds," says Bill Taylor, CEO of NuFuture.TV. "Every fifteen or twenty seconds, the reporter must renew that contract, or risk losing the audience."[30] The use of strong natural sound gives the video journalist a way to renew the contract: Nothing beats it to help heighten a story's sense of realism. The sharp, crisp sounds of life give us a sense of being there and of having experienced the moment (Figure 1.6).

BUILD IN SURPRISES

When you report, try to build surprises into your stories to help sustain viewer involvement. A surprise is any device that helps viewers feel something about the story, helps lure uninterested viewers to the screen, or connects them more directly with the story's subject or main character. John DeTarsio, National Photographer of the Year,

FIGURE 1.6

In television news, sound is a primary form of communication. The microphone is thus a form of "writing" instrument that can be used to heighten the story's sense of realism.

San Diego, launches a fire rescue story with natural sound of the rescuer's words, "Gimme air! I need air!" John Goheen, three-time National Photographer of the Year, Denver, lets audiences peer into the bottom of a small bucket as the rancher holding the bucket says, "I call this my rain gauge. I reckon it rained an inch and a quarter or so." Surprises can be compelling visuals, unusual or unexpected sound, short sound bites, or poetic script, such as Bruce Morton wrote for a piece on atomic radiation: "Once upon a time on a Pacific Island, the sun exploded."[31] Always, surprises are little moments of drama, regardless of their form, that help renew the contract with viewers and lure them back to the screen.

KEEP SOUND BITES SHORT

Sound bites, or short excerpts from an interview, public statement, or spontaneous comment, can help prove the story you show. They are less effective when they are used as substitutes for your own reporting. An effective approach is to think of the sound bite as an exclamation point, both to help enhance the visuals and to punctuate story content. Especially in television, sound bites work best when they're kept short (five to fifteen seconds, or around the same one or two sentences as the quotes in newspapers and magazines), and when they are not used as an essential part of the main story. Otherwise, they may transfer editorial control to the speaker. For that reason, sound bites should enhance the report, but rarely should a specific sound bite be so essential that a report would fail without it. Remember that stories are different than reports, however, and offer more leeway. In stories, the sound bite may even function as a main point.

ADDRESS THE LARGER ISSUE

Most people will watch a story that tells them "Vacations are fun," but they may wonder subconsciously, "So what?" if that's all you tell them. Few viewers will forget your story if you address the larger issue: "The typical family vacation creates more stress than it relieves." Even routine traffic accident stories can address larger issues if you look beyond the event and search instead for the event's meaning.

CHALLENGE YOUR FOCUS STATEMENT

You can check whether you've addressed the larger issue by asking the "So what?" question: Immediately after you have stated the story's focus to yourself, immediately ask yourself "So what?" If you believe the audience also will say "So what?" when your story airs, look for a stronger, more interesting focus before you begin to report.

Often, it's as simple as challenging your original focus statement. Some reporters strive to "focus their focus" by asking the magic question, "What's most interesting or important about that?" repeatedly until their focus gels and they're confident they have the strongest story line possible.

VIDEO PACKAGES ARE FACTUAL MINI-MOVIES

You can think of video packages as miniature movies with a beginning, middle, and ending. Just as any other visual story, they tell the viewer where the story is headed, deliver the main points and prove them visually, and they build to a strong visual close. In some ways, they are similar to television commercials, which have a beginning (to establish a problem or a need), a middle (to introduce the product and show it in use), and an ending (to resolve the problem). Typically, the thirty-second television commercial delivers its messages with strong, often unforgettable, visual proof. Effective commercials further integrate strong sound, memorable writing, and creative editing to enhance the message. The same principles are true of the best television and Hollywood films—and of the strongest television and video stories.

THE LEAD

The beginning of any **package** is the **lead**. Like all story leads the first shot should instantly telegraph the story to come. Ideally, the lead is visual. If the story subject is a stranded rock climber, the package will better serve viewers if it begins with a shot of the stranded climber, not of bikers pedaling down a nearby highway. If the subject is the hardships of poverty, show something more meaningful than a shot of the county courthouse in which the welfare office is housed.

PROVIDE VISUAL PROOF FOR ALL MAIN POINTS

Throughout the package, one of the visual storytellers' or reporters' greatest obligations is to tell the visual story and to prove its main points visually. The main body of the story, the middle, cannot be constructed until the journalist has identified the story's main points.

"So often journalists find themselves with a notebook full of facts and a half hour of interviews, and they still may not have the story firmly in mind," says Dotson. "The trick is to realize that all those facts are your research, not your story. Then you can sit down and ask yourself, 'All right, what are the three or four main points I've learned today about this story?' Once you've identified those main points, you can then find ways to prove them visually."[32]

Perhaps a main point in your report about child abuse is that some 300 elementary students are abused each year in your community. Through voice-over narration you can tell your audience that figure, but the audience may soon forget what you said. No member of the audience can so easily walk away from that number if you communicate it visually.

A simple standup can accomplish the objective: A reporter in an empty school gymnasium points out the rows of bleachers those abused children would fill each year, then cuts to an extreme long shot to show that about every five years enough children are abused in just this one community to fill the entire gymnasium.

With sufficient thought and hard work, almost any main point in any story can be proven visually. The alternative, which will never amount to good television, is to write and narrate the main points verbally and illustrate them with generic video.

Even abstractions like inflation can be brought to life through pictures in ways that will stick in the viewer's mind. Say you've been given a half-hour to shoot a story on inflation. "The typical approach is to crank up the graphics machine and make some charts with arrows that point up or down," says Dotson. "But if you can think through a way to report the story with visuals, your report will have far greater meaning for your audience."[33]

On assignment to show inflation's effects, Dotson entered a Fort Worth meat market, with the camera running, gave the butcher a ten-dollar bill, and asked how much stew meat that ten dollars would have purchased a decade earlier. The butcher displayed a hefty portion of beef. "Now," Dotson said, "show me how much beef that same ten dollars would buy five years ago." The butcher grabbed his cleaver and chopped the once generous purchase approximately in half. "Now show me how much stew beef I could buy today with the same ten dollars," Dotson prompted.[34] The butcher again apportioned the meat in half and handed Dotson the remaining tidbit. It is one of those storytelling approaches that "make it memorable."

As another example, perhaps a main point in a story is that new restaurant openings suggest that eating out is becoming a way of life for busy people. In yet another story, a main point is that trucks exceeding state load limits are damaging interstate highways in your region. In either case, your creativity and imagination can provide an effective way to prove those main points visually. In the first instance, you might simply show the number of new entries in the telephone company's restaurant listings. In your story about road damage, an interview with an expert who only tells you what happens to roads when trucks exceed their legal carrying capacity won't effectively prove your main point. Neither will voice-over narration, illustrated with trucks traveling down the interstate. What may work to make the message memorable is something like a close-up of hot pavement in the summertime, bending and stretching in slow motion as truck tires hammer their way through the potholes.

THE CLOSE

The story's **close**, the ending, should be so strong that nothing else can top it. Ideally, the moment you first arrive on scene, you will begin to look for a closing shot. You can then build the rest of your story toward the close when you write it because you already know how the story will end.[35]

The closing shot of a story on poverty might be of a woman on Social Security as she sits at her kitchen table one night, before her a pile of monthly expenses she must somehow cover with her meager income. The story of a national figure who has just died might build to a closing shot of file video of that person, waving a final good-bye to a crowd of admirers.

Generally, avoid ending your story on a sound bite or standup. Save that for traditional reports. Stories demand satisfying endings with strong closing images and strong closing sound from the environment. Standups and sound bites that end a story abruptly rarely satisfy.

BE HARD ON YOURSELF AS A WRITER

The most inviting newspapers and magazines contain "white space," and the most inviting television and video scripts contain frequent pauses in narration (audio **white space**) to let a moment or two of natural sound play out or to allow a compelling moment of video to make its point. Unnecessary words destroy the impact of otherwise memorable moments. Yet, few television journalists use silence or pause narration to let a few seconds of strong storytelling sound and picture play out.

The moment of drama that plays without narration may be something as simple as five seconds of video and **nat sound** (natural sounds from the environment) as a passenger jet with damaged landing gear approaches for a landing. Perhaps the drama is that final moment in a pro golf tournament as the front-runner sinks a complicated putt for the grand prize—no words, just that pregnant moment as the ball snakes across the green and finally plops into the cup.

"When the pictures are telling the story, we should be able to get an idea of what the story is about, even [without narration]," says Fidel Montoya, former KUSA news director.[36]

WFAA photographer Tom Loveless and reporter Scott Pelley (now with CBS News) vividly demonstrated that concept in a report titled "Boaters' Rescue." The report, which earned a National Press Photographers Association (NPPA) First Place Spot News Award, shows the rescue of two persons who had been pitched from their open boat into a storm-tossed lake. Time and again, two volunteers on the bow of a pitching rescue boat reach into the water for the survivors—a twenty-year-old man and a nine-year-old boy. Finally, after eight hours in the water, the two survivors are pulled into the boat, brought to shore, and given artificial resuscitation. The story runs two minutes, twenty-seven seconds. It features forty-seven seconds of narration, a nine-second sound bite with an eyewitness, and segments totaling eighty-nine seconds that consist exclusively of pictures and natural sounds of the rescue, with no voice over. Two of the most compelling segments play for more than thirty seconds each with only pictures and natural sound telling the story.

In television, the reporter's larger commitment must be to clarity, and to attract and hold the audience's attention. Fresh, conversational writing, delivery, and powerful storytelling visuals help achieve these goals, as does a commitment to eliminate the unnecessary in every report. Audiences that fail to see much difference between competing newscasts and anchors these days will appreciate your originality and your memorable stories—and perhaps return until it becomes a habit.

WRITE FROM THE VISUALS

Some reporters might contend that the audience is at fault for not remembering or understanding the stories they see. But it's more probable that the blame lies with reporters whose stories flow over and around their audiences and fade quickly from memory because there was no drama, no compelling story, and few devices to engage the viewer's attention.

Even when words are essential to help tell the story, writers frequently put up with too much laziness and uncritical thinking from themselves. It is difficult to be harsh with oneself, but every television writer can eliminate information the viewer already knows or that the visuals communicate more eloquently. A more workable approach is to *write from the visuals*. In a story on homeless Americans, for example, the pictures might show a man in tattered clothes as he walks down the sidewalk with a liquor bottle in a brown paper bag. If you write *from* the visuals, whose message is "Whiskey numbs loneliness," your voice over might say something like "Joe's best friend is always at his side. Already it's robbed Joe of his family and given him cirrhosis." The opposite approach is to write the script first, talking about alcoholism in general, then find visuals that support the script. But this approach tends to damage visual and story impact. Words can more easily be written *from* the visuals than pre-shot visuals can be found to accompany the narrative script.

LOOK FOR A STORY WHILE CAPTURING UNCONTROLLED ACTION

So often, we think of an event as the thing we should photograph. If the president comes to town or a big fire breaks out, that's where many video journalists point their cameras—and keep them pointed. The same thing can happen on non-news events that occur outside your control, be it a cattle drive or a pilot's first landing on a Naval aircraft carrier. Event-driven video is one reason so many stories look the same.

BOX 1.1 CREATING AUDIENCES WITH EFFECTIVE STORIES[37]

Audiences appreciate thoughtful, well-produced stories with strong visual elements. Sometimes such criteria seem impossible to achieve, given the four-hour or less news cycle that dictates reporters' and producers' lives on television and the web.

The trick is to remember television's strengths and play to them. "If reporters spend their time covering the 'people' angle of a story, the anchors can then play a more meaningful role in the newscast by giving us some of the latest information and video on a story," says KLAS news director Ron Comings. "They can use graphics for information such as numbers in a story about budget cuts while the reporters focus on the people sacrifices that will follow.

"Now you have a newscast where the anchors are seen and heard delivering significant information and playing a more meaningful role as the station's most recognized reporters. They move away from the 'Vanna White' duty of introducing one package after another. They 'own' a piece of every story. Audiences actually get to see and hear them at work," adds Comings.

Remember also to seek minor victories in every story, advises NBC's Bob Dotson. Find the right word, record storytelling sound, write a phrase that works, shoot sequences that give viewers a sense of "being there," or shoot a scene that tells the story. Anything you can do to enhance viewers' sense of vicarious experience and understanding advances television's mandate.

Be mindful that some stories are best treated as reports that neither merit more than "an account of an event" nor a team's time investment to produce a package that emphasizes the story's focus on human perspectives. Other stories, such as school shootings and hurricane devastation, may require the entire newsroom's efforts to update the human stories for days or weeks on end. ■

LOOK FOR THE LARGER STORY

To find that larger, more interesting story, a good approach is to first capture the main event and anything else that happens only once: a wall collapsing, firefighters rescuing a pet from a burning home, or the president waving to admirers as he exits Air Force One. In the non-news uncontrolled event, you could show how six cowboys can drive a thousand cattle down a highway, how far the herd stretches, the stopped traffic, and the cowboy assigned to keep cows from bolting to freedom. Certainly, you'd want to be rolling as the Navy pilot makes her first carrier landing. None of those video images will help position your work as unique or exceptional, however, because anyone with a camera would be photographing such moments.

Once you've captured all the good stuff from the main event, then stop for a moment to look around—and think. Whatever the story, *look for people who are trying to get something done.* Such people help you find the story's soul. Now, it's not just a report about the 'President Comes to Town,' or 'Local House Burns Down,' but 'Local Family Loses Home, But Learns How Much Neighbors Care."

Maybe you're covering a house fire in which the hard news is the blaze itself. Look about and you may discover dramatic storytelling details wherever you glance. The telling detail, the story's journey, might lie in a neighbor's vigil from the sidewalk, as she waits to hear whether everyone escaped the burning home. Her vigil now becomes a channel that can elevate shots of leaping flames and falling walls into a narrative story with a beginning, middle, and an unknown ending. Most viewers won't stop watching such stories until they learn the outcome, in which, in this example, the woman's neighbors escape unharmed.

As you explore the story environment, also look for little two- and three-shot sequences that can add subtext and enhance the story's energy and pace. In our example, you might also happen upon a firefighter struggling to free a snagged hose. Maybe he loosens it in a few seconds and goes about his business, but that little tussle is a moment of detail, a small step along your journey to find and show human struggles and their resolutions unfolding on camera. Viewers will appreciate your efforts to help them become even more involved in the story as eyewitness observers and participants.

SUMMARY

In television news, there are only two ways to tell stories. One is with pictures. The other is with sound. Photojournalists, who may be both photographers and reporters, use the television field camera and microphone as writing and reporting instruments to tell compelling visual stories. In television news, the written word, although crucial to the storytelling process, seldom stands alone but is part of a complex package of information made up of images, colors, actions, sounds, and silence.

The most effective visual stories typically communicate a sense of experience to viewers by incorporating matched-action sequences and natural sounds. Something happening can be seen to happen. When the camera is closely involved in the action, the process somewhat duplicates how eyewitness observers and participants would experience the event.

Crucial to the visual story is a story focus, the journalist's equivalent of the script-writer's story line or premise. In news, the focus statement is a declarative sentence that summarizes the story to be told and helps give it clarity. Each story also requires a beginning, middle, and ending. Often the strongest stories are told through people engaged in visual and interesting activities. In most stories, it also is desirable to build white space or pauses in the voice-over narration to allow compelling pictures and sounds to involve the viewer more directly in the story.

Besides the camera, microphone, and computer console, another essential tool of photojournalists is the edit console. Here, ideas are put in relationship to one another, story pace is adjusted and refined, and the story's emotional outlines are given their emphasis.

KEY TERMS

close 19	package 18	storyboard 14
commitment 12	photojournalists 12	visual proof 14
focus statement 11	reportorial editing 13	white space 19
lead 18	sound bites 16	
nat sound 19	spot news 15	

DISCUSSION

1. What qualities separate the photographer from the photojournalist?
2. In what sense are the camera and microphone "writing and reporting instruments"?
3. Why can the edit console fairly be called a "rewrite" machine?
4. How does the nature of a television news report differ from a newspaper story?
5. What is the role of the written word in television news?
6. To what extent should television news stories be anchored around the word? Around the picture?
7. What is the important role of picture sequences in television communication?
8. Why is sequential video usually more engaging and compelling than illustrative video?
9. What is the story commitment or focus statement, and what are the procedures for determining it from one story to the next?
10. Why can most television reports benefit from a focus statement?

11. Explain the value of learning to write from the visuals.
12. What is the role of natural sound in television news reports?
13. Why are short sound bites often preferable to lengthy bites?
14. What techniques can the photojournalist use to help make news stories more memorable?
15. What purpose lies behind the need to "address the larger issue" in news stories?
16. In a television news story, what is meant by the term visual proof?

EXERCISES

1. Using only natural sounds and visual imagery, photograph or script a sequence or two that captures the moment and communicates a sense of experience about the subject. You might choose to capture the mood on a ski slope at opening time, the feeling of test-driving a used car, or of planting and watering a tree or flower. At all times, keep the camera involved in the action. The key is to help viewers feel as if they have participated in the event and experienced something of the story's environment.
2. Study the field reports in a television newscast and determine the percentage of stories that contain sequences and matched action. Note how many stories contain sequences and how many rely primarily on illustrated scripts (illustrative rather than sequential video).
3. Study television stories and commercials for the "visual proof" of their main points. How frequently are the main points proven verbally when they might have been made far more memorable with strong visuals?
4. View several television news stories and define the story focus for each. If the story's focus seems vague and uncertain, supply a story focus that would have given the story a clear meaning.
5. Turn your back to the television set during a newscast and listen for examples of the effective use of natural sound and sound bites in news stories and commercials. Pay attention to how often the sound or voice-over narration entices you to look at the screen.
6. Analyze sound bites and compare the impact of short, five- to ten-second bites with interviews of thirty seconds or more.
7. Study news stories and commercials for examples of "surprises" or moments of drama that reengage the viewer and make the story more memorable. If the stories you watch lack such moments, consider what elements could have been added to make the story more interesting and memorable.
8. Study a newscast and its commercials with the sound off to determine how "intelligent" or literate the visuals are. As a photojournalist, how might you have improved the level of visual literacy in the stories you viewed?
9. Watch a newscast and determine how many stories address "larger issues" as discussed in the text.

NOTES

1. Roy Peter Clark, "Making Hard Facts Easy Reading: 14 Steps to Clarity," *Washington Journalism Review*, January/February 1984, 24–26.
2. Diane Ackerman. *The Zookeeper's Wife*, (New York: W. W. Norton & Company, Inc., 2007), 237.
3. An indirect quote from James McGaugh by Lesley Stahl, *CBS 60 Minutes*, "Endless Memories," December 19, 2010. Stahl is quoted verbatim from the *60 Minutes* transcript accessed December 20, 2010 at http://www.cbsnews.com/stories/2010/12/16/60minutes/main7156877_page6.shtml?tag=contentMain;contentBody.
4. Dwight V. Swain. *Techniques of the Selling Writer* (Norman: University of Oklahoma Press, 1965), 39.
5. Thomas Griffith. "Goodbye to All That," *Time*, April 1988, 47.
6. Laurel C. Sneed. "Make Your Video Tell a Story (People are irrational, they reason by stories)," *Training*, v29 n9 p58–60, 62–63 Sep 1992: Quoted from *In Search of Excellence* by Tom Peters and Robert Waterman.

7. Ray Farkas. "Letter to Sean (Last name withheld to protect privacy)," excerpted from comments written in his private letter to a friend, April 9, 1992.

8. Bob Priddy, "The Courage to be Serious," from an interview with Jim Lehrer and Robert MacNeil, by Bob Priddy *RTNDA Communicator*, September 1990, 15.

9. Robert MacNeil, comments on the original MacNeil-Lehrer Report, from an address at the University of Kansas, February 10, 1982.

10. Linda Ellerbee, "And So It Goes: My Adventures in Television," *Playboy*, April 1986, 196–198.

11. Reuven Frank, "Almost Nobody Writes Silence Anymore," an address to the Radio and Television News Directors Association, Hollywood, FL, December 4, 1980, as quoted in *Vital Speeches of the Day*, Vol XLVII, No. 10, March 1, 1981, 293.

12. Ibid.

13. Ellerbee, Linda. "And So It Goes: My Adventures in Television," 196.

14. Edward Dmytryk, *On Film Editing*. (Stoneham, MA: Focal Press, 1984), 79.

15. Shannon Brownlee. Horizons Section, *U.S. News & World Report*, May 7, 1990, 66.

16. Mitchell, James D. "Touching the Senses," a presentation at the Oklahoma Writers' Federation 22nd Annual Conference, Oklahoma City, Oklahoma, 04 May 1990.

17. Dotson, Bob. *In Pursuit of the American Dream*. (New York: Atheneum, 1985).

18. Anonymous author. Cited by James D. Mitchell, "Touching the Senses," a presentation at the Oklahoma Writers' Federation 22nd Annual Conference, Oklahoma City, Oklahoma, 04 May 1990.

19. Brad Woodward. "Writing News for Radio, *RTNDA Communicator*, December 1986, 42.

20. Bamber, James. "Importance of the Word/Text in Reporting," an address at the SRC Storytelling Workshop, Montreal, Canada, 02 February 1991.

21. An address to journalism students at Colorado State University, Fort Collins, CO, October 22, 1991.

22. Fred Shook and Don Berrigan, "Glossary: Television Field Production and Reporting," Atelier Sur le Récit Visuel, Service National de la Formation et du Développement, Bureau de Montréal, Société Radio Canada, Montréal, Canada, 1991.

23. Shellie Karabell. Comments at the NPPA Advanced Team Storytelling Workshop, Lexington, KY, April 22, 2003.

24. Jack Bickham. *Scene & Structure* (Cincinnati: Writers Digest Books, 1999), 24.

25. Larry Hatteberg, "People Oriented Photojournalism," a presentation at the NPPA TV News-Video Workshop, Norman, OK, March 17, 1998.

26. Ibid.

27. E-mail correspondence with the principal author, June 27, 2007.

28. Eric Deggans. "WFLA-Ch. 8's move to drop fleet vehicles craters morale at the TV station," *Tampabay.com (The Feed)*, published on the Internet December 16, 2010, and accessed December 20 at http://www.tampabay.com/blogs/media/content/wfla-ch-8s-move-drop-fleet-vehicles-craters-morale-tv-station

29. Bickham, *Scene and Structure*, 2.

30. Bill Taylor. Conversation with the principal author, June 28, 2007.

31. Cited by Ed Bliss in his address, "Newswriting," to the 42nd Annual Radio-Television News Directors Conference, Orlando, FL, and September 3, 1987.

32. Quoted from e-mail correspondence with the author, September 14, 1998.

33. Ibid.

34. Bob Dotson. Comments in a live video presentation to Australian journalists, Sydney, Australia, August 11, 2010.

35. Jim Redmond, Fred Shook, Dan Lattimore, and Laurie Lattimore-Volkmann. *The Broadcast News Process*, 7th ed. (Denver: Morton Publishing, 2005), 109.

36. Fidel Montoya. Quoted from "National Press Photographer's Best Photography Awards" videotape presentation. This and similar tapes are available from National Press Photographer's Association, P.O. Box 1146, Durham, NC 27702.

37. Ron Comings. Comments during telephone interviews with the lead author from early March though mid-August 2004.

2

The Visual Grammar of Motion Picture Photography

The goal of visual communication is to expand the viewer's consciousness. The photojournalist seeks to reconstruct events in such a manner that viewers develop a sense of having observed and experienced the moment, and learned something from it.

Throughout the reporting and visual storytelling process, the emphasis is on *reconstruction* of events from raw material shot in the field, rather than on the *re-creation* of events. And in television, just as in theatrical filmmaking, photographic reconstruction works best when it embodies a sense of continuity or consecutiveness to help heighten the viewer's sense of experience.

To accomplish such feats requires an understanding of the **visual grammar** that enables the field journalist to break simple action into its complex parts for later reconstruction at the edit bay. In television and other visual media, no one can excel without an ability to previsualize and properly manage this reconstruction process.

THE SHOT

In motion picture photography the basic unit of expression is the **shot,** or the single, continuous take of material recorded each time the camera is turned on until it is turned off. Depending on action and content, the "average" shot is recorded in the field for some eight to ten seconds and occasionally longer. The guiding rule maintains that it is easier to shorten a shot during editing than to lengthen it. When recording in the field, hold the shot long enough for the action to conclude, or to portray subject matter adequately within the shot, and remember to give the editor adequate length in every shot. During editing, each shot assumes larger meaning in relation to the shots that come before and after it.

THE SEQUENCE

Shots are the building blocks from which the editor builds a representative composite of the event. A number of shots, related to each other to convey a single message, are combined to form the **sequence** (Figure 2.1). Action flows across the edits from one shot to another to create the

FIGURE 2.1

The sequence is a series of related images that shows an event as it unfolds. The process duplicates how an observer in real life might take in the event. In an edited motion sequence, action continues smoothly from one shot to the next with no disruption in continuity.

illusion that viewers are watching a continuous, uninterrupted action. Sequences help a viewer feel he or she has experienced an event because they represent the activity much as eyewitness observers would experience it.

Surprisingly, some videographers have never shot a sequence, and others cannot identify a sequence with any reasonable certainty—the consequence of scripts that are first written and then illustrated, sentence-by-sentence, and paragraph-by-paragraph, with random, nonconsecutive bits of video.

BASIC SHOTS

In essence the photographer has only three shots with which to build sequences: the long shot (LS), the medium shot (MS), and the close-up (CU) (Figure 2.2). All other shots, including the medium close-up (MCU), extreme close-up (ECU), and extreme long shot (ELS), are variations of these three.

LONG SHOT

The **long shot (LS)**, or wide shot, provides a full view of the subject. Accordingly, the long shot may show a full view of an individual from head to toe or perhaps be a view of an entire mountain valley. Whatever the subject, the distinguishing feature of the LS is its ability to show an entire view of the subject.

FIGURE 2.2
The three basic shots in motion picture photography are the long shot (top left), medium shot (top right), and close-up (bottom left). All other shot compositions are variations of these three shots.

MEDIUM SHOT

The **medium shot (MS)** brings subject matter closer to the viewer and begins to isolate it from the overall environment. Although a LS might show us an entire federal courthouse building, the MS might show only the main entrance. Whereas a LS of an individual might show the person from the feet up, a MS would show the individual from the waist up. The MS can be used to place the viewer's general attention where the photographer or editor wants it, without the jolting effect that might result from cutting directly from an ELS to an ECU.

CLOSE-UP

The **close-up (CU)** isolates the subject entirely from its surrounding environment. It shows a person from about the shirt pocket up and may show nothing more of a building than the doorway or a sign that identifies it.

CUs can help the viewer achieve a greater sense of intimacy and vicarious involvement with the subject. This suggests that if you want close, intimate shots, move the camera physically close to the action. If you wish to involve your audience in the action, you must involve your camera.

HOW THE BASIC SHOTS WORK TOGETHER

The basic shot designations of LS, MS, and CU identify shots according to their image size and composition. These basic shots function together in sequences in a manner roughly equivalent to how the eye works. Whenever we first encounter a situation, we normally make a visual overview to acclimate ourselves to the surroundings. When we first walk into an airport, we see the crowds of passengers and long rows of ticket counters (long shot).

Once we have taken in the full view and oriented ourselves, we begin to inspect the environment more closely, perhaps searching, through medium and close views, for an overhead TV monitor that displays flight departure information. For detailed visual inspection, we may walk closer to the monitor for very close-up views.

Even without moving physically closer it is sometimes possible to create the photographic equivalent of a MS or CU in our mind's eye through our ability to isolate an object of interest within the environment and concentrate primarily on that object with our full attention.

Beyond the basic LS, MS, and CU, other shot designations derive their names from particular camera movements or how shots are used within the storytelling process.

CAMERA MOVEMENT

The main job of the motion picture camera is to record action, not to create it. The photographer can animate otherwise static shots with pans, zooms, and tilts, but the goal is to record actual motion whenever possible rather than to infuse the scene with artificial camera movement. Nevertheless, camera movement has its place, as you'll soon see.

PAN

In the **pan,** the camera is swiveled on a tripod to show an overall scene, or the handheld camera is moved in similar fashion to "show all the scene" in a single shot. The pan is an artificial device that tends to call attention to itself. Although our heads can swivel, our eyes never pan, just as they never zoom. They only take individual shots. Try to pan a view with your own eyes: Notice how your eyes cut from one part of the scene to the next as you move your head. Even when we view a pan shot on the screen, the eye darts from one "shot" to the next within the pan as it isolates various views and builds a composite image.

BOX 2.1   RULES FOR PANNING

Rules that govern the pan are intended to help keep the viewer's attention on the subject matter rather than on the techniques of artificial camera movement.

Avoid panning altogether unless the pan is motivated by action within the scene.

Shoot static footage before and after the pan to give the editor a range of cutting points.

Always have something on the screen as you pan. Compose the shot so that as one object leaves the screen, a new object comes into view.

Adjust the speed of the pan to the subject matter in order to make camera movement less obvious.

Let each object you pan remain on the screen long enough for viewers to have a clear view of it.

Feather the start and stop of the pan, so that camera movement begins and ends smoothly and imperceptibly.

Alternatives to panning include building an overall composite of the entire environment to be shown, in LS/MS/CU, just as the eye builds its own composite of reality. ■

When you do pan with the camera, hold the shot steady for at least three seconds before you begin to pan, and again hold the shot steady for another three seconds after you end the pan. Editors appreciate this technique because it gives them options about where to begin and end the pan. Shooting a few seconds of footage before and after the pan also gives the editor static footage that can be used separately if necessary as static shots.

MOVING SHOT

If the camera swivels on a tripod or other fixed support to follow action, such as to follow a bicycle race, the result is a **moving** (or follow) **shot**. The moving shot is sometimes called a "pan with a purpose," but because the photographer's motivation here is to follow action rather than show a static object in panorama, the moving shot is technically not a pan.

COMBINATION SHOT

A variation of the pan and moving shots is found in the **combination shot**. The camera follows the action until a new moving subject enters frame, then picks up the new subject and follows it. The camera, for example, might follow a jet plane as it taxis; when a second plane appears in frame, taxiing in the opposite direction, the camera then follows the second plane. The combination shot produces a relatively long "take," which the editor on tight deadline can substitute for two or three shorter shots that otherwise would have to be edited together separately.

TILT SHOT

The **tilt shot** is the vertical equivalent of a pan: The camera tilts up; the camera tilts down. The tilt is commonly used to show an entire object that would be too tall to photograph in a single shot, or to reveal some new aspect of the subject: the unveiling of an artist's mural that covers the entire wall of a hotel lobby three stories tall, or from a close shot of clapping hands to the square-dance caller's face. The tilt shot also keeps subjects in frame, such as when football fans stand to cheer a touchdown, or to follow a firefighter's ascent up an extension ladder.

TRACKING SHOT

In the **tracking shot**, the camera actually moves through space to keep moving subjects in frame. No longer does the camera merely swivel to follow bicycle racers as it would in the pan. In the tracking shot the camera is mounted on some means of conveyance and physically moved through space to keep, for example, the bicycle riders in frame. For a tracking shot of a pedestrian walking down a sidewalk, the camera could be mounted in a car or other conveyance to keep pace with the subject.

TRUCKING SHOT

In the **trucking shot**, the camera itself moves past fixed objects. A trucking shot would result if, for example, a camera were mounted atop a cargo van and driven down a neighborhood street past Victorian homes or if the camera were mounted in the seat of a wheelchair and moved past a row of students in a classroom.

DOLLY SHOT

In the **dolly shot,** the camera moves either toward the subject or away from it: The camera is said to dolly in (toward an object) or dolly out (away from the object). To achieve smooth movement, the camera tripod is attached to a dolly, a simple frame or platform mounted on wheels. Anything from a professional dolly to a wheelchair or snow sled can be used for dolly shots, provided the device glides smoothly without bumping or jerking the camera. In some shops, the dolly shot may be called a *tracking shot.*

CHANGES IN CAMERA PERSPECTIVE

Perspective reflects the apparent sizes of photographed objects in relationship to one another as they appear at certain distances, in comparison with how the human eye would view the same scene from the same distance. No change in perspective is possible unless the camera itself moves through space. On occasion, the **zoom shot** may serve as a passable substitute for the dolly shot, provided the zoom is introduced coincidentally with subject movement. The zoom is a shot produced from a fixed location with a continuously

(a)

(b)

(c)

(d)

FIGURE 2.3

Note the change in perspective between the close-ups, taken from a distance with the zoom lens set on a long focal length (Figures 2.3a and 2.3c), and the close-ups on the right, taken by moving the camera physically close to the subject (Figures 2.3b and 2.3d). Subjects shot with the camera physically close look almost three-dimensional by comparison.

BOX 2.2   INCORPORATE ACTION IN EVERY SCENE

The great strength of video is movement. Children smile. Flags flutter and ripple in the breeze. Rabbits scutter through the grass. Rockets climb into the sunrise. The alternative to movement is still life and static subject matter, the stuff of every slide show. For this reason walls and signs make poor establishing shots in television.

In visual stories, the goal must be to incorporate movement into every scene. If you have decided to shoot an establishing shot of the courthouse, photograph people as they walk up to it in an establishing shot, rather than photograph the static side of the courthouse building. If the subject is a sheer rock cliff, follow an eagle's flight with the cliffs in the background. If the assignment is to photograph a lifeless fence, show it as it moves in the wind or as a bird takes flight from a corner post. ■

variable focal-length lens. If a child on a bicycle turns onto a country lane and pedals toward camera, for example, the camera can be zoomed back to keep the child in frame in an effect similar to the dolly's. A substitute shot is possible in a reporter standup if the camera zooms out to preserve proper composition as the reporter walks toward the camera.

Because the camera remains in one physical location in the zoom shot, there can be no change in perspective. For this reason, if you wish to take a close shot of an object, move the camera physically close to the subject. Although you can keep the camera at a distance and zoom in for what appears to be a close-up, the lack of true closeness to the subject is immediately apparent (Figure 2.3).

The **aerial shot** is achieved by placing the camera in an airplane, helicopter, aerial balloon, or even a flying robotic camera system. Aerial shots are unequaled in providing overall, bird's-eye views of traffic, floods, fires, terrain, and related subject matter. Because the camera physically moves through space, the aerial shot also can be used to produce both tracking and trucking shots.

STABILIZATION OF SHAKY IMAGES

Camera movement inevitably introduces the possibility of unwanted shakiness on the screen, especially when shooting scenes from vehicles and aircraft. Professional and amateur photographers alike rely on the **gyro-lens** to electronically steady otherwise shaky images. Special circuitry constantly monitors the image being photographed, electronically counteracting unexpected shifts and shakiness in the image from one moment to the next. Even handheld, walking shots can look smooth and fluid. If the camera is moved or shaken violently, however, the image may take a moment or two to stabilize. The gyro-lens takes its name from the gyroscope that allows planes and ships to maintain a steady course despite the contrary effects of wind, water, and gravity. Editing software also can help stabilize shaky images.

Chapter 4 explores in detail how to achieve steady images in your photography.

SHOTS THAT HELP TELL THE STORY

The LS is commonly used as an **establishing shot** because of its easy ability to introduce viewers to the story's locale or to the story itself. Among professional photojournalists and editors the practice is to avoid establishing shots of walls and buildings, which rarely tell viewers much about the story to come, and to concentrate instead on shots that help engage the viewer and instantly communicate the story to come.

Whereas an establishing shot can be a wide shot, it can also be a close shot, for example, of a foot tapping to the music at a bluegrass festival. A jury foreperson reading a verdict may be a more effective "establisher" than a LS of the federal courthouse building with a sign in front.

From time to time within a scene, the **reestablishing shot** is useful to introduce new action or subject matter or to reestablish a sense of the setting in which the action occurs. In a typical example, we might first see a motorist looking under a car hood at the engine, followed by a reestablishing shot of the overall scene in which a patrol officer pulls up to help. In another example, we might see a close shot of a little girl blowing a party horn, followed by a reestablishing shot to show her mother as she enters frame with a birthday cake and walks toward her daughter.

The **insert shot** provides the audience with close-up, essential detail about some part of the main action. If, in one shot, we see a woman slip something into her purse, the insert shot shows us the object in close-up detail.

The **point of view (POV) shot** shows the view as seen through the subject's eyes (Figure 2.4). If a ship captain looks out to sea in one shot, the point of view shot shows us the view as seen through the captain's eyes.

You can use the camera from the perspective of someone physically involved in the action or from that of the uninvolved observer. Whenever the camera represents the participant's point of view, the style is called **subjective camera**: The screen shows action as the subject would see it. If the screen portrays action as an observer on the sidelines would see it, then the style is called **objective camera**. (Note: POV also is a useful device to motivate legitimate camera movement, as explained later in this chapter.)

Action and reaction are critical components in the visual storytelling process. An action occurs, followed by a reaction. A woman looks down and smiles at an object off screen. In the next shot, the **reaction shot**, a baby coos and smiles in response. A food server accidentally drops a tray of dishes on her return to the restaurant kitchen.

FIGURE 2.4

The point of view shot (POV) depicts a view from the observer's perspective.

Action–reaction is a useful device to heighten viewer interest in a story. Left, (the action); right, next shot (the reaction). Many reaction shots also can also serve as cutaways.

In the reaction shot, diners pause in their conversation at the sound of the breaking glass and then applaud as the server takes a bow. Yet again, a baseball player knocks a home run. In the reaction shot, the team's coach jumps for joy. Reaction shots tell us how people feel about what happened (Figure 2.5).

The face and the eyes mirror the soul and the depth of feeling. Therefore, if you show action in your photography, look for the reaction as well. "The reaction is where most things happen," writes filmmaker and author Edward Dmytryk. "Reaction is transition, change, movement—and movement is life."[1] Often, the heart of the most memorable visual stories lies in the reaction shots.

The **reverse-angle shot** (Figure 2.6) is commonly used to introduce new action or to advance the action within a scene. Assume a scene in which a barber has just finished cutting a patron's hair. The patron pays the barber and exits frame. The barber yells "Next!" and a second patron enters frame with his back to the camera. The reverse-angle shot can then be used to give viewers a frontal view of the new patron as he approaches camera. To accomplish the reverse-angle shot, the camera simply shoots back along the axis line as originally established in the first shot.

FIGURE 2.6
A reverse-angle shot is accomplished by shooting an establishing shot (left), then shooting a second shot from behind a the subject in the opposite direction along the same axis line.

ONE SHOTS TO CROWD SHOTS

Other shot designations are defined according to the number of people who appear in the shot. Into this category fall the one shot, two shot, three shot, group shot, and crowd shot. In the group shot, anywhere from five to a dozen people or more, it is possible for viewers to identify individual faces. In the crowd shot, it is difficult to differentiate among individuals.

MASTER SHOT WITH CUT-INS

Over the years in traditional theatrical filmmaking, directors have commonly relied on the **master shot,** in which a single camera records a continuous take of the entire scene from one location and at one focal-length lens setting (Figure 2.7). After the main action is recorded in one take, the action is then repeated (or the photographer waits for the action to reoccur) in order to photograph **pickup** or **cut-in shots**. Typical cut-in shots include the CU or insert shot, reaction shot, and POV shot, as well as new camera angles to emphasize particular elements of the action. You might create the look of a two-camera shoot with a single camera, for example, if you were to make your master shot of a chorus singing holiday carols at a 9 o'clock religious service, and then wait for the 11 o'clock service to shoot cut-ins when the choir again sings those same songs.

A variation on the master shot with cut-ins occurs in the television studio or at outdoor sporting events whenever multiple cameras are used to record different facets of the action as it unfolds. Video signals from the various cameras are fed simultaneously to a central switcher in the control room or field production van and displayed on a bank of video monitors. At the central switcher a director looks at the

FIGURE 2.7

A master shot (left) is used to record an uninterrupted take of the entire action. The photographer then asks for the action to be repeated, or waits for it to repeat, and photographs insert or pickup shots to emphasize detail and improve story pace.

FIGURE 2.8
When an action is edited so that it continues smoothly and without interruption from one shot to the next, the result is matched action.

monitors and decides when to punch up a particular shot "on air" or to record it for later broadcast. Because the various cameras view the same action from multiple angles and compositions, it is relatively simple to cut from one camera view to the next as the action progresses.

Even when photographing with a single camera, the photographer can produce shots that can be edited together in **matched action** (Figure 2.8), if the photographer shoots **overlapping action** in the field.

Using one camera, the photographer must move it from one location to the next, corresponding to the locations of the various cameras as they would have been placed in a multiple-camera setup. Either the action is repeated or the photographer waits for the action to repeat itself in order to capture the developing action from each of the various angles. Done correctly, the result can be virtually indistinguishable from the action recorded in a master shot with cut-ins or through multiple-camera photography.

OVERLAPPING ACTION

Overlapping action means simply that action in one shot occurs identically in at least one other shot (Figure 2.9). If a fly angler throws a line into the river in an idyllic backlit shot, a close shot might show the fishing fly as it lands on the water's surface.

Because the line can be seen to land on the water's surface in both the LS and the CU, the action in the two is said to be overlapping. The editor can produce matched action between the two shots by cutting out of the LS at a point in the action identical to the continuation of the action in the CU.

MATCHED-ACTION SEQUENCES CAN BE SHOT IN SPOT NEWS

Even in spot news, the action often repeats regardless of whether it is of firefighters battling an apartment house fire or a police officer directing cars away from a flooded intersection. Even events that happen only once can be shot sequentially if the photographer anticipates the action. The photographer might decide to hold a defendant

FIGURE 2.9
Many activities in life, including those in most news events, are repetitive. Photographers who look for repetitive action can record shots of overlapping action in the field and use such shots to create matched action at the editing console.

entering the courthouse in frame during a continuous shot, **snap zooming** to the defendant's feet or to the grim face of the accompanying marshal, or the photographer might determine to shoot the action in such a way that the defendant will enter and leave frame a certain number of times. Snap zooming is a technique in which the photographer snaps the zoom lever, instantly zooming in or out for a new shot of an

BOX 2.3 TIPS FOR SHOOTING SEQUENCES

Even if the story moves in real time, there are ways to acquire sequences. The best way is to anticipate the action, to have the camera one step ahead of what's going on. If a woman goes to the ATM to get money out, you would probably begin with her walking up to the machine. You would also know that she'll pull out her ATM card. Maybe you should skip ahead and have the camera ready for the card going into the machine. With anticipation, you can be ready when the card comes into frame. You also know she'll have to push buttons to enter her pin number. At that point you may go to a wider shot, and then to the woman's face, always trying to anticipate the action, staying one step ahead of it, so you can build your sequences.

When you shoot, one of the biggest rules is not to interfere with real life. It's never appropriate to interrupt subjects with a "Hey, wait a minute," to catch up with the action because when we interfere with real life, it goes away.

The other way to shoot sequences in real time is through action–reaction. Whatever is going on you can build sequences by shooting the action, and then shoot reactions to that action. Examples include: someone speaks to a class and the students listen, cookies come out of the oven and a child watches with anticipation, or a high school basketball player shoots the winning basket and the crowd goes wild. ■

action. Later, the editor eliminates the few frames of video in which the snap zoom appears and edits together the action as though it had been shot simultaneously with two cameras, one set for a MS or LS, the other set for a CU.

The result of such planning in the field is overlapping action—the raw material that will enable the editor to cut together matched action.

JUMP CUTS

Jump cuts in finished video occur when action jumps unnaturally forward or backward in time or when an object jumps unnaturally into a new position on the screen. If in one shot the speaker at an outdoor rally has on a hat but in the next shot an instant later has lost her hat, a jump cut has occurred. Technically, a jump cut is an action that could not occur in real life. The action "jumps." A woman at the beach is seen wearing sunglasses in the first shot but no glasses in the shot immediately following, or a computer screen displays text in an establishing shot, followed by a MS of the same screen that is now blank (Figure 2.10 shows still another example).

When the action cannot be edited together seamlessly, or when it must be abridged, the editor often can fix the problem with cutaways, inserts, reverse-angle shots, and reestablishing shots.

THE CUTAWAY

A common device to eliminate jump cuts and to condense time is the **cutaway**, a shot of some part of the peripheral action that diverts the viewer's eye for a moment so that when the eye returns to the main action, the "jump" will be less obvious. In the case of the woman at the beach who wears glasses in the first shot, a shot of the setting sun and perhaps a second cutaway of a sandpiper hopping along the beach could be inserted just before shot 2 of the same woman now seen without glasses. Viewers can be expected to assume that while they watched the sunset and sandpiper, the woman had time to remove her glasses. In the story of a chess match, the cutaway could be a shot of the clock that measures the time allotted each player to contemplate the next move. At a news conference, the most hackneyed cutaway

FIGURE 2.10

A jump cut occurs when an object changes position or appearance on the screen instantly and unnaturally from one shot to the next. This example also produces a false reverse in the action.

shows a bank of television cameras recording the event or a close shot of a reporter taking notes. Besides using a cutaway, an optical device such as a dissolve or wipe can be used to eliminate the jump cut. A **dissolve** occurs when a scene fades to black on top of a scene that fades to full exposure (one scene into the next). A **wipe** creates the illusion of one shot being shoved off the screen by an incoming shot. As you will read elsewhere, straight cuts often are preferable to dissolves and wipes, which provide only artificial continuity.

THE MOTIVATED CUTAWAY

The typical cutaway is simply a device the photographer shoots to help the editor eliminate a jump cut and/or to condense the action (as when editing together two short cuts from a lengthy speech). Even more ideal is the **motivated cutaway,** which contributes desirable or essential new information to the scene. Instead of the gratuitous shot of television cameras at the news conference, a motivated cutaway might show the proud faces of the speaker's relatives as she announces her candidacy for office. Whatever the setting, the essential contribution of the motivated cutaway is to help drive the story forward and help sustain story development by providing new information.

THE TRANSITION OR REVEAL SHOT

Another way to link scenes is with a **transition shot,** also called a **reveal shot.** Transition shots give the editor a way to pivot from one sequence to the next, a way to link separate scenes without dissolves or wipes. Transition shots can be used to disorient the viewer momentarily, as in this example from film editor Michael Kahn, who describes a scene in which a group of people are sitting around the table, followed by a scene in which the same people are in line waiting to go to a movie:

> Normally you'd cut to the marquee to show a geographic reference, but in this case you cut to a close-up of the counter and hands exchanging money for tickets, or even a close-up of somebody's face. You [the viewer] don't know where you are, but you know you're somewhere different. Then you cut back to the master (shot) of all of us in line waiting to enter the movie. You go right to a close-up and then cut back to reveal the new scene.[2]

In another example, a CU shot of a ship's whistle could be used to move the story from a fish market along the wharf to shots of canning operations aboard a fishing ship.

Similarly, in a video package about diseases in ponderosa pine and elm trees, the transition shot might be used to move the story from a mountain setting to an urban area. In this example we first see a logger with a chain saw cutting down a ponderosa pine in a forest setting. Next we see the transition shot, a CU ostensibly of the same chain saw the logger used in the previous shot, followed by a cut to a long shot of an elm falling in an urban setting.

You can shoot the equivalent of an optical wipe in the field during a tracking shot in a newsroom; for example, the camera might move past a white pillar that fills the screen. The pillar creates the illusion of a screen wipe from left to right. In the midst of this wipe, while the pillar is still full screen, you might cut to a tracking shot that reveals your main character striding into the newsroom. The result is a natural wipe without the need for studio effects.

To photograph such transitions in the field, the photographer must already be thinking like an editor as he or she shoots. "Create a mental bank account of what you have shot and what you need to shoot," advises documentary producer Mary McCormick Busse.[3]

USING CAMERA MOVEMENT TO ENHANCE STORYTELLING

Shooting an unfolding story requires that you shoot with the camera off tripod, and that you have good reason—a motive—to move the camera physically or to zoom and pan. Let action or reaction motivate where and how the camera moves. Use such movements to take viewers along with you, or otherwise show where you want them to look. Let's assume that a wide, establishing shot shows a burning house, while the voice track talks about someone inside that house. In this example, the wide shot might zoom in toward the house to visually take viewers inside or at least suggest that someone remains inside. The same zoom in without purpose might distract or confuse viewers.

If we see a person walk down the street, or drive past in a car, we might follow the action with a camera, or concentrate on other essential movement or details, much as we would focus our attention in real life. We could photograph a woman as she walks through frame at a wedding rehearsal, then shoot a CU of her face and then her shoes, and finally take a wide shot as she walks away from camera.

Elsewhere the camera might record the bridesmaids' limousine in a wide shot as it glides through wine country. If we let action motivate camera movement, the next shot might show the limo approach the wedding location and stop; the shot after that might show the driver opening the limo door; then the bridesmaids exiting the limo in a MCU shot and walking out of frame.

As the bridesmaids walk away from camera toward the wedding site, their action might motivate a reverse angle shot of their "walk away"; and finally, the camera might follow the limo driving into the late afternoon light and disappearing from view. Instead of directing the action, action now directs the camera.

Indeed, we could stage, rehearse, and direct every shot, but anyone who shoots uncontrolled action rarely has the time or opportunity. Even then, viewers can tell the difference. On screen, we believe real-life actions and behaviors—far more than the stiff, deliberate, self-conscious behaviors of nonprofessional actors, or everyday folks who are told to "just act natural."

POINT-OF-VIEW MOVEMENT

The subjective camera perspective can further enhance storytelling by showing something from a moving subject's POV. Suppose a woman leaves her house and walks to her car. Within this sequence you could make a shot from her POV, with the camera positioned at her eye level, set to a lens focal length that duplicates what the human eye sees, thereby putting viewers in her shoes and seeing life from her perspective as she walks toward the car.

THINKING CAMERA

Another moving-camera technique is "the thinking camera." In a sense, the camera reacts to the moment as a person might. If an interview subject says something airworthy, but unusually intimate or heartfelt, the camera might drift downward, much as a respectful listener might look down at the subject's hands in her lap before looking back at the speaker. A reverse angle of the interviewer's reaction also would work, serving as a way to look at something else for a moment to honor the other person's feelings. Perhaps the subject might look off to the left, as if reliving a poignant moment. Audiences might accept the camera looking there as well, perhaps to show a picture on the mantelpiece, before it looks back at the person. The goal is to let the camera see and process the moment just as any person might. Used properly, the technique can help make television more intimate and sometimes less obtrusive.

SCREEN DIRECTION

In real life, subjects move in predictable directions. Yet on many news and "reality" programs, subjects swap directions on the television screen like Ping-Pong balls. The rule of thumb regarding screen direction is to keep the subject moving in one consistent direction—either screen right or screen left. Otherwise, viewers may be left confused and consciously or subconsciously frustrated.

The underlying cause of illogical changes in screen direction begins in the field, when photographers unwittingly "cross the axis line" to produce shots in which a subject first faces one direction on the screen, then in the next shot is shown to face the opposite direction. To envision the phenomenon, ask two people to face one another while you photograph them. In the camera viewfinder, the person on your left (subject A) will face screen right and the person on your right (subject B) will face screen left. Now, go to the opposite side of the two individuals, again viewing the shot through the camera viewfinder. This time subject A will face screen left; subject B will face screen right. The result is called a **false reverse**.

HOW TO AVOID THE FALSE REVERSE

The only way to avoid the false reverse is to avoid crossing the **axis line**. When the first or primary shot is made of a subject in the field, an axis line is established. One form of axis line is an imaginary straight line projected from the tip of the camera lens through the center of the subject and beyond (Figure 2.11). Some photographers use

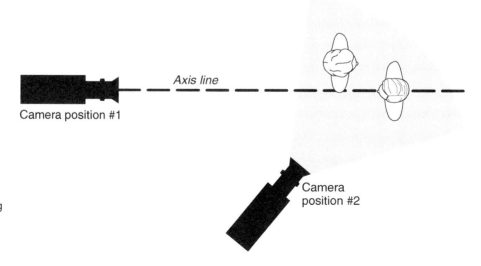

FIGURE 2.11

Eliminate false reverses in the subject's screen direction by remembering to establish an axis line, then consciously shooting on only one side of that line, not both.

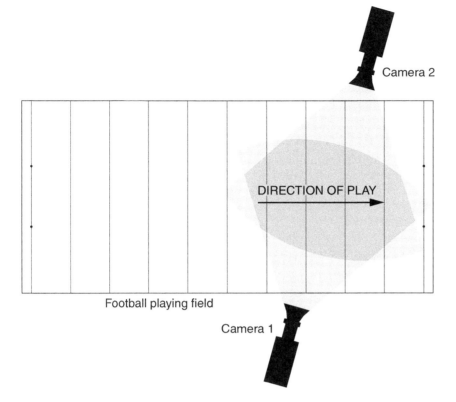

FIGURE 2.12
A false reverse in the action will result if the shots from camera positions on both sides of an axis line are spliced back to back. Shots made from camera 1 will produce action that progresses from screen left to screen right. Shots from camera 2 will produce action that moves screen right to screen left.

the term *vector line,* a similar concept used to describe the compass direction along which planes and ships move. Still other photographers simply call the axis line "the line." After the first or primary shot is taken, the photographer must commit to shoot on one side of the line or the other, but not both. If shots are taken on both sides of the line, a false reverse in the action will result.

Another form of axis line occurs when the action plays out parallel to the camera, for example, at a football game. The photographer can shoot on one side of the line or the other, but never on both sides of the line (Figure 2.12). Conflicts in screen direction can be eliminated in the field if the photographer simply remembers to keep the subject facing the same direction in the viewfinder at all times.

VARY CAMERA ANGLES

Variations in camera angle give the photographer a way to enhance visual interest from one shot to the next and are essential to help maintain viewer interest. Viewers will soon feel a monotonous sameness in the photography if every shot is taken from a flat, straight-on angle, with the camera at the same unvarying height from the ground. In every shot, work to find angles that are exactly right, even if you must climb a tree or lie on the ground. Your angle is too extreme if it makes viewers tilt their heads to see your picture.

"When you're shooting down the railroad tracks, don't just stand and shoot. Put the camera down low, on the rail. That way you build in some foreground interest and a more dramatic angle," says Boston photojournalist John Premack. "Or when you're shooting down a supermarket aisle, move over against one side of the aisle, close to the shelf, and note the increase in visual impact."[4]

PHOTOGRAPH PEOPLE AT EYE LEVEL

The rule of thumb is to photograph people at eye level, and to show both eyes. When you photograph children, lower the camera so that it looks straight into their eyes. Similarly, photograph adults straight on, not looking up or down at them with the camera unless, of course, you want to achieve a particular psychological impact (Figure 2.13).

ANGLES PROVIDE PSYCHOLOGICAL IMPACT

Camera angles also influence the viewer's psychological response to subjects. **High-angle shots,** taken with the camera high and looking down, tend to diminish the subject. The effect is similar to the relationship that occurs when one person stands and talks to someone who remains sitting. The person who stands maintains a psychological dominance. Such is the situation when the supervisor stands but the employee is told to sit, or in an adult–child relationship in which the adult dominates simply by virtue of his or her greater height.

Low-angle shots, taken with the camera low to the ground and looking up at the subject, make the subject more dominant and may even destroy the viewer's sense of control or superiority. Low-angle shots of an earth mover on a highway project can make the machine seem overwhelmingly powerful and destructive, whereas a high-angle shot taken from atop a nearby hill can make the same earth mover pale to insignificance against the terrain's enormity.

FIGURE 2.13
The angle of the camera, whether high or low, affects how viewers perceive the subject. In the picture on the left, emphasis is on the top of the subject's head because the camera was allowed to remain high and look down at the subject. A more desirable composition (right) is to photograph the subject at eye level.

CONTRAST AND COMPARISON

Visual sameness is the equivalent of dullness. In most areas of life, including visual communication, we seek variation. Just as a meal made up of four bowls of potatoes and gravy lacks interest, so does a story with four back-to-back shots of elderly residents at a nursing home. Do show us the faces of the older people, but show us also the unwrinkled youth and vitality of the children who come to visit or photographs of the elderly residents when they were younger. If your story is about the desert, try occasionally to show viewers something cool and green or perhaps simply the drops of water that slide down a bottle of beer as moisture condenses in the heat. In all stories, contrast and comparison are powerful devices to help give your subject additional screen presence.

COMPOSITION

Videography is a way of seeing on behalf of others. **Composition,** or the placement and emphasis of visual elements on the screen, lets the photographer control what viewers see and helps clarify the messages to be communicated. In motion picture photography, composition may be less noticeable to viewers because no shot stands by itself or communicates an entire story as it does so often in still photography. In motion picture photography, only when all the shots have played out is the story complete.

SUMMARY

Visual grammar comprises the rules that govern the visual reconstruction of events, including both the raw material shot and recorded in the field and the process of editing the material for broadcast. In television, the basic unit of expression is the shot. A matched-action sequence of long, medium, and close-up shots can be linked to convey a message.

Shots are further defined according to camera movement and function. Shots that incorporate camera movement include the pan, tilt, dolly, tracking, trucking, and aerial shots. Shots classified according to their function include the establishing, insert, point of view, reaction, reverse-angle, and master shots.

Matched-action sequences can be created at the edit console only if the photographer has shot overlapping action in the field. In other words, identical action must be present in at least two shots. If overlapping action cannot be photographed, or if action must be compressed, then unnatural jumps in the action—jump cuts—can be avoided with cutaways or optical effects.

Transition shots allow the editor to create transitions from one time, location, or subject to the next within a story. Angles and composition further affect the treatment of subject matter and how viewers will react to the subject.

Always, the goal is to create a visual reconstruction of events so compelling and involving that viewers are unaware of technique.

KEY TERMS

action and reaction   32
aerial shot   30
axis line   40
close-up (CU)   27
combination shot   28

composition   43
cutaway   37
cut-in shots   34
dissolve   38
dolly shot   30

establishing shot   31
false reverse   40
feather   29
gyro-lens   30
high-angle shots   42

DISCUSSION

1. Explain the meaning of the term *visual grammar*.
2. List the three basic shots in motion picture photography and describe their functions.
3. Explain how the three basic v can be joined to achieve a sense of continuity or consecutiveness in a scene.
4. What considerations help determine when a shot or the image size of a subject should be changed in a visual story?
5. Explain why it is important in film and television to have action in virtually every scene.
6. List and define the various shot categories, describing each shot according to its function. Be certain to differentiate between the pan and the moving shot.
7. Describe when an insert shot might also serve as a reaction shot.
8. Can a reaction shot ever serve simultaneously as a point of view shot? If your answer is yes, provide an example. If your answer is no, explain why not.
9. Provide an example of a master shot and list six possible related pickup or cut-in shots.
10. Explain the essential distinction between matched action and overlapping action.
11. Explain how jump cuts can be eliminated (a) when shooting a scene and (b) when editing a scene.
12. Describe the functions of the transition or reveal shot, and give an example as part of your discussion.
13. How can the photographer avoid the false reverse (a) when shooting action and (b) at the edit bench?
14. Define the psychological impact of variations in camera angle as a function of camera height in relation to the subject.
15. What unique considerations of composition affect television photography?

EXERCISES

1. Shoot a simple sequence of a subject that is under your control, using a long shot, medium shot, and close-up.
2. Shoot the same sequence, but this time purposefully cross the axis line so that you create a false reverse in the action.
3. Purposefully photograph two shots that would result in a jump cut if edited together and a related cutaway. First, edit together the two shots to produce a jump cut, then edit them so that the cutaway separates them. View and analyze the result.
4. Make two shots of an action plus a generic cutaway that can be used to divert the audience's attention from the main subject. Now shoot a motivated cutaway that also diverts the audience's attention but contributes useful new information to your story.
5. Pan a static subject, then reshoot the same shot, this time while following a moving subject with the camera to motivate the pan. Compare the result.
6. Shoot a master shot with at least six related pickup or cut-in shots.

7. Shoot a sequence in which the subject progresses through space, this time allowing the action to move into-frame, out-of-frame.
8. Shoot a matched-action sequence that contains an insert shot. Be certain each shot has overlapping action so that action can be matched at the editing bench.
9. Shoot a matched-action sequence that contains action–reaction shots.
10. Shoot a matched-action sequence that contains a point of view shot.
11. Find a subject that is not under your control and shoot a matched-action sequence. Remember to anticipate the action rather than to react to it.
12. Shoot a story in which you can move from one time, location, or subject to the next. Shoot at least three transitions or reveal shots that can be used to move the story to the next time or location.
13. Experiment with camera angle on a subject and note the variations in psychological impact that result.
14. Learn to critically inspect all elements within the viewfinder. Practice consciously composing scenes so that you show viewers only what you want them to see.
15. Practice composing a shot with two people in an interview situation until the shot is pleasing and well balanced and good enough to be used on television.
16. Find a routine subject and photograph it in a new way. As an example, you might show a knife from a Halloween pumpkin's point of view or a fast-food restaurant from a transient's point of view.

NOTES

1. Edward Dmytryk, *On Film Editing* (Stoneham, MA: Focal Press, 1984), 65.
2. "Michael Kahn: Film Editor at the Top," *Moving Image* 1 (September/October 1981): 46–47.
3. Mary McCormick Busse, "The Beginning, Middle and End: Continuity," in *The TV Storyteller* (Durham, NC: National Press Photographers Association, 1985), 4.
4. John Premack, comments to a critique group, NPPA TV News-Video Workshop, Norman, OK.

Video Editing: The Invisible Art

Video editing has gone mainstream. It's easy to edit video and add basic effects, even on a smart phone or tablet, and stream it via broadband at resolutions sufficient for web and commercial broadcasts. Such technology makes it easier to overlook the artistry and creativity involved in great editing. Because true art conceals art, the best editing is invisible. People see the video, but not how beautifully put together it is. Viewers notice bad editing, too, for it can disrupt their mood and jolt them out of otherwise engrossing narratives.

This chapter looks at editing's purpose and how it weaves the magic carpet that transports viewers through the screen and into the story. Most great editing is seamless and transparent, yet potent and magical, for it gives stories their heartbeat. It is the process of thinking and seeing, of finding interrelationships among shots and sound to create new meaning.

There is no right or wrong way to edit, however. Consider adopting guidelines, rather than obeying rigid rules about editing. Good editing is what works. This perspective is your invitation to edit with your heart and your innate storytelling skills. Whenever you edit, trust what you think and feel about every shot, scene, cut, effect, sequence and their timing and pacing, regardless of what the rulebooks say.

EDITING IS ANOTHER WRITING TOOL

Video editing is another of the visual storyteller's writing tools. Few viewers ever watch newscasts for the editing, and just as certainly the editor's name on a film rarely sells tickets at the movie theater. Those who have never edited may think of editing as a mere joining of scenes, or as an "elimination of the bad parts," but unless you truly understand editing you'll find it difficult to preplan the story in your mind; and it will be more difficult to shoot raw footage that tells a story.

Hollywood editor Glenn Farr speaks of editing's critical role in the storytelling process: "Photographers and reporters need to understand [editing's] importance as much as editors need to know what good photography and writing can do to help shape the idea being communicated," says Farr.1

VIDEO EDITING FOR WEB SITES

Video's power has led many web designers and editors to model web sites after television, rather than text models.[2] The web is a visual medium, after all, where high demand exists for those who can shoot raw video and transform it into blockbuster visual stories. Even radio and print-media web sites depend on video or other wide-screen imagery to attract viewers, and upon visibility in social media to further drive audience growth. Many web sites take the best from all digital platforms—using blogs, magazines, video, stills, and audio—and converge their content into strong, memorable brands with loyal audiences. Web managers know they're in a race for dollars by creating content that will attract the most valuable visitors, and the highest quality ads. The savviest have shifted their editorial focus to video, realizing that compelling visual stories and frequent major story updates, lure regular clients more often, and can help convert casual viewers into regulars.[3]

You can view just one example among hundreds of web sites that emphasize video at The New York Times Online, http://video.nytimes.com/ ■

TOWARD A PHILOSOPHY OF EDITING

Editing is vital to every visual storytelling platform because it lets us use all visual and audio media to their maximum potential. The art of **editing** therefore lies in reconstructing and condensing reality, and stimulating and sometimes controlling emotional responses (Figure 3.1). Even cutting together two unrelated shots creates meaning not present in either shot alone. Think for a moment about two individual video shots, recorded months apart. One shows a woman running toward camera. The second shot shows a snarling grizzly bear standing on hind legs. Cut them together in that order and you've foreshadowed probable tragedy. Reverse them, and you've made the woman seem a bit unhinged. Who in their right mind would run toward certain death?

EVERYONE IS AN EDITOR

Editing, in its simplest definition, is selection, arrangement, timing, and presentation.[4] Only through editing can one enhance the story and the storytelling process. Editing, then, begins not at the final stage of the storytelling process but rather at the beginning.

Your choice of shots and how you compose them is one form of editorial selection. Only through selection is emphasis possible. The order in which the shots appear is a form of editorial arrangement. Shot length is a form of editorial timing, a way to control dramatic tension through quick cutting or a more relaxed mood that lets the eye wander across the screen. Even your preplanning for matched action and for transitions in subject matter and through time and space will determine whether presentation is harsh and noticeable or smooth and seamless.

Shots and sounds, their timing and arrangement, and their framing and composition should become part of your thinking the moment you finalize your story focus, or as you see the story's focus changing in the field.

FIGURE 3.1

The picture and sound editing process allows journalists to emphasize, reveal, pace, and structure the various elements that make up a television news story.

THE CUT

In editing, the **cut** is the most basic, yet most important edit of all. Nonlinear editing makes it simple to add wipes and effects, but in real life our eyes and minds work in cuts, not wipes and dissolves, and never in wiggles or flips.

As we walk into a room our eyes naturally see a wide shot of the room, then perhaps a group of people, before we focus on an individual's face. In real life, we experience this sequence in cuts. We look at one thing, and then another, always in cuts, never in zooms and pans.

You can reaffirm how humans see if you look at something far away, and then imagine your eyes are the camera lens as you try to zoom out to a wide shot. It's impossible to zoom with your eyes. Now pick out objects to look at on opposite sides of a room or other environment. Look at the object on the right, then on the left. Did your eyes and head do a slow pan from one side of the room to the next or did your eyes naturally make a "cut" from one object to the other?

In real life, humans can choose what to look at, when, and how much emphasis to give whatever they view. Psychologists call this process selective perception. As we first enter a familiar room, we might not take a wide shot with our eyes had we misplaced our house keys. Even standing fifteen feet distant, we might focus our attention only upon a shelf across the room where we normally place those keys, obliterating all awareness from our view but that empty shelf. This is the mind at work, not the eyes, but we can do the same thing with the camera and editing process.

Just as the eye works, cameras, photojournalists, and video editors can serve as extensions of the mind. They too can show viewers what to look at, when, for how long, and from what angles and perspectives. In the lost-key example, the camera might replicate the subject's selective attention on that empty shelf in a close shot that screams, "No, not there either!"

The next time you watch a movie, pay special attention to the editing. Unless a change occurs in time, or sometimes in location or subject, you'll rarely see anything other than a cut edit. Unnoticeable cuts, however, require thoughtful field photography, which makes seamless cuts possible rather than trying to "fix it in the edit" with dissolves and wipes.

CHOOSING EDIT POINTS

The point at which one shot is surrendered and a new shot begins is called the **edit point**. Every shot that contains action has an ideal moment when it should begin and another ideal moment when it should end. If you will "listen" to the action and observe it closely, the action itself will suggest where the cuts should be made. Suppose that we have two shots: (1) a college student approaches a mailbox and deposits a letter, and (2) a close-up shot of the mailbox in which the student's hand enters the frame and we see that the letter being stuffed into the slot is addressed to "Navy Recruiter."

The scene could be edited in as many ways as there are editors, yet there is only one ideal edit point. You would cut out of shot 1 just as the student approaches the mailbox and her body language indicates that she is about to post the letter (letting her arm motion determine the edit point), then cut to the close shot in which we see action that has already begun in scene 1 continue smoothly and conclude in scene 2.

You also could cut the action out-of-frame/into-frame. In this approach the student would exit scene 1, followed by a cut to scene 2 (close shot of the mailbox), and the shot would hold for a moment until the student's hand came into frame. This technique is perhaps less desirable because there would be little motivation to cut from the shot of a student walking down the sidewalk to a static shot of the mailbox. In effect, the editor would be saying, "Here's a shot of a student about to mail a letter. Now let's cut to a shot of the mailbox and wait for her to catch up with us."

THERE CAN BE NO MATCHED ACTION WITHOUT OVERLAPPING ACTION

Few stories can unfold naturally if individual field shots lack the basic raw material that video editors need to produce **matched action** sequences. Editors worship photographers who bring back video shots that contain recurring or **overlapping action**. In other words, an action present in one shot also appears in a related shot, in a similar manner and rhythm. Such shots contain cutting points that allow action to flow smoothly, without interruption, from one cut to another.

If, for example, in a long shot a swimmer dives into a swimming pool and presently surfaces near the pool's edge, a close shot might show the same swimmer surfacing after the dive. Because the swimmer can be seen to surface in both the long shot and the close shot, the action in the two is said to be overlapping. The editor can produce matched action between the two shots by cutting out of the long shot at a point identical to continuation of the action in the close shot.

Even a simple reaction shot or a motivated cutaway can help the editor build a more natural-looking story. But without overlapping or recurring action, or even reaction shots or cutaways to use, that editor will end his day with a story full of unrelated jump cuts.

Equally regretful, the jump-cut story will lack a meaningful sense of experience, because as humans we see and experience real-life activities in uninterrupted time— the equivalent of television's matched-action sequences. In the end, good video stories are just little reconstructions of human experience, composed as we might encounter them ourselves in real life.

CUTTING ON ACTION OR AT REST

Whether the action is a fistfight or a horse race, if the edits or cuts (or shot changes) occur while the action progresses, the technique is called **cutting on action**. If the edits occur at a moment in which the action on the screen has stopped, the technique is called **cutting at rest**. Cuts might be made with the action "at rest," for example, in a three-shot sequence of a woman being served coffee at a resort hotel. In the first shot the server would enter frame and place coffee before the woman. The coffee cup is at rest. In the next shot, the camera might cut to a close shot of the same coffee cup (still at rest), then to a shot of the woman's face as she looks at the cup.

Even a fistfight can be cut at rest if the cuts are made at that moment when the fighter's arm is fully extended during a punch or when a scene change is made from a shot of a fighter who takes a hard blow to the face and collapses, to a shot of the fighter lying unconscious on the floor.

The decision whether to cut on action or at rest lies with the editor. Generally, action scenes should be cut on action if the editor wishes to sustain pace and provide fluid story development and continuity. If the subject matter should be treated more deliberately and at a slower pace, cutting at rest may be appropriate. Here, the axiom that "performance follows content" holds true. Let content dictate the proper treatment.

Regardless of the choice you make, the action must be edited so that it flows smoothly and effortlessly across the cuts without the editor's work calling attention to itself. The editing will be strongest if it is as seamless and transparent as when we look at an event with our own eyes, unaware even of the process by which we are observing it. For this reason, be cautious about cutting out of a moving pan, tilt, or zoom to the middle of another zoom, pan, or other shot that contains artificial camera movement. If you must edit such shots together, consider linking them with a dissolve, fade-in or fade-out, or similar optical effect to soften the edit (optical effects are explained in detail later in this chapter).

INTO-FRAME/OUT-OF-FRAME ACTION

In cutting matched action, most editors try not to let a continuing action "fall out of the splice" at shot changes. In other words, they cut from an outgoing scene while the subject is still visible in frame, then cut to the incoming scene at a point where the subject has obviously entered frame. If the action disappears from view at splice lines, pace will drop and viewers may wonder why the subject disappeared momentarily.

Exceptions occur frequently, however. Photographers may be forced to maintain continuity when shooting uncontrolled action by shooting into-frame/out-of-frame action. In such cases they begin to shoot before the subject enters frame and continue to shoot after the subject has exited frame. Once the subject has left frame, the editor can cut to virtually any new scene without a jump. Cutting into-frame/out-of-frame action also is useful to create a transition from one time or locale to the next or even to move a subject through time or space, because the editor can cut from an empty frame to anything else.

JUMP CUTS

In the previous chapter you learned that **jump cuts** in action occur when action jumps unnaturally forward or backward in time. The most common device to eliminate jump cuts is the **cutaway,** a shot of some part of the peripheral action that diverts the viewer's eye for a moment so that when the screen returns to the main action, the jump will be less obvious.

Sometimes you can render jump cuts less noticeable by cutting from one shot to another shot during motion. Look for movement in each shot and see if the movement contains edit points. Say the camera is on a wide establishing shot from across the street. In this shot, the subject walks screen left to right toward his car, which is about 20 feet away. You can next cut to a shot of the person entering the car, assuming the camera changes focal length and the action still moves from left to right at about the same pace. This approach tricks the viewer into believing the scene continues seamlessly, although you compressed time and advanced the action by 20 feet.

If all else fails, editors can once again call on optical effects such as dissolves and wipes to eliminate the jump cut. Such effects may still diminish audience involvement, however, by making the editing technique more obvious.

POP CUTS

Be vigilant not to confuse the jump cut with the pop cut. They're different animals. **Pop cuts** occur whenever you edit together two or more shots that were photographed along the same axis line, even when the action is perfectly matched. Maybe the photographer first photographed a long shot, then zoomed in for a medium shot, and then a close-up.

The solution is to "shoot and move" while taking shots in the field. For each new shot, move the camera to establish a new axis line. When you shoot and move, matched action edits together more naturally. The result is smooth, seamless, distraction-free matched action.

DEVICES TO COMPRESS TIME AND ADVANCE THE ACTION

Any shot that diverts audience attention lets the editor cut back to the main action at a moment further ahead in time than could be the case in real life. The **insert shot** is an example. Unlike the cutaway, which diverts audience attention from the main subject, the insert provides the audience with close-up, essential detail about some part of the main action. At a news conference that continues in real time for nearly a half hour, for example, a politician announces he will end his candidacy for office. In the edited report, we see the politician announce his decision (the statement is edited from a point early in the news conference), followed by a close-up insert shot of the candidate. In the insert shot a reporter asks, off camera, whether the candidate wishes to comment on published reports that he has been unfaithful to his wife, and the candidate replies "No comment." The insert is followed by a final shot in which the candidate turns and leaves the news conference. With the help of an insert shot, a half-hour news conference has been depicted in just three shots totaling thirty seconds or less.[5]

Two other shots, the **reaction shot** and the **point of view shot,** can be used in similar fashion. In the reaction shot, the subject reacts to something that has just happened in the previous shot: In a medium shot a doctor gives a child a flu vaccination; the reaction shot shows the child's stoic response to the pain.

In the point of view (POV) shot, the subject sees or reacts to something offscreen, and we see the thing from the subject's point of view. For example, shot 1 shows a woman sitting in an airport-waiting lounge as she looks down at her wristwatch; shot 2 provides a close-up of the wristwatch from the woman's point of view. From that point, the editor can advance the action by cutting to another shot of the woman taken some minutes later and thereby condense time. Note that in this example, the point of view shot also functions as an insert shot.

On occasion, you may want to use the first part of a scene, cut to another shot, then cut back to the original scene. The sequence might be of a football player running for a touchdown, then a cutaway to the cheering crowd, then back to the original scene of the football player. Or perhaps the scene shows a hot air balloon passing before a sheer rock cliff. In either event, remember to advance the action so you don't cut back into the shot at the same point you left it. If we last saw the football player at the twenty-yard line, the football player must have advanced a logical distance beyond the twenty-yard mark following a two-second cutaway to the crowd. Conversely, the hot air balloon must be shown to have advanced through space when we cut back to it after a cutaway shot of onlookers, rather than being shown still positioned at the same reference point against the rock cliff.

A good rule of thumb in such cases is to advance the action at least the same amount of time as the cutaway remains on-screen. If the cutaway is left on-screen for two seconds, an equal length of footage should be eliminated from the primary scene before the action is resumed (Figure 3.2). Usually, though, you can advance the action further than it might have gone in real life, provided the object's progression through time and space appears natural and logical.

FIGURE 3.2

Proper pacing and screen logic result when the editor cuts shots to reflect a logical progression in the action. In this example, the editor has used the first part of a shot (top left), cut to another shot (top right), then cut back to the original scene at a point about two seconds beyond where audiences last saw the action (bottom).

PARALLEL CUTTING

If neither overlapping action nor appropriate cutaways or other shots are available in the raw field video, at least the illusion of matched action can sometimes be accomplished through **parallel cutting,** or intercutting between separate but developing actions. Parallel cutting was routinely employed in early westerns as the screen cut back and forth between an out-of-control stagecoach and bandits in hot pursuit.

Today, the technique can be just as effectively used in television news in situations where overlapping action is difficult or impossible to photograph—for example, in a hostage situation in which little matched-action footage is available. In this case, footage that may be little more than a series of "grab shots" (shots taken on the run as action unfolds before the camera) can be intercut to first show police officers surrounding the building where hostages are held, to shots of efforts to evacuate nearby citizens from the neighborhood. This back-and-forth cutting as the action progresses can help impose a continuity otherwise unavailable.

SHOT ORDER IMPACTS THE ILLUSION OF CONTINUITY

Acceptably edited matched action sometimes can look wrong, even when a close, frame-by-frame inspection of the edit shows the action to be perfectly matched. If the eye doesn't accept the match, you have a problem.

One solution is to follow the advice of Seattle photojournalist Phil Sturholm. "If you have a problem matching your action perfectly, edit the action from a close-up to a long shot rather than a long shot to a close-up," says Sturholm. "The long shot has so many things coming at you it's hard to see if something doesn't match exactly."[6]

CONTENT DICTATES PACE

We often hear that in video reporting and storytelling, pace is everything. The truism means simply that audiences will lose interest if story development is too slow or predictable. Although few guidelines exist about what constitutes acceptable pace, most video editors and virtually all viewers know it when they see it. The story's pace either feels right, or it doesn't.

The key to good pacing is to recognize that content dictates pace. Slow does not necessarily mean dull. Fast does not necessarily mean interesting. Good editors listen to their feelings and let the story suggest its own pace. Depending on the photographer's commitment and the story's point of view, a motorcycle hill-climbing event may be told better either in a series of slow-motion shots that play out on the screen over long seconds or in a flurry of action, colors, and sounds that hit the screen with the staccato beat of machine-gun fire. Only visual content and story commitment can determine which treatment will be more effective.

CUTTING TO CONDENSE TIME

The average television newscast contains twenty to twenty-five elements, excluding commercials. Packages and reader copy must be kept short if story count is to remain acceptable. One of the great virtues of visual communication is its ability to expand or compress time, an effect known as **filmic time**. Such a simple event as a police officer leaving the patrol car, entering an apartment building, walking upstairs, and entering an apartment can be accomplished in two or three shots: officer leaves car and walks out of frame, officer enters frame at top of stairs and exits frame, officer walks into frame and enters apartment. In television and film, time can be compressed or expanded far beyond the constraints of real time. An action that required up to a full minute in real life is accomplished in as little as ten seconds of filmic time. Sequences can just as easily be expanded beyond real time using slow-motion shots, cutaways, point-of-view, insert, and reestablishing shots.

COMPOSITION AFFECTS PACE

Compressing time is but one element of pacing. Equally important is the composition of the various shots in a story as the framing switches from long shot to medium shot and close-up.

In the past, because of original small screen size, television was considered a close-up medium. Today, as screen size increases, the size of subjects on the screen can be varied more dramatically. Larger screen size allows the editor to place emphasis on subject matter more precisely and permit greater control of the "distance" to be created between audience and subject.

From one shot to the next, however, the speed of an action on the screen can be altered by such factors as focal length, distance from subject, and the relative lens perspective. If the action is unfolding at one speed in the first shot, then at a different speed in the next shot, the editor has another problem. Composition influences not only visual and dramatic impact, but also the amount of information that can be delivered. Consider the story that hinges on the make of a gun used to murder a holdup victim. A medium shot of the gun may be insufficient to show an important trademark crucial to the jury's deliberation. A close-up of the gun may be necessary, held on the screen for several seconds so that the viewer's eye may discover and study the all-important trademark.

Conversely, a close-up of a single rose might deliver its entire meaning in a couple of seconds, whereas a long shot of tulip beds in Holland may require triple that screen time to deliver its message. Clearly, both the editor's intent and the story's content will dictate individual shot length and the story's final pace. After all, the editor's responsibility is to reflect not only the story's information, but its feeling and atmosphere as well.[7]

SCREEN DIRECTION

In real life, subjects move in predictable directions, so the rule of thumb regarding screen direction is to keep the subject moving in one consistent direction—either screen right or screen left. Otherwise, viewers may be left confused and consciously or subconsciously frustrated (Figure 3.3).

You can avoid screen direction conflicts in the field if you keep the subject facing the same direction in the viewfinder at all times. If a subject moves screen left in the first shot, then it must continue to move screen left in all the other shots. Otherwise, the result is a **false reverse** (Figure 3.4).

EDITING TO ELIMINATE THE FALSE REVERSE

The most obvious solution to a false reverse is the cutaway. A shot of a football player running screen right can be followed by a shot of the crowd or a referee, preferably looking somewhat toward the camera rather than obviously right or left, followed by a cut to the player running screen left. Another device to neutralize the false reverse is a **head-on shot** of the action coming straight toward camera or a **negative-action shot** of the subject moving away from camera. Yet another device is to continue photographing the shot as the camera moves across the axis line, taking the audience with it. If such a shot is unavailable, the editor can again use an optical effect such as a dissolve or wipe.

FIGURE 3.3

In real life, most subjects move in predictable directions, hence the need for consistent screen direction of subjects in motion picture photography and editing.

FIGURE 3.4
If a subject suddenly and illogically swaps directions on-screen, the result is called a false reverse.

THE TRANSITION SHOT

The typical news package, even the typical theatrical film, is a series of sequences. **Transition shots** give the editor a way to pivot from one sequence to the next, a way to link separate scenes.

In a video package about a glassblower, for example, the transition shot might be used to move the story from the artist's studio to a retail shop. In this example, we first see the artist twirling and transforming molten glass into a vase. Next we see the transition shot, a close-up ostensibly of the vase being turned (as if the close-up were a continuation from the previous shot), followed by a cut to a long shot of a customer holding the vase in her hands as she examines it in the retail shop.

A memorable illustration of a transition forward in time occurs in the classic film *Little Big Man*. A young Cherokee played by Dustin Hoffman rides down to a mountain stream on horseback, dismounts, kneels by the stream, and scoops water to his face. The screen cuts to a close shot in which Hoffman's hand covers his face. When Hoffman lowers his hand to reveal his face, we see it is the same person, but he's now eighty years old.

Film director David Lean fashioned an equally memorable transition in *Passage to India*. A young Indian doctor leaves a wealthy enclave late at night after treating an upper class British woman. He sees a horse-drawn carriage leaving the area, and calls out, but the driver does not stop. The doctor looks into the night sky, where a brilliant moon hangs in still life. We next see the moon, as if from the doctor's point-of-view. As the shot holds, a hand comes into frame, as if reaching behind the moon itself, and scoops water, in a match cut, to the doctor's face. Viewers realize that what they mistook as a shot of the moon itself was its reflection, lying motionless upon the surface water in a horse trough.

Occasionally it is useful for video journalists to study such transitional techniques, even those in theatrical motion pictures, to better apply the principles to their own videography and editing.

Even if the photographer has failed to record transition shots in the field, transition opportunities may still be possible during editing, as in the story of a black swan that sticks its head beneath the water. In a closer shot, in which camera angle and action are exactly matched with the previous shot, a white swan pulls its head from the water.

Such opportunities occur frequently enough that it pays to be alert. Always, the goal of such efforts is to preserve visual continuity while inviting and reengaging viewer participation.

SOUND AS A TRANSITIONAL DEVICE

Another transitional device is the use of what is known variously as the sound overlap, sound bridge, or incoming sound. The technique allows incoming sound to be heard for a moment or two before the accompanying shot appears on screen. Normally, the incoming sound begins over the last second or two of the outgoing shot, although it can be introduced even earlier.

Consider how this technique would work in connection with the shot of a cruise ship lying idle at dockside, then a close shot of a ship's whistle followed by shots of passengers coming aboard the ship. Sound could be laid in so that viewers would hear the incoming sound of the ship's whistle over the last two seconds of the shot showing the ship lying idle. At the conclusion of the lying-idle shot, the ship's whistle would appear on screen with its accompanying sound continuing.

In addition to its utility as a transition device, the sound bridge can provide a moment or so of white space or breathing room in voice-over narrative to help give the package greater realism.

COLD CUTS

The sound bridge also helps the editor eliminate tiresome successions of cold cuts. **Cold cuts** occur when a shot ends and its accompanying sound ends, only to be replaced at the splice line by a new picture with new sound. To avoid cold cuts, let outgoing or incoming sound carry over the splice line or make edits on words or other sounds. Avoid edits on silence at the end of a sentence of voice over, and strive to avoid edits during a pause or at the conclusion of other sound. If the phenomenon is difficult to imagine, watch television newscasts and notice how often the shots in news packages end coincidentally with the end of sentences in the voice over.

FLASH CUTS

Some video stories go better with music. With its smaller-than-theater screen sizes and audiences taught to thrive on pace, television is well suited to an editing style called **flash cutting**, or "rapid montage cutting."

In this technique, brief fragments of shots are cut to exact rhythm against a musical beat or sound. The visual information comes quickly, but not so fast that it fails to leave an impression or message, whether on an 80-inch TV or a 40-foot theater screen.

CUTTING TO LEAVE SPACE FOR AUDIENCE REACTION

Wall-to-wall narration has become a hallmark in many videos and news packages. In part, the phenomenon occurs because conscientious reporters hope to communicate as much information as possible in the little time available. But no communication is complete until there is understanding. Remember the need to "write silence," to give your viewers time to assimilate information. When facts are fired at them as if from a scattergun, the information washes over them and soon fades from memory.

For that reason, all packages need white space or breathing room, occasional moments in which pictures and sound play while the viewer takes a momentary respite from the narration. If, in a shot, a plane with crippled landing gear is about to touch down on the runway, the editor owes his or her audience a moment or two of silence during the landing, even if it means eliminating a sentence or two of voice-over copy from the package.

Always, common sense is essential. If those five seconds of voice-over audio are more essential to the story than a little breathing room, keep the voice-over. But, if viewers need that little moment of dramatic impact more than audio that only tells them what they can see for themselves, they should have it.

COMMUNICATION PAYS

In shops that use crews, photographers are sometimes heard to say, "The editor used my worst stuff yesterday and made me look bad." Most oversights involve no malice but are a consequence of the editor's unrelenting deadlines. Too often, the editor must simply "edit off the top" of the field video to make airtime.

Elsewhere it has been suggested that photojournalists should photograph only what they want on air. In fact, photographers who avoid indiscriminate shooting can endear themselves to video editors who have too little time and too many packages to edit. Editors love photographers who anticipate the action, who preplan what they'll shoot, who wait for action to occur and are already shooting when it does occur. And if the video contains no meaningless shots, soft focus shots, or shaky footage, then the photographer has become at least a silent partner in the editing process.

If, as a photographer, you would like to see certain shots aired or avoided in a story, tell the reporter or editor. If you can't talk face to face, at least write a note to the editor. If, as reporter or editor, you see your photographer shooting too many unnecessary shots, express your concerns.

DISSOLVES AND OTHER OPTICAL EFFECTS

A simple straight cut may be adequate to move viewers along even from one unrelated scene to the next, but at other times the editor may want to use such optical effects as fades, wipes, dissolves, or more elaborate digital video effects to indicate that scenes, although significantly different, are related.

In general, the **dissolve** indicates a change in time, location, or subject matter. One scene melts into another. In other words, one scene optically fades to black on top of another scene that optically fades from black to full exposure. The longer the dissolve, the more obvious is the separation. Common dissolve lengths are from one-half second to two and a half seconds or more. Occasionally, editors use dissolves to more artistically connect scenes or eliminate jump cuts within a real-time sequence, but the result may be confusing to audiences who have been conditioned to understand that dissolves mean a change in time, location, or subject matter.

Wipes and flip wipes, whether horizontal or vertical, are used to indicate a more noticeable separation between scenes. Wipes tell the viewer that a new subject, idea, or location is being introduced.

Fades, including the fade-in and fade-out, are among the most obvious transitions. The scene fades to black, or sometimes to white, or fades from black to full exposure. The fade is seldom used in news, although it is commonly found in public affairs and documentary programming and is used at some stations just before commercial breaks.

Because no rules exist regarding how or when to use optical effects, editors can profit from the axiom that true art conceals art: The best optical effects may be those that go unnoticed because they are used so logically. Remember, also, the beauty of the straight cut, which is the most transparent optical effect of all.

Ultimately, the key to good editing is to make all your work go unnoticed. If your technique is invisible, if continuity is present, and if your pace is smooth and flawless, then you will have helped viewers achieve that incomparable feeling of "being there."

SUMMARY

Editing is important to the visual storytelling process because of the ways in which it duplicates how the mind works. Shots, or fragments of reality, are combined to form a composite understanding of the original experience or event. Everyone involved in the reporting process is an editor and uses editing to emphasize, pace, structure, and reveal the story.

The most fundamental editing technique is the cut, the joining of one scene to another. Deceptively simple as a creative device, the cut creates new meaning. A shot of a child crawling on the ground, intercut with a shot of a snake crawling toward camera, creates meaning that was not present in either shot by itself. If the two shots are reversed, their meaning is again altered and new meaning created. Editing also allows the journalist to expand or condense time, an effect often called filmic time. The essence of an event that occurred over hours or days in real life can be reconstructed on the screen in only a minute or so. Similarly, events that happened during the span of a few seconds can be depicted for far longer times on the screen by repeating the action through shots from multiple cameras and slow-motion photography.

Pace, a critical component in all visual communication, is affected not only by shot length but also by composition, cutting points, and the content itself. Normally, in scenes with action, pace is more natural if scenes are cut on action, or in other words, while the action progresses.

Various shots can be used to emphasize and reveal action and control pace. Among them are the insert shot, reaction shot, and point of view shot. Common editorial devices to eliminate unnatural jumps in action, or jump cuts, include the cutaway and insert shots. Like the photographer, the editor also is responsible for helping preserve screen direction. Generally, pictorial continuity is best served when subjects move logically in one direction on-screen, rather than randomly swap directions from shot to shot.

Editing also encompasses sound, which can be used as a transition device to move from one shot to another, as in the use of incoming sound a second or so before its accompanying scene is shown. Sound also helps provide perspective in a scene and helps heighten the viewer's sense of realism. Optical effects such as fades, wipes, and dissolves offer further means of visual punctuation.

Competency in video reporting and photography relies on more than a passing acquaintance with editing. Editing is not simply the final process in the art of visual reconstruction: It guides the reporting process from start to finish.

KEY TERMS

cold cuts 56

cut 48

cutaway 50

cutting at rest 49

cutting on action 49

dissolve 57

editing 47

edit point 48

fades 57

false reverse 54

filmic time 53

flash cutting 56

head-on shot 54

insert shot 51

jump cuts 50

matched action 49

negative-action shot 54

overlapping action 49

parallel cutting 52

point of view (POV) shot 51

pop cut 50

reaction shot 51

transition shots 55

wipes 57

DISCUSSION

1. Why are the best editing techniques often invisible to home audiences?
2. Describe how editing can be used to help enhance the visual storytelling process.
3. Explain why an understanding of picture editing is important to all members of the reporting team.
4. Describe the role of the *cut* in video editing.
5. Explain the meaning of the phrase "pace is everything" as it applies to video stories.
6. Explain what is meant by the term *filmic time* and provide an original example.
7. Describe the considerations that influence the length of individual shots in an edited television news story.
8. Distinguish between the terms *cutting on action* and *cutting at rest*.
9. What considerations guide determination of the edit point in beginning and ending a given shot?
10. Define *parallel cutting* and provide an original example of the concept.
11. Explain how sound can be used as a transition from one time, subject, or location in a story to the next.
12. Explain the difference between cold cuts and flash cuts.
13. Describe typical uses of the most common optical effects.

EXERCISES

1. Arrange three video shots, each with separate but related subject matter, and consider them to be shots A, B, and C. If you lack access to a video editing console, use still photographs and place them side by side.

   An example of three shots might be: A—a mobile home in perfect condition sits on a well-manicured lot; B—a woman removes the lid from an empty quart jar and holds the jar in the direction of something offscreen; C—a mobile home that has been overturned by high wind. Notice how the linkage of shots A and B produces new meaning that neither shot by itself contained. Notice further the new meaning created when shots B and C are linked. Now, if the visual result will make sense, relink your three shots in the following orders and compare the outcome: A-C-B; C-A-B; B-A-C.

2. Analyze television news stories, commercials, and theatrical films to determine what factors motivate the cut or edit that transfers the viewer's attention from one shot to the next. Note to what extent the content influences the pace of the editing.

3. Find an event that occurs over the course of several minutes or hours in real life, then photograph and edit a reconstruction of the event into a one-minute presentation. Reedit the one-minute version into a thirty-second reconstruction, and finally into a twenty-second reconstruction.

4. Ask a video editor, preferably a willing acquaintance, to determine the proper screen length for a long shot and a close shot of identical action. Compare the running time of the two shots.

5. Edit footage of an action, first on action, then at rest. Analyze the result.
6. Edit together two versions of out-of-frame/into-frame action from the same footage. In the first version, take care to avoid letting the action "fall out of the splice." In other words, surrender an outgoing shot while the subject is still visible at the edge of frame, and pick up the incoming shot with the subject already in frame.

   In the second version, recut the action so the subject disappears entirely from frame in the outgoing shot and does not reappear for several moments after the incoming shot has begun. Compare and evaluate the two approaches.
7. Edit together precisely matched action from raw field shots that contain overlapping action. View and discuss the raw and edited footage with the photographer.
8. Using footage from separate events, cut together an example of parallel cutting.
9. Insert a cutaway in the middle of a shot in which the action continues to progress, such as an athlete running down a playing field. Pick up the action after the cutaway precisely where it ended in the outgoing shot just before the cutaway. Now recut the scene, this time eliminating from the action scene following the cutaway a length of footage equivalent to the length of the cutaway. Compare and discuss the result.
10. Edit together two scenes that result in a false reverse in the action. Use any other appropriate shot available to you to soften the impact of the false reverse.
11. Use sound or a video shot of your choice as a transitional device from one sequence in a story to the next.
12. Edit together two examples of the cold cut, followed by examples in which you have eliminated the cold cuts you originally created.
13. Practice editing flash cuts. Cut footage of your choice to the beat of music of your choice.
14. Study examples of the effective use of optical effects as they are used in television and film.
15. Practice editing voice-over narration against video pictures, leaving white space with natural sound in the track as appropriate.

NOTES

1. "An Interview with Cheri Hunter," in *Editing* (Eagle Eye Film Company, 4019 Tujunga Avenue, Studio City, CA 91604) (July 1986), 1, 2.
2. Nick Denton. "Why Gawker Is Moving Beyond the Blog," *Gizmodo*, accessed December 28, 2010 at http://gizmodo.com/5702374/why-gawker-is-moving-beyond-the-blog.
3. Ibid.
4. Karel Reisz and Gavin Miller, *The Technique of Film Editing* (New York: Hastings House, 1968), 46–48.
5. Matt Williams, "Academy Winner Extols Editing," *Rangefinder* (Utah State University, Spring 1985), 40.
6. Phil Sturholm, "Creative Photojournalists—They Are the Future," a presentation at the NPPA TV News-Video Workshop, Norman, OK, March 20, 1986.
7. Reisz and Miller, *The Technique of Film Editing*, 142.

CHAPTER

4

Shooting Video in the Field

Photojournalists often discover that small changes in their work produce big improvements on the screen. As one element after another comes under control, an individual style begins to emerge. The process affirms that professional development never ends and that no detail is too unimportant to master.

COMPOSITION GUIDELINES

The rules of composition that have served artists over the centuries remain valid for the photojournalist. Balance, harmony, depth, scale, and perspective are virtues to be preserved in all photography, but video adds a few twists because of motion and video's horizontal format. This section thus addresses approaches to composition that can enhance the photography in video reports and stories.

TELEVISION IS A HORIZONTAL FORMAT   Everything on television happens within a horizontal format. Rarely does turning the camera sideways to record a vertical shot make sense. Although the horizontal-only format may require some adjustment, for most photographers it is seldom limiting because the entire horizontal field needn't be used all the time.

THE RULE OF THIRDS

The **rule of thirds** identifies "Golden Spots" within the viewfinder frame to improve the composition of individual scenes. Many camera viewfinders can display these "golden spots," or locations within the frame where the lines intersect. Figure 4.1 identifies these golden spots (one, two, three, four on the diagram). If your camera viewfinder lacks such lines, try imagining them superimposed upon the viewfinder.

These areas serve as focal points where our eyes naturally go whenever we view or take a picture. Most times, compose the shot so your main subject or center of interest occupies one or more golden spots, or lies along a horizontal or vertical line.

Referring to Figure 4.1, a water-skier moving screen left to screen right might be placed on the imaginary line identified by numbers 1 and 2. This composition gives the skier room to move into the frame. A man petting a dog might be placed at intersection 2 with the dog

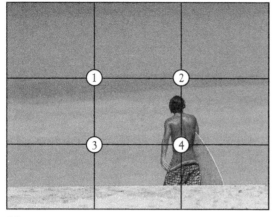

(a)

(b)

FIGURE 4.1

The camera viewfinder, divided into imaginary lines, with "Golden Spots" where the lines intersect, permits composition of scenes according to the rule of thirds. Note how the rule of thirds strengthens composition in Figure 4.1C.

Graphic Copyright © 2012 Laura Schaub Designs

(c)

at intersection 3. A speaker addressing a large crowd might be placed at intersection 1 with the crowd filling the remainder of the screen.

Using the same approach you can place horizon lines either on the line identified by numbers 1 and 2, and thereby emphasize the foreground, or on the line identified by numbers 3 and 4, and thereby emphasize the sky or background.

Notice the absence of a Golden Spot in the frame's dead center. That's the "Bermuda Triangle" in your viewfinder, where good composition often goes to die. Note, however, that recommendations are only guides, never hard and fast rules. You may want a rocket standing smack in the frame's dead center, so you can capture flames spitting frame right and left as the rocket ignites. You may wish to place a face in the frame's dead center, to create the POV of an amateur photographer or yes, even as a professional approach to heighten impact (see Figure 4.3).

SHOW VIEWERS WHAT YOU WANT THEM TO SEE   One of the most freeing rules of composition is to show viewers only what you want them to see. Although the mind concentrates on what it wants to see and filters out the rest, the camera records everything before it, so show the camera only what you want viewers to see. "Study the viewfinder just as if you are at home watching the scene on television," advises KCNC photojournalist Gary Croshaw, "and never let anything on the screen take you by surprise."[1]

ON EVERY SHOT, THINK BEFORE YOU SHOOT   Ask yourself, as you peer into the viewfinder, "Is this important?" "Is this relevant?" If the answer is yes, push the button.

FIGURE 4.2

Notice how composition affects the viewer's perception. The randomly composed image (left) is less pleasing to the eye than its companion. Notice how the photo on the right has a more powerful center of interest and "feels" more balanced. Note its use of "Golden Spots" suggested by the rule of thirds; its overall balance; and its obvious visual impact.

ELEVATE THE ORDINARY   "Don't turn on the camera unless what you see in the view finder makes you say 'wow,' or otherwise impresses you with its impact," advises photojournalist John Premack.[2] Such advice helps explain how some photographers make the mundane seem extraordinary and memorable. Skilled photographers can make even an ordinary hen's egg or ballpoint pen an object of great beauty.

SCREEN SPACE   In shots with action, **screen space** and visual balance change constantly as subjects move about in the frame. To maintain a visual treatment that is relatively transparent and unnoticeable to home viewers, some vigilance is necessary.

- Make good use of the entire screen when composing a shot. Fill the screen with important subject matter.
- Avoid tilted horizon lines. Use the leveling bubble on the tripod or line up the camera viewfinder with a horizontal line to be certain the camera is level.
- Avoid cutting the screen exactly in half with the horizon line.
- Remember that movement or bright lights in the background pull the viewer's eye away from the subject. Eliminate these distractions from the frame whenever possible.
- If the background is distracting, move the subject or the camera if possible; otherwise, throw the background out of focus by changing the focal length and focus point of your lens or by reducing light so you can shoot at a wider aperture and thereby reduce depth of field.

FIGURE 4.3

Powerful composition sometimes results from ignoring composition guidelines. Here the main subject occupies the frame's dead center with powerful effect.

- Avoid placing the speaker's face dead center in the frame when shooting sound bites. Place the speaker's eyes above the center of the frame and provide "looking room" within the frame. Also, leave room at the bottom of the shot to superimpose the speaker's name.
- When doing over-the-shoulder shots, avoid filling the frame with the back of the person's head.
- Composition can be unconsciously disturbing if the subject appears to be moving or looking out of frame instead of into frame. As a rule of thumb, action moving frame right should be positioned in the left third of the frame, or at least slightly to the left of center, and vice versa. This leaves space for the subject to move into.
- Avoid big gaps of space between people, such as in interview settings. If wide spaces exist, either recompose the shot by physically moving the camera or, if ethically warranted, by repositioning the subjects themselves. Normally, people can position themselves closer together on screen than would be customary in real life.
- Photograph individuals in full facial shots that show both eyes, rather than in profile shots that show one eye and one ear. In real life we normally see eyes in pairs but are only subconsciously aware of ears. Side profile shots incorrectly emphasize the ear.
- Create the illusion of depth in your photography by including foreground interest in the shot and by photographing shots that contain two or more planes of focus for the subject to pass in front of and behind.
- Maintain crisp focus on your subject.

POINTERS FOR WIDE SCREEN COMPOSITION

Composing for any format has always been subjective. You may find the following aesthetic and practical approaches useful in taking your composition for wide-screen media to the next level.

- Paint to fill your canvas. Place people and interesting backgrounds edge-to-edge in your frame.
- Be mindful that a 55-mm lens will more closely approximate the normal field of view in wide-screen formats. If you're seeing too much of the background around the edges, tighten up the shot.
- Use care in interview situations where the interviewer is off screen. With such a wide frame to work with, the interviewee may appear to be looking off into space if the eye line is too far left or right of the center of the frame. You can place yourself (or another interviewer) almost directly behind the camera to help avoid this disturbing appearance.
- Allow for TV Cutoff. Whenever you compose a shot in the camera viewfinder, remember that some home screens clip off the edges of the transmitted image. To avoid TV cutoff problems, some camera viewfinders show a "safe area" or else show less of the image than is being recorded, which can cause other problems, as you'll see in Chapter 11, Video Journalism: Storytelling on Your Own.
- If the viewfinder does show the entire picture being recorded, then compose shots that are slightly looser than normal.[3]

TRUST YOUR INSTINCTS   The world's libraries are filled with advice for developing artists and photographers on how to become more artistically sensitive and proficient. No one must wait to be taught these things, of course. Often the best approach is to move ahead, experimenting with new approaches, adopting what works for you, and discarding what doesn't. Rather than doubt yourself too often throughout this process, learn to trust your instincts.

USE A TRIPOD WHENEVER APPROPRIATE

Sometimes a tripod is most appropriate, sometimes not. In general, use a tripod for extreme tight shots; for shooting sequences free of shakiness; or when shooting video that requires thoughtful composition. Also use a tripod when shooting a sit-down interview or whenever you have time to compose the shot (Figure 4.4). Most photojournalists keep a tripod close by, wherever they go.

If no tripod is available where you work, or if the tripod assigned to you is wobbly or inadequate and repair or replacement appears unlikely, consider buying your own tripod.

THE HANDHELD CAMERA

When the story is moving, switch to handheld so you can move with the story. Wide-angle lenses help reduce shakiness in handheld shots. The closer you are to the action and the wider the shot, the steadier and smoother the pictures will look. Use a tripod if you have to stand more than 10 or 20 feet away from your subject.

If you find yourself without a tripod and the action isn't moving, convert your body into a tripod. Find a wall, a telephone pole, a tree, or whatever else is handy and push the camera up against this object. Indoors, if a straight-backed chair is handy, sit backward on the chair and use the chair back as a camera support. Further support the camera with a sandbag, pillow, or cushion.

For steadier shots, you can also kneel, a technique that provides good perspective on many shots. When kneeling, sit on your heels and rest elbows on your knees,

FIGURE 4.4
The steadiest shots are created when the camera is mounted on a tripod.

BOX 4.1   HANDHELD VERSUS TRIPOD SHOTS

It's important to shoot appropriately to the action going on around you. If the subject is moving, you should be moving as well. If I am away from the action, I want my camera on a tripod.

When action is happening or when the character is involved in a real-life moment, I want to be handheld, up close and personal. I keep my camera loose so I can move with the character.

The whole purpose of a tripod is to have rock-steady pictures. Tripod shots often are scene setters—"this is where we are now." Tripods are also invaluable for shots made on extreme telephoto, composing a scenic shot, or setting up a shot through which action will flow.

Handheld shots are most useful in very close situations when you're right up next to your subject, with the lens on a very wide shot. It's almost like you're dancing with the subject and the movement

is all with the feet. It's all tracking, side to side, front to back, zooming and panning with the feet and not with the fingers on the zoom control, and the shoulders pivoting around, and always with the camera on a wide shot and always used up close. It's a person walking down the hall and me walking with him—never standing and panning as the person goes by, but walking along in a tracking motion.

Ideally, I want shots to last at least ten seconds, so there's plenty of usable footage in the middle. This gives the camera time to settle down if there's a little shaking in the beginning and toward the end, and still leaves plenty of usable video. You can be confident about having "enough meat in the middle," especially when deadlines are tight and all you can do is just lay down long-running shots with everything already there.

—John DeTarsio ∎

or even set the camera on an equipment case. You can also place the camera on the ground or floor, straddle it with your knees, and use a wallet or similar object as a wedge to position the camera properly.

You also can hold the camera at waist level (cradle it in your arms) or at arm's length. Most viewfinders can be swiveled to virtually any angle the photographer might need to compose the shot conveniently.

If all else fails, you can adjust stabilization in your video editing software to make shaky video look steady. This step may add more time to the edit job, however, depending on your software.

BALANCE THE CAMERA

When handholding, balance the camera's weight on your shoulder. Some cameras have adjustable shoulder pads. This way you need only support the camera gently, rather than hold its full weight with your arms (Figure 4.5 shows correct stance).

USE A WIDE STANCE

A wide stance gives the body more support. Stand with feet about shoulder-width apart. Keep the body straight, with the pelvis tucked forward and elbows close to your chest. The "rear end out, elbows flying in the breeze" stance is unacceptable. It produces wavering shots.

CONTROL BREATHING

As you prepare to shoot, relax. Breathe in, let half the air out, then hold your breath like a target shooter. If the shot is long, breathe in shallow breaths.

PREPLAN BODY MOVEMENT

Preplan your body movement for pan shots or whenever you follow action with the handheld camera—to follow a plane taking off, for example, or to follow a person moving past the camera. Position your feet in the direction the shot will end, then swing your body back around to capture the approaching action. As you shoot, your body will "uncoil" much like a spring. Otherwise, your body will bind up as you "coil up."

FIGURE 4.5

Proper stance is vital to produce steady shots with the handheld camera. Balance the camera until it rests comfortably on the shoulder and use the left hand to make focus adjustments. Note that the steadying right arm remains close to the chest.

WALK IN LOCKSTEP

Another trick to minimize the shakiness of handheld shots is to photograph only objects that move. Subject movement renders camera movement less obvious. For smoothest action whenever you follow a subject in a walking shot, stay in lockstep with the person you're photographing. When the person steps on the right foot, you also should be stepping on your right foot. If you are walking backward, reverse this procedure.

AVOID UNPLANNED CAMERA MOVEMENT

When you zoom, avoid bumping the camera as you reach for the zoom button or lever, and take care to avoid hard starts and stops at the stop limits of the zoom range. And when shooting spot news, take your hand off the camera's start-stop button so that if you're frightened or startled, you don't accidentally shut off the camera. Finally, for video that captures more of the action, and for greater personal safety, try shooting with both eyes open so you know what's going on around you.

HOW TO USE THE ZOOM LENS

Use zooms with care, and to achieve a goal. Some zooms can help you communicate with the viewer. A **zoom in** (zooming from wide shot to tight) can show viewers what you want them to see. Perhaps you're shooting a detective looking through a case file. After an establishing shot, you might shoot over her shoulder. Now viewers see a document from her point-of-view, as the camera zooms in to show pertinent information.

If you must zoom while working handheld, try to avoid using the zoom motor on your lens. Instead, zoom by *physically moving your body with the lens set to a wide-angle view.* The wide-angle setting will keep the shot in focus and minimize shakiness as you physically move closer to your subject. In general, use the electronic zoom on the lens only when the camera is on a tripod.

The **zoom out** (zooming from tight shot to wide) works best in two situations. If you find nothing better, you can shoot a zoom out to alert viewers the story is ending. A better closing shot, though, is **negative action**, as in old westerns that end with the main character riding into the sunset, a train pulling away from the station, or a hero walking into the distance. Another caution: negative action shots often supply better closing audio than zoom out shots.

A second zoom technique is the **reveal**. The camera zooms out to reveal a change or visual surprise—something unexpected for the viewer. Perhaps we see the main character at a polo match. The next shot on screen cuts to a close-up of our main character, then pulls back to reveal the subject in a new location. Thus, the reveal shot can serve to surprise or disorient the viewer, or serve even as a transition shot.

AVOID CALLING ATTENTION TO THE ZOOM

Normally, the best zoom shots glide so smoothly and slowly that viewers seldom notice them. One trick is to introduce the zoom simultaneously as subject movement begins, as when a jet at the end of the runway begins to gather speed for takeoff.

Another device to help make the zoom shot less noticeable is to use only a portion of the zoom range, rather than zooming through the lens's entire focal-length range from wide angle to telephoto. The shot's purpose may suggest the appropriate zoom range for a particular subject.

ADJUST SPEED AND DURATION OF ZOOM TO STORY MOOD AND PACE

Remember also to control the speed, length, and duration of the zoom so that it will match the overall pace and mood of the larger sequence in which it is to appear. Sometimes "snap" zooms are most appropriate. At other times, a slow, lazy zoom will work best. Zoom shots that are always made at the same speed, and are predictably long and artificially slow, will inevitably damage the story's pace.

Also try to "feather" the beginning and end of your zoom shots: Accelerate slowly to predetermined zoom speed, then gradually decelerate the zoom as you come to the end of the shot. This avoids the hard stops and starts that occur when zooms begin and end instantly.

RECOMPOSE THE SHOT AS YOU ZOOM

As you zoom, remember to tilt the camera up or down as necessary to keep such factors as headroom in acceptable composition. Beginners often start a zoom shot with the subject centered close-up in the frame, then zoom back to a longer shot without tilting down the camera to keep head room above the subject in acceptable proportions. The result is a long shot of the subject in dead center of frame, with most of the top half of the frame wasted on empty space.

Remember, also, the good advice of professional photographers: "When you zoom, don't 'play the trombone.' Don't zoom in, then back out, during the same shot."

STORYTELLING AND PLANNING

It is possible for the photographer to shoot everything that moves and still not have a story. Photographers who have learned to think as reporters produce not just a succession of pretty pictures, but pictures that tell stories. Identify the story. Research the subject. Decide what you want your audience to learn, see, and experience. Know the story so you can tell it effectively to others with your camera. Ask yourself as you shoot, "What offers visual proof of the subject, of my point of view, the story's main points, and my story focus?"

Remember also to give every story you shoot a beginning, middle, and ending. Stories without an ending are the visual equivalent of unsigned letters.[4]

ESTABLISH COMMUNICATION IN THE FIELD

Once you have identified the story in your own mind, talk over your ideas with other members of the reporting team. Contribute as appropriate to the story and how it is to be covered and edited. Only if you establish communication with other members

---

BOX 4.2 JOHN DETARSIO TIPS

From the minute I first get my assignment, I start brainstorming the story's focus, how it will begin, what's likely to happen in the middle, and how it will end.

The focus will change until we start to shoot, and will often change again at least once after shooting begins. That's because visual focus depends on the real life that plays out on location, and what I'm able to capture.

Before leaving the location, I must know what my open is, and what the opening shot or shots are. How are we going to start this story—the first layer of the onion for this story? I must also know I have at least one good closing shot (often negative action) and a good closing statement or sound bites that can sum up the day—a statement, a period to the piece. ■

FIGURE 4.6

A CBS crew on location in Brazil sets up to shoot a *CBS 60 Minutes* interview. Reporting in team situations is a collaborative effort among all team members. Ongoing communication is essential on every assignment, whether crew size is two or ten.

of the reporting team can you know what they are thinking and reach final agreement on the story to be told (Figure 4.6).

Communication with the subjects in your story is just as vital. The contributions of subjects who trust the reporting team, and who feel safe enough to share something of their inner selves, can elevate the story from the routine to the exceptional.

THINK BEFORE YOU SHOOT

To further separate your work from the competition, exercise imagination every time you shoot. Try to make your photography communicate not only what you see and experience in the field, but also what other observers may have missed. Show the event, but also give viewers a reason to want to watch the story, and look for ways to help viewers feel as if they have participated in it.

SHOOT SEQUENCES

A proven method to heighten the viewer's sense of involvement in the story is to shoot matched-action sequences. Through sequences, photojournalists can reconstruct an event much as first-person observers would see the action. To shoot sequences, learn to recognize action that repeats itself and break "simple" action into its complex parts. If the assignment is to show a child boarding a school bus, show the child's face, a close-up of her scuffed tennis shoes, the sapphire-chip ring on her finger, her fingers tightly curled around her lunch box handle, her point of view of the approaching bus, the driver's smiling face, the cars stopped behind the bus, her father waving good-bye, the bus door closing, and the bus resuming its journey. During editing, the shots can be used in any given selection and order to emphasize particular aspects of the message.

SHOOT AND MOVE

Remember to help the editor avoid "pop cuts" (also see Chapter 3). After every shot you make in the field, try to physically move the camera to a new location and angle. They result most often from using the zoom lens to shoot a long shot and medium shot of a subject, or a medium shot and a close-up, without moving the camera off the original axis line.

To avoid the pop cut, simply remember to shoot and move. When you first photograph the subject, establish an imaginary axis line projecting from the lens through the center of the subject. Shoot the subject, and then physically move the camera to a new setup position for each new shot (Figures 4.7A, 4.7B, and 4.7C).

ANTICIPATE ACTION

If you can study the action before you shoot and learn to anticipate what happens next, your photography will have originality. If you find yourself shooting behind the action, try to preplan your shots. Wait for the action to occur and be shooting when it happens. "Don't let yourself get behind the story," in the words of network freelance photographer Bob Brandon. "Otherwise you will always be shooting aftermath."[5]

SHOOT ONLY THE SHOTS YOU NEED

Most photographers have seen their worst shots make it into a presentation, broadcast, or onto the web. Usually they blame the editor: "The shot was out of focus/too shaky/too fuzzy/too green. *Why* did you put *that* shot on the air?" In turn, the editor usually blames deadlines that prevented a more critical review of the footage. If a shot with

(a)

(b)

FIGURE 4.7

To avoid "pop cuts," remember to shoot and move. In other words, physically move the camera to a new location and angle after every shot you make.

(c)

poor focus or an unsteady zoom resides in your video, it will often make its way onto the screen. The answer to such problems is to be found in the wisdom of professionals. "If you don't want it aired, don't shoot it," says Atlanta editor James Townley.[6]

This means that when you focus the camera, focus it before you pull the trigger to begin recording. Sometimes, things will happen so fast you may have to roll while you're focusing the lens, but in general try to work out all your shots, including zooms and pans, and rehearse them before you turn on the camera.

AVOID INDISCRIMINATE SHOOTING

With twenty- to sixty-minute field cassettes, hard drives, and memory sticks, many photographers overshoot their subjects. They simply shoot until the video is full, sometimes shooting twenty minutes of video or more for a simple thirty-second spot. This practice of shooting "editing fodder" wears down field batteries and forces editors under tight deadlines to handle unnecessary footage. As every editor knows, less footage is easier and quicker to edit.

Even if every shot is award-winning material, the editor faced with a ten-minute deadline may still have to cut the spot from the first two minutes of raw video anyway. If you discover that your best footage often is near the end of the shoot, become more selective and avoid shooting the camera randomly. The goal is to assess the story visually in your mind before you shoot each scene and to have a purpose for every shot you take, a process made easier if you have first identified the story to be told, and its essential points.

EDIT IN THE CAMERA

The best videographers are also experienced editors. Their experience at the edit console allows them to previsualize or edit a scene in their mind before they shoot it. This ability allows the photographer to **edit in the camera,** shooting sequences and overlapping action in generally the same order in which they later will be aired (Figure 4.8). The technique can save valuable editing time on stories that originate close to airtime. The technique can even help ensure that a story will be edited as the photographer wants it to be aired.

When you edit in the camera, it is important to concentrate on three shots at a time: the shot you're taking, the shot you just took, and the shot you will take next. With this approach, you will intuitively shoot more sequences and can more naturally maintain continuity in the action from one shot to the next.

FIGURE 4.8

Cameras that record on optical disc make editing in the camera faster and easier than ever. Video and audio files can be accessed directly on nonlinear editors without the need to digitize video to hard drive. Cuts-only editing is sometimes possible within the camera deck itself.

SHOOT TO ELIMINATE THE FALSE REVERSE

As you edit in the camera you can eliminate false reverses in the subject's screen direction by remembering to establish an axis line, then consciously shooting only on one side of that line. If the axis line is a confusing concept, just remember to keep action moving in the same direction in the viewfinder from one shot to the next. If the train is moving screen right, keep it moving screen right in every shot. If a person's nose points screen left, keep it pointing left in all shots.

If you retake a shot without altering composition, avoid the inadvertent airing of identical takes by placing your hand to the lens to blank out the screen or by recording a few frames of color bars between your identical takes. When you edit against deadlines, or whenever someone else edits your footage, these visual separations will help prevent jump cuts from making air.

Just as important, when you want particular footage to be aired, especially when the editor is on deadline, submit your footage for editing or digitizing with the video already cued to the best footage.

INVOLVE THE CAMERA IN THE ACTION

Try to move in close to your subjects and involve the camera in the action as intimately as possible. Go for detail and try to include full facial close-ups of people, in views that approximate how we see people in real life during our everyday, one-on-one encounters. Otherwise, the audience may feel cheated.

Full facial shots create high impact because of their emphasis on eyes. Close-up, detailed shots of eyes help reveal what the subject is thinking and feeling, so try to show both of the subject's eyes, rather than a profile shot that shows one ear and one eye (Figure 4.9).

In this context, telephoto shots seldom count for actually moving the camera close to the subject. Shots made on long focal length settings magnify the subject but tend to produce an artificial and unappealing sense of perspective. Telephoto shots rarely involve the audience as intimately as the camera that is truly close to the subject.

FIGURE 4.9

Full facial composition in which both of the subject's eyes can be seen is preferable to the often observed shot that shows only one of the person's eyes and an ear.

BOX 4.3 WORKING WITH STORY SUBJECTS

As I get to know the main characters and try to make them comfortable, I always talk with them throughout the story, either giving them questions regarding the story or explaining what we are doing. If, as I shoot cover footage and see they are nervous because the camera is on them, I sometimes turn my head away from the camera's eyepiece and caution them not to talk right now, explaining they might look like they're talking to themselves. They then begin to understand how the video will be edited and be-gin to feel part of the process. Explaining what may seem like a mysterious and glamorous process instead of just snapping, "don't talk" helps win the person's confidence in your mission. I always try to explain what I'm doing and try to relate to them and their comfort level by letting them know "I understand this is uncomfortable, but you are doing a great job" as I continue to gather the story all the while, keeping them on focus.

—John DeTarsio ▪

WORKING WITH PEOPLE

Because video is often about things that happen to people or otherwise affect their lives, an emphasis on people helps give most stories larger meaning. Without people in your stories, your reporting will tend toward institutional treatment, which many viewers may find dull and uninviting. Often, when you tell your stories through people, you can use their presence to help illuminate the larger meaning of events.

Working with people is essential for photographers to master because the most intimate relationship in the reporting process often develops between the photographer and subject. The process is less intimidating than it might at first appear to be. Most strangers will be willing to cooperate, provided you treat them with courtesy and respect.

To understand that relationship, consider having someone stick a camera in your face, stand two feet away, and follow every move you make. Now try to act natural while under that microscope and you'll understand why it's so important to develop rapport with your subject.

To make people feel comfortable you have to like people. Look for common ground with the subject, something you both have in common, something you can share with the other person. Unless you establish a comfortable relationship and your story subject is able to open up, the story will be stiff, period.

Confidence in yourself and your ability helps you avoid being intimidated by your gear or by onlookers or even by the subject of your story. If you do feel inhibited or intimidated, remember that self-confidence develops through experience. In a short time you should feel entirely at ease telling other peoples' stories.

AVOID DISTRACTING THE SUBJECT

Because the camera and other hardware interrupt reality, try to avoid drawing attention to yourself or any of your equipment whenever you work with people. Set up sound and lighting equipment with as few distractions as possible, preferably before your subject arrives, and try to make yourself "fade into the wallpaper."

If people are worried about how they'll look or how they should behave in front of the camera, they won't give you their best heat or white light. **Heat** is present when sound bites are spontaneous and believable and when they embody moments of emotional and intellectual intensity. **White light** occurs whenever the subject is natural, unaffected, and emotionally transparent while on camera. When white light occurs, viewers know they are experiencing something of the real person in a real environment.

FIGURE 4.10
The handheld or "stick" mike (left) can draw attention to itself and unnecessarily act as a barrier between the audience and reporter. The miniature lavaliere microphone is much less intrusive (right).

To further preserve spontaneity, try not to emphasize the microphone. Hand-held and shotgun mikes intimidate many people and create barriers between you and the subject. Furthermore, mike flags (station logos affixed to handheld microphones) tend to pull the viewer's eye away from the person and the person's emotion. Mikes are the only reporting equipment journalists still routinely photograph. Unless station policy dictates otherwise, consider substituting a wireless mike instead (Figure 4.10).

STAGING VERSUS MOTIVATING

When working with people, you have at least three options when photographing their activity. The first is to photograph people as they go about their affairs. This technique results in perhaps the most honest and natural depictions of the subject. A second approach is to ask the subject to perform a particular activity on camera. If the wood carver has decided not to work on the day you show up, you may have to ask him to carve anyway so you can shoot the video you need and get on to your next story assignment. Most photographers consider this practice ethically acceptable, because the subject performs only as he or she normally would in the photographer's absence. A third alternative, unacceptable at most operations, is to **stage** the action and ask people to do what they don't normally do or direct them to engage in activities that are out of character.

The far more preferable alternative to staging is to motivate people to do what they normally do. The process can be as simple as making an observation: "I'll bet you can still outrun your grandkids." If the photojournalist's luck holds, Grandpa may reply, "It's a fact. Here, let me show you."

THE ONE-PERSON BAND

The **one-person-band** defines anyone who shoots video and records audio *alone*, often while serving as both photographer and reporter Not only must those who labor alone simultaneously photograph and conduct the interviews for their stories, they may even photograph themselves in standups before the camera. Yet with only a little practice in the field, both techniques are easily mastered.

HOW TO SHOOT AND CONDUCT INTERVIEWS SIMULTANEOUSLY

Interviews are most easily conducted if the person to be interviewed remains busy at a familiar task. This allows the reporter-photographer to carry on a discussion with the person, sometimes without even formally asking questions, and without the need to

BOX 4.4 INTERVIEW STYLES

Interviews are an everyday fact in reporting and storytelling. They show people to people, and help give stories immediacy, authority, and spontaneity. The most common interview styles come in three flavors.

1. **Process interviews:** This approach lets the photojournalist have a conversation with story subjects as they go about a familiar task or some activity they've mastered. In formal interview settings, folks who seldom appear on camera or prefer not to appear, often fuss over what to wear or how their hair and makeup look. They focus attention inwardly, upon themselves, rather than the topic. Process interviews help such individuals feel less self-conscious.

   They also will become more comfortable around the camera(s) and microphones if you first shoot a couple of sequences while they perform some activity. After you've taken a few shots, you might throw out a simple observation, "That looks delicious," or "I know you've pulled this old ferry back and forth across the Rio Grande for a long time." Questions also work, "What happens next?" or "If people no longer need your ferry to enter Mexico, how will you earn a living?".

2. **Sit down interviews:** Once interview subjects know you better, and trust you, they may be willing to proceed to a quiet place for a formal, sit-down interview. Here, you would frame and light the subject in the most appealing ways possible, and compose the shot in a head-and-shoulders frame. Here you can ask the person more reflective questions about the story and perhaps uncover a meaningful emotional response that will help viewers more closely relate to the subject, "What were you thinking when that happened?" or "Tell me about the day you learned about your cancer."

3. **"Non-interview" interviews**: Throughout process and sit down interviews, try as well to conduct the "non-interview" interview, or as some call it, "the non-question question," which is nothing more than nonverbal language that encourages subjects to explain what they just said, state what remains unspoken, or encourage them to continue. It may be nothing more than holding their gaze without saying anything—looking directly, eye-to-eye; or giving the subject a gesture. Maybe it's a raise of the eyebrow in surprise, a positive gesture that suggests, "You're doing great!" or even a shrug or small smile. Storytellers sometimes discover those little nonverbal moments yield the best material. Your subject may not realize that little nod you gave them was an interview question, but it was.

—John DeTarsio ■

"interrupt reality" by placing the person in a staged interview setting. People usually are less self-conscious in this setting, so interviews can be more spontaneous.

Holding the camera during the interview seems to result in greater spontaneity than if the photojournalist mounts the camera on a tripod and concentrates most of his or her attention on the viewfinder. Preferably, the photojournalist can hold the camera while asking questions or commenting from off camera. The shotgun mike supplied on most field cameras usually is sufficient to pick up remarks from both the interviewer and interviewee. Because the camera mike is close enough to pick up your "I see's" and "Uh-huhs," you can indicate your interest and understanding of the interviewee's comments with an occasional and barely audible "Mmmm."[7]

You can work the camera quite close to the interviewee, provided you've established rapport with the other person. To help keep the subject from looking straight into the camera lens as you photograph the interview, you can try holding your left index finger to your left ear. Most subjects will obediently attach to this visual reference point during shooting, rather than to the camera lens, especially if they have been told in advance what to expect.

HOW TO PHOTOGRAPH YOUR OWN STANDUP

If you are shooting yourself in a static, nonmoving standup, simply place a light stand in front of the camera to mark the spot where you will stand. The top of the stand can extend to within a couple of inches of your height. Tape a business card or other small object to the stand at the same height as your eyes. Use this card or other object to help focus the lens and to establish correct framing and headroom. Clip a lapel mike to your clothing, set sound levels, roll video, and step in front of the camera to deliver your standup. Your body will block out the light stand you used as a reference point during the setup. If you must use a handheld mike, hang it on the mike stand before you roll the camera. When you step in front of the camera, simply grasp the mike, turn so that your body is centered in front of the light stand, and deliver your standup to the camera.

If you are doing a walking standup, frame the shot so that you leave room to move into and out of frame. Again, you can use the light stand to help you establish proper framing and headroom height. Set up the light stand where you want the right side of the scene to be framed, then move the stand and use it to help find where the left side of the frame ends in the viewfinder. You can mark both right and left limits of where you will enter and exit frame with a couple of rocks or with some gaffer's tape or any other suitable object. At this point, remove the stand so it doesn't appear in your shot. (Some cameras, you'll remember, show more than you see in the viewfinder)

Now, with the lens set on the desired composition, roll the camera, walk into frame, and "root" yourself, meaning that you set your body so that you don't begin to sway as you address the camera. When you are finished talking, give yourself an edit point before you exit frame or else exit frame naturally as you finish talking.

Network correspondent John Larson offers more guidelines about shooting your own interviews and standups in Chapter 11, Video Journalism: Storytelling on Your Own.

SHOOTING IN COLD WEATHER

When shooting in cold weather, keep batteries, camera, and recording media dry, covered, and as warm as possible. Especially try to avoid storing tapes or batteries in the car during cold weather. When you move the camera inside from the cold, give it adequate time to warm slowly to room temperature (Figure 4.11).

Humidity and condensation can occur on the camera lens and inside the camera itself as the equipment is moved from a cold environment to a warm, relatively moist room. Some cameras shut down when moisture levels climb too high, until the moisture has evaporated or the video record mechanism is physically dried.

Cassettes that become too cold can tear or break during taping, and if they are exposed suddenly to a warm environment, moisture may condense inside the cassette. Clogged video heads soon follow. During heavy rain or snowfall, the best solution seems to be a kind of fairly loose "raincoat" that allows excess moisture to escape before it can damage the camera lens or condense inside the camera. This so-called raincoat is nothing more than a loose cape that you can buy, or make from waterproof materials to fit the machinery at hand.

FIGURE 4.11
Plummeting temperatures take their toll on field equipment, batteries, and people.

When you must work in the cold, try to install batteries in the camera at the last possible moment, and then try to spend as little time making your shots as necessary. Try to keep batteries and recording media as warm as possible, preferably under your winter coat next to your body. When the shots are made, remove the batteries from your equipment and if possible return to a warm car and let warm air from the car's heater or defroster blow across them. If you must shoot outdoors in frigid weather for long periods, consider covering the camera housing with a padded cover. Some covers are available or can be made to order with pockets specially built to accommodate portable hand warmers.

SAFETY FIRST

When you cover spot news you learn when it's wise to avoid risky, sometimes hazardous situations. If you are to expose yourself to danger while covering events, the cause must be terribly worthwhile. Possibly no event is worth risking death or serious injury. Train yourself to be aware and learn to recognize that the brick wall in front of you may collapse at any moment or that you are in the middle of the SWAT team's line of fire or that noxious fumes and smoke are creeping your way. Also carry what gear you need to help protect yourself and your equipment (Figure 4.12).

Although you can be physically hurt while covering the news, it is just as possible to be emotionally hurt. Perhaps a man's wife has just died or a family has lost its home in a fire, or perhaps a three-year-old girl in a story you cover suffers from terminal cancer. No one says journalists must be the tough, silent type. The important thing is to admit your feelings and if something bothers you, talk it out with someone you trust.

FIGURE 4.12
Video journalists encounter hazards that range from dust storms, cave-ins, and fire, to oil spills, enraged crowds, tear gas, and military combat. Here, videographers encounter a New Mexico sandstorm while shooting a television series.

DISTANCING

Also of potential concern when you cover the news is a phenomenon called **distancing**. As you watch the action unfold in the camera viewfinder, a feeling develops that you're watching the event on TV. The event may seem remote, even unreal, and at such moments you may almost feel that nothing can hurt you. Dozens of photographers have looked up to find parade floats and football players almost upon them, all because of the erroneous sense of distance that resulted from the false perspectives of wide-angle and telephoto lens settings.

SAFETY IN NUMBERS

An extra set of eyes can offer the photographer an important margin of safety. Whereas the photojournalist's attention is focused in the viewfinder, the reporter or someone you enlist can be alert to action that develops outside the viewfinder frame. This person also can watch your back in dangerous crowd situations, making paths through crowds as you record the action, or acting as driver while you make shots on the move.

PLAN TO MAKE MISTAKES

Every photographer encounters common problems the first few times in the field. With only slight exaggeration, some photographers suggest you're not a professional until you've committed every mistake there is to commit, at least twice. The following list of most common mistakes forms a starting point; you may wish to add additional notes based on your own field experiences.

SHAKINESS   Tripod all shots until you learn to hold the camera rock steady. If you can't use a tripod, shoot on wide angle and support the camera and your body by leaning or resting against stationary objects. Remember never to hold the camera when the lens is set on telephoto.

COLOR BALANCE   Set the camera's white balance to achieve an absence of color at white. Adjust white balance each time the light source changes. Some cameras have a memory chip that allows you to preset indoor/outdoor white balance values. Thus, if you're following a suspect from fluorescent light inside a courthouse hall to bright sunlight outside, you can hit the white balance switch as you move outside and be assured of proper white balance.

WRONG FILTER   If needed, determine that the proper camera filter is in place under each source of light—sunlight, fluorescent, artificial, mercury-vapor, athletic playing fields, and so on.

RECORD COLOR BARS   Remember to record color bars for ten to fifteen seconds at the start of each tape or disk. Color bars provide a reference of the field camera's color output, contrast, and video signal strength. Color bars also provide space at the start of videotape for edit prerolling. Without space for the edit preroll, the beginning of the first scene on tape cannot be edited.

EXPOSURE PROBLEMS   Guard against under- and overexposure and hot spots in the frame. Use the automatic camera meter to set exposure, but then shoot on manual iris, in order to avoid the exposure "bloom" that results from moving objects when the lens is set on auto iris.

FOCUS PROBLEMS   Establish crisp focus; avoid zooming in to unintentional soft focus or zooming out to soft focus.

CONTRAST PROBLEMS   Avoid high-contrast backlit scenes that occur when the main light is behind the subject you are shooting. Use front fill light if necessary. Some examples of backlit scenes: shooting the person's face against the background of a bright sky; shooting the subject against a light-colored background; shooting a subject in front of a window (close the curtains behind your subject).

COMPOSITION PROBLEMS   Compose each shot carefully. Avoid distracting backgrounds. Adhere to the rule of thirds to avoid placing subjects in the dead center of frame. Leave room at the bottom of the shot for superimpositions of the speaker's name. Avoid tilted horizon lines.

TOO MUCH PANNING AND ZOOMING   Practice self-control when you zoom and pan. Hold the beginning of your shot steady for about three seconds, then zoom or pan, and again hold the shot steady for another three seconds before you stop the camera.

SOUND PROBLEMS   Monitor sound quality in the field through earphones. If you hear high-quality sound while you are recording, you know the sound will be usable for broadcast.

WIND NOISE   Protect against wind noise when recording sound in the field. Use the foam rubber windscreen furnished with the microphone, or wrap a dark-colored cloth neatly around the microphone. When fashioning a homemade windscreen, avoid white because it may bloom, or appear to be overexposed, on home screens.

SPOT-CHECK TAPES AND DIGITALLY ACQUIRED IMAGES IN FIELD   Preview video in the field before you return home. Most systems feature instant playback through the camera viewfinder. Playback lets you spot troubles that have developed during shooting while you're still in the field, where reshooting may still be possible.

LABEL ALL VIDEO   Immediately label each cassette, hard drive, or memory stick with subject matter and date. Unlabeled video can drive you and the editor up the wall.

DEAD BATTERIES   Number field batteries and use them in sequence so you know which ones are still charged. When working some distance from the news car or helicopter, take extra recording media and one extra battery, fully charged.

PROTECT FIELD EQUIPMENT   Field equipment is extremely sensitive and the quality of pictures and sound depends on careful handling. Regularly clean and check all equipment, including front lens elements. See that no one bangs, jars, or drops equipment. Protect cords and cables against rough treatment. Fragile electrical connections may short-circuit or come loose, resulting in loss of power, picture, and/or sound. Neatly re-coil all cords and cables and return them to their proper cases. Replace the lens cap on the camera. Don't leave the lens cap in the field by accident.

ON RETURNING TO THE STATION

- *Charge batteries.* Immediately recharge all batteries that have been depleted in the field.
- *Be considerate of the next person or crew.* Be certain to leave blank recording media with each camera so the next person or crew doesn't enter the field unprepared.
- *Store equipment properly.* Store equipment in its assigned place on returning from the field.
- *Report damage.* Report any damage or malfunctions immediately.

SUMMARY

Attention to small details in photographic technique can markedly differentiate the work of one photographer from the next. Often, the most professional techniques are transparent to home viewers. A hallmark of professional photographers is their ability to hold the camera rock steady. Use of a tripod or appropriate stance and breathing techniques are necessary to produce a steady image. Professionals always have a reason to pan and zoom: Leave excessive panning and zooming to amateur photographers.

Beyond mastery of technique, skills in storytelling and planning are essential requisites for the professional video journalist. Discrimination in the order and choice of shots made in the field helps preserve story focus, reduces the amount of unnecessary footage and time wasted in the field, and speeds the editing process.

Television is a medium of close-ups, textures, and details, so the viewer's greatest sense of involvement and first-person experience naturally results when the camera is involved in the action. Equally important is the need to focus more on people than on institutions during the reporting process. The photographer also must learn to work comfortably with people in order to portray them naturally and with spontaneity, and to work safely and prudently whatever the environment. Ultimately, success depends on mastery of creative and technical principles through unflagging attention to detail.

KEY TERMS

distancing   78
edit in the camera   71
heat   73
negative action   67
one-person band   75

reveal   67
rule of thirds   61
screen space   63
stage   74
TV cutoff   64

white light   73
zoom in   67
zoom out   67

DISCUSSION

1. List the advantages and disadvantages of using a tripod when shooting television news.
2. What are the most important techniques that can be used to steady the handheld camera?
3. Explain the primary considerations that govern panning and zooming.
4. Why is it important to establish interactive communication in the field between the photographer and reporter?
5. What techniques can be used to avoid the pop cut?
6. Define the term *editing in the camera,* and discuss situations in which the technique can be useful.
7. Why is it important to involve the camera in the action?
8. What approaches can you use when working with people to make your stories more natural and interesting?
9. What is the difference between staging action and motivating it?
10. Explain the steps involved in shooting your own standup in the field.
11. Explain how to simultaneously shoot and conduct an interview in the field.
12. What precautions must the photographer observe when shooting in a cold environment?
13. Discuss the elements of safety you should observe whenever you cover news events.

EXERCISES

1. Continue to practice holding the camera until you can hold it rock steady. Adjust the camera until it is balanced on your shoulder; observe proper breathing technique and stance. Shoot a shot while standing up; shoot the same shot while leaning against a support. Rest the camera against the back of a chair or other support while you shoot. Compare handheld shots taken with the lens set on wide-angle and telephoto focal-length settings.

2. Practice panning and zooming a subject at differing speeds. Then photograph the same subject without panning or zooming. Compare the result.

3. Create a pop cut for analysis: First shoot a long shot of a subject under your control, then physically move the camera toward the subject along the same axis line as you shoot medium and close shots. Now, move the camera back to its original position. Again shoot a long shot of the subject, but remember to move the camera off the original axis line as you shoot and move to photograph the medium and close shots. Edit the scenes together and compare the results.

4. Shoot a simple sequence in which you edit action in the camera. Shoot only those scenes you want on the air, in the order you want them to appear, with action as closely matched as possible. Show the result without editing any of the scenes.

5. Shoot close shots of action from a distant location with the lens on a telephoto setting. Now, involve the camera in the action by physically moving it close to the action to record shots. Compare the screen results.

6. Working with a friend or willing stranger, try to motivate an action that would be familiar to your subject without letting the subject know your intent, such as the observation made to a spelling bee champion, "I'll bet you can even spell chrysanthemum." Next, stage the action, perhaps telling your subject, "Okay, why don't you sit here, and I'll tell you a word to spell. Ready?" Compare the spontaneity in each approach.

7. Practice photographing yourself in a field standup, using the suggestions offered in this chapter and Appendix B.

8. With the help of a friend who can act as your interview source, practice holding the camera while you interview your friend.

9. Ask a couple of friends if you can follow them around with the camera. Practice photographing moments of heat and white light.

NOTES

1. Gary Croshaw, comments to journalism class, Colorado State University, Fort Collins, April 11, 1995.

2. John Premack, "Avoiding Mistakes," a presentation at the NPPA TV News-Video Workshop, Norman, OK, March 14, 1994.

3. Kirk Bloom, cinematographer, Los Angeles, CA, in undated correspondence with the lead author.

4. Darrel Barton, network freelance correspondent, comments to journalism students at the University of Oklahoma, Norman, OK, November 5, 2005.

5. Bob Brandon, comments in a critique session at the NPPA TV News-Video Workshop, Norman, OK, May 20, 2003.

6. James Townley, "Videotape Editing: The Basics," a presentation at the NPPA TV News-Video Workshop, Norman, OK, March 14, 1994.

7. Larry Hatteberg, "Working with People," a presentation at the NPPA Television News-Video Workshop, Norman, OK, March 16, 1992.

5

Writing with Light

Light has as much substance as words or gale force winds. Light is real stuff, as real as ink and sound, and in television and video, light is the communicators' primary medium. Until the advent of photography, we could never see or hear the past or present.[1] Since photography's invention, the past has been recalled not simply from memory, or through words, but from a tangible record the original photons created when they glanced off the actual subjects of our stories and were captured on video. Through videotape and digital recordings, the past can be captured, condensed, and reviewed at will. This is the magic embodied in the word *photography*, which is taken from Greek root words meaning "writing with light."

As the artist's palette in this electronic medium, light is thus far more important to the work of the video journalists than merely as a source of illumination to provide an exposure. Light does illuminate, but when properly controlled it also lends texture, emphasis, and emotion. In video journalism, light is form. Light is mood. Light is meaning.

The most "natural" light is natural light (Figure 5.1). The best lighting is invisible. In fact, the strongest and most honest stories often contain little or no lighting. But, when natural light wanes, and your story fades, you'll profit from understanding the following lighting techniques.

You'll encounter basic but essential lighting concepts and patterns here. You also can achieve the most important patterns outdoors, under natural sunlight. At first blush, they may appear complex, perhaps unnecessary. Don't be fooled. Learning to control light, and work smart with available light, is akin not only to learning a native language, but figuring out how to whisper, speak, and shout while using it.

PHOTOGRAPHY IS THE ART OF CONTROLLING LIGHT

In many ways, then, photography is the art of capturing and controlling light. Until the advent of electronic cameras, the photographer was forced to manipulate light, its intensity and color, to suit the whimsy of film stock. With today's technology, the photographer can adjust electronic circuitry to accommodate a greater range of light conditions and color.

Color Temperature

The **color temperature** of lighting sources is measured according to a scale of degrees Kelvin (°K), which indicates the proportion of red to blue light the light source radiates. Daylight is a combination of all the light rays in the visible spectrum, but daylight contains a higher proportion of blue than some other sources. Tungsten halogen lights, commonly used in video and television lighting, contain all the light rays of the visible spectrum, but with a higher proportion of red hues than daylight produces.

Some cameras automatically monitor color balance. Other video field cameras are set up to reproduce colors accurately only under light sources with a color temperature of 3200°K. If light entering the lens is anything other than 3200°K, the scenes will be either too green or blue (at color temperatures above 3200°K) or too red or orange (at temperatures below 3200°K). This means that outdoors, without compensating filters or auto monitoring, the camera will "see" sunlight as overly blue.

An understanding of color temperatures is important for photojournalists because professionals often need to fine tune settings for proper white balance to reproduce pure white and accurate colors under each of the various light sources. **White balance** is defined as the absence of color at white.

The laws of physics that influence color temperature are different from our psychological and physical reactions to color and temperature. Human experience leads us to associate the color blue with cool or cold objects and the color red with warm or hot objects. In the case of color temperature, *just the opposite is true* (Figure 5.2). As the color temperature increases, the light becomes progressively more bluish. As color temperature decreases, the light becomes progressively more reddish. Thus, with color temperatures, blue is "hot"; red is "cool."

FIGURE 5.1

Natural light is often most natural, even under sunlight, and even indoors. Otherwise, you can achieve natural lighting patterns by understanding how to position artificial lights indoors, and even outdoors under natural sunlight by knowing how to position your camera and your subjects.

Tungsten Halogen Light Sources

The artificial light source frequently used in television news is the tungsten halogen bulb. Many professionals just call them quartz, tungsten, or halogen lights. Small, lightweight, and portable, tungsten halogen lights produce brilliant illumination at a relatively constant color temperature of 3000°K to 3200°K (see Figure 5.2). The color temperature can be held constant because the bulb is filled with an inert gas that prevents the glowing tungsten filament from discoloring the inside of the bulb as it burns. Because of the inert gas tungsten halogen bulbs have the capacity to "renew" themselves. In an atmosphere in which virtually no combustion is possible, particles that evaporate from the filament redeposit onto the filament.

Filters

Videographers and photojournalists rely on three basic **filter** applications to control light, color temperature, and sometimes depth-of-field. These applications encompass filters used on cameras, artificial lights, and windows.

Color Temperature Scale		
	DEGREES KELVIN	**TYPE OF LIGHT SOURCE**
Reddish hues	2000–3000°K	Sun at sunrise or sunset
	2500–2900°K	Household tungsten bulbs
	3200–3500°K	Quartz lights
	3200–7500°K	Fluorescent lights
	3275°K	Tungsten lamp 2k
	3380°K	Tungsten lamp 5k, 10k
Bluish hues	5000–5400°K	Sun: direct at noon
	5500–6500°K	Sun (sun + sky)
	5500–6500°K	Sun: through clouds/haze
	6000–7500°K	Sky: overcast
	7000–8000°K	Outdoor shade areas
	8000–10,000°K	Sky: partly cloudy

FIGURE 5.2

The color temperature of various light sources is measured in degrees Kelvin (°K) as an indication of the proportion of red to blue light radiated by the light source. As light sources change, the television camera's white balance must be adjusted to produce an absence of color at white under these varying hues of color.

Source: "Kelvin Color Temperatures," www.3drender.com/glossary/colortemp.htm (accessed February 13, 2011). Based on information by Jeremy Birn, *Digital Lighting & Rendering*, (Indianapolis: New Riders Publishing, 2000).

Camera-mounted filters: filters that are mounted on the front of the camera lens or just behind the lens inside the camera.

Light-mounted filters: gel or optical glass filters that are positioned directly on the light head in a mount or clamp-type holder.

Window-mounted filters: filters mounted directly on windows and normally used to change the color temperature of sunlight entering a room to 3200°K.

In each case, the goal is to correct the color temperature, or else to change the quantity of light entering the camera so that a different aperture can be used to control depth of field. No filter is required on the camera when a light source has an intrinsic color temperature of 3200°K. Under all other color temperatures, some form of filter or compensating electronic circuitry is required.

Camera-Mounted Filters

The most traditional camera-mounted filters are the amber (#85), fluorescent (FLB or FLD), and neutral density (ND) filters. On some older video cameras, these filters are built into a filter wheel that can be clicked into proper position behind the lens according to a reference chart printed on the side of the camera body. Commonly, digital cameras provide automatic white balance without filters, with high-end cameras permitting manual white balance for even more precise color control. Understanding how filters work is still important, however.

#85 B Filter   The amber-colored #85 filter converts sunlight in the vicinity of 5400°K to 3200°K. Average daytime sunlight, which otherwise would appear overly blue to the camera, is reduced to the same color temperature as the artificial light from tungsten bulbs so that normal color results. An amber filter must be used anytime the light source, regardless of whether it is natural sunlight or artificial fill light, is 5400°K, or reasonably close to that figure.

Practically speaking, in average daylight conditions, the #85 filter can be used anytime from a couple of hours after sunrise to within a couple of hours before sunset. It is best, however, to use no filter or a clear filter within one hour after sunrise or one hour before sunset. At these times of day, color temperature is already between 3200°K and 3500°K, a range that closely parallels the camera's preset preference for color temperature.

FLUORESCENT (FL) FILTERS Two designations of camera-mounted fluorescent filters can be used to accommodate fluorescent light that otherwise would be reproduced with an undesirable greenish-blue cast. The first of these is the FLB filter, used under fluorescent bulbs that produce color temperatures in the range of 4500°K. The second is the FLD filter, used under "daylight" fluorescent bulbs that produce color temperatures in the range of fine to cloudy daylight, or 6500°K. Once again, FL filters produce the appearance of a color temperature around 3200°K.

NEUTRAL DENSITY (ND) FILTERS A third type of camera-mounted filter, the ND filter, reduces the amount of light entering the camera but otherwise has no effect on either color temperature or the colors of objects within scenes. The primary function of this dark, smoke-colored filter is to cut exposure—either to help reduce depth of field by permitting a wider lens aperture (resulting in less emphasis on the background and greater emphasis on the subject), or to reduce exposure under very bright light sources to acceptable limits.

LIGHT-MOUNTED FILTERS

The *dichroic filter* is most commonly used on lights. This filter, made of gel or optical glass, has a pronounced bluish hue. It boosts the color temperature of quartz-halogen lights (3200°K) to the approximate color temperature of sunlight (5400°K). The filter helps achieve balanced color temperatures when sunlight and artificial light are mixed. Artificial **fill lights** outfitted with dichroic filters are useful outdoors, with the sun used as the key light, and indoors regardless of whether sunlight entering through a window is used as the key or the fill light.

Window-Mounted Filters

Semiflexible panels and flexible sheets of #85 amber filters sometimes are used on exterior windows to convert sunlight to 3200°K. The sheets also can be taped to car windows, thereby allowing the use of 3200°K fill lights inside the car—for example, to photograph an interview with a police officer as she patrols a neighborhood. These filters also can be taped over house and office windows to convert the sunlight entering a room to 3200°K. It is then possible to supplement the sunlight with artificial lights with a color temperature of 3200°K. If sunlight at 5400°K is allowed to enter the interior of a car or room, then artificial fill light must be pumped up to 5400°K by means of a dichroic filter mounted on the light head. This alternative is less desirable because more lights and higher wattage bulbs may be required to overcome the exposure-reducing effects of the dichroic filter.

Filter Factors

All filters, even clear glass, filter out some light. With clear filters, the light loss is virtually unnoticeable, but with other filters the light loss can be significant enough to result in underexposure. The amount of loss for a given filter is expressed as the **filter factor**.

Each factor of 2 cuts the original amount of light in half, an amount equal to one f/stop decrease in the amount of light entering the lens. Thus, if a scene were being photographed at f/16, a new exposure of f/11 would be necessary if the scene were to be rephotographed using a filter with a filter factor of 2. Cameras with automatic exposure circuitry compensate automatically for this light loss, but an understanding of filter factors is still important to the professional photographer.

The ND filter, for example, allows the photographer to achieve normal exposure in extremely bright light conditions. ND filters also allow the photographer to shoot at wider lens apertures in any given lighting environment than would otherwise be possible. Wider apertures, in turn, result in reduced or shallow depth of field.

Filters Used in Combination

Note that each filter factor of 2 results in the equivalent of one f/stop of light loss. To determine the light loss that occurs when filters are used in combination, it is necessary to *multiply* the filter factors. Because some picture quality is lost when two filters are used together, manufacturers commonly combine dyes with the characteristics of two filters into the physical properties of one filter.

One of the most common filters of this type is the 85N6 filter, which combines the color conversion characteristics of the #85 amber filter (with a filter factor of 1.5)

BOX 5.1 TRY YOUR HAND WITH FILTERS AND LIGHTING

The following situations and discussion are provided to illustrate how you can use various light sources and camera filters in combination. (Assume your camera has no auto color balance.)

Situation 1: Outdoors, under normal sunlight, set up an artificial fill light and balance its color temperature to sunlight.

Situation 2: You're shooting an indoor scene in front of a window. Across the street, in sunlight, is other important action that can be seen through the window. What combination of lights and filters can be used to achieve balanced color temperatures?

Situation 3: You're shooting an interview inside a moving car. You've placed a #85 gel filter on the driver's window to convert sunlight to 3200°K and have decided to use a quartz fill light with a color temperature of 3200°K. Which filter do you use on the camera?

Discussion

In situation 1, the sun, with a color temperature of around 5400°K, serves as the key light while the fill light produces a color temperature of 3200°K. A dichroic filter must be mounted on the light head to boost the artificial light to the color temperature of sunlight. In addition, you would want to place a #85 amber filter on the camera lens.

In situation 2, two solutions are possible. If sunlight is the dominant light source inside the room, the camera should be outfitted with a #85 amber filter. To match the color temperature of sunlight, all quartz fill lights should be outfitted with dichroic filters.

If, in situation 2, artificial quartz lights provide the dominant light (3200°K), then no filter should be used on the camera lens. Sunlight entering the room should further be converted to 3200°K by use of #85 filter sheets placed on the window.

In situation 3, you would simply shoot the scene as is, with no filter of any kind on the camera lens. ■

and the light-reducing properties of the ND 0.6 filter (filter factor of 4). Thus, the combined filter factor of the 85N6 filter is 6:

$$1.5 = \text{filter factor of #85 filter}$$
$$\underline{\times\ 4} = \text{filter factor of ND 0.6 filter}$$
$$6 = \text{combined filter factor}$$

MIXING LIGHT SOURCES

Poor color reproduction can result when light sources are mixed. Indoors, the photographer should avoid mixing fluorescent light (greenish hue) with daylight (bluish hue) or tungsten lights (reddish hue). Outdoors, an inadvertent mix of sunlight and tungsten light also produces undesirable results. Any of the light sources used alone—fluorescent, daylight, or tungsten—are acceptable, but they should never be mixed unless they can be balanced with filters.

Check for the presence of various light sources as one of the first steps after you arrive on location. If daylight in the room is strong enough, you can use it as the only light source. If different light sources are present, perhaps you can turn off all fluorescent lights in the room, close curtains in the room to block unwanted sunlight, and light the scene only with tungsten lights. If the fluorescent lights can't be turned off, use them if they provide sufficient illumination. Otherwise, you will have to overpower them with artificial lights or perhaps a combination of sunlight and artificial light color-balanced to the temperature of sunlight.

BASIC LIGHTING PATTERNS

Most lighting patterns borrow from nature's design. The most frequent pattern is one dominant light source (the sun or an artificial light) combined with a secondary light source. The dominant source produces direct light rays that throw strong highlights and distinct shadows in an effect called **specular light**. The goal is to make the light look as though it originates from one source, even when three lights are being used, and to light in such a way that subjects have dimension, not flatness.

The secondary light source, whether artificial or from the sun's rays that reflect off objects in the environment, is soft and diffused. Secondary light yields no hard shadows and no distinct highlights because it has been broken up and randomly scattered as it reflects off the multitude of objects and surfaces within an environment.

THE ROLE OF ARTIFICIAL LIGHT

For most photographers, the sun remains a favorite light source. But for all its charm, sunlight is never reliable or under a photographer's control, and it seldom is available in sufficient quantity when the shooting moves indoors. In such conditions artificial light gives the photographer control over illumination, and when properly controlled, can recreate the natural look of available sunlight. Proper light control also gives the illusion of depth in scenes and makes possible the creation of textures and interesting highlights and shadows.

KEY LIGHT

For natural-looking news scenes that replicate the look and feel of available light, almost all artificial lighting setups have one dominant light source called the **key light**. This light represents the function of the sun and provides the distinctive highlights and shadows in the scene.

When using the older, more traditional tungsten lights, the key light is usually placed higher than the subject to be photographed and to one side of the camera, somewhere between 30° and 45° over from the camera axis and high enough so that the light can be aimed down 45° or steeper at the subject, in a pattern called *high side lighting.*

When using a Chimera® (described in this chapter) or Lowel Rifa® soft box, for example, the key light is placed much lower (see Figure 5.3). Irrespective of light source, the key light is placed properly when it throws a triangle of light on the shadow side of the subject's face.

Outdoors the photographer can achieve the same effect using the sun as the key light. In this approach you can reposition the subject until the triangle appears on the shadow side of the face.

Variations to the high side light pattern include the *side light*, sometimes called **hatchet light** because it splits the subject in half, and *side-rear lighting*, in which the key light is placed to the side and somewhat behind the subject.

Another variation is *top lighting*, with the key light almost directly above the subject. This technique throws deep shadows beneath the eyes, nose, and chin. A variation of top lighting is called **butterfly light** (Figure 5.4). The light remains high but is

FIGURE 5.3

Butterfly or glamour lighting occurs when the light is positioned high but slightly in front of the subject. Note the modeling in the subject's face created by shadows beneath the eyebrows, nose, lips, and chin. A single light will produce a butterfly pattern if you position it until you see a "butterfly" pattern beneath the subject's nose.

FIGURE 5.4

High side lighting occurs when the key light is placed high and to one side of the camera in front of the subject. Note the triangle of light on the shadow side of the subject's face.

slightly in front of the subject so that no harsh shadows appear in the eyes or under the lips. This lighting pattern takes its name from the butterfly-shaped shadow that appears beneath the subject's nose and can be an excellent choice of patterns when only one light is used. Butterfly lighting is also called *glamour lighting* because it is commonly used with models and actors.

CONTRAST CONTROL

Analog video is less sensitive to detail than the human eye, and in dark shadow areas it may lose detail altogether. High-definition video is far more sensitive to detail. Irrespective of the primary light source, most photographers use a fill light (the secondary light source) to create depth and dimension in the subject's face. The fill light often is set to produce illumination about half as intense as the key light (Figure 5.5).

You can achieve the same fill effect outdoors with a reflector or with a battery-powered light equipped with a dichroic filter that raises the color temperature of tungsten lights to that of sunlight. For soft fill outdoors, use a white reflector with a matte surface (Figure 5.6), or for hard fill light, an aluminum foil reflector. White walls and other objects also can be used outdoors if they reflect light of the same approximate color temperature as the key light source.

THE INVERSE-SQUARE LAW OF LIGHT

The fill light is located approximately mirror opposite the key light and adjusted so that it illuminates the subject at about half the intensity of the key light. To arrive at this intensity, the photographer can use the **inverse-square law of light**. This law states

FIGURE 5.5

A key light is used to illuminate the right side of the subject's face (left). In the picture on the right, a fill light has been added to open up detail in harsh shadow areas on the subject's face.

that at twice the distance from a subject, artificial lights provide only one-fourth their original level of illumination (Figure 5.6).

Stated another way, if you have two identical lights, one twice as far from your subject as the other, the farther light will be only 25 percent as bright on the subject as the closer light.

This would provide a key-to-fill contrast ratio of about 4:1. The key light is four times brighter than the fill light. For analog television lighting the normal contrast ratio

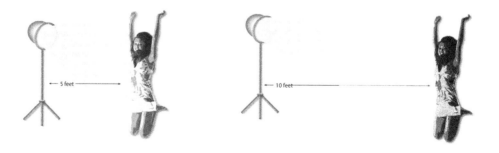

FIGURE 5.6

The inverse-square law of light can be visualized by looking at the diagrams. Doubling the original distance between your light and the subject reduces light intensity to one-fourth its original level.

© 2012 by Laura Schaub Designs

Lighting ratios are expressions of the difference between the most brightly illuminated areas of a subject and the areas of least exposure. Calculations are based on the difference in intensities between the key and fill lights. In the following table, a 1:1 ratio indicates that key and fill light intensities are identical: There is no difference in

illumination on either side of the subject's face. A 4:1 ratio indicates that light on the key side of the face is four times brighter than on the fill side. In the case of the 4:1 ratio, the key light determines exposure. If the key light were to be turned off but the fill light left on, the subject would be two stops underexposed. ■

should be approximately 3:1 for best color and contrast control. To achieve this, the fill light should be placed about one and a half times the distance of the key from the subject.

Assume, for example, that the key light is six feet from the subject to be photographed. To maintain proper contrast control for video, the fill light in this case should be placed about nine feet from the subject.

BACKLIGHT

To the key and fill lights, the photographer can add a **backlight** (also called the *accent* or *separation light*). This light is placed opposite the key and shines down on the subject from behind to give the subject's hair added texture and sheen and to separate the subject more obviously from the background. A fourth light, the *background light*, illuminates the background to provide even greater separation of the subject from its background.

BROADLIGHTING AND SHORT LIGHTING

When the key light shines on the side of the face closest to the camera, the effect is called **broadlighting**. Generally, broadlight is the preferred lighting pattern for interviews and news conferences. In **short lighting,** the fill light shines on the side of the face toward the camera. The technique is used widely in portrait photography, and it can be used as warranted in visual stories to achieve a different mood and feeling.

LIGHTING FOR HIGH DEFINITION

High-definition television brings viewers face to face with people's physical imperfections. With clarity roughly six times greater than analog television,[2] high-def cameras magnify everything from acne scars to wrinkles, bags under the eyes, and poor makeup jobs. High-def studio lighting and adjustments in makeup help hide those imperfections for news anchors, but without similar lighting adjustments in the field an anchor, reporter, or virtually anyone else can suddenly appear 10 years older.[3]

The backlight separates your subject from the background. When shooting indoors, you might use a window as your key light (light coming from a window is often pleasantly soft), and use one

light as a backlight/sidelight. If a lamp is available in the room, you might use that as a sidelight or backlight. ■

HMI Lights

Professionals shooting high def often use **HMI** lights (Figure 5.7), short for Hydrargyrum Medium Arc-Length Iodide. Aside from their high cost, HMIs offer several advantages. They produce a soft, natural look, and full, rich color, while using only about a fifth the energy of quartz lights. HMI bulbs produce full-spectrum, bluish light much like noon sunlight (5600°K). Photographers and subjects alike also appreciate how much cooler they operate.

FLAT LIGHTING

When the photographer must shoot fast-moving action, there often is not time to properly light the scene. For this reason most digital cameras can power a single battery-operated quartz light that mounts directly to the camera. This approach frees the photographer's hands to make camera and lens adjustments, but it results in a pattern called **flat lighting**, which produces uninteresting pictures with little depth or modeling.

A better solution, whenever possible, is to use the single light high and to one side of the camera. In this position the light produces shadows that lend depth and interest to the face.

A common mistake with the single light is letting harsh shadows fall on the background behind the subject. At least three remedies are possible: Hold the light so that shadows fall outside the viewfinder frame, move the light and the subject farther away from the background, or compose a closer shot in such a way that no shadows are visible within the viewfinder.

LIGHT DIFFUSION

In all lighting patterns, some kind of diffusion material over the lights can produce softer, more pleasing natural light. Diffusion materials include spun glass, heat-resistant plastic, metal window screen, and metallic mesh. These materials reduce glare and harshness in the scene by breaking up direct light rays and radiating them in random directions. Diffused light also is less noticeable to persons who otherwise would be uncomfortable and self-conscious under the harsh glare of direct television lights.

Umbrella lighting offers a quick, inexpensive way to convert a single light into a viable soft light source. With an umbrella reflector, the light head is pointed *away* from the subject. The light is then reflected back to the subject via a metallic-colored, heat-resistant umbrella attached to the light stand or head (Figure 5.8). In a sit-down interview, the light can be placed above the reporter's head or where the reporter would be if present.

FIGURE 5.7

Short for Hydrargyrum Medium Arc-Length Iodide, HMI lights produce a soft, natural look with the color temperature of sunlight while using only about a fifth the energy of quartz lights.

Light from this single source wraps naturally around the subject. Shadows are soft and smooth, and in close-up shots only a single highlight or catchlight is obvious in each of the subject's eyes. The light from umbrella reflectors is virtually unnoticeable to home audiences. Interview subjects appear more at ease, and they are more comfortable because of the cooler temperatures that result from indirect light. Umbrella reflectors are available at most camera and photo supply stores for fifty dollars, a relatively small investment considering the improved lighting that results.

BOUNCE LIGHTING

Bounce light is another way to produce soft, natural lighting. Bounce lights can be reflected (bounced) off a ceiling, wall, or some other reflective surface. Bounce light is diffused and less harsh than direct lighting, but take care to avoid unwanted color temperatures when bouncing the light off colored surfaces.

EYE REFLECTIONS

In real life and in natural portraiture, each eye normally contains only one highlight. When lights are improperly placed, however, the subject's eyes frequently contain two highlights (catchlights), which make it obvious that the subject is being "lit." The problem is compounded when eyeglass lenses and frames produce still other distracting highlights. Although dual highlights and unwanted reflections cannot always be eliminated, they can often be minimized. The most common solution is to move the camera or to change the projection angle of the lights, or to use some form of indirect lighting that may solve the problem altogether.

FIGURE 5.8
An umbrella reflector can produce dramatic improvement in lighting quality.

BOX 5.4   LIGHTING FOR HIGH-DEFINITION TV

The key light is most often a soft light, which produces a more flattering and appealing look. Several approaches can help soften the key light. Chimera®, Lowel®, and other companies manufacture a collapsible light box with a reflective silver interior and a front diffusion screen. Such boxes fit on a variety of light heads and produce soft, pleasing light (see Figures 5.9 and 5.10).

Setting the Key Light for Sit-Down Interviews
Sunlight is often most pleasant when it's low. To recreate that same look with the Chimera® Lightbank, bring the key light down low, about a foot above the subject's eyes. At this angle, the light is perfectly placed (see Figure 5.11). It also illuminates more of the subject's lower body. If the subject looks into the key light, the camera can see the shadow molding

on the other side of the subject's face, an effect that lends three-dimensional perspective. Try it and experiment. The less moody you want your story to be, the more light you fill into that dark side. ■

FIGURE 5.9
Light boxes produce soft, natural-looking light, without calling attention to the lighting pattern.

FIGURE 5.10
A typical soft-light setup for a high-definition television interview. The key light in this photo is positioned on the left side of the camera, a fill light on the right, and a backlight behind the subject.

FIGURE 5.11
Figure 5.11A The key light produces full, rich lighting.

Figure 5.11B The fill light side of the face is somewhat underexposed to provide a three-dimensional look. The darker the fill side of the face, the moodier the resulting light.

Figure 5.11C The soft box key and fill lights produce a more three-dimensional appearance. Note the triangle of light beneath the subject's eye on the fill (darker) side of the face.

EXPOSURE

At their most basic, scenes are correctly exposed, too light from overexposure, or too dark from underexposure. Proper exposure results in a rich cross section of pleasing colors and details.

BOX 5.5   STAR QUALITY CLOSE-UPS WITHOUT LIGHTS

Lighting Tips from John DeTarsio
Network Freelance Photojournalist

Ready for My Close-Up!

Notice the star's close-up shot next time you watch a movie. Study how the camera focuses on the actor's eyes. Whenever we look at someone close to us, we look first at the eyes, or wherever the sharpest focus on the video screen guides our attention. Film and television close-ups thus usually show the person's face, hair, and shoulders in sharp focus, while retaining soft focus on the background behind the subject. Most people look best in compressed shots like that.

Shallow depth of field emulates how we naturally see others whenever they are close to us. You can confirm it yourself while you read these very words. Remain focused on the text as you transfer your attention (but not your focus) to your peripheral vision. You can see that by focusing on something close, only what you look at directly remains in focus.

How to Shoot Effective Close-Ups

The best close-ups show people (and sometimes animals) as they appear in real life. The goal is to capture your subject so naturally that viewers might recognize that person a few days later at the supermarket. An ideal approach is to position your subject at least 10 feet in front of the background in your shot, and place your camera on a tripod at least 10 feet in front of the subject. Next, zoom into the subject and frame the shot to achieve a "movie star close-up" look (Figure 5.12). Enclosed or difficult shooting environments may sometimes render this general rule of thumb impractical, but honor it as closely as you can. ■

A   B

FIGURE 5.12

Depth of field in close-ups affects our impressions of people, and reveals much about the photographer. Figure 5.12A (left) reflects undesirable depth of field that occurs when the subject is positioned too close to the background and the camera. This setup often leads to unnecessary shadows and unwanted background detail. A better approach in close-ups is to set up the shot for shallow depth of field, and focus on subjects' eyes (Figure 5.12B). Shallow focus portrays people much as you would see them up close in real life. In this setup the subject is about 10 feet from the background, and the camera is on a tripod about 10 feet in front of the subject.

In the case of cameras with automatic exposure control, electronic circuitry behind the lens "sees" only what the lens shows it. If the main subject shows up against a dark background, the scene may be overexposed as the camera struggles to properly expose the predominantly dark area in the background. The same subject in front of a white background might be underexposed because light backgrounds may fool the camera.

The solution in both cases is to move in closer with the camera or zoom lens to eliminate the background and let the camera meter see only the primary subject. Once exposure is properly adjusted, the exposure control can be clicked from automatic to its manual position. The exposure will remain until the control is readjusted or switched back to the automatic mode, so the shot can now be recomposed and recorded.

ESSENTIAL LIGHTING EQUIPMENT

Surprisingly little equipment is necessary to produce professionally lit scenes in the field. Boston photojournalist John Premack recommends the following essentials[4]:

- Two focusing quartz lights such as the Lowel Omni (see www.lowel.com/) with stands, barndoors, dichroic filters, 650- and 300-watt lamps, and extra-small Chimera soft boxes (see www.chimeralighting.com). An alternative to the Chimera is Lowel's RIFA™ eXchange System™, a small, folding softlight box complete with bulb, socket, and stand-mounting bracket
- One focusing mini light (such as the Lowel Pro) with stand, 2-leaf barndoor, and diffusion filter
- One folding fabric reflector to provide fill light from the primary light source, indoors or out

The quartz light heads should include at least one head that can be mounted directly to the camera body for fast-breaking news events. Especially useful are the small reflector lamps that mount on the camera body and can take power from the camera battery. Round out the list with spare lightbulbs, two-inch-wide silver cloth gaffer's tape to hang lights and to tape cords to the floor to keep people from tripping, and plenty of extension cords. Also desirable is a package of mixed gels, a portable, 12-volt battery-operated light and battery pack for covering big stories at night, as well as scrims and other diffusion materials.

LIGHTING IN SUNLIGHT

Bright sunlight produces distinct highlights and black shadow areas with little or no detail. The problem worsens when subjects are silhouetted against the sky. In these situations, fill light will be required—either from an artificial quartz light outfitted with a dichroic filter or from fill light supplied by a portable reflector or similar source.

Some of the most pleasing lighting patterns occur when the subject is lit with indirect sunlight. If the sun is behind the subject, the backlight on the person's hair and shoulders may be used to especially flattering effect, with quartz light or reflector fill light used to enhance illumination on the subject's face (Figure 5.13). If the sunlight is especially bright and straight overhead, a 1,000-watt quartz light with dichroic filter may be required to balance illumination levels to the same intensity of sunlight. Another pleasing form of indirect sunlight is **open shade**, in which the subject is photographed in shade, well away from direct sunlight, but with nothing above the subject to obstruct secondary light from the sky itself.

FIGURE 5.13
A portable reflector is used to kick fill light into the shadow side of the subject's face.

Strong sunlight also can overpower artificial light being used to photograph subjects indoors, converting the subjects to silhouette. The problem is most evident when subjects are photographed in front of open windows. In such situations try to close the curtains behind the person to be interviewed. If there are no curtains or they cannot be closed, try to reposition the subject in front of a more neutral background. Failing that, you may have to boost illumination with artificial lights on the subject's face to the same intensity as the sunlight behind the subject, a process called **balanced lighting**.

HOW TO LIGHT A NEWS CONFERENCE

Most news conferences can be nicely lit with a three-light setup. Set up key and fill lights and add a backlight to help separate the subject from the background. If your lights will be more than seven or eight feet from the subject, use at least 650-watt bulbs.

If time or equipment is at a premium, two lights will do an adequate job. Eliminate the fill light and cheat the backlight by setting it on "flood" and opening the barndoor a little more. If you have only one light available, use it to bounce light onto the subject or to create a butterfly lighting pattern. The single light also can be used high and to one side of the camera, ideally with a scrim to help diffuse the light and make it softer, or else move the light back toward the side of the speaker's face.

If you must work with only one or two lights, shoot at the lowest level of illumination that produces acceptable skin tones. If you find it impossible to achieve light levels of f/8 on the subject and f/8 on the background, consider settling for an illumination level of f/2.8 on the background. If the skin color of the main subject is accurate and if illumination of the main subject is acceptable, little harm will result if exposure levels and color temperature of the background are allowed to stray. Once again, it is important to turn off existing lights or to filter your own lights to match the color temperature of the existing light source.

As you adjust the lights, you can ask your soundperson, your reporter, or a volunteer to serve as a stand-in. If it's obvious the speaker will throw unwanted shadows against the background, try to move the podium away from the background or reposition the lights and/or camera to eliminate unwanted shadows from the frame.

As you position your lights, set a chair or other object by each light so the stands won't be inadvertently bumped or knocked down. It also is advisable to tape extension cords securely to the floor so passersby don't trip and break their legs or send your light stands crashing to the floor.

SETTING UP LIGHTS IN COOPERATION WITH OTHER CREWS

Although news conference lighting is not art, inept lighting calls attention to itself and distracts viewers' attention from the speaker and what is being said. For that reason, be alert for the damaging influence of other crews who arrive and set up their own lights without regard for the lighting patterns and levels of illumination you've already established. Gentle negotiation to establish acceptable lighting patterns will work to everyone's benefit.

If you must work within the confines of **pack journalism,** arrive early enough to stake your claim to an ideal camera position and hold your ground. Newspaper and radio reporters may swirl around you and complain that you're blocking the view, but their requirements are different from yours and they may not understand your needs.

LIGHTING ETIQUETTE

Regardless of the situation you are lighting, remember to practice lighting etiquette. If the room is already set up and lit before the subject walks in, so much the better. Most people will adapt quickly to the lights and soon forget about them. Otherwise, when you first plug in the lights, try to tilt them down to the floor, then swing up the light heads gently so as not to blind your subjects suddenly. Another approach is to use your hand to block the light when it is first switched on, then slowly lower your hand from the light head to permit gradual, full illumination of your subject.

LIGHTING SPOT NEWS AT NIGHT

No matter whether you're photographing a nighttime political rally outdoors or covering spot news at night, the most logical place for the light is on the camera. Spot-news photography demands that the photojournalist move quickly to keep up with the action, which means that light stands are generally out of the question. Further, the camera-mounted light may be the only illumination available when the camera is diverted from the main action to shoot cutaways.

Especially at night, it's important to use no more light than you need (Figure 5.14). This means the camera-mounted light is an excellent choice for night photography because of its relatively low level of intensity. If light levels on the main subject are too high, the background at night will be pitch black. "The more light you put on your subject at night, the greater

FIGURE 5.14
At night, try to use relatively low levels of illumination. The more intense the light used to illuminate a subject at night, the less visible the background will be.

discrepancy there is between your subject and the dark background at night," says photojournalist John Premack. "You're trying in effect for balanced light, even at night, so shoot with the aperture wide open if the image looks clean and acceptably exposed."[5]

PHOTOGRAPHING SUBJECTS WITH DARK SKIN

Whenever you light subjects with dark skin, look for backgrounds slightly darker than the subject. Another practice is to keep as much light as possible off the background, in order to keep contrast ratios to acceptable levels. If the background is too light or too brightly lit, essential detail may be lost in the subject's face, or the subject may even be reproduced in silhouette. Keep light levels as low as comfortable, and if possible, err slightly on the side of overexposure rather than underexposure.

LARGE-SCALE LIGHTING

Occasions may occur when you have to photograph uncommonly large areas, such as hotel ballrooms, auditoriums, showrooms, and supermarkets. In such cases, the rule of thumb is to work with the light you have and to supplement existing light rather than bring in an entirely new overall light source. If the predominant light source is fluorescent light, for example, consider adding your own portable fluorescent fixtures to provide additional fill or accent light. Color temperature should remain relatively constant if the lightbulbs are all the same type. Otherwise, you may need to use a correcting gel filter.

If sufficient illumination is unavailable or if extremely deep areas are to be lit, enough lights will be needed to light foreground, middle ground, and background adequately. If the area is very large, high wattage lights of 1,000 watts or more may be necessary. If an examination of the viewfinder shows that certain areas within the scene are too bright, the photographer can use **barndoors** (Figure 5.15), or **flags** (opaque panels that block light from certain areas), or **cookies** (flags with regular or irregular cutouts that form patterns of light and shadow on the background) and nets to enrich or subdue particular areas within the scene, a practice called *painting with shadows*.

CAUTIONS

Lights are extremely bright and hot, and they pull lots of electricity when plugged into wall outlets. The obvious precautions apply when using artificial lights:

FIGURE 5.15
A portable light with "barndoors" that can be moved to control light falling on the subject and background.

BOX 5.6   TOO HOT TO HANDLE

Imagine going to someone's home to cover a story, and burning down their house. It can happen if you overload the home's electrical circuits. Plug in too many lights, overburden an old fuse box, add one too many extension cords, and you could send an entire family's way of life up in smoke. Imagine the misery you might cause were you to overload the circuits in an apartment building, or a horse barn, or an airport hangar.

Basic savvy can help you avoid such tragedies. Building codes require 20-amp circuits in most U.S. structures built since the mid-1980s. Before that, the standard was 15 amps. Remember that your equipment rarely is the only electrical appliance on a circuit. If you exceed those loads by plugging in

too many lights, stand by to call the fire department. What to do?

Just remember the rough formula for converting watts to amps: divide by 100. If you're using a 1,000-watt light, divide by 100. This tells you the light draws 10 amps. You are good to go. If you were to use three 1,000-watt bulbs, however, that would be 3,000 divided by 100, or 30 amps. Run for your life.

The consequences might not be life-threatening. You could just blow fuses or trip the circuit breakers. But you could start a fire. Even your extension cords could break into flames. Why risk the danger? Divide the number of watts by 100. It's the smart way to operate. ■

- Never touch quartz bulbs. Serious burns can result, and bulbs can be damaged from the natural oils on fingers.
- Allow bulbs to cool before packing them away or setting on objects (including carpeting, camera cases, and vinyl-topped tables).
- Serious retinal damage can occur if bright lights are used closer than three feet to human or animal subjects.
- Avoid shining bright lights directly into the lenses of older cameras. Cameras with pickup tubes can be permanently damaged.
- Avoid plugging more than three lights into an electrical circuit. Excessively high-voltage drains can cause overheated cords or tripped circuits.
- Avoid 1,000-watt bulbs whenever possible, because they tend to blow fuses.
- Use only extension cords that are large enough to handle the job. Cords that are too small cause voltage drops and can overheat to the point of causing fires. Voltage drops also alter the color temperature of artificial lights.
- Never discharge batteries completely or overcharge them.

In the final analysis, lighting creates mood. Mere illumination destroys it. Within every shot, light is the most visually important element—the raw material for every television journalist, the essential substance of every television story. As documentary historian William Bluem observed, "A photographer who cannot light is not a photographer. A reporter who underestimates the importance of light is a fool."[6] Happily, in today's environment, light is a commodity more easily controlled than ever before in the history of photojournalism.

SUMMARY

One of the photojournalist's most important writing tools is light. A primary characteristic of light is its color temperature, an expression of the proportion of red to blue light that the light source radiates. Under each varying light source the camera must be white-balanced to produce an absence of color at white. Avoid mixing light from sources with different color temperatures.

When shooting field video, the artificial light source most commonly used is the quartz bulb, which produces a color temperature of 3200°K. Under light of any other temperature, the camera must be white balanced or filters employed. On older cameras, lens-mounted filters are used to correct the color temperature of sunlight, to filter out the excessive greenish-blue hues of fluorescent light, or to reduce the quantity of light entering the camera so a different aperture can be used to control depth of field.

Light-mounted dichroic filters are used to boost the color temperature of quartz light to the approximate color temperature of average daylight. Semiflexible sheets of filter gel also can be mounted on windows to convert sunlight to 3200°K. All filters reduce light to some extent; the amount of loss is expressed by the filter factor. Each factor of 2 cuts the original amount of light by one-half.

Basic lighting patterns involve use of a key or dominant light and a fill or secondary light. The key light normally is positioned 30° to 45° over from the camera axis and high enough so the light can be aimed down 45° or steeper at the subject. Variations include side light, side-rear light, and top light, with further refinements available, such as butterfly or glamour lighting.

The intensity of illumination between key and fill lights helps determine contrast ratios within the scene. Generally, the key light is set one and a half to two stops brighter than the fill light. Often, diffused light is softer and more pleasing to the eye. Sunlight is naturally diffused on overcast or foggy days or when subjects are in open shade. Diffusion of artificial light also can be achieved through bounce light or umbrella lighting or with any of various diffusion materials.

Although most lighting assignments can be accomplished with a key, fill, and backlight, large-scale interiors and night lighting present special challenges. In the final analysis, light creates mood and meaning. Mere illumination destroys it.

KEY TERMS

backlight 91	fill lights 85	key light 88
balanced	filter 83	lighting ratio 91
lighting 97	filter factor 86	open shade 96
barndoors 99	flags 99	pack journalism 98
bounce light 93	flat lighting 92	short lighting 91
broadlighting 91	hatchet light 88	specular light 87
butterfly light 88	HMI 92	umbrella lighting 92
color temperature 83	inverse-square law of	white balance 83
cookies 99	light 89	

DISCUSSION

1. Discuss the extent to which light is the true medium of television, web, and nonbroadcast video.
2. What is color temperature and how does it affect the video image?
3. List the filters most commonly used in television photography (camera-, light-, and window-mounted) and describe their uses.
4. Explain filter factors and how they are used to determine the light-reducing properties of filters.
5. Explain what happens when light sources with different color temperatures are mixed. How can the photographer avoid the problem?

6. Describe the differing roles of the key light and the fill light.
7. Describe the basic lighting patterns commonly used when shooting video.
8. How are key-to-fill lighting ratios (lighting contrast ratios) determined?
9. Explain the difference between broad lighting and short lighting.
10. How can light rays be diffused or otherwise controlled to create softer, more pleasing lighting patterns?
11. What minimum lighting equipment should the photojournalist have available for field assignments?
12. What special considerations are necessary when using supplementary artificial lights outdoors under bright sunlight? Why are artificial lights sometimes necessary under such conditions?
13. Explain how to light a news conference or similar gathering.
14. What considerations should you keep in mind when lighting subjects outdoors at night? When lighting large-scale subjects such as warehouses and supermarkets?
15. What safety precautions should you observe anytime you work with lights?

EXERCISES

1. Color-balance the camera for 3200°K light, then without altering color-balance, photograph scenes illuminated by a normal 60-watt household bulb, under sunlight at noon, and one hour before sunset. Compare the results.
2. With the #85 filter in place and the camera properly white-balanced, shoot a scene under sunlight at noon with and without the #85 filter. Repeat the exercise indoors under artificial quartz light with the camera properly white-balanced for a light source of 3200°K. Slate or otherwise identify each scene.
3. Shoot a scene indoors under artificial quartz light with no #85 filter on the camera. Again shoot the scene, but this time with a dichroic filter on the artificial quartz light.
4. Shoot a daytime scene of a driver from inside a car using a battery-operated, 3200°K artificial fill light and no filter on the camera. Shoot the scene again with the same light and camera setup, but this time with a #85 gel filter taped to the window that is visible behind the driver.
5. Shoot a subject indoors silhouetted against the sunlight or other backlight coming through a window behind the subject. Set up an artificial fill light with dichroic filter to balance exposure on the subject's face against the light in the background.
6. Set up a key light on a subject. Properly position the key light so that a triangle of light appears on the shadow side of the subject's face. Now, set up a fill light of equal intensity, but position the fill light approximately twice as far from your subject as the key light. In this configuration, what is the approximate key-to-fill ratio?
7. Reposition the fill light in example 6 so that your key-to-fill light is approximately 3:1. A good way to accomplish this feat is to set the key light first and take an exposure reading with an exposure meter or by letting the camera circuitry determine proper exposure. Jot down the f/stop setting that would be required for proper exposure when using the key light by itself.

   At this point, turn off the key light. Adjust the intensity of illumination from the fill light by moving the light stand forward or backward until the exposure reading on your subject's face is one and a half stops less intense than the key light reading.

   In other words, if proper exposure for the key light alone is f/8, position the fill light so that proper exposure for the fill light alone would be halfway between f/4 and f/5.6, or one and a half stops less intense (thus the need to open the aperture to a larger setting). The fill light is always farther from the subject than the key light, if both lights are of equal intensity.

   Finally, turn on both lights and shoot the scene. Remember to stop down so that you shoot the scene at the proper exposure value for the brightest light.

8. Using a single light, shoot and record a scene using a flat, front-on lighting pattern, then move the light to create high side lighting, and finally, butterfly or glamour lighting on the subject. Play back the video for review.
9. Outdoors, under bright sunlight, use a reflector fill or artificial quartz light with dichroic filter to provide fill light on the shadow side of the subject's face.
10. Photograph a subject using broadlighting and short lighting and compare the result.
11. Light a scene to create first a low-contrast image, then a high-contrast image.
12. Practice diffusing artificial light with a diffusion screen or other material, bouncing light from the ceiling, and using a heatproof lighting umbrella.
13. Inspect the shots you have made of people during practice lighting sessions for the presence of single highlights in each eye. If two highlights appear, relight the subjects properly and again photograph them.
14. Light a person outdoors at night, first using brilliant illumination, and then consciously subdue the illumination to the lowest intensity possible. Compare the results.
15. Attend a news conference or other media event and observe lighting techniques and practices. View the scene that night on television.

NOTES

1. Isaac Asimov, "The Third Sense," *American Way* (May 28, 1985), 15–16.
2. Diane Holloway, "That's Harsh: Hi-Def TV Is Changing Our Views of the Stars," Cox News Services, March 29, 2007.
3. Ibid.
4. John Premack, in correspondence with the author, June 8, 2003.
5. John Premack, "Lighting—Making It Work for You," a presentation at the NPPA TV News-Video Workshop, Norman, OK, March 19, 1986.
6. A. William Bluem, *Documentary in American Television* (New York: Hastings House, 1965), 274.

The Sound Track

T oday's viewers spend millions of dollars on HDTVs and surround sound systems, and expect full, clean sound in everything they watch. Sound, like words and pictures, is another of the symbols that reporters and storytellers use to communicate meaning and to enhance the impact and intrinsic drama of their reports. Other than images, as you have seen, video reporters and storytellers have only one other way to communicate. Herein, we encounter the wisdom of acoustic specialist Ned Hall, about how to isolate and harvest audio—the kind that comprises the other half of the image and that lets us see with our ears.

Ned Hall, Audio-Recording Engineer

The late Ned Hall traveled the world as an audio-recording engineer for NBC, ABC, CBS, PBS, Fox, Disney, HBO, and MTV for such programs as *48 Hours, 60 Minutes, Prime Time Live, and Today.* Ned espoused author Diane Ackerman's philosophy that the world would not be nearly so interesting if it were silent. He brought home a rich fabric of sounds from the Arctic Circle and the Gulf of Mannar to the Cape of Good Hope. His work included music videos for artists from Neil Young to the Royal Philharmonic Orchestra. In the dark, windowless world of postproduction, he sweetened shows like PBS's *Creation of the Universe* and the syndicated series *The Story of Rock and Roll.* In his own postproduction facility, he generated several Random House Audio Books and composed music for NBC News videos and for documentaries for the Discovery channel. Friends and colleagues knew Ned as an artist who sculpted audio, revered it, and shared his love of life's sounds with all of us. Ned rewrote and contributed much new information for this chapter before his death. You will recognize his humor in the following pages, and his wisdom. We have dedicated this chapter to Ned's memory and to those who will follow in his footsteps in the pursuit of storytelling audio, wherever that pursuit may take them.

For all the bandwidth we dedicate to imagery, both in our airspace and in our minds, the stubborn fact remains: Sound carries much of the meaning of our stories. We are thinking creatures; one thing that separates us from animals, and science from art, fact from feeling, is

BOX 6.1   DOUG DREW EXECUTIVE EDITOR NEWS DIVISION 602 COMMUNICATIONS

How Six Seconds Can Make a Newscast Special[1]

I tuned in to see LeBron James return to Cleveland. It wasn't the game I wanted to see. I simply wanted to see how the Cleveland fans would react. I knew they would probably boo him, but I wanted to see to what extent they would "let him have it."

So, there I sat, in front of my TV, waiting for that big moment. But the moment came, and the moment went, and just like that, it was over. Gone. "That was it?" I said to myself. Really? It's not that the moment didn't happen, it's just that it didn't become a magic moment, either in the arena or on TV. It could have happened, but why didn't it?

As the player introductions began, I could hear the boos already starting. When James was introduced, the fans really opened up, but you never really got the drama of it by watching the broadcast. The magic moment never really happened, and I blame two producers for this: the person producing the opening ceremonies and the person producing the broadcast. They had to know that many viewers were tuning in just to see it. All it would take to make this come alive for those in the arena and for those sitting at home was for the announcer to just pause for a few additional seconds after saying

James's name. But that didn't happen. Instead, the announcer said his name, and as we saw James run onto the court, the announcer was already announcing the next player. Couldn't they have just taken six seconds to let the natural sound of the fans booing be heard? Instead, the fans jeered, but the announcer kept talking, so it became anti-climatic.

This same technique applies to newscasts. If you have a special piece of video, sound, or copy, do something special with it. Too often in the haste of putting a story or a newscast together, we just go about doing it the way we always do. That's what happened in Cleveland. They did the player introductions the same way they did it the night before, and the same way they will do it for the next game. They had something special, but they didn't do anything special with it.

When someone asks me "Doug, what makes one producer or reporter better than another," this is what I talk about. The most talented people are the ones who recognize they have something special and do something special with it.

Conclusion: Not every second has to be filled with copy. If you have something special, give it special attention.

our ability to distill our perceptions into words and to reconstruct an experience from the shorthand of speech.

When a passenger jet crashed into the wooded hills outside Pittsburgh, the pictures of the aftermath could only frame the words: "The plane was on an approach to the airport when the aircraft apparently banked sharply to the left and dove 6,000 feet, in twenty-three seconds, to the earth."[2] Without the words, we see a trash dump in the woods. With them, we see a tragedy. And when the flight recorder was recovered, the Federal Aviation Agency decided not to release the audio contained thereon in order to "spare the passengers' loved ones" the sounds of human suffering.[3] Such is the power of audio.

The most spectacular images of an exploding oil refinery cannot answer some very important questions: Where is the refinery? When did this explosion occur—last weekend? last year? fifteen minutes ago? Was anyone hurt or killed? How many? Who is in jeopardy right now? Is the neighborhood being evacuated? The most revealing shots of the fire chief's face as he arrives at the scene will tell you no more than the tone of his voice as he dispatches the firefighters.

Recording sound, like recording images, is fishing, casting about for the best story elements you can coax from the world's undergrowth. You can catch a trophy fish on a bent pin and a string, but chance favors the angler armed with experience, patience, and the necessary tackle.

HOW MICROPHONES WORK

The magic of recorded sound begins with the microphone. Sound is vibrating air, and microphones convert those vibrations into electrical energy. The diaphragm of a **dynamic microphone** moves a coil of wire in the field of a magnet, rather like a dynamic speaker, in reverse. Dynamic microphones commonly are used in news reporting and in stage and music applications. Dynamic mikes produce high-fidelity sound at reasonable cost and are among the most rugged units of all.

Ribbon microphones operate in a fashion similar to dynamic microphones, but use a thin ribbon of metal foil inside a magnetic field for a diaphragm. Ribbon microphones can be "warm" sounding, and thus are commonly encountered in audio booths and radio studios.

A *condenser* microphone's diaphragm acts as one of the two plates of a capacitor in an electronic circuit. When the diaphragm vibrates, the capacitor changes value in the circuit. This type of mike requires power, supplied by the mixer/preamplifier or a separate power supply and sent through the mike cable, or by a battery in the mike itself. Condenser mikes can be the most sensitive of microphones and are used in a variety of music and voice applications.

DIRECTIONAL PATTERNS

The simplest microphone, suspended in open space, can "hear" sound equally well from any direction. You might imagine the directional pattern of that mike as a sphere. Microphones can be designed to favor specific areas in a sphere, allowing you to point the mike at the sound you want to record while lessening to some degree the pickup of sounds you don't want. Unfortunately, this is not like a camera lens that sees only where you point it. A camera can take a picture of a clear mountain stream without revealing that the idyllic brook runs six feet from the highway. A microphone will report faithfully the traffic density on that highway, complete with a truck count, no matter what the directional pattern of your mike.

The directional characteristics of mikes are more pronounced as the frequency of the sound increases. Low-frequency sounds will "leak" into any mike regardless of its type or orientation, and sound reflects off objects in thousands of unpredictable ways.

Light may be stopped with an upraised hand or a dropped eyelid; sound can be stopped only with mass or distance.

Omnidirectional

A mike with an **omnidirectional** pattern picks up sound equally from all directions. The majority of handheld and lavaliere microphones are omnidirectional. However, an "omni" mike mounted on a person's chest becomes hemispherical in pattern—the mass of the body blocks sound coming from behind the subject.

Unidirectional

A mike with a **unidirectional** pattern tends to reject sound from the rear and sides. Unidirectional mikes are good for news conferences and meetings because of their ability to minimize audience noise and feedback. They come in these basic flavors, each more directional than the last:

- cardioid (sound is picked up to the front and sides of the mike)
- hypercardioid
- short shotgun
- long shotgun

Bidirectional (Figure Eight)

Sound is picked up in front and back but not to the sides of the **bidirectional** microphone. The user must correctly position the microphone to record desired sound while rejecting unwanted sounds.

ON CHOOSING A MIKE

At first consideration, given the incredibly cluttered soundscape in which we live and work, one might be tempted to grab a shotgun mike and be done with it. In fact, many soundpeople seem to settle on a short shotgun mike as the one first pulled from their kit and mounted on the end of their boom pole. Indeed, if you are fishing for sound bites in an unknown sound environment, that's a good choice. However, there are other points to ponder.

A key point to bear in mind when placing a mike is this: When you halve the distance between a mike and a sound source, you increase the level by three **decibels (dB)**. One reason lavaliere mikes, though omnidirectional, seem to reject so much extraneous sound is that they are positioned so close to the source of the sound. The closer you can get your microphone to the sound, the less unwanted sounds will intrude.

IMPEDANCE

Microphones also are designated according to their **impedance**, a characteristic related to, but not to be confused with, electrical resistance. The **ohm** is the measure for both. Low-impedance microphones (generally in the range of 50 to 250 ohms) are standard for field sound recording and include most dynamic mikes. These mikes can be used with any practical length of microphone cable. Consequently, it is possible to work several hundred feet from the camera or live transmission facilities without noticeable loss in sound quality. High-impedance microphones (in the range of 1,000 ohms and higher) are limited to cable lengths of twenty feet or less. Generally, modern high-quality mikes are low impedance.

FREQUENCY RESPONSE

The human ear is said to be capable of hearing frequencies ranging from 20 **hertz (Hz)** to 20 **kilohertz (kHz)**. There is considerable but conflicting evidence that we can sense overtones much higher. Be that as it may, a microphone company that boasts of a mike with a frequency response from 20 Hz to 20 kHz is suggesting that its mike can "hear" any sound your ear can. Microphones with the same published frequency response can sound very different, though, so make your selections based on what you hear in your headphones.

MICROPHONES FOR THE VIDEO JOURNALIST

At a minimum, solo reporters and crews should carry an omnidirectional hand mike, a unidirectional mike for stand use (to exclude audience noise at news conferences and meetings), a shotgun mike, at least one miniature lavaliere mike, and at least one wireless transmitter-receiver system. Some organizations provide their crews with far less than this basic complement, although wireless transmitters and inconspicuous lavaliere mikes lead to more spontaneous interviews and even to more compelling demonstration standups. Almost always, progress depends on performing at a higher level of excellence than your competitors. If the station refuses to provide you with the tools you need in this endeavor, you might want to consider buying those tools yourself.

FIGURE 6.1

The handheld microphone is an indispensable field reporting tool. Such microphones can intimidate some news subjects, however, and they can draw unwarranted attention, especially when outfitted with a mike flag that carries the organization's logo.

Handheld Microphone

Both directional and omnidirectional hand mikes are the workhorses of the video storyteller. You can tape them onto tree branches to record the passing sounds of the parade, position them at the edge of the gym floor to record the squeak of basketball players' shoes, or tape them to the speaker's stand at a news conference. Rugged, reliable, and affordable, dynamic handheld microphones are indispensable tools for the video journalist. The standard electronic news gathering (ENG) mike is usually an omni because it is rather like a hand grenade: You don't point it so much as heave it in the general direction of whatever is making the noise. They are often chosen for their bulletproof construction and for how they look wearing a **mike flag**, that little box imprinted with the station logo that pops into view so frequently (Figure 6.1).

Often, however, the handheld mike is used with such little thought that it intrudes on news content. Journalists continually thrust handheld mikes into people's faces and further compound their intrusiveness with mike flags. The effect is intimidation, which will silence a wise man but will incite a silly one to greet his mother.

Given today's technology, there is less need for viewers to see the microphone. Its presence can remind viewers that the story is being reported, thereby reducing the viewer's level of involvement in the story. Occasionally, management requires a logo to appear on the hand mike and encourages the presence of the mike on-screen. But, as managers find better ways to promote the station's presence in the field, we can hope that mike flags will become just a curious footnote in the history of television journalism.

Lavaliere Microphone

During interviews, reporter standups, and similar applications, the use of a **lavaliere microphone** often is more appropriate than using a hand-held mike. These small microphones clip to the speaker's clothing or can be taped directly to the speaker's chest and are easily hidden from camera view (Figure 6.2). Lavaliere mikes are designed to be used close to the speaker's chest cavity, never handheld, and their output may become less vibrant and more tinny the farther they are used from the sound source.

Shotgun Microphone

Other microphones are used in situations where you can't move close enough to the speaker. News conferences are an example. Here, you may have to use the so-called **shotgun microphone,** which picks up sound from a relatively narrow area in front of the microphone. This mike derives its name from its resemblance to a miniature shotgun barrel (Figure 6.3). The shotgun mike has a pickup pattern vaguely similar to the angle of view of a telephoto lens and allows usable quality sound to be recorded from quite a distance in a perfectly quiet environment. Because the shotgun mike is highly directional, you must "show" it precisely what you want it to hear. If your aim is poor, you may pick up the sound of a taxiing jet and miss the speaker's most important comment at a news conference. To help keep the microphone accurately pointed at the sound source, you must listen carefully with headphones.

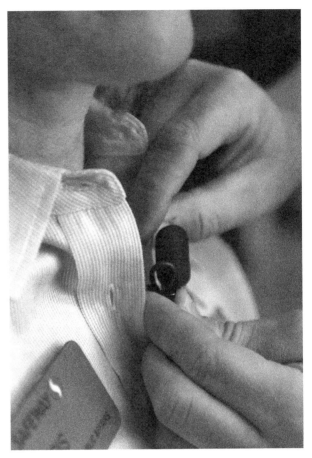

FIGURE 6.2
Small lavaliere microphones can be clipped to the speaker's clothing or can be hidden entirely from view by taping them to the speaker's chest or inner clothing.

FIGURE 6.3
The shotgun microphone is highly directional. It has a pickup pattern somewhat similar to the angle of view of a telephoto lens. The microphone seen here is equipped with an acoustic foam windscreen.

THE WIRELESS TRANSMITTER-RECEIVER

Useful in many situations and crucial in some is a miniature radio transmitter and receiver set, commonly referred to as a *wireless*. Used most often in conjunction with a small lavaliere mike connected by a short, thin cable to a small transmitter worn inside a pocket or hooked to a belt, the wireless can be invisible or no more obtrusive than a pager. Transmitters can also be used with a handheld mike or with a mike placed inconspicuously in a likely spot (often referred to as a "plant" mike), or, with a special cable, to public address (PA) systems or hi-fis.

Wireless transmitters provide speakers with great mobility and give reporters the freedom to move about during standups and interviews. Using two wireless systems, the reporter and interviewee can walk and talk during interviews without the restriction of microphone cables and without the annoyance of microphones intruding on the interview process (Figure 6.4). The transmitted sound is picked up by a matching receiver(s), which in turn feeds directly into the camera, an audio mixer, or live broadcast transmission facilities.

Range

In a perfect world, a wireless transmitter would have infinite range. In reality, its working range often seems to be about two feet less than you need. Several factors limit wireless range. One is the relatively small power output of the transmitter, measured in fractions of a watt, and, like all radio transmitters, regulated by the Federal Communications Commission (FCC). Another is the possible presence of interference.

Interference

Although wireless transmitters are relatively expensive, they cannot deliver the sound quality of a regular hardwired mike. For one reason, a wireless introduces special signal processing circuits into the signal path in the interest of delivering a clean, usable signal. The transmitter has an audio circuit called a compressor that "squeezes" the signal into a very narrow dynamic range, a term relating to variations in intensity. The receiver contains an expander that then restores the signal. Although these components function as intended, they limit the frequency response and the dynamic range that could be preserved by a simple microphone cable. Another reason sound quality is poorer is because the transmitted signal is susceptible to any outside electrical interference that may be present, whether

FIGURE 6.4

The wireless transmitter-receiver system allows reporters and subjects to move about freely without the restriction of microphone cables.

it's electrical ignition noise from poorly maintained cars in the area, the periodic snap-snap of an electric cattle fence in the country, the unwanted intrusion of **radio frequencies (RF)** that carry radio and some TV signals, or from another crew across the street using the same frequencies you are. Further, the physical mike cord wire that feeds into the wireless transmitter can act as a radio antenna and serve to convert the field recorder into an AM or FM radio receiver, which can pick up perfectly clear reception of broadcast programs. Some units also are susceptible to occasional interference from shortwave broadcasts, walkie-talkies, and microwave transmissions.

Dropouts and interference also can occur when the signal from the main transmitter arrives at the receiver just as a secondary signal reflected from a wall or other nearby reflecting surface reaches the receiving antenna, so monitor your sound and move the receiver if necessary. Occasionally, even fluorescent or neon lights produce interference. If you can, turn off the lights. Otherwise, if you suspect the lights as a source of interference, reorient the receiver or move it to a different location. Murphy's law postulates that the interference will be intermittent and will occur in direct proportion to the status of the person being recorded. Often the problem will exist on one frequency and not another, making a spare wireless a lifesaver.

Interference often increases as the distance between the transmitter and the receiver increases. As the signal becomes weaker, the receiver is less able to discriminate between the desired signal and a spurious one. In general, it is best to keep that distance as short as possible. Remember that you are broadcasting a radio signal, and that you will occasionally "take a hit" and hear a pop, zizz, whistle, crackle, tick, ding, hash, or clang. En garde!

Frequency

The FCC assigns the frequencies available for wireless use. Although these units output very little power, the FCC requires that radio transmitters be licensed in the frequencies made available for wireless use. Certain areas of VHF band (from about 169 to 216 MHz) were home for these devices until some spots in the UHF band (470 to 890 MHz) were more recently made available, and this higher frequency, coupled with the relatively (for now) uncrowded condition of these wavelengths, makes for some desirable improvements in wireless performance. Back when wirelesses were mostly in the VHF band, a buyer who planned to use the units in locations all around the United States was urged to buy them in the 169 to 172 MHz range. These "traveling frequencies" are safe from interference from VHF television stations. But be aware that when dozens of news crews are working at the same location, many of them may be using those traveling frequencies.

Antenna Placement

Whenever you use a wireless transmitter, placement is important. When the antenna, or the mike cable that serves as an antenna, is poorly positioned, some wireless units tend to cut off or "clip" certain frequencies, making voices sound thin and artificial. Try to keep the wire straight and, ideally, keep the antenna on the front of the person, facing the camera, so signals don't have to pass through the speaker's body on their way to the receiver. To help reduce dropouts, keep the antenna away from metal (is your subject playing with car keys and change in his pocket?) and, if your transmitter has both antenna and mike cable, keep them as separate as possible.

To further reduce interference, place the receiving antenna as high as possible, preferably atop the camera or on the shoulder strap of the mixer, or even, in desperation, on a pole placed high enough so that it is above the subject. If you are in a nightmare situation and your wireless will work only for a few feet, tape the receiver to the end of a pole and "boom" the antenna, keeping it just outside the picture frame.

Wireless mikes also can quickly eat up batteries, so remember to carry plenty of spare batteries into the field. The crackle and static you hear in your earphone may be simply the sounds of a battery growing weaker. Some photojournalists use fresh batteries on every assignment, having learned that batteries are less expensive than failed productions.

THE MIXER

As a photojournalist, you may find yourself sometimes working by yourself, and at other times with a reporter. In these situations, the mike mounted on the camera and one wireless velcroed to your battery pack may be all you need to capture the audio required to tell your stories. Sometimes, though, the story may demand more complex setups. When the assignment calls for interviews by a reporter with one, two, or three or more people, multiple microphones in different locations can dramatically enhance the pictures you take. These assignments may take the form of a discussion between two or more people walking down the street, a question-and-answer session after a speech (including a telephone call-in), a conversation, or even situations where one shot pans from a summit conference to an angry protest just outside the window.

Note the difference between a wireless link between mixer and camera and a true "double system" of audio recorder rolling in sync but separate from the picture recorder. A double system puts control of the sound recorder in the hands of the soundperson; this allows audio to be recorded even when the camera is not rolling. Small pieces of incidental audio, or "wild track," can add greatly to a finished piece; **nat sound** needn't be merely street noise recorded while the camera shoots an exterior shot of a building. A double system also gives the soundperson the opportunity to roll on dialogue that the camera operator might not be aware of; in casual, less

BOX 6.2 USING MULTIPLE WIRELESS MIKES

Wireless microphone setups have been in use for many years but, since the mid-1980s, have been put into increasingly complex setups. Before the one-piece camcorder came into common use, camera people were connected to their sound operators with a thick video cable. The sound operator carried the video recorder as well as the various accouterments that soundpersons invariably accumulate. For more ambitious productions, the sound kit grew to include a four-channel mixer and two or three channels of wireless as well as a boom mike. Then, when camcorders became common, sound operators added two wireless transmitters to their mixers, sending their two-channel mix to two receivers affixed to the camcorder.

This "cutting of the cord" gave video the freedom that film crews have had since recorders like the Nagra IV allowed them to discard the sync cable that had camera and sound recorder joined until the end of the 1960s. Relegated to fireside fable are tales of "clothes-lining," when the cameraperson and the sound operator race off in opposite directions (most entertaining when working in front of a large audience, say, at a football game) or on documentary shoots when the camera squeezes onto an elevator with the subject but the soundperson doesn't . . . quite . . . make . . . it.

structured environments you may be documenting a conversation rather than shooting a formal interview. Sometimes your subject will say the most telling things just as the camera stops rolling (see Murphy's law).

In a double system, the soundperson's headphones can monitor the sound as it is being recorded; in a wireless link, only the camera operator, only while at the camera, can hear any interference that occurs between the mixer output and the camcorder. This risk must be regularly evaluated (check playback often!) to help determine the best method to use. Most crews using a wireless link are ready at a moment's notice to abandon the wirelesses and revert to an audio "snake" that, in addition to sending two channels of audio to the camera, will as well return the mixed audio from the camera's earphone jack back to the soundperson. In fact, it is best to hardwire in this manner for any situation that does not require mobility. If you are riding around in the back of a police car, wireless links will prevent the clothesline phenomenon; if you are doing a sit-down interview of the Dalai Lama by the pope, hardwire.

Whenever you have more potential audio sources than you have channels, the mixer becomes an essential tool, as does the need for a soundperson, who can devote all attention to whomever is speaking, to whomever might speak next, or where the best place might be to record the sounds of a passing marching band. It is a soundperson's job to choose microphones expertly and decide where and how to place them, and to see that good-quality sound is being recorded at the appropriate level.

The microphone mixer is the tool used to choose the appropriate audio sources, to control the levels of those sources, to assign and mix those sources to an appropriate channel on the recorder, and to monitor those sources via headphones. A good mixer can provide power for condenser mikes and can accept both mike- and line-level signals of various strengths as well as output signals at mike or line level for more than one recorder. It can insert high-pass filters on individual channels separately, and it can generate the tones used to record a reference level to tape.

ESSENTIAL POINTS FOR AUDIO

How to Dress News Subjects with the Miniature Mike

Concealing the microphone is almost an art form in itself. When the microphone is out of sight, the reporting process itself is less intrusive. In fact, if you are not careful, it may be inadvertent. A completely concealed microphone can create ethical questions, so if you find yourself concealing a microphone to record someone without his or her knowledge, be sure you have some good ethical reasons.

There are many approaches to mounting a mike on a person. Often, unobtrusive mounting might prevail over invisible mounting, because seeing a lav in a news interview is more common than seeing one on a character in a movie. When a reporter speaks to the camera there is no point in pretending that he or she is not on television. But when you follow a subject through the paces of a "typical day" (typical except for, of course, one or more people bristling with video gear tagging along behind), it is best to see no mike at all. In any case, a black lav clipped to the middle of a white shirt with the cable dragging off to one side summons images of 1950s newscasts. A mike clipped to a tie or to a collar will have much less chance of being rubbed and scraped by other clothing than will a mike you have tried to hide completely. Some degree of "clothes rustle" may be present no matter what miking technique you employ; a nylon windbreaker can play havoc even with a boom mike. Your headphones will tell you whether you have an intolerable problem or not.

BOX 6.3   NED HALL ON MICROPHONE PLACEMENT

In ENG work the handheld or "stick" mike is often, but not always, an omnidirectional, dynamic mike. This is usually a good choice for a correspondent or presenter honoring the Hand Grenade Principle. If the hand that is holding the mike is waving the mike around, as during an impromptu interview, the background noise can change drastically. For example:

Your reporter is interviewing a farmer standing out in his field (for being outstanding in his field, one supposes). The field is bordered on one side by a busy freeway. On the opposite side of the field is the farmer's son idly gunning the engine on his rusted all-terrain vehicle (ATV). Behind you is a barn, containing six newborn calves, lowing for suck. Directly next to the farmer is his shiny Behemoth MkIII tractor, which shakes the ground slightly as it idles. What to do?

Well, first, ask the farmer to shut off his beautiful Behemoth. Then, send the producer over to talk Sonnyboy into turning off the ATV, preferably after he has driven it far away. This leaves you with the barn and the freeway to deal with. If the reporter has a directional mike in her hand and she is facing the freeway, then when she points it away from her, the freeway's roar will be much louder under the farmer's comments than under her questions. If you can reorient the pair so that the mike is always pointed away from the freeway, you will have largely farm sounds under your whole interview. This is desirable, as the background noises will then reinforce the location as seen by the camera. If the mike is omnidirectional, the background noise won't change

so drastically, but just how annoying the freeway noise is depends on how far you are from the road.

The only way to ameliorate this is to move further from the road and closer to the barn. The omni will pick up a more consistent background, but it also must be much closer to the mouths of the speakers to achieve an acceptable difference between the volume of the speech and the volume of the lowing calves. If you could get that omni mike very close to the desired sound source, you would minimize the volume of most of the background sound, but that big object in the picture would be quite distracting.

Enter the lavaliere. Usually omnidirectional (because the omni is less susceptible to handling noise and is more forgiving of head turns and other sound source anomalies), the lav will usually achieve the most isolation from background noise of any miking technique. Remember, if that farm is located four miles from the closest road, then a cardioid condenser mike held over the heads of your subjects may yield the most pleasing, open, and natural sound, complete with crickets cricking, grasshoppers whirring through the moist grass, cows softly lowing in the barn, the breeze rustling the rushes down by the creek, the old windmill cranking and banging in the next pasture, the bed sheets the farmer's wife hung on the line billowing and snapping, the flies buzzing on the compost heap back by the truck garden, the phone ringing in the next farmhouse over. . . . Yes, you're going to need a good-quality, sturdy mixer that will accommodate as many channels of input as you foresee needing.

Different lavs conceal more effectively than others; you will find a favorite that mounts the way you like, sounds good, and seems to yield the cleanest track. There are some general methods that apply to any mike you choose: Lavs usually sound good mounted at about sternum height; a mike mounted too high on the neck may sound muffled, with the subject's chin blocking some sound; a mike mounted too low may sound thin and distant. (If your goal is to pick up both sides of a conversation with only one mike, a low position might be better because both subjects' mouths may then be about the same distance from the mike. Be willing to experiment.)

If necessary, tape the mike firmly to the shirt or body to keep it from producing extraneous noise when the person moves, and tape in an isolation loop to keep the mike cord free of stress. Gaffer's tape, folded into two "sticky-side-out" triangles and sandwiching the mike, makes a flat, sticky package that can easily be concealed beneath a shirt or blouse, or under a lapel or a tie.

If you clip the mike to a coat lapel, choose the side where the speaker is most likely to be looking during the interview (body right or left). Sound quality will diminish if the microphone is attached to the person's left coat lapel but he or she looks mostly to the right.

If the speaker wears a low-cut blouse or sweater, fasten the microphone right under the lapel or neckband with a safety pin or a small piece of gaffer's tape. Keep the mike cable out of sight, preferably beneath the person's clothing. Women can be directed to an area where they will have privacy and asked to drop the mike plug down the front of their dress or blouse. The cable need not necessarily run down the subject's front. It might be easier to tape it at the shoulder or under a collar and let it trail down the person's back. If the speaker is wearing a tie, you might conceal the mike cord by running it through the tag on the back of the tie.

If the person wears casual clothing, a jogging outfit for example, or will be active, use safety pins and tape to hold the microphone and cable in place. If the safety pins show through the clothing, bend them to conform to the clothing and the person's body and cover them with gaffer's tape.

Place the transmitter wherever it is least obvious—in the person's pocket, for example, or in the back of a bra. Sometimes the transmitter can be taped to the small of a person's back or even inside the person's thigh. Tuck all cables and wires neatly out of sight (and don't tangle the mike wire with the antenna).

Work quickly, but remember that Murphy's law states that if you wire someone in the belief that he or she will never be seen on camera from the waist down or from the back, the subject will stand up during the wide shot to retrieve a photo album from the bookcase behind him or her. Remember that you are invading your subject's personal space when you mount a mike. How you handle the process can make the person more nervous or less nervous. It's up to you.

Tips for Good Sound

Achieving good-quality sound is a matter of learning to listen for sound and to differentiate between what is acceptable and what is not. "Good sound is the absence of bad sound; bad sound is sound that is distorted," writes Murray R. Allen, president of Universal Recording Corporation in Chicago. "Distortion is any signal that unintentionally sounds different on output as against input."[4] Listen to sound recordings for hiss, buzz, boomy sound, low volume, and distortion. If you hear any of these elements, take steps to eliminate the unwanted sounds.

Experiment with Microphone Placement

One of the most important steps in achieving good-quality sound is to experiment with microphone placement. Take time to move the mike closer to the subject, then farther away. Change the sound volume. Move your subject away from walls and the center of rooms to avoid unwanted sound reverberations. One of the most frequently committed errors is to work the mike too far from the sound source. The rule of thumb is to work the microphone close to the speaker and to involve the microphone in the action just as you would involve the camera. The nearer the mike is to the sound source, the better the recording will be. Moving the microphone closer allows you to lower the volume and thereby cut down the background noise. Each microphone reproduces sound best when used in a particular way, and you will need to experiment to discover which position yields the best sound quality.

Monitor Recording Levels

Often, **distortion** occurs because volume levels are set so high that the recording equipment becomes overloaded. All professional video gear has audio-level meters that indicate the recording levels. Unfortunately, there is more than one type of meter and more than one way to calibrate the meters internally. Also, the maintenance and alignment of the audio portion of a camera generally isn't performed with the regularity and diligence devoted to the "tweaking" of the video components. This means that the same meter reading that yields a clean, well-modulated recording on one camera may indicate distortion on another. Experiment with your own equipment and listen to playback.

In general, if your high-end camera has a mechanical meter, that is, with a pivoting needle indicating the audio level, that meter is calibrated in volume units (VU). Speech should be adjusted to peak at zero, just before the needle moves into the red area of the meter face. If your equipment has a liquid crystal display, its meters may read peak levels and may be adjusted to indicate somewhere to the right of 0 on the meter for normal speech.

In various camera viewfinders a red light flashes when the signal level approaches or intrudes into distortion. Experiment so that you know what your meters are telling you. For all their differences, most audiometers are marked in decibels (dBs), a measure of sound intensity that corresponds roughly to the minimum change in sound level that the human ear can detect. Even a change in speech levels of 2 dB, for example, may not be noticeable to anyone who is not listening for it. Sound recorded from −10 to 0 dB generally is acceptable. To avoid further sound distortion, try to avoid automatic level controls because of the alternating levels in volume and the increases in background noise that result.

It is important to record a tone at the beginning of each session while you are recording color bars. All mixers contain a tone generator. Set the mixer so that its meters read the tone at 0 dB and then set the recorder's meters to 0 dB. This will allow the editor to calibrate the playback machine's audio output.

FIGURE 6.5

To determine whether field recordings are clean and free of dropouts and distortion, continual monitoring of the sound with earphones is essential.

Monitor the Sound with Earphones

Whenever you record in the field, it is critically important to monitor the sound with earphones (Figure 6.5). Photojournalists by the hundreds fail to monitor their sound, but the practice can be professional suicide. There is no other way to determine whether the sound you're recording is good enough unless you monitor it with earphones. The best earphones enclose both ears and block out much unwanted sound, but, if you are shooting video as well as recording sound, smaller, in-the-ear plugs may be more comfortable. High-quality ear buds designed for portable media players can be pressed into service if full-sized headphones interfere with your shooting style.

TECHNIQUES TO REDUCE WIND NOISE

Wind makes noise only when interacting with some object. The undesirable artifact we refer to as wind noise is not the sound of the wind, but the sound of a microphone diaphragm literally flapping in the breeze. Obviously, the windiest conditions offer quite a challenge; recording on a boat under sail or in stormy conditions on land calls for elaborate measures. The lightest breeze, though, will ruin a track if you are not prepared.

The first line of defense in battling the breeze is foam. This substance is sold as *acoustic foam,* so called because it is open-celled; that is, the little bubbles in the material touch each other and thus allow air to pass through them, albeit in a convoluted path. Closed-cell foam, which may appear quite similar, will not work. The test is to hold the foam to your mouth and blow through it. Open-celled foam will allow your breath to pass through easily; but note that the puff of air has lost its power after its trip through the foam. Manufacturers normally supply their microphones with **windscreens** made of gray foam or of a metallic mesh that has the same effect (Figure 6.6).

In an emergency, should the wind guard be absent, you can use the foam used to protect quartz bulbs in your lighting kit, but keeping a piece of acoustic foam in your kit is inexpensive and will come in handy. If you are having wind problems with a lavaliere mike and its tiny windscreen is not up to the task, you can try moving the mike under a layer of the subject's clothes, making a larger windscreen from your stock of foam, or repositioning the subject with her back to the wind.

In high winds, the best solution might be to revert to a boom-mounted mike encased in a large mesh cage, called a *zeppelin* or *blimp.* These work in higher winds by creating a large pocket of still air around the mike. They are often augmented further by a cloth sock and further still with a jacket of long synthetic fur. When installing your mike in this device, you can slip a foam windscreen on the mike itself and add one or more layers of foam sheet inside the zeppelin. If you still have a wind noise problem, take cover because there's a tornado right behind you!

Windscreens can have a slight dulling effect on the recording if you use several layers of blocking material. The odds are, though, that if you are in a situation where you need all that protection from the wind, your subject will be shouting just to be heard.

The second step is a *filter.* A **high-pass filter** (or low-cut filter—two names for the same thing), so called because it sharply attenuates low frequencies and allows the highs to pass through, is almost always used in field recording. This function is usually built into a mixer, mike power supply, or into the mike itself. Some amount of high-pass filtering may also be built into a wireless transmitter—it may or

FIGURE 6.6

A microphone windscreen is the first line of defense to help dissipate the wind and absorb its shock. Here the windscreen is normally concealed beneath the metallic mesh microphone cover.

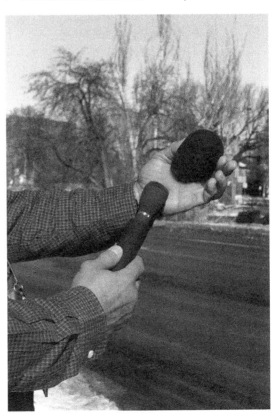

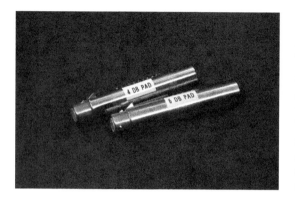

FIGURE 6.7

A high-pass, or low-cut, filter can be installed in the mike line to diminish wind, air condition-ing, and other low-frequency noises.

may not be externally adjustable. There are simple, nonadjustable high-cut filter "barrels" designed to be placed in-line on the microphone cable (Figure 6.7), but more versatile circuits usually provide you with three choices: no filter at all and two different degrees of attenuation. The most severe of these settings is useful in a stiff breeze; the more moderate setting can be handy even indoors, to lessen the obtrusiveness of furnace or air conditioning rumble. More than one filter may be used in tandem for even more pro-nounced effect, useful if you insist on shooting that tornado.

These filters do affect the quality of your record-ing, most obviously in music, but also, to a degree, when recording the voice. A low-cut filter will remove some of the depth of a reso-nant male voice, but the trade-off of also removing the worst of a distracting roar from a refrigerator or from a crowd of people must be considered. The conscien-tious recordist will eliminate as many distracting noises as possible. Turn off the air conditioner and shut off the refrigerator right before the interview starts—but remember to turn them back on before you leave! (You'll never forget if you put your car keys in the refrigerator when you shut it off.)

Bear in mind that, once you eliminate the booming rumble of wind hitting the microphone, you may still hear the wind rustling the subject's clothing. Wind can render a location undesirable even after you have solved the immediate problems with the mike. Be aware of possible problems before you become wedded to a location; the only way to know for sure is to listen carefully through your headphones. Wind in the tree-tops can make a terrible racket even though it is beautiful, and still, on the ground. Careful headphone listening will also reveal that most condenser microphones are so sensitive that just moving them around in still air will cause them to rumble. These mikes are therefore always used with at least a foam windscreen.

BE AGGRESSIVE

As a soundperson, be aggressive but unobtrusive. Strive to identify the small things that make sound in the environment in which you are recording. And don't give up if the sound is bad: Keep trying different variations until you get clean, usable sound. You are the person who makes the difference between unacceptable and excellent sound and be-tween merely technically correct sound and something truly exciting. Your instincts can guide you to story elements that might otherwise be missed. If a tree falls in the forest and you weren't rolling, does it make a sound? Your audience will never know!

THE MICROPHONE HEARS DIFFERENTLY

Remember that the microphone is as different from the ear as the camera is from the eye. The microphone "hears" differently, just as the camera "sees" things your eyes and mind screen from your consciousness. Be especially aware of sound that comes from outside the camera frame. For example, it is possible for the sounds of a lawnmower to intrude during an interview conducted on a battleship berthed at dockside. Routinely, the microphone will pick up buzzing flies, air conditioners, distant airplanes, and the rumble of heavy equipment in the background, even if you fail to notice such noises while you're conducting the interview. Careful monitoring with headphones is the only way to be sure you haven't ignored a stray sound that will return to haunt you.

Sometimes there is no complete solution to a sound problem. If you do a feature on anti-abortion picketers and interview people on a busy street in front of a clinic, you will not be able to avoid traffic noise in the sound track. If the camera chooses to frame the interviews with the fine old oak tree growing next to the clinic, your subject might appear to be standing in a peaceful glade, and the car noise will make no sense and will distract the viewer. If, however, the camera includes the traffic zooming past just two feet from the protest, the noise then becomes perfectly appropriate and will even add a feeling of tension to the scene. And, if you are prepared and have a proper mike at the ready, you might even catch a shout from a passing driver that will speak volumes about the situation you are trying to document. Can you keep one eye on your surroundings and catch the first words of an irate neighbor as he crosses the street to engage the protesters?

SOUND PERSPECTIVE

Sound should have the same perspective as the pictures they accompany. If the shot is a close-up of a basketball smacking the backboard and the mike was in the bleachers, some effect is lost. One danger of using wireless lavs is that all perspective is lost; the listener's ear is resting on the speaker's chest. If your reporter is standing on a desolate and wind-swept plain and the camera is pulled way back to reveal the bleak and stormy conditions, the reporter should not sound like someone speaking from an isolation booth. Either put an open mike on another channel or record some wild track of that moaning wind.

Similarly, take the case of a scene and accompanying sound of a woodpecker hard at work on a tree in the Okefenokee Swamp. If the woodpecker is photographed in a long shot or with a wide-angle lens, the bird will appear to be some distance from the camera. At that distance in real life, there would be a slight delay in the sound of the tapping because it must travel some distance to the observer. In the edited video, the same delay can be incorporated into the sound track if the editor simply slips sync slightly to create a perspective of distance, even if the original sound of the woodpecker's tapping was field recorded in dead sync with a wireless microphone hidden in the tree.

STEREO AND SURROUND SOUND

Even with video cameras that can record three-dimensional images that reveal detail and nuance flat pictures can't even suggest, it may be years before we all have three-dimensional television receivers in our homes. It will be years before the broadcast industry can agree what standards to adopt for this innovative medium. Yet the technology for delivering three-dimensional sound to our living rooms is already in place. Most television shows, including news programs, have stereo theme music if not surround sound. At professional production houses, edit bays have been equipped to do stereo for years. Even the most basic of editing systems is stereo-ready, and computer-based editing systems are engineered to handle stereo audio automatically. Yet most sound in the field is often recorded monophonically.

If you were to decide to produce a program in stereo, much of your field procedure might remain the same. A mono sound can always be placed in a stereo image, and an interview or standup may best be recorded in mono. But imagine yourself at an antiwar rally at the Vietnam memorial in Washington, DC. The camera shows a somber man tracing a name sandblasted in the stone. The sound records a sniffle or two, but far off to the left, you can hear a man's voice, singing a song he heard years ago on the radio, and to the right, the murmuring of a crowd listening to someone speaking with anger and conviction into a bullhorn. The camera turns and moves through the crowd, and you can feel the people pass by you on both sides. You hear a yell from off-camera, but you know where it came from, and as the camera pans to the source of the shout, you can hear the crowd move past the lens. This is life in surround sound and, if you find yourself in the position to experiment, you will be rewarded with sound that will make you sure the quality of the picture has magically improved.

Many stereo microphones are available, and the ones that use a technique called M-S (for mid-side) are perfectly suited for work in television. These mikes use one unidirectional mike capsule pointing forward and another figure-eight capsule with its lobes pointed to the left and right. The mikes combine these signals in a special way to produce an accurate stereo image. Should that stereo signal be combined into mono, as in a television with a single speaker, all that will be heard is the forward-facing unidirectional mike.

COVERING NEWS CONFERENCES

One secret to covering news conferences is to arrive early and stake out your territory. If a number of camera crews are expected, use your tripod to help create a buffer area for yourself. To keep other crews from moving in front of you, try leaving them a place—even make a hole for them and offer it when they arrive. You may want to be less accommodating, however, for the "radio and print people who want to get right up in front and get good shots with their pencils," advises freelance photographer Darrell Barton.[5]

Normally, news conference sound is recorded in one of three ways: You can use a shotgun mike, tap into the public address system fed from the podium mike, or you can add your handheld or stand mike to the thicket of microphones already taped to the podium. If you are taking the main sound from a common junction box or amplifier, find out in advance which adaptors you will need (Figure 6.8).

If you are the only organization at the news conference, or the first to arrive, consider placing the mike where you'll want the subject. "They'll come to the mike," says Barton. "It's like bait."[6] And if possible, talk to the speaker in advance and get to know the individual. That way, when the person speaks during the news conference, he or she may look in your direction somewhat more than in the others'.

FIGURE 6.8
Recording sound at news conferences presents special challenges of acoustics and microphone placement. Come prepared, arrive early, and expect the unexpected.

RECORDING GROUP DISCUSSIONS

If your task is to record a roundtable discussion or a full circle of speakers, then a different approach is required. To mike a group of people sitting in a circle will be most simple if the individuals sit around a table. You may be able to capture normal sound by placing the mike flat on the table. If no table is present, perhaps you can dangle a microphone from a ceiling fixture above the center of the group, or else use a shotgun mike and keep it as low and as close to the middle of the group as you can. Experiment with microphone placement until the sound is acceptable.

THE TWO-PERSON INTERVIEW

The "sit-down" conversation between two people is a staple in television and usually lends the most opportunity to control extraneous sound. Often, the crux of an issue is stated in this main interview, and the sound recorded here may be used over other pictures, so it is doubly important to eliminate distracting sounds. Check the air conditioners; close the doors; unplug the telephones; shut off the pagers and mobile phones. Try to make a quiet nook for serious exchange. Generally, it is best to use the same kind of mike on both parties, so the tracks will blend well. Also, because everyone is sitting down, and the camera(s) is tripod-mounted, there is no disadvantage to "hardwiring" your subjects—that is, using cables instead of wirelesses—to improve your chances of avoiding an ill-timed "hit."

RECORD ROOM TONE

Whenever you record sound in the field, remember to record some **room tone** or ambient sound for the editor. Room tone is the ambient undertone peculiar to each environment. It is the "silence" of the forest, the calming sound of the distant river, the fan noises in a room full of computers, the sound of people breathing in a quiet classroom. During editing, gaps of silence in the sound track will draw unwarranted attention if the track suddenly goes dead. To prevent a dropout, the editor has merely to insert room tone, provided you recorded it in the first place.

THE SEDUCTIVE QUALITY OF NAT SOUND

The need for nat sound as a storytelling tool—that is, all sound other than speech that occurs naturally in our environment—is an expression of our desire for realism. Good sound is compelling, involving, and engaging. Often, good sound builds on prior experiences that viewers themselves bring to the screen. When we hear sounds on television that imitate or draw from our own life experiences, we bring to the story a more profound and intimate depth of understanding. Although it is inaccurate to say that experience is the equivalent of understanding, sound is a vital component of direct observation and a source of much that we know. Often, sound serves as an equal partner with pictures in helping viewers experience the great potential of video reporting and storytelling.

WATCH WHAT YOU SAY

Perhaps one of the most important cautions whenever you record sound is to say nothing around the microphone that you wouldn't want broadcast. Around the country, broadcast journalists compile video of the spoonerisms ("It's snowing tonight on Rabbit Ass Pierce" when the weather reporter meant to say "Rabbit Ears Pass") and obscenities of other journalists—and share them widely, including on YouTube. Some of the best-known names in U.S. television are on those videos, and some of their utterances would make a deckhand blush. Even worse, in the rush of deadlines, some of their obscenities and unwarranted religious and ethnic comments, although made privately during the reporting process, have been inadvertently broadcast to home audiences. Consequently, the guiding rule must be, "If you don't want it on air, or the web, don't say it."

SOUND AND VIDEO ACCESSORIES

Returning home with usable sound is sometimes a matter of being able to fix problems that occur in the field. Many professionals carry a car kit with the following items. You can pack them in a standard shaving kit or a small drawstring hiking bag. Such items can be especially valuable in remote areas or when you travel overseas, far from the nearest repair shop.

You cannot check the kit on board, of course, when you travel by air; if you're worried about losing the kit should your checked luggage go astray, consider creating a backup kit and check it through in a second bag. Your kit might contain the following items:

- battery-operated penlight
- spare batteries for everything you operate (penlight, mikes, wristwatch, microphone mixers, wireless, etc.)
- spare bulbs for portable lights and your penlight
- video and audio connectors and adaptors (mini, phono, etc.) (Murphy says you will either carry every adaptor except the one you need or, to make the desired connection, you must use all the adaptors you carry.)
- alligator clips
- straight/Phillips screwdrivers
- pliers
- jeweler's screwdrivers
- miscellaneous small screws, bolts, nuts, pins, washers, etc.
- extension cord adaptors (3-prong to 2-prong)
- foreign electrical adaptors and power converter
- locking needlenose pliers
- small soldering iron
- good electronic solder
- scissors
- sharp pocketknife (Swiss Army knife is de rigueur)
- Allen wrench set
- masking or other form of paper tape
- gaffer's tape (furnace duct tape is acceptable, but it can mar delicate surfaces)
- nylon strapping tape
- instant bonding adhesive
- heat-shrink tubing
- cleaning swabs or chamois
- magnifying glass (small)
- earphones (take a spare pair)
- loose waterproof cover or plastic garbage bags for camera and mixer
- wooden wedge or steady bag to put under the camera when shooting low angles
- log books to jot down footage locations as you log video and audio
- pens/pencil(s)/felt-tipped markers
- electrical wire
- spare mike cables
- labels for video and hard drive recorders
- adjustable nylon fastening straps
- 75- to 300-ohm converter
- 75-ohm coaxial cable

- in-line line-to-mike adaptors to match level from auditorium amplifiers to a mike-level input
- in-line transformers to match impedance
- in-line high-pass and low-pass filters

SUMMARY

Conscientious professionals use audio in special ways. Sound imparts a sense of realism and life to news stories, and viewers have come to expect natural sound and crystal-clear interviews in their news reports and other videos. Microphones have various pickup patterns. Whereas some pick up sound from a full 360-degree circle, others pick up sound only from a narrow angle in front of the mike or both in front of and behind the mike.

Handheld microphones, although versatile and reliable, may intrude on news content when they act as barriers between the reporter and interview subjects or, in the case of standups, between the reporter and home audience. The problem is further compounded when the mike flag with station logo distracts the viewer's attention from the reporter or interview subject.

More appropriate in such situations is the lavaliere mike, an unobtrusive miniature microphone that can be clipped or pinned to clothing or taped to the speaker's chest. Shotgun microphones, which take their name from their appearance, can be used to record faraway sounds, such as at news conferences and athletic events. For the least distraction and most freedom to move about during standups and interviews, a good option is a wireless transmitter-receiver system. Sound can be transmitted over a range of several hundred feet, although wireless units are more sensitive to electrical interference than hardwired mikes.

Poor sound quality will result from improper microphone placement and from recording levels that have been set too high or too low. A dependable rule of thumb is to work the microphone close to the sound source and, as appropriate, to involve the microphone in the action. Set recording levels and monitor sound quality with earphones.

Frequently, wind noise destroys otherwise high-quality sound. Techniques to reduce or eliminate wind include placing foam or metallic mesh windscreens on the microphone, installing high-pass filters in the microphone line, or physically shielding the mike from wind gusts. As a further consideration, a recording should have the same perspective as the pictures it accompanies. If the picture is a close-up, the sound should be recorded in close-up, and vice versa. Sound is a vital component of the best visual stories, and in real life, a source of much that we know.

KEY TERMS

bidirectional 107
decibels (dB) 107
distortion 116
dropouts 111
dynamic microphone 106
hertz (Hz) 107
high-pass filter 117

impedance 107
kilohertz (kHz) 107
lavaliere microphone 109
mike flag 108
nat sound 112
ohm 107
omnidirectional 106

radio frequencies (RF) 111
room tone 121
shotgun microphone 109
unidirectional 106
windscreens 117

DISCUSSION

1. Of the various microphones, which types are most frequently used to cover news and field events? Compare the strengths and weaknesses of each type.
2. Discuss the most common microphone pickup patterns and their relative merits.
3. Explain the distinguishing features of the dynamic microphone.
4. Discuss the typical uses of the handheld, lavaliere, and shotgun microphones in news applications.
5. Discuss the major strengths and weaknesses of the wireless transmitter-receiver system.
6. When you work with news subjects, what considerations are most important to remember in concealing the miniature microphone beneath their clothing or in other personal effects?
7. Overall, what are the most important considerations to follow if you are to achieve good-quality sound in the field?
8. Explain why it is essential for the photojournalist or soundperson to constantly monitor sound in the field with earphones.
9. Discuss the full range of techniques you can use to reduce wind noise in the field.
10. Explain the concept of perspective as it applies to the sound that accompanies visual images.
11. List the steps that are helpful to follow when you record sound at news conferences.
12. Discuss the potential of stereo ENG and the limitations it faces in today's production world.
13. Explain the role of nat sound in helping lend a sense of realism to television news stories.

EXERCISES

1. Attend a news conference and observe procedures that professionals use to record high-quality sound. Examine microphone placement. Determine whether cords and cables are properly taped to the floor to reduce the risk that passersby will trip or fall. Notice what techniques the professionals may use to entice speakers to look in their direction.
2. Visit with the chief photographer or a sound engineer at a television station and inspect the various microphones used for news and sports reporting. Prepare a report based on your discussions with the photographer or engineer about the uses and relative merits of each type of microphone.
3. Record a person's voice with a dynamic handheld microphone located approximately two feet or more from the speaker's mouth. Make a second recording with the microphone about ten inches from the person's mouth. Determine which microphone position results in the best quality sound.
4. Practice concealing a miniature lavaliere microphone and its cord beneath a willing subject's business and leisure clothing, on the neck of a pullover sweater, and beneath a necktie.
5. Experiment with microphone placement in a room with poor acoustics. While you monitor the sound with earphones, have a friend reposition the microphone in several locations until you find the best position to record quality sound.
6. Intentionally record sound at too low a volume, then boost volume to acceptable levels during playback. Note the distortion that results. Repeat the exercise, this time recording at too high a level and lowering volume to acceptable levels during playback.
7. Record sound outdoors in high wind. Use the mike with and without a windscreen. Block the wind with your body or other object, then again with and without the windscreen. If possible, record sound with a high-pass filter installed in the mike line.
8. With and without the high-pass filter in the mike line, record the sounds from the tailpipe of an idling car or motorcycle.
9. Practice installing a wireless transmitter on a willing participant. Make practice recordings with the system, changing the transmitting antennae from the front to the back of the person, from horizontal to vertical position, and at various distances from the wireless receiver.
10. Note the variations in sound perspective that result when the microphone is involved in the action.

11. Record a series of room tones from various environments and study these respective "sounds of silence."
12. Watch editors at work as much as you can. Witness the problems caused by poor sound recording techniques.

NOTES

1. Doug Drew. "How Six Seconds Can Make a Newscast Special," December 09, 2010; accessed December 9, 2010 at http://602communications.com/site/2010/12/how-six-seconds-can-make-a-newscast-special. Substantive excerpts quoted with permission.
2. National Public Radio, November 11, 1994.
3. Ibid.
4. Murray R. Allen, "Is There a Place for Good Audio in Video?" *Follow Focus* (official journal of the Professional Motion Picture Equipment Association, Toluca Lake, CA) 3, no. 2 (Fall 1983), 24.
5. Darrell Barton, "Anticipation: The Key to Success," a presentation at the NPPA TV News-Video Workshop, Norman, OK, March 16, 1994.
6. Ibid.

7

The Video Interview
Shooting the Quotation Marks

Although images communicate much of the visual story, interviews provide the little moments of emphasis that punctuate the story. Interviews provide essential detail, help give stories spirit and atmosphere, and impart vital spontaneity. Part of the interviewer's function is to gather facts, but an equivalent obligation is to reveal the person being interviewed. The best interviews are often so strong that viewers would recognize the main subject days after seeing the story. Inevitably, some interviews feature the world's mayors, ambassadors, and other authorities. Still, the most poignant and memorable interviews often are with ordinary people who have never been on television and may never be on television again. KAKE's Larry Hatteberg observes that people listen most closely when they hear folks like themselves talking.

Whatever your story assignment, interviews usually play a valuable role. The following discussions apply whether you are a "one-person band," an employee at a station where reporters are expected to shoot video for one another, or a partner in a traditional reporter–photographer team.

ESTABLISH TRUST

As a video journalist you're most often an outsider, yet your job as an interviewer depends on your ability to establish trust and gain acceptance from perfect strangers quickly. The job is sometimes less difficult for print reporters, who can walk up without a camera and immediately establish rapport, than for the photojournalist who pulls up to a story burdened with camera, lights, microphone, and other gear.

Because your presence is so obvious, some people will be curious about you; others may be hostile, frightened, or indifferent. To achieve their cooperation, you will have to be open enough to let people come to know and trust you. "People will talk to a friend long before they'll talk to a stranger," says photojournalist Art Donahue.[1]

The process can take as little as five minutes and be as simple as a brief chat over coffee, but it can never happen unless you have a genuine interest in people and have the self-confidence to reveal something of yourself. If you are afraid to approach people as you launch your interviewing career, remember that most people feel flattered to be on TV even if they seem nervous at first.

PRACTICE GOOD MANNERS

In a sense, the audience will be peering over your shoulder throughout the interview. Your conduct will determine how the subject reacts, so even when you are in a rush to meet deadline, practice good manners and treat subjects with genuine courtesy. Arrive on time and take leave before you wear out your welcome. Leave the chewing gum at home, and refrain from sitting unless you are invited. Be friendly but not overly familiar. Journalists are always invited guests. Because viewers may identify more with interview subjects than with the reporter, how you treat the interviewee may translate into how viewers subconsciously feel you have treated them.

THE MOST IMPORTANT INTERVIEW QUESTION

Often the people you interview have never been on television, so your first task is to do everything you can to get their mind off why you're there. So great can be the anxiety that one of the West's most gifted poets routinely suffered bouts of diarrhea before television interviews and once fainted before anyone could ask him a question.

Because the objective in television news is communication of ideas through visual action, and because the most compelling stories and interviews reveal personality, it is well to remember that the interview itself is not the thing that happened. It is supporting structure for the larger story. For this reason, sometimes the most important question you can ask an interview subject is, "Show me what you do."

Interviewees are more at ease if they can focus on familiar work and surroundings than if they are forced to focus on themselves, their appearance, or their performance during the interview. Often you can interview people while they're engaged in familiar activities rather than standing them in front of a blank wall and thrusting a stick mike in their face. People are more relaxed doing something other than watching you photograph them. To avoid the appearance of staging in such situations, remember not to ask for or suggest action unless the person already routinely performs the activity in your absence.

SAVE YOUR QUESTIONS FOR THE INTERVIEW

The best interviews carry at least the illusion of spontaneity. Often, however, the reporter sets up the interview and determines in advance the subject matter to be covered, the time of day the interview will be conducted, and even the location for the interview. To help preserve the feeling of spontaneity, try not to share questions in advance of the interview. That's because subjects ordinarily put most of their energy into their first response. Once the camera rolls they may leave out the detail because having told you once, they assume you already know what they said. Although it's natural for interview subjects to want to think through their answers in advance, the best interviews address the moment and the feelings of the moment and grow naturally from the honest interaction between you and the subject.

DO YOUR HOMEWORK

The more you know about your source, the more confidence you give the person and the more you can concentrate on listening without having to worry about the next question you'll ask. Anyone can ask anyone else questions, but the interviewer can succeed only by asking informed questions that are based on knowing everything possible

BOX 7.1 HELP INTERVIEW SUBJECTS FORGET ABOUT THE HARDWARE

Many people you interview will have little experience with reporters, microphones, lights, and cameras. Predictably, their first reaction will be to become almost painfully self-conscious and to direct their focus inward. To help put interview subjects at ease and keep their focus off themselves, the following strategies may help.

- If you have the time, leave your equipment out of sight until you've had a chance to talk with the person you plan to interview.
- Spend as much time as possible getting to know the subject, whether you have only a few minutes or a half hour. Often, this interaction is the most valuable time you can spend on a story because it

gives you and the interviewee a way to come to know and trust one another.

- Talk about things that interest the subject; try not to talk about yourself unless the subject first expresses an interest in you.
- Preferably, use a miniature lavaliere microphone and wireless transmitter.
- Try to avoid talking about your equipment and how much it costs.
- Give the subject time to become accustomed to the camera, recorder, tripod, light case, and cables.
- Let the subject do as much of the talking as possible.
- When you record, turn off the tally light so people won't know the camera is rolling. ■

about the subject. Author Cornelius Ryan believed journalists should never interview anyone without knowing 60 percent of the answers. Do all the homework you can before the interview. The person you're interviewing has, and will be, prepared.

Among the resources available to most reporters are encyclopedias, almanacs and yearbooks, government manuals, directories, magazines and newspapers, the public library, the Internet, and, of course, phone calls and visits with acquaintances, friends, and relatives of the person to be interviewed. The absence of full and certain knowledge about a subject virtually guarantees an interview far beneath its potential.

HOW TO FRAME INTERVIEW QUESTIONS

So often, reporters think up the questions they'll ask on the way to the interview. The result is an interview without focus. "When you start asking questions, the other person immediately wonders, "Why does she want to know that?" If your purpose is unclear, your subject may be reluctant to talk. Ask a few questions to warm up, but save the best and strongest or most controversial questions for the last part of the interview and actually build the interview to a climax. The interview must lead to a given conclusion, somewhat like a story with beginning, middle, and end. Never should it be simply a series of unrelated questions.

USE A WIRELESS MICROPHONE

When you conduct one-on-one interviews at close range with people unaccustomed to the bright lights and hardware of television, try to avoid the handheld mike and even the shotgun mike because such hardware reminds people they're being recorded (Figure 7.1). If you can use a wireless mike instead, subjects are more likely to forget about the microphone. They'll feel and act more natural and may engage in more unguarded conversation.

To further keep the hardware low profile, arrive early to set up the equipment. Whenever necessary, use low-intensity lights, and set them up ahead of time to give interview subjects time to adjust. Long-time interviewer Bill Moyers suggests that

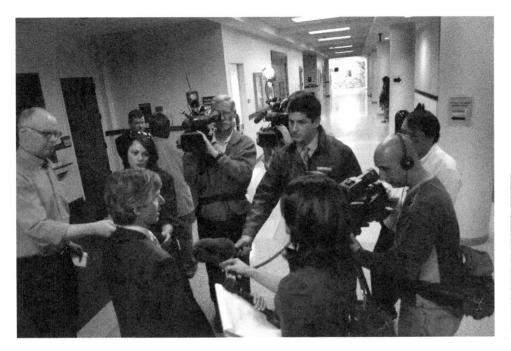

regardless of the camera, lights, and other gear, try to operate in such a way the person forgets it's a TV interview and has a conversation.

THE ART OF LISTENING

The most powerful interviews originate from conversations, yet there can be no conversation without a listener. Most obviously, that job falls to the interviewer. Listening, in fact, is one of the reporting arts. If you're prepared, listen well, and show interest in what people say, good interviews will follow. People will give part of themselves to you if you give part of yourself to them, observes Larry Hatteberg.

Listening also helps you frame more meaningful questions. A spontaneous interview is most likely if your questions build naturally off the other person's responses. Attentive listening also frees you from having to concentrate so hard on formulating your next question that you miss what the other person is saying.

As a further payoff, good listening can help you identify potential "edit points," even while you are in the field. When you feel something about what the person says, for example, it's generally a strong bite. "Whenever I interview someone, I try to identify the emotions I feel, and which points during the interview I feel them," says NBC News senior correspondent Bob Dotson. "Inevitably, when I go back to those moments in the interview while I'm editing, that's where I find the strongest statements."[2]

AVOID THE EASY QUESTIONS

It would help all interviewers to talk with a celebrity or two about interviewing. Whether they are screen stars or football quarterbacks, all celebrities have endured countless questions so similar and predictable that they become clichés. Especially when you work with people who appear frequently on television, think up fresh questions. Again, the task is easier the more you know about the subject.

If your research leads you nowhere, perhaps you can call one of the subject's old college classmates for background information that may point you in new directions. Along the way, you can ask questions and dig for details based on your curiosity about the interviewee, even when they lead you beyond the subject under discussion.

When shooting sit-down interviews, for example, and you have time, be alert for the moment when your subject becomes more than just an expert on the story and reveals personality and humanity. When you dig for details, you'll likely throw away 98 percent of what you unearth, but the more small details interview subjects reveal, the more you learn what matters to them. Sometimes, the small details will become the most touching and memorable moments in your story. Avoid interviewing someone for more than a few minutes, however, if you know you can only use one or two short informational sound bites in your story. Know what you need. Get in, get out, and move on.

Build Questions around the Five W's

The strongest interview questions solicit information and often arise from queries that begin with the "Five W's" familiar to all reporters: Who, Why, Where, When, What (and How). Such words compel informative responses. The question that begins "Why did you oppose reinstating the draft?" is vastly superior to the question or observation that results in a simple yes or no response: "I understand you opposed reinstating the draft." Another good technique is simply to prompt the person for clarification, "Really? Tell me about that," or "I know you oppose the draft. Tell me why."

AVOID TWO-PART QUESTIONS

The strongest interviewers ask their questions one at a time, building each new question on the subject's last response. Inevitably, whenever you ask two-part questions, one of them is left on the table: "How likely are we to see prefabricated factory-built houses dominate the new home market in the United States this century, and if they do come to dominate the market, will financing be provided mostly through private lenders or through government agencies?" Most subjects will answer the first question, then having answered, will ask the interviewer, "What was the other question?"

"HOW DO YOU FEEL?"

The question most likely to pop from the reporter's mouth at inappropriate times is, "How do you feel?" The question is asked of grieving parents, air crash survivors, and losers of football games. Perhaps the question is inappropriate because the answer normally is so obvious: "I feel like hell/sad/miserable/alone/scared/angry." Given story context, any viewer can fill in the blanks.

Sometimes a better approach is to make an observation, "I know it's tough for you right now," or to ask a question that probes the subject's emotions less deeply, such as "What do you think about this?" At other times, the best approach of all is simply to walk away. Some interviews aren't worth the invasion of privacy and loss of dignity they would require.

ANTICIPATE QUESTIONS THE VIEWERS WOULD ASK

As the reporter or solo journalist, try to anticipate questions your viewers would ask the subject if they had the opportunity. You are the viewer's representative in the field, and you will frustrate viewers if you overlook obvious or important subject matter in your interview. Conversely, because you are the viewer's representative, remember to keep your questions in good taste and to the point.

PRACTICE THE FINE ART OF HESITATION

Silence can be golden as an interviewing technique known as the "non-question question," described from the photojournalist's point-of-view in Chapter 4, Shooting Video in the Field. Experienced interviewers know the single most interesting thing they can do in television is to ask a good question and then just wait for two or three or four seconds after the answer as if they're expecting more. Typically, interview subjects become a little self-conscious and reveal more about themselves than intended. Even experienced interview subjects, who have "heard it all before," sometimes give their best response to a question that was never asked.

PITCH REPORTING OPPORTUNITIES

When conducting interviews for "people stories," professionals follow two rules. **Rule #1**: Don't interview people only in one location; move them around. A change of location can help rejuvenate the interview, and it provides a good chance to go from soft questions to the tough ones. **Rule #2**: Don't interview people. Have a conversation. Use little conversational questions and observations to which subjects can automatically respond, and in responding, define the moment. The observation "I'll bet it's cold in there" may elicit just as meaningful a response as a direct question. Remember, however, to use this technique as a way to elicit a response, not as a way to lead the subject to any particular response. Television journalist Jim Hanchett recommends four standard questions to foster this more conversational process:

> What's happening?
> What's going on?
> What do you think of this?
> What happens now?

Normally, the questions are asked of interview subjects as they sweep out the mud from their flooded storefront or sift through tornado debris for their possessions, while Hanchett's photographer uses a camera-mounted shotgun microphone to pick up their answers. No time is wasted setting up a formal interview, no spontaneity lost because reality has been interrupted (Figure 7.2).

To capture responses in the aftermath of a flood, for example, Hanchett might drive the news car along a street where flood cleanup operations continue while his photographer sits on the car hood and takes pictures. At opportune moments, either of the two will call out to people sometimes fifteen or twenty feet from the camera: "*How's it going?*" Back comes the response: "*This is terrible. I just got flooded out of my house; I lost everything.*" Extemporaneous questions give people no time to become nervous or to rehearse their answers.

PREARRANGE SIGNALS BETWEEN REPORTER AND PHOTOGRAPHER

A similar technique sometimes is possible even in more formal interview situations. Sometimes interview subjects will be at their most spontaneous and energetic best before the interview begins. If you work alone and your camera already is on a tripod,

FIGURE 7.2

A good way to interview people unaccustomed to appearing before the camera is to carry on a conversation with them while they continue to work at a familiar task.

focused, composed, and ready to record, you can capture the subject's energy and feeling without interrupting the moment. You can start recording on some cameras with a remote. (You did remember to put a wireless on your subject first thing when you arrived?)

The technique also works for reporter–photographer teams. Using a prearranged gesture as simple as replacing a ballpoint pen in a purse or shirt pocket, the reporter can signal the photographer to begin recording, even without the subject's knowledge. By the time the interviewee asks, "When do we start?" it's sometimes possible to reply, "We've just finished. Thank you so much."

HOW TO REACT WITHOUT APPEARING TO AGREE

Part of the art of conducting the interview is to react, but without indicating agreement or showing inappropriate displays of sympathy with the subject. Into this category fall nods of the head or responses such as "I see" and "uh huh." Most often your intent is to indicate your understanding, or to prompt your subject, through body language that communicates "keep going," but audiences may see such actions as agreement. As a further problem, your own utterings may make it impossible during editing to cleanly pick up the start of a sound bite if you have stepped on that part of the audio with your voice.

To avoid such problems, some reporters tilt or cock their head slightly to one side to show interest in the subject's response, or perhaps even utter an occasional "mm-hmm," provided it's low enough in volume not to be recorded on the sound track. Also be mindful to blink your eyes occasionally, and to allow your interest or concern to show in your eyes as appropriate. It is also acceptable to change body position, even to lean forward to indicate your interest in the subject's responses, but do skip the "I see's" and "uh-huhs," no matter how well intentioned.

RETAIN CONTROL OF THE INTERVIEW

It is important for the reporter to retain control of every interview, even when the interviewee is assertive enough to grab the handheld mike and hold it as a means to seize control. In such moments, the best defense is a good offense. Firmly and forcefully, take back the microphone. If the interviewee refuses to yield, then stop the interview so you can explain, "I have to hold the mike and ask the questions. Now, let's try again."

At other times it may be hard to interrupt a nonstop talker. In this situation, be assertive enough to interrupt the interviewee so you can ask another question. Take a deep breath and hold it, until the interview subject stops talking long enough to breathe. When that magic moment happens, seize it as your cue to ask the next question.

INTERVIEWING CHILDREN

Few NBC *Today* viewers who watched that day will forget the report about Bill Samples, a patrol officer stationed at Philadelphia's Children's Hospital who spent his off-hours helping make the dreams of very sick children come true. NBC News correspondent Bob Dotson told of Samples and his wife, Helene, who helped find money so dozens of terminally ill youngsters could see the mountains or visit the ocean before they died. The report, titled "Sunshine Child," enabled viewers to accompany tiny Christina Wilson, who suffered from leukemia, on a visit to Disney World where she hoped to meet a mouse named Minnie.

On the plane from Philadelphia to Orlando, photographer Warren Jones showed Christina the wireless microphone that would be in her purse when she met Minnie, and he let Christina hold the camera he would be using to tell the story. The camera was valued at more than $30,000. When they landed in Orlando, the lens was covered in fingerprints. But by the next day, the lens had been cleaned and Christina was all but oblivious to the reporting crew and the hardware that surrounded her.

"Have you seen Minnie?" Christina asked the next morning, amid the crush of children who had gathered to meet the Disney characters. Suddenly, a big black foot stepped into frame behind Christina. The little girl turned. "Hi, Minnie," she whispered. Minnie Mouse held out her arms and the two hugged each other for long moments. Once more Christina looked up at the big mouse. "Minnie, I love you," Christina said. Minnie knelt down to offer her big black nose, and a moment later Christina kissed Minnie.

Jones's technique with Christina is central to the success of visual storytellers who interview and work with children. The camera and other reporting hardware fascinate younger kids, so a good approach is to sit down with them and explain the equipment, even to let them look through the camera viewfinder if possible (Figure 7.3). Soon they will be their natural selves, oblivious to the camera and sometimes even to the reporting process itself. This approach often leads to stronger interviews and may even result in less time spent on the interview itself.

Specific questions work best with children (Figure 7.4). A usable response is more likely if the reporter asks, "What did Minnie's nose feel like?" than if the child is asked, "What did you like most about Disney World?" Children often give vague answers if questions are too vague.

FIGURE 7.3

KUSA photojournalist Brett Alles helps a young story subject become familiar with the camera and accustomed to his presence. This technique helps subjects forget the camera and reporting process.

THE TALKING HEAD

FIGURE 7.4

The strongest interviews with children commonly result when questions are specific and to the point.

The viewers' inherent interest in people can help lead them to an expanded interest in news. Although interviews are never substitutes for the story, they are an essential component of stories told through people. For the most part, whenever you edit interviews, keep bites short. Use them to provide emphasis rather than as substitutes for the story or for your own reporting. Many strong bites will run less than ten seconds to little more than twenty seconds, but use good judgment. Depending on content and pace, even two-hour interviews can be compelling and memorable.

Some organizations instinctively deride the **talking head,** as though a speaker on-screen is boring by definition; however, legitimate talking heads can enhance the story's meaning, sometimes even serve as a main point. Such talking heads may serve to

- provide insight into the speaker's personality
- show that what is said is less important than why and how the speaker says something
- show the person as he or she is
- show speakers who are compelling and dramatic or who have dramatic statements
- help prove the visuals

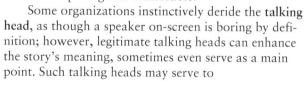
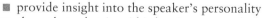

By contrast, the talking head can become a handicap in the video report when it displays the peculiarities that have created its bad reputation. Such characteristics are to be seen whenever the sound bite

- substitutes for the report
- substitutes for legitimate visual communication
- substitutes for a succinct script
- fails to enhance the visuals
- is long-winded and boring

INFLUENCING HOW VIEWERS PERCEIVE THE SUBJECT

It is vital to represent the interview subject honestly and to make the interview technically acceptable. How you structure and photograph interviews and their environments will affect how viewers react to interview subjects and what they remember about them.

Interviews by their nature are meant to reveal personality and, for the most part, call for reasonably close shots. But avoid shots that place the viewer uncomfortably close to the subject. "The viewers are entitled to look as closely at newsmakers and strangers as they look at the anchors," says Boston photojournalist John Premack. "Yet extreme close-ups flatter no one."[3]

ONE-EYED TALKING HEADS

Compose shots so viewers can see both the subject's eyes throughout the interview. Eyes are among the most eloquent indicators of the inner self and state of mind. Too often, however, photographers compose shots so viewers see only the side of the subject's head, a shot that incorporates a full view of the subject's ear but only a single eye. Ears, in and of themselves, rarely communicate much meaning.

BODY LANGUAGE

Finally, the interviewer's body language and attire inevitably affect how viewers perceive the interview subject (Figure 7.5). If interviewees are open and generally friendly, no purpose is served by inadvertently portraying them otherwise. To generate context about your interview subjects, consider the following behaviors as appropriate.

BOX 7.2 MAKE YOUR SUBJECT THE CENTER OF ATTENTION[4]

With every sit-down interview, when the camera is on the tripod, I try to create as much space as I can between the subject, the background, and myself. This lets me deemphasize the background in two ways: It lets me keep the key light off the background, and it gives me distance enough to zoom into the person's head and shoulders, making the background even less noticeable. With more separation and less emphasis on the background, the more the subject's face becomes the center of attention. Watch any movie with Tom Cruise and you'll notice that most close-ups are shot on a long focal length. The face really stands out when the camera is far away and the background is fuzzy.

—John DeTarsio,
freelance network photojournalist ■

FIGURE 7.5

The reporter's appearance and body language influence how viewers perceive both the interviewer and the interview subject.

If the mood of the interview is open and friendly, and you will appear on camera with the interviewee:

- Take off your coat, roll up your sleeves, and if you're a man, loosen your tie should you wear one.
- Open up visually and physically; show your friendship and your concern; move closer to the subject.
- Sit beside the source with nothing between you, not even a stick mike.
- Angle your body toward the person, rather than face the person head on.
- Create a sense of freedom by taking the person outside; communicate a clear impression that the person is with you of his or her own free will.

If the mood of the interview is investigative or adversarial, then the atmosphere and body language change accordingly and can be reflected through the following behaviors:

- Place something between you and the source (a desk, a stick mike, etc.).
- Place more distance between yourself and the other person.
- Wear a coat and tie, or dress in a similarly businesslike way.
- Face the person straight on, instead of at an angle.

AFTER THE INTERVIEW IS OVER

By day's end, video reporters and storytellers who cover five or six stories a day find it difficult to remember who said what, let alone have time to preview the various interviews before writing the stories. Yet an exact knowledge of wording is necessary to write naturally into and out of sound bites and integrate them properly into packages. Some reporters solve the problem by making a backup recording of the interview with an inconspicuous, handheld audio recorder. They play back the interview in the car on their way to the station or to the next story and note the exact wording of the sound bites they will need for the story.

The process can be streamlined even more if you train your ear to listen for sound bites during the interview itself. Listen for edit points and note the moments when you feel something about what has been said. Later, it will be easier to locate the statements you need and, if necessary, to communicate that information to an editor. If your field camera is equipped with a time-code generator, you can even set the generator to correspond to the time on your wristwatch. Then, as usable statements are made, a simple glance at your wristwatch during the interview can help you identify where in the video the statements can be located.

INTERVIEWS ALLOW REPORTING THROUGH DIRECT OBSERVATION

In the final analysis, video journalism is the art of reporting through direct observation. Through the broadcast interview, participants in news events can report their own observations, firsthand and with an intensity and believability unparalleled in other forms of journalism. Sometimes journalists have a rare opportunity to see into a person's soul, but that moment happens only if people feel comfortable enough on camera to reveal their innermost selves. If you have established a comfortable working environment, prepared yourself for the interview, and allowed your source to see that you are a reasonable and caring human being, then you will have set the stage for powerful reporting.

SUMMARY

Interviews impart a sense of authority and spontaneity to visual stories and provide intimate detail that otherwise would be unobtainable. Interviews further help reveal something of the person being interviewed. None of these goals is possible unless the reporter first establishes trust with the interviewee. An atmosphere of trust is most easily created if the reporter is open and courteous and exhibits a genuine interest in people.

Interviewees usually are more at ease if they can focus on familiar work and surroundings rather than on themselves or their "performance." Thus, interviews may progress more smoothly if a subject continues with a familiar task, and if the reporter makes observations and has a conversation with the subject rather than attempts to conduct a formal interview. Such exchanges progress even more smoothly when lights, microphones, and other reporting hardware are unobtrusive.

Few interviews achieve their full potential unless the journalist has conducted sufficient research to learn everything possible about the subject. Preparation is a prerequisite to success. Full knowledge of a subject also frees the reporter to listen closely to responses as the interview develops, another critical interview skill. As you listen to responses, react as appropriate but strive to avoid indicating agreement or showing inappropriate sympathy with the subject. Remember also that the reporter's body language influences how viewers will perceive the subject.

Because you are the viewer's representative, anticipate the questions viewers would ask if they had the opportunity. Interview questions can be constructed around the Five W's—who, why, where, when, what (and how)—to help elicit informative responses. Questions that elicit simple yes or no responses are less desirable, as are two-part questions, which can be confusing and difficult for the interviewee and audience to remember.

In all interview situations, good taste and courtesy are mandatory. If the audience feels uncomfortable with a reporter's conduct or questions, the interview may fail. When interviews are lengthy, consider interviewing subjects in more than one location. A change can help rejuvenate the interview, and it provides a good opportunity to change the subject.

Retain control of the interview, even when subjects seize the microphone or refuse to stop talking. If necessary, stop the camera or use a prearranged but unobtrusive signal between reporter and photographer to cut the sound and recompose the picture, as, for example, during a live shot.

Children represent special interview challenges. Good strategies include explaining the equipment before the interview and asking very specific questions during the interview.

Although interviews are never substitutes for the story, they are an essential component of stories told through people.

KEY TERM

talking head   134

DISCUSSION

1. Explain the essential role of the interview in video stories.
2. Discuss ways that will help you establish trust with an interview source.
3. What personal conduct and manners are important to observe whenever you are in someone else's home or office?
4. What is the most important question you can ask during an interview?
5. Discuss ways to help put the interview subject at ease.
6. Why is it important not to reveal the questions you intend to ask until the actual interview begins?
7. Describe the most important steps you can take to help interview subjects forget the microphone, lights, camera, and other hardware involved during the interview process.
8. Explain why research and planning are so important to the interview process.
9. Describe a good way to structure the interview questions you intend to ask.
10. Why is listening such an important part of the interview process?
11. What constitutes a "dumb" interview question?
12. Describe the difference between asking an interview question and pitching a reporting opportunity.
13. Devise and describe some prearranged gestures that a reporter–photographer team could use to signal one another during interviews without interrupting the spontaneity of the moment.
14. What are some good ways to react to an interviewee's statements without appearing as though you agree with what is being said?
15. What steps can you take to retain control of the interview, even when an interviewee seizes the microphone?
16. Explain the special challenges that arise when you interview children.
17. Describe the characteristics that make for a legitimate talking head interview.
18. Discuss how environment, lighting, composition, and even your body language can influence how viewers perceive the interview subject.

EXERCISES

1. Study professional television interviewers such as Diane Sawyer, Conan O'Brien, Oprah Winfrey, Katie Couric, and Craig Ferguson. Pay special attention to how they put interview subjects at ease, elicit meaningful information, and move the interview along.
2. Arrange to interview a news source or someone who will play the role of a news source. Research the person and the topic you wish to discuss, schedule a time for the interview, arrive on time, and take a few minutes to become familiar with the interviewee. This time, take just a notebook and pencil and leave the camera at home. Concentrate on being relaxed, knowledgeable about the subject, interested, and friendly.
3. Repeat exercise 2, but with a different person. This time take the camera, lights, and microphone.
4. Interview someone while the person continues a familiar task. Make observations or offer "reporting opportunities" rather than ask formal questions.
5. Construct two lists of questions: (1) questions you would expect an informed interviewer to ask you about your life interests and activities and (2) questions of the same nature that you would like to ask a friend based solely on your existing knowledge of that person. Compare the two lists of questions. How do the questions differ? Now, experience the value of research firsthand by calling your friend's parents, old schoolteachers, close friends, classmates, and brothers and sisters, and ask them questions about your friend. Using this new knowledge, expand the list of questions you will ask your friend.
6. Practice listening to people more attentively, even in everyday conversations. Develop your ability to listen to people into a fine art.

7. In your everyday conversations, practice listening to people without appearing to agree. Act interested, but suppress any body language that tends to communicate agreement.
8. Practice conducting interviews and working with children until you are able to routinely elicit broadcast-worthy responses.
9. Study television interviews to determine how interview environments, lighting, camera composition, and body language can influence the viewer's perceptions of interviewers and interview subjects.
10. Listen to interviews on radio and television to practice identifying alternative "edit-in" and "edit-out" points in sound bites. Often, the routine sound bites in news stories can be shortened with no loss in meaning and sometimes can even be improved.

NOTES

1. Art Donahue, "Utilizing a Creative Eye for Everyday Assignments," a presentation at the NPPA TV News-Video Workshop, Norman, OK, March 21, 1986.
2. E-mail correspondence with the principal author, Norman, OK, June 27, 2007.
3. John Premack, "What's Wrong with Interviews," *RTNDA Communicator* (September 1984), 17.
4. DeTarsio expands on this advice in Chapter Four, "Shooting Video in the Field." See examples of his work for CBS *60 Minutes*, such as "Brazil's Rising Star," at http://www.cbsnews.com/video/watch/?id=7143554n&tag=mncol;lst;5 accessed for this reference December 21, 2010.

8

Video Script Formats

—Luan Akin

Most organizations use script-formatting software. Competing software programs may produce slightly different formats, but if people writing the scripts draw from a common pool of abbreviations and phrases, the differences won't matter. The various terms will be synonymous, and anyone familiar with those terms in general will understand the script.

The following scripts represent the various ways stories can be formatted, even on a word processor or a personal computer with a script template, or a program such as Final Draft AV®. They're not meant to be seen as the only way each type of story should be laid out, nor do the techniques apply to television alone. Most of us now have greater access to low-cost cameras, studio-like environments, computer graphics, video editing, electronic effects, good audio recording methods, prompters[1]—even on iPads® and other tablet devices—and the ability to broadcast our own stories around the world via the Internet. The following scripts, therefore, are specific to television journalism but equally adaptable to any organization's needs. Once you become familiar with the material, you'll be well on your way toward reading and recording a script from any source and understanding the technical instructions that accompany the script.

READER

A **reader** is as simple as a television story can get, but it's still a valuable format. In just a few well-written lines, viewers can get an overview of a story. And by keeping the copy short, producers can increase the story count of their show and keep the pacing up as well. If a story worth running isn't visual, or if the pictures simply aren't available, a reader may be the answer.

Scripts for television are written in two columns. In simplest terms, the column on the left is primarily for instructions to the director or editor. The column on the left does not appear in the prompter. The column on the right contains information for the anchors and the actual copy to be read out loud.

The first instruction in this script, "Live Jean," indicates the story is "on camera." We'll see Jean live from the news desk or studio, looking into the camera, delivering the story. Some newsrooms may use the abbreviation "OC," or on camera, rather than "live."

The name "-Jean-" at the top of the right-hand column clearly indicates to each anchor who's reading which story. This is especially important for dual anchors. The anchor's name is bracketed with hyphens or parentheses to separate it from the copy.

Slug: Cabbie/Dentures

Live Jean	-Jean-
S/Jean	

A Denver cab driver may owe his life . . . to his false teeth.

The driver for Yellow Cab was shot in the mouth during a robbery overnight.

Police say the man's dentures deflected the bullet.

The cabbie was treated at Denver General Hospital and released. No suspects are in custody.

The only other instruction on this script, "S/Jean," calls for a graphic, a "super," of the anchor's name. The anchor doesn't need to know his or her name is appearing at the bottom of the screen, so the super instruction appears in the left-hand column only.

VTR VO (VOICE-OVER VIDEO)

Television is pictures. As often as possible, producers will include even short pieces of video that help "bring the story home." That's the job of a **voice over** (**VO**). VOs as short as twelve to fifteen seconds can tell a story. That's only three or four shots. But if the shots are well crafted, they can definitely leave an impression.

"Live Ed": In the left column, this VO begins just as the reader did: The top of the VO is live, with the anchor on camera.

"-Ed-": At the top of the column on the right, we see the name of the anchor delivering the story, just as at the beginning of the reader. The name must be distinguished

Slug: Kicker/Pet-a-Cure

Live Ed	-Ed-
S/Ed	Have you ever thought of giving your cat a pet-a-cure? It's not what you might think.
VTR VO	-VTR VO-
S/Jacksonville, Fla.	A Jacksonville, Florida, pet clinic is putting press-on nails . . . on cats.

They're glued on, just like the artificial nails many women wear.

Veterinarians say the press-on nails help cats that have been de-clawed protect themselves if they go outside.

When the cats come back in, the artificial claws can be removed, so the furniture can't be scratched. As to polishing these nails . . . the vets say you're on your own.

from the copy with hyphens or some other mark to make it clear the word is not to be read out loud as part of the story.

"S/Ed": Instructs the director to superimpose the anchor's name briefly in a graphic at the bottom of the screen. The anchor doesn't need to know about this super, so there's no mention of it in the right-hand column.

Next, our first instruction for video: "VTR VO," video "voice over" by the anchor. At this point in the story, the audience will continue to hear the anchor's voice, but instead of seeing the anchor on camera, viewers will see a piece of edited video—a VO.

Hyphens or parentheses are again used in the right column to bracket the indication to the anchor that the on-camera section of the script is over, and the "-VTR VO-" is beginning. This instruction already appears in the column on the left, but it needs to be repeated here for the anchor because only the right-hand column of a script appears in the prompter.

The final instruction, "S/Jacksonville, Fla." calls for another super. Until now, the only graphics we've used have identified people. This graphic is a "locator." It identifies the place pictured in the videotape, in this case, Jacksonville, Florida.

VTR VO (VOICE-OVER VIDEO) VO/SOT/VO (VO SOT OR A/B FOR SHORT)

A VO SOT or A/B is a VO that includes previously recorded sound or **SOT**. It's usually a "sound bite," that is, a short piece of an interview recorded earlier. Some newsrooms edit the first video, the sound bite, and the video following the bite onto one tape. That means the script needs to be carefully timed by the anchor, so just the right amount of video can be included before the bite. If too much video is used, there will be "dead air." The anchor will have read the first section of copy, but there will be a painful silence before we hear the bite. If too little video is used, the anchor will "up-cut" or talk over the first part of the bite. Both mistakes are distracting.

To prevent such problems, many newsrooms put the first section of video (plus an extra shot or two for pad) on one tape. That becomes the A roll. The sound bite and the second section of video (plus pad) are edited onto another tape. That's the B roll.

As soon as the anchor finishes reading the first section of VO and reaches the point for the sound bite, the director calls for the video operator to roll the second video segment, the B roll. The bite plays just where it should. There are no problems with dead air, and the anchor doesn't risk up-cutting the bite. In short, the newscast is cleaner, tidier, and looks more professional.

The use of A/Bs does mean editors have more videos to keep track of, but the results are usually worth it.

The following script is written to be edited as an A/B.

By now, the instruction "Live Kathy" should be familiar. This script begins with the anchor live, on camera. This is the beginning of the A roll.

Instead of seeing the anchor's name appear at the bottom of the screen, for this story the producer has called for an OTS, an over-the-shoulder graphic. Often, it's a single frame of video taken from the story—a freeze frame. It could also be a computer-generated drawing—flames to accompany the story about a fire, for example. An OTS will always include a cutline, a word or two that describes what the story is about. The cutlines are simple and direct: "Severe Weather," "Police Chase," or a

Slug: ATM Cash

Live Kathy	-Kathy-
OTS: Free Money	A bank giving away money? Sounds impossible, but it actually happened in Missouri this past weekend.
VTR VO	-VTR VO-
S/St. Louis, Mo.	Students at Washington University in Saint Louis couldn't stop cheering. A foul-up at the campus automatic teller machine left many of the students twenty dollars richer.
VTR SOT	-VTR SOT-
S/Melissa Hammond, Student	"From what I hear . . .
In: 07:14:44	. . . at the ATM." (Runs: 11)
VTR VO	-VTR VO-
	The problem happened after twenty-dollar bills were placed in the A-T-M's five-dollar bin.
	Some of the students reported the error to the bank, but most of them simply pocketed the extra cash.
	Bank tellers say the error has been corrected and the extra money has been deducted from the students' accounts.

well-known person's last name, to cite only a few examples. The cutline for this story is "Free Money." In short, that's what the story is about.

"-VTR VO-": Another familiar instruction: voice over video, followed by a locator graphic.

The instruction "-VTR SOT-" in the right column marks the top of the B roll—the point in the script where the sound bite belongs.

The graphic "S/Melissa Hammond, Student" gives us the name of the person speaking in the sound bite. Her name is Melissa Hammond. The graphic will further identify her as a student.

The instruction "In 07:14:44" tells the editor where to find the sound bite on the video used to shoot the interview. If the story was shot on more than one tape or disc, the person writing the script should also tell the editor which sources to use. The director doesn't need this information, but including it on the script makes it easy to find the bite again if the story is updated or rewritten for later use.

The short phrases "From what I hear . . ." and ". . . at the ATM" are the "in cue" and the "out cue" for the sound bite, in short, the first few words and the last few words. The out cue is the most important. It tells both the anchor and the director when the bite has finished and the anchor should resume reading. It's also helpful for both the anchor and the director to know how long the sound bite lasts.

INTROS TO LIVE SHOTS

In a sense, an introduction to a live remote is a short reader. Producers can dress up the intro with various production techniques—running a short VO that segues into the package, for example. (A *package* is an edited, self-contained video report of a news event or feature, complete with pictures, sound bites, voice-over narration, and natural sounds.) But the intros are simple and straightforward. So let's make this more interesting, and cover more ground at the same time.

Instead of dissecting a plain intro to a package, we're going to look at an anchor intro, or **toss**, to a reporter who's live at a remote location. Then we'll examine the reporter's intro to a package shown within that live shot. These intros will contain a lot of detailed information, but most of it is material that we've already talked about, used in a slightly different way.

Slug: Wheat Farmers/Intro

Live Bill	-Bill-
S/Bill	Damage is adding into the millions of dollars following a powerful storm yesterday that pounded wheat crops in northeastern Colorado.
Side by side	-Side by side-
	Newsfour's Ann Thompson is live in Copter 4 over Washington County with more on how serious the loss is there.
Remote full	-Remote full-
S/Live Ann, Copter 4	
S/Live Ann, Wash. CO.	
VTR SOT pkg	-Cue to pkg-
	Through here yesterday.
Remote full	-Cue to remote full-
	In business very long.

"Live Bill," "-Bill-," and "S/Bill" should be old, familiar friends by now. They show which anchor is reading; and indicate the anchor appears on camera, with a super of the anchor's name at the bottom of the screen.

A "Side by Side" shot is one of several production techniques a producer can use as a transition from the studio to the reporter in the field. The instruction means just what it says. The shot of the anchor live on set is switched to a shot where the screen is split down the middle, the anchor on one side, the reporter at the remote location on the other.

"Remote Full": at this point, the anchor's intro has been read and it's time to hear from the reporter. The side-by-side shot is switched to a full-screen shot from the remote location, and the reporter's intro begins.

Most newsrooms use what is called a "live sequence" of supers (S/Live Ann, Copter 4, S/Live Ann, Wash. CO.) for remote shots. This will include a small "live" graphic that's on-screen (usually upper left corner) throughout the shot. The sequence also includes the reporter's name and location, supered during the first few seconds of each live appearance (i.e., before and after any video).

"VTR SOT pkg": In short, roll the package!

"-Cue to pkg-" is the cue for the director to roll the package. The cue to package includes the final few words of the reporter's live intro. The director doesn't need to see the reporter's entire intro—just enough to call for the package when it's needed.

"Remote full," "-Cue to remote full-": Once the package is over, it's time to see the reporter again in a full-screen shot of the remote. The director listens for the reporter's cue to remote full to take that shot. The cue to remote will be the last audio on the package. Usually, it's the final few words of copy or the end of a sound bite, but the cue to remote full could also be natural sound (i.e., the sound of a siren as an ambulance pulls away). If the **crossroll**, the video within the live shot, is a VO or A/B instead of a package, the cue to remote full will be the final few words of that script.

LIVE INTROS TO PACKAGES

As you'll note again in Chapter 13, reporters' live intros should flow easily from the anchor's toss. The reporter's intro should be brief; it's important to get to the video. But it's also important to make good use of the live presence with a meaningful reference to the backdrop or setting.

Slug: Wheat Farmers/Live

S/Live Ann, Copter 4	-Ann-
W/Live Ann, Wash. CO.	Bill, from the air, the damage is clear: wheat field after wheat field flattened by the strong winds, rain, and hail that moved through here yesterday.

In most cases, the director won't see this script. But the information in the left-hand column, "Remote full," is still worth including. This is a simple live shot, to and from the news set. But if this live reporter was supposed to toss to another live location, that reminder should be included in the left-hand column.

Just as with the other formats, the name of the person reading the script ("-Ann-") appears at the top of the right-hand column.

PACKAGE SCRIPTS

We've seen and heard the anchor and reporter lead up to a package on the wheat damage. Now let's see the package, or more specifically, the package script. Even though this package was intended to run as crossroll within a live shot, the format for the package is the same as if the story was introduced from set. The only difference is we won't hear the reporter "lock out" or sign off at the end of the story.

Slug: Wheat Farmers/Pkg

	It wouldn't be so bad if Rick Lewton's wheat field looked this flat after the harvest. But Rick hasn't harvested his wheat yet.
S/Rick Lewton Wheat farmer Tape 1, 03:50:54	"It was about 2 . . . 2$^{1/2}$ feet tall. About this tall. But there's nothing left." :08
	That same hailstorm blasted buildings and barns all over Washington County yesterday.
S/Marge Corman Wash. CO. resident Tape 2, 05:57:27	"We had brick-sized hail. It was in ice balls this big . . . Bricks of ice. It was just terrible." :07
Shot of bldg. damage Shot of wheat damage	It's no wonder weather that powerful . . . can leave a wheat field looking like this.
Rick Lewton Tape 1, 03:58:49	"You could hear the hail in the cloud. It was just roaring . . ." :04 And once it had roared through Rick's field, not much was left.
CU Wheat as Rick talks Rick Lewton Tape 1, 03:53:12	"This is the stem of what used to be a head. This has some of the wheat still left on it. This is what happened after the hailstorm." :10
SU Bridge Tape 2, 04:15:32	"Yesterday's storms were especially widespread. But that's not the worst of it. The hail pounded Colorado's top two wheat-producing counties." :10
	Kit Carson and Washington counties provide 20 percent of Colorado's wheat crop. The loss here will hurt statewide.
Darrell Hanavan Tape 3, 06:43:03	"We're already down to the second-worst crop in 14 years." :04
	Darrell Hanavan is the director of the Colorado Wheat Board. He says more damage like this could set a record.
Darrell Hanavan Tape 3, 06:54:59	"We would be looking at the worst crop in 14 years." :02
	Hanavan says Colorado's wheat crop was already in trouble because of severe drought this spring.
	But for people like Rick Lewton, the hail has made a bad situation even worse.
Rick Lewton Tape 1, 03:54:59	"Most farmers can expect to have a little hail every year, and that's what they plan for. That's just part of farming. But you can't stand this kind of hail loss and stay in business very long." :10

In a script for a package, the instructions in the left-hand column are for the editor. If the photographer who shot the story is also editing the piece, the instructions generally don't need to be as detailed. But if there's any room for confusion, it's better to have too many instructions than too few.

"S/Rick Lewton Wheat farmer Tape 1, 03:50:54": This instruction serves several purposes. It tells the editor who's talking in the sound bite and where that bite can be found. It also indicates that a graphic of that person's name will go here. That's important because it's up to the editor to fill out a "cut sheet" for the package, a list showing how far into the package (in minutes and seconds) certain graphics should appear. Generally, sound bites need to be at least five seconds long before a graphic is used. If the first sound bite with a particular person is too short, the graphic can wait until a second, longer sound bite from that person. If none of the sound bites are long enough, the person should be identified in the copy, as we'll see in a moment.

"It was about 2 ... $2^{1/2}$ feet tall ...": Writing out the entire sound bite takes more time, but it's a good habit to get into. It helps the reporter remember just how the sound bite was phrased. That means the copy leading into the sound bite can flow more easily, and the reporter won't end up repeating the phrasing inside the bite.

Some reporters like to distinguish their narration track from the sound within the story by writing one in lowercase and the other in capital letters. This helps the editor get a better sense of how the story is laid out. When all of the type on the page looks the same, it's surprisingly easy to overlook a section of track or a piece of sound.

It's also a good idea to note the length of the bite. It gives the reporter a better sense of how long the story is likely to run. People talk at dramatically different speeds. A bite that looks as if it should take six or eight seconds might take twice that long if it's full of pauses. Incorrectly judging the length of a package can force a sloppy rewrite or reedit at the last minute.

"Shot of bldg. damage Shot of wheat damage": When the reporter has a certain shot in mind for a particular phrase or sentence within the copy, it's best to tell the editor. Here, the reporter has called for a certain type of shot: video of building damage in one case, and wheat damage in the other. There will be times when the reporter wants a very specific shot. When that happens, the editor needs to know exactly what that shot is and where it can be found.

"SU Bridge Tape 2, 04:15:32": At this point in the script, the reporter has called for a standup bridge recorded earlier when the story was being shot. A "bridge" implies that the reporter's standup is within the story, rather than at the beginning or end. A package used as crossroll for a live shot shouldn't have a standup open or close.

"Darrell Hanavan": Notice there's no "S/" in front of this name. The name is there to help the editor identify the speaker, but neither bite from this speaker is long enough for a graphic. Instead, the person is identified by name and position in the copy.

It's actually a good habit to identify the people speaking within a story even if you do plan to super their name. That way, if the graphics computer fails, and they sometimes do, the story can stand on its own without supers.

REPORTER AND ANCHOR CLOSES

Generally, reporters will close out their live shots with another sentence or two live, then toss back to the anchor on set. Often, the reporter close is only loosely scripted, if it's scripted at all. The director doesn't need written instructions to know when to return to the camera on set. The reporter will make it clear by using the anchor's name at the close of the live report.

THE CASE FOR CAPS AND LOWERCASE

Some television writers prefer to write their stories entirely in capital letters, as demonstrated in the following story.

> THERE MAY BE TROUBLE AHEAD FOR A PROPOSED CITIZEN REVIEW PANEL TO OVERSEE JOHNSON CITY POLICE. MAYOR WEBB SAYS CITY COUNCIL APPEARS LIKELY TO VOTE DOWN THE IDEA IN WHAT MAY BE A STORMY MEETING TONIGHT. THE MEETING BEGINS AT SEVEN O'CLOCK AT THE CITY AND COUNTY BUILDING.

Other writers and anchors prefer their scripts in "caps and lowercase," as the following script demonstrates.

> There may be trouble ahead for a proposed citizen review panel to oversee Johnson City police. Mayor Webb says city council appears likely to vote down the idea in what may be a stormy meeting tonight. The meeting begins at seven o'clock at the City and County Building.

Station policy, prompter limitations, or the preference of on-air personnel may answer the question as to which format is "best." Otherwise, you will have to choose which format you most prefer. Some journalists find that caps and lowercase helps them find their place in the copy more easily, regardless of whether they record voice tracks in a sound booth or present the news live from a studio. Other journalists seem to find all caps easier to read, although if that were actually the case it might seem as if newspapers, magazines, and book publishers would print their stories in all capital letters. Ultimately, the choice seems to boil down to which style can help make on-air presentations the most seamless and flawless. Which format makes words that demand special emphasis most obvious? Which format reveals the strength and meaning of individual words most definitively? Your answers will help determine which style you select.

SUMMARY

Script formats vary from one station to another, but virtually all stations follow some variation of the prototype formats described in this chapter. From the simplest voice-over script, to VO/SOTs, and to the most complex scripts for packages, every writer needs an understanding of script structure.

In addition to the formats discussed in this chapter, you may wish to include features from other formats you are familiar with to custom design a script structure that is most comfortable for you.

KEY TERMS

crossroll 145	toss 162
reader 140	voice over (VO) 141
SOT 142	

EXERCISES

1. Obtain samples of television news scripts from one or more local stations. Compare the scripts with examples provided in this chapter; also compare with each other if you have samples from more than one station. Determine what formats you most prefer and analyze the reasons for your preferences.

2. Following the example in this chapter, write five separate on-camera "readers," each on a different newsworthy topic. Limit each of your stories to twenty seconds in length. You may wish to use a web site, newspaper, or news magazine as your source of information for this assignment.

3. Following the example in this chapter, write three separate VTR VO stories of approximately thirty seconds in length, each on a different newsworthy topic. Follow the format of the VTR VO example in this chapter. You may wish to use a newspaper or news magazine as your source of information for this assignment, or use information from any other legitimate source. Assume you have at your disposal all video you would need for each story.

4. Write three separate VO SOT stories for television or the web, following the format of the VO SOT example in this chapter. You may wish to use a newspaper or news magazine as your source of information for this assignment, or use information from any other legitimate source. Determine an appropriate length for each story you write. Assume you have at your disposal all video you would need for each story.

5. Write intros to three live shots, following the format example in this chapter. Determine an appropriate length for each intro. You may wish to use a newspaper or news magazine as your source of information for this assignment, or use information from any other legitimate source.

6. Write a video news package, following the format example in this chapter. Use quotations from newspaper or magazine stories as the source for your "sound bites." Assume you have all video you would need for this assignment.

NOTES

1. See, for example, the free computer/tablet prompter at http://www.cueprompter .com/promptr/php

CHAPTER

9

Writing the Package

Package. An edited, self-contained video report of an event or feature, complete with pictures, sound bites, voice-over narration, and natural sounds. The package is a form of narrative storytelling with a beginning, middle, and ending.

Some reporters start with the pictures whenever they "write" a package. Others start with the words. But the most efficient reporters first block the package as a story with a beginning, middle, and ending. The blueprint looks something like this:

1. Focus (the story stated in a sentence)
2. Beginning (lead)
   a. Studio lead-in
3. Package lead
   a. Visual lead
   b. Voice over (VO)
4. Middle (three or four main points)
   a. Main point A
   b. Main point B
   c. Main point C
   d. Main point D
5. End (close)
   a. Final visual
   b. Final VO
   c. Strong closing sound

   Following this approach, you first emphasize the ideas you wish to communicate, and only then begin the search for images and words that will most effectively tell the story. You structure the story through four distinct stages of development: (a) reviewing existing knowledge and new information obtained from story research before you leave for the field;

(b) conducting field research and interviews; (c) viewing and editing field video and sound bites; and (d) writing the final package. Structuring a package thus becomes much more a way of thinking than of writing.

DEFINE YOUR FOCUS

Once you understand the story, you can define its **focus**. The focus is a simple, vivid, declarative sentence expressing the heart, the soul, of the story as it will appear on air.[1] Until you know the story yourself, it will be difficult to tell it to anyone else.

In the following example of how to structure a package, assume you are assigned to cover a story on smart ways to lose weight. Perhaps as you research the story, you begin to understand that the story focus is, "The secret to weight loss lies in eating a healthy diet from the four basic food groups."

WRITE THE BEGINNING (STUDIO LEAD-IN)

The package, like all stories, will need a **lead-in**. It could take several forms:

- the introductory copy an anchor reads on camera from the studio before the package airs
- as explanatory printed copy for web viewers to read for themselves before they click to activate the accompanying video
- a recording of someone reading the copy on camera within a totally self-contained video package for a web page or public presentation
- voice-over copy with accompanying graphics within a totally self-contained video package for a web page.

Audiences are best served if the studio lead-in instantly and intrusively begins the story, rather than serves merely as an introduction to a story yet to come. In a studio setting, the video package then continues the story as the screen cuts from the anchor's studio lead-in to the package.

Studio lead-In:

If you want to lose weight and become healthy for life, you'll never need a fad diet again. In fact, you never did. You learned the secret in elementary school. (Reporter) has the story.

The anchor has disclosed the heart of the story in the studio lead-in. At this point the package begins to air and audiences see the story's first video, which is a continuation of the story a continuation of the story rather than its beginning.

WRITE THE PACKAGE LEAD

Again, as you plan the "visual lead," or first video of your package, identify the central idea you wish to communicate before you worry about the words. In general, the thought process focuses first on (a) an idea to communicate; (b) images to prove the idea visually; and (c) words as necessary to interpret and explain the images.

If you want to indicate in your first visual that healthy diets are instinctive, you may decide your first video should be of children eating healthy foods. You might further decide to emphasize close-ups that show healthy faces and foods. Now that you have the images defined, you can write the voice over.

Voice Over To Accompany The "Visual Lead":

Nutritionists now tell us the only diet we ever needed is to follow the four basic food groups, and to eat a variety of food from those groups. It's how healthy people just naturally eat...and it can become a way of life for almost anyone.
(Video [close-ups]: Children eating healthy foods: apples, vegetable snacks)

WRITE THE MIDDLE OR MAIN BODY

After the package lead, begin the middle or main body of your report. In a 1:10- to 1:30-minute package, try to limit yourself to no more than three or four main points. Again, focus on the ideas to be communicated before you worry about the images or words.

In this example about healthy diets, perhaps after finishing your research you know that you wish to emphasize four main points, as follows:

1. You can eat anything you want, just not everything (eat in right amounts).
2. Exercise plays a role, although you don't need to be obsessive.
3. Healthy diets and foods are tastier. Fatty foods actually are less satisfying. If you cut fat in your diet, you begin to crave healthy foods.
4. If you find you can't control your eating, you may be using food as a substitute to fill other needs in your life.

Again in the main body, focus first on (a) the ideas to communicate, (b) images to prove the ideas visually, and (c) words as necessary to interpret and explain the images.

Now that you have your idea clearly focused for *point one,* "You can eat anything you want, just not everything (eat in right amounts)," you begin the search for images. Perhaps you decide to visit a supermarket and obtain permission to photograph a shopper as she buys apples and whole grain foods. As part of your report you interview the woman and she admits to having the occasional urge for a hot fudge sundae. In the sound bite, the woman tells you, "I've found that diets based on deprivation will not work, so I try to eat healthy foods but also occasionally reward myself with a hot fudge sundae. It's no big deal that way."

Even while you are in the field, you decide to build off the woman's interview as a way to incorporate a reporter standup at this point. "Try to integrate the reporter standup so the story doesn't come to a stop," counseled network freelance television producer and photojournalist Ray Farkas. "Make it flow visually."[2] In this story, perhaps you decide the standup gives you an excellent transition from point one ("Eat reasonable amounts of whatever you want") to *point two* ("Exercise plays an important role"). You "script" the standup either in your mind's eye or perhaps jot down the main idea on a note pad and deliver your standup to camera. Normally, in a 1:10- to 1:30-minute story, two or three sentences will provide sufficient length for a standup. Avoid one-sentence standups, however, because they may feel too abrupt, and can even diminish the reporter's authority.

Standup (At Fast-Food Take-Out):

"So the occasional indulgence in a healthy lifestyle is normal . . . and inevitable. Just one caution: Know when to say enough . . . and remember to exercise."

The standup in this example helps introduce *point two*: "Exercise plays a role, although you don't need to be obsessive." Again, after you define the main point, look for images that will help prove it. In this story, perhaps you decide to photograph people walking along the exercise path; people running around an exercise track; and a basketball game you happen to spot as you drive by. Perhaps you decide to interview a person walking along the exercise path and record the following sound bite for the report.

Bite:

"Five months ago, I weighed thirty-eight pounds more than I do now. Once I started working out, my body began to crave healthier foods."

Remember to block in visual transitions as you move from one main point to the next, and remember to insist on "visual proof" for each of your main points. Because *point three* states that "Healthy diets/foods are tastier," you will need one or more shots that prove this idea. The transition shot that begins point three after the sound bite could be of an ultra close shot of mist-covered red delicious apples. As the shot holds on-screen, a hand comes into frame. The next shot, in matched action, shows a shopper reaching into the fruit bin at a natural foods store as she selects apples. The next shot, a close-up, might show the woman's hand coming into frame. In a matched-action shot, this time a medium or long shot, the woman places an apple on the kitchen counter at home. As the sequence continues, she cuts the apple, arranges it on a plate with some cheddar cheese, and hands the plate to her four-year-old daughter.

Voice-over narration throughout this sequence would make the following points: Natural foods, those without much processing, often are the healthiest and the tastiest. Further, when people cut fat in their diets, they begin to crave healthy foods; fatty foods actually are less satisfying.

At this stage, you begin *point four* in your package: "If you find you can't control your eating, you may be using food as a substitute to fill other needs in your life." Because point three ends on the idea that fatty foods actually are less satisfying, you could launch point four with video of fatty foods. The shot might be of dessert cakes on a bakery shelf, rows of potato chip products in a supermarket, fried chicken in a deli display, or any other shot that proves the main point visually. If you use such a shot, you will need voice-over narration that helps you make the transition to point four: "While fatty foods won't kill you, they can leave you craving more. Worse yet, with high-fat temptations around, it's easy to lose control with these foods." At this point, you might cut to another sound bite that helps prove point four. Perhaps during your field interviews, someone told you:

Sound Bite:

"Food is a powerful drug. Often we eat to satisfy needs that have nothing to do with food. To live a healthy lifestyle, you may have to learn why you're eating when you're not hungry."

The person who gave you such a sound bite might be a dietician, a specialist in addictions or eating disorders, a dieter you meet at a weight-loss clinic, or some other person with the close knowledge or experience to make such an observation. A word of caution: The bite must occur spontaneously in the field during the interview process, without coaching from the reporter. Ethical reporters never steer an interviewee into making a statement to help substantiate a main point in a story.

Based on your own research, however, it might be permissible during an interview to observe, "I suppose some people use food almost like some people use drugs." In this way you have suggested subject matter, but not the response itself. Every interview question follows such a process.

WRITE THE CLOSE

Next, write the **close** to your package. The close makes it obvious to your audience the story is ending. Without a strong close, the package will stop but it will not end. As soon as you arrive in the field, begin your search for a closing shot—a visual close you can build toward throughout the entire piece, something so strong it's obvious the story is finished. Lazy reporters sometimes end stories on interviews or standups, but such endings resemble unsigned letters.

If you must write from video someone else shot in the field, search it carefully for a closing shot. If you are under extreme deadline pressure, ask the photographer or editor to help you identify a strong closing shot. Once you have identified the shot, you can then build every component of the report toward that final moment.

In this example, you might want to leave audiences with the idea, "If you learn how to eat and live healthily, you will live a happier life, and possibly a longer life." The close not only wraps up the story but also reinforces the story's focus. In this example we stated the original story focus to the effect, "The secret to weight loss lies in eating a healthy diet from the four basic food groups." Note how the story close, "If you learn how to eat and live healthily, you will live a happier life, and possibly a longer life," reinforces the focus and brings the story to a decisive ending.

Again, in the close, give your audience visual proof of the point you wish to communicate. Images that show an elderly person playing with a grandchild might address the idea of a longer, happier life. You also might photograph senior citizens having the time of their life at a square dance, or perhaps find a fit, trim couple in their 70s jogging in a park, and some closing sound as the woman says, "Let's go for twelve laps." The more articulate you can make your images and audio, the more memorable your message will become.

PREPLAN THE PACKAGE

Often, you can plan many elements within a package before you enter the field, based on your existing knowledge and new information obtained from story research. We are not talking about making a story, or writing the story in advance, but rather about nailing down all the information you can before you enter the field, then filling in the holes as you shoot field video and conduct your field research and interviews (Figure 9.1).

The term *preplanning* thus refers to planning that occurs before you enter the field. "You can do a lot of effective reporting without leaving where you are—kitchen or station—by letting your fingers do the walking," says reporter Chuck Crouse. "The more extensive your use of the phone, the more finesse you may need to apply. For instance, your city councilors are probably experienced at talking to you, and see each call as a chance to communicate with their constituents. An attorney involved in litigation, however, may be wary of talking to you."[3]

You also can gather information by reading newspapers and magazines, talking with friends and acquaintances, and just from living. "You must reflect on the story before the need to write it occurs. Otherwise it will be difficult to speak with

FIGURE 9.1
The most complete and authoritative reports build on the reporter's research, planning, and knowledge of the community.

authority," says Bob Moon, senior business correspondent for *Marketplace*, public radio's daily magazine of business and economics. "As a given, we assume you know everything you can about the local community: what crops come from the fields, what goods emerge from the factories, and the like."[4] The same need for reflection and understanding applies even when you are covering institutions and issues. The late Peter Jennings, anchor for ABC *World News Tonight*, became convinced during years of international reporting, that prior acquaintance with developing country issues— not to mention knowledge of the tastes and smells in those lands—is indispensable to covering the news. Jennings believed it simply wasn't possible to catch up with events by reading official reports and calling government officials.

In such discussions, note the distinction between preplanning and "prewriting" the story. "Planning is essential. But it is no substitute for the reality of what a reporter finds on location," says NBC's Bob Dotson.[5] Basically, when you preplan a story, you plan the story on paper or as a **storyboard** (reproduction of a single frame of video that represents one scene or sequence in a video story) in the mind's eye that treats only those elements you feel reasonably certain about. But if conditions change in the field, you must change with them. "Prewriting is an easy way to laziness," believes Martha Raddatz, senior foreign affairs correspondent for ABC news. "Skill in reporting comes from the ability to rapidly organize your story once you've arrived and had time to digest what is happening."[6]

Another form of laziness occurs when reporters wait to understand the story until they return from the field and begin to write. By then, it's too late because the story happens in the field and can never be more than you bring back from the field. "A good visual story is made in the field by competent reporters and photojournalists," says KAKE's Larry Hatteberg. "Reporters must be concerned with the story and not the standup and how it will play. You have to cover the story to write it."[7] Using this approach, you focus first on ideas, then on images and words.

SPOT-NEWS PACKAGES

Spot-news packages can follow the same planning process, although fast-breaking news offers less time for contemplation and reflection. Often the reporter and photojournalist do well to capture what's happening. Still, once the breaking event has ended, some time usually remains to identify the story and its focus, assess what

---

GRAIN ELEVATOR EXPLOSION (FIELD REPORT)

	(VTR WITH VO NARRATION)
:04 LS Rubble & fire-fighters	The explosion occurred about nine o'clock this morning at the McMillan Grain Company just outside Abilene.
:03 MS Firefighter scales tower	Police say five workers were inside one tower at the elevator when grain dust exploded.
:04 CU Grimy faces	Four of the men were killed instantly. One survived.
	(SURVIVOR ON CAMERA)
:18 Sound bite	We were leveling out wheat by hand at the top of one of the storage towers. I heard one of the guy's shovels hit another shovel. There must have been a spark because all of a sudden that dust exploded. Why I'm not dead, I'll never know.
	(QUESTION FROM OFF CAMERA)
	How did you escape?
	(SURVIVOR)
	The west side of the tower was still standing … and that's the side with the emergency ladder. When I came to, I was being hauled out by a firefighter who'd come up the ladder to look for survivors.
	(REPORTER STANDUP)
:04 Reporter standup	The explosion shook buildings and rattled storefront windows in a five-mile radius around Abilene. Officials estimate property damage at more than two million dollars.
	(VTR WITH VO NARRATION)
:04 LS Damaged trucks :03 CU Driver inspects damage	Trucks from the summer wheat harvest were dumping their loads when the explosion occurred. Falling debris damaged 15 of these trucks.
:05 Injured driver sits on running board	Several truck drivers suffered minor injuries.
:15 Trucks drive past damaged elevator	Farmers who had been using these facilities will now have to deliver wheat to storage elevators in surrounding towns. At the McMillan Grain Company in Abilene, Tina Roberts, 9-News

happened, and record pickup sound and additional video. Even while covering spot news, the video journalist can identify (a) story focus, (b) the story's three or four most important main points, and (c) how the story will close. If raw field material is unavailable to prove the story's crucial beginning, middle, and ending, or if the VJ or field crew has insufficiently identified these points before returning from the field, the story will suffer. In the accompanying spot-news story, note how the package has a beginning, middle, and ending, and how the visuals "prove" every main point. The studio lead-in has been omitted to help make the package's essential structure more obvious.

SET A HIGH STANDARD FOR PACKAGES

If you do make your story into a package, you are obligated to set high standards for your work. Not every story justifies a package or even a reporter's presence, and many stories work well as simple anchor VO or VO with previously recorded sound (VO SOT). Conversely, if you are assigned to write, report, or photograph a simple VO but think the story would make a good package, tell your producer or assignment editor you think it should be a package. To help guide your decision, you can think of stories as falling into two categories[8]:

1. A video story that can be told by the camera and through sound bites. Into this category fall spot news, fires, overturned tanker trucks, and similar "event-driven" stories.
2. Stories that require explanation, analysis, or the reporter's observations of the environment—stories the camera alone cannot tell without a reporter to help tell it.

If the anchor can do what the reporter is doing, and do it better, then the reporter must justify his or her presence in a package. Otherwise, the anchor can simply read a VO SOT VO. "When reporters tackle a complex story, they chronicle the sequence of events, flesh out the personalities, explain the issues and the implications, and put all the pieces of the puzzle together," says journalist Peter R. Kann.[9] They know more about the story than the anchor and can bring such stories to life. Such television reporters can justify their presence in the story. Furthermore, if the television reporter experiences the story, senses it, and serves as an eyewitness in some way to explain the smells and sights of an event, then audiences may feel they need the reporter in the story.[10]

Ultimately, it's not how many stories you crank out that counts, but how memorable you make them. "You pick timeless subjects and treat them properly, and people are going to be looking at them 200 years from now. We are stockpiling history," said Canadian documentary filmmaker Donald Brittain.[11]

Fifty or a hundred years from now, for example, historians may look back on Ron Mitchell's reports about construction of Denver's International Airport, the last U.S. airport to be built in the 20th century. When construction began, Mitchell, a KUSA reporter, took viewers into the empty fields east of Denver. In subsequent reports, using standups and even the routine sounds from public address systems at other airports, he crafted reports to "show" viewers where the various concourses, taxi ramps, baggage claim areas, and concession stands would someday be located. Today his series chronicles the airport as it rose from empty fields to become a hub for international travelers.

FIGURE 9.2

Images and sound from the natural environment lend a sense of realism to video reports and stories, and help give viewers a closer sense of connection.

USE NATURAL SOUND LIBERALLY

To help involve viewers and listeners in your story, and to help them feel as if they're experiencing the events you show on-screen, remember to use natural sound through-out your package (Figure 9.2). Natural sound at the very start of a package, even before the first voice over, can help draw viewers into the story. Such natural sound could be an athlete's labored breathing, a young boy yelling "Ice cold lemonade, 25 cents!," or the purr of electric clippers at a pet grooming boutique. "When we go out, we don't often enough listen for the little sounds," observed Ray Farkas, the network television freelance producer and photojournalist. "Too often, we go for the bite at the sheriff's news conference versus the sense of what it felt like to be in the sheriff's office or the marriage license bureau."[12]

In the end, every package should capture something of the news environment and communicate that experience to viewers. Universally, storytellers seek to communicate a sense of experience to their audiences. The news package is simply another form of narrative storytelling with a beginning, middle, and ending. "Television journal-ism is uniquely a combination of storytelling, photographic, and cinema-editing skills which can be specifically learned and clearly articulated," says news producer John Haydock.[13] Routinely, at television organizations around the world, the most memo-rable journalism often takes the form of compelling news packages.

SUMMARY

The package can be defined as an edited, self-contained report of an event or feature, complete with pictures, sound bites, voice-over narration, and natural sounds. It is a form of narrative storytelling with a beginning, middle, and ending. Before they write the words for a package or shoot the pictures, the most efficient video journalists first create a blueprint or structure for their packages. Ideally, the thought process will concentrate first on the main story idea, then on images to prove the idea visually, and finally on words as necessary to interpret and explain the images.

Typically, a 1:10- to 1:30-minute package includes a focus statement, a beginning or lead, a middle section with three or four main points, and an ending or close. The strongest packages normally begin and end on visuals and sounds from the environment rather than with standups or sound bites, except for tosses to and from live shots and remotes.

The package takes form during four stages of development: reviewing existing knowledge and facts obtained from story research before you leave for the field, conducting field research and interviews, viewing and editing field video and sound bites, and writing the final package.

To tell the story effectively, you must first understand it yourself. A good way to do that is by defining your focus statement. The focus is a simple, vivid, declarative sentence expressing the heart and soul of the story. When you can distill your understanding of a story this succinctly, you are ready to report it. The best reporters exchange ideas for the story with others involved in the storytelling process so that everyone works toward a common goal.

The strongest packages begin with a studio lead-in that instantly and intrusively begins the story, rather than serves merely as an introduction to a story yet to come. The main body of the package typically contains three or four main points, each with visual proof, and with a visual transition to help the package flow smoothly from one main point to the next.

Identify the closing shot early, so you can build the package to an obvious and definitive ending.

Plan elements within a package before you enter the field, but never go so far as to write the story in advance: The goal is to gather information and reflect on the story before you write it. Breaking news offers less time for reflection and contemplation, but often you will have time after the main action subsides to identify the story and its focus, assess what happened, and record pickup sound and additional video.

Not every story justifies a package or even a reporter's presence. To guide your decision, you can think of stories as falling into two categories: The first category includes "event-driven" stories or spot news that can be told by the camera and through sound bites. The second category includes stories that require explanation, analysis, or the reporter's observations of the environment.

Use natural sound liberally in all packages as a way to help involve audiences, and to help them feel as if they're experiencing the events you show on-screen. Remember, too, the more articulate you can make your images, the more memorable your messages will become.

KEYTERMS

close   154   lead-in   151   storyboard   155
focus   151

EXERCISES

1. Record a television news package and analyze its structure. Prepare a two-page, printed, double-spaced report that addresses the following considerations:

   ▪ Length of the studio lead-in, in seconds
   ▪ Your analysis of how effectively the studio lead-in discloses the heart of the story

- How effectively the first video communicates the story to come
- Whether the package lead-in continues the story as expressed in the studio lead-in or actually begins the story
- Number of main points in the story, listed individually
- Use of visual transitions between main points
- Use of sound bites
- How well the story integrates a reporter standup, if any, without disrupting the package's visual flow
- How well the story builds to an obvious, definitive conclusion
- The presence of an obvious and easy-to-articulate story focus

2. Using a newspaper story that contains quotes from one or more sources, write the script for a 1:10-minute video package. Include all elements for the package: a studio lead-in or lead-in copy for a web page, all VO narration, scripted sound bites transcribed from quotations in the story, notes or a script for the standup, and a brief description of all visuals you would use, complete with visual transitions between all main points in the body of your package. Follow the script format example in Chapter 8, Video Script Formats.

3. Record a television news package or similar web video and write a script that reflects how you would make the package more informative and interesting. Change any components of the package as it now exists: You may want to rewrite the studio lead-in, for example, so that it's more interesting and addresses a wider audience or that discloses the heart of the story more immediately. You may wish to indicate changes in the existing video, or perhaps you may want to eliminate or shorten some sound bites. You may want to build a stronger close for the package. You may decide to shorten the package itself. All changes you make should make the story more interesting, more informative, and more memorable.

4. Record and view five television news packages and write a one-sentence focus statement for each, based on what you understand about the story after watching it. Next, analyze how a stronger focus statement could have made each story even more memorable and relevant to viewers.

5. On a given day, study a front-page newspaper or substantive web story and decide to what extent you could preplan the various story elements before you enter the field. Choose a story you think a local television station, cable channel, or web site will cover as a video package that day. Identify the story; try to write a focus statement for it; list what you already know about the story, all the facts you still need; and decide what sound bites you might use. Include a reporter standup, if possible. Next, write a script that contains everything you know about the story, leaving holes as necessary in the script for missing information. That evening, watch the story on television. Compare your treatment of the story, based on your own preplanning, with your sources' video field coverage.

6. Compare the structure of a spot-news package with the structure of a package that addresses a nonbreaking news event. Discuss how package structure differs between the two examples, and what influences might account for the differences.

7. Apply the "Story Blueprint" on page 150 to the script you wrote for assignment #2. Rewrite the original script as necessary to incorporate as many of the checklist elements as possible.

NOTES

1. Fred Shook and Don Berrigan, "Glossary: Television Field Production and Reporting," Atelier Sur le Récit Visuel, Service National de la Formation et du Développement, Bureau de Montréal, Société Radio Canada, Montréal, Canada, 1991.
2. Ray Farkas, "Looking through the Lens Differently," a presentation at the NPPA TV News-Video Workshop, Norman, OK, March 21, 1991.
3. Chuck Crouse, "Doing It by Phone," *RTNDA Communicator* (September 1987), 66.

4. Bob Moon, "Bringing the World to Main Street," a workshop for students and professional journalists at Colorado State University, Fort Collins, CO, November 9, 1990.
5. E-mail correspondence with the principal author, June 27, 2007.
6. John Premack, "Straight from the Shoulder," *RTNDA Communicator* (December 1985), 28.
7. Ibid.
8. John Haralson, in remarks to students at the Talent Performance Development Workshop, Colorado State University, Fort Collins, CO, February 22, 1992.
9. Peter Kann, quoted in an undated letter to *Wall Street Journal* subscribers.
10. Bob Kaplitz, "Managing Creative People," a presentation at the NPPA TV News-Video Workshop, Norman, OK, March 19, 1991.
11. Terry Kolomechuk, ed., *Donald Brittain: Never the Ordinary Way* (Winnipeg, Canada: National Film Board of Canada, 1991), 54.
12. Farkas.
13. John Haydock, "Developing an Evaluation System for Daily News Packages," *RTNDA Communicator* (November 1987), 17.

10

Write Like a Storyteller

—By John Larson
© 2011, 2012 John Larson

Have you ever attended a class in which a teacher dutifully lists names, facts, equations, or dates but fails to interest you? The information never connects in any meaningful way? Can you remember walking out of that class, relieved to be out in the fresh air?

At its worst, reporting is similar to that lecture. It fills the air with important sounding names and facts, but fails to make them matter very much. Storytelling, on the other hand, is a bit like walking out into the fresh air—it feels natural, interesting, and a little like recess. When a great story begins, your senses come alive, as if an adventure lies ahead of you.

Great reporting borrows from the best of both of these worlds—reporting important truths and revealing this information in interesting, powerful stories. Learning to write like a storyteller can help any journalist.

An important first step is to understand that although a reporter learns facts, storytellers pay attention to what they experience while learning those facts, and what the people in their stories are experiencing. They pay attention to what they see, hear, and feel. This is important in any form of journalism—newspaper, magazine, radio, blog—but is especially important in video journalism.

TRANSMITTING THE EXPERIENCE

You know by now that good video storytelling shares, or transmits, an experience. It gives viewers a sense that they are there. You see, hear, and experience a story. Good storytellers also are aware their own experiences can be powerful tools to help tell stronger stories.

Why choose storytelling over other forms of communicating information? The advantage of sharing experience and information through video storytelling is that it takes advantage of our senses. People are *hardwired* to be curious about what they see, and intrigued by what they hear. It is less like the lecture mentioned previously and more like going out for recess. If journalists could capture smell, taste, or touch in order to tell a more powerful story, we certainly would—but that is for some future medium. Much is written about the importance of pictures and sound, but they are important only because they mimic the way your viewer experiences the world. Use this to your advantage. Ignore it, and your stories will falter. How do you do this? Some of the ways follow.

BOX 10.1   JOHN LARSON, NETWORK CORRESPONDENT

Recognized as one of the country's best storytelling reporters, network correspondent John Larson excels in investigative, breaking, and feature news reporting. He reports and produces stories for PBS *Need to Know*, and is a former *Dateline NBC* correspondent. At *Dateline NBC*, he traveled to the corners of the world. He investigated and reported on corrupt police in Mexico City; terrorism in Morocco, Spain, and Central Africa; a sinking ferry in Indonesia; and a five-year-old Buddhist monk in Nepal. Larson also has become an international "backpack" or Video Journalist (VJ) since he joined this book's previous edition as a co-author, and shares what he has learned on that front here and in Chapter 11, Video Journalism: Storytelling On Your Own.

Larson's numerous accolades include national Emmys for investigative reporting of the Louisiana police and breaking reporting coverage of the Houston floods. Most notably, Larson is a four-time winner of the prestigious duPont-Columbia Baton, the equivalent of television's Pulitzer Prize; in 2001, for "A Paper Chase," an investigation of the insurance industry and one of the most honored works of journalism in broadcast history; in 2004, for "A Pattern of Suspicion," an exposé on racial profiling; in 2006, for his work with other NBC reporters covering Hurricane Katrina; and the 2011 duPont-Columbia Baton, honoring Larson and other team members for a KCET investigative series. Their three stories exposed the negligence and fraud of local, state, and federal officials in preventing the "often illegal growth of medical marijuana shops in Los Angeles."

The *Philadelphia Inquirer*, in 2001, called "The Paper Chase" "shocking and delightful. Larson skewers executives with an understated, yet relentless technique that could teach Mike Wallace a thing or two." The *Florida Sun Sentinel* declared it was "stunningly impressive. John Larson breaks down executives . . . in a way that would make Perry Mason envious." Judges for the 2011 awards cited the series' thorough sourcing, excellent

FIGURE 10.1

Network correspondent John Larson is recognized as one of television's most gifted storytellers.

Source: Copyright © 2012 John Larson

writing, strong production, and "clear, thorough and well produced reporting that brought change to the community."

Before his selection as a *Dateline NBC* correspondent in 1994, Larson spent eight years at KOMO-TV in Seattle, Washington, where he won sixteen regional Emmy awards for his reporting. His creativity and powerful writing have made him a sought-after speaker, teacher, and motivator at workshops and newsrooms across the country and abroad.

Larson lives with his wife, two children, and terrier in San Diego, California. ■

Be a Tour Guide

You can think of this as the "tour guide" school of storytelling and writing for video. Think of the last time you took a guided tour. It might have been in a museum, an historic district, or a national park. Along the way, you may have discovered that the best tour guides are great storytellers. They lead you up to each revelation and help you pay attention.

A tour guide might say, for example "On your left is the Washington Monument. Notice the three birds sitting on the very top edge? The monument is 555 feet high, the cornerstone was laid in 1848, but it took 40 years before the first person ever set foot inside." While the tour guide says this, everyone looks at the monument, wondering, "Why did it take so long?" The tour guide might then tell a deeper story: "You can't see it from here, but inside the monument, buried in the walls, are 193 special stones, each one different, each one hand-crafted, each one a memorial stone made with the soil of one of the nation's 50 states. The monument's builders thought the soil of every state seemed a good way to say 'thank you' to the man who gave birth to a nation. What do you think?"

Take your audience by the hand and walk them into the story. Use your words to verbally show them around; point out the pictures and sounds that are important. Help them focus and understand what they see. And then, while they watch, tell deeper stories.

This is sometimes more difficult than it sounds. Reporters are often so busy trying to cram as many facts as they can into a story, they forget to transmit their experience—what they saw, heard, and felt. They forget how their audience is hardwired to experience the world. They deprive their audience the fun of experiencing a story.

Use "Wows!"—The Things That Turn You On

The way *you* experience a story—the things that intrigue you and bore you—are excellent hints about how your audience might experience a story, and how you might construct your story. Don't underestimate this. Pay close attention to your own reactions. This is the beginning of transmitting an experience—your experience—realizing your reactions are often similar to your viewers'.

For example, pay attention to what happened when you were first introduced to a story. What bored you or interested you? What made you laugh, moved you, or made you say, "Wow!"

Say your assignment is to write a story about a factory that was closed, the jobs exported overseas. You've done your research and know the facts: the number of jobs that were lost, the cost to the local economy, and so on. You meet a company supervisor at the shuttered plant. He takes you into the factory and you are immediately struck by the immensity of it—the huge, silent room, silent machines, assembly lines, and workbenches. You think, "Holy *&!$#!" I call these moments "wows." Good writers notice wows and write to them. When I experienced this in a shuttered pulp mill in Washington State, I wrote it this way,

"The first thing you notice about the ATT-Rayonier Plant—is the silence."

Let Your Audience Experience the Wows

Once you've identified a wow, make sure you shoot it. Take video as you walk through the door that reveals how huge, empty, and silent the factory is. You need video of the empty workbenches, and the work gloves left behind. Then, write to it. Allow several long moments of silence so the audience can "look around," appreciate the emptiness, and experience the same sense of loss that you did. This requires you to stop talking for a moment, and let the shot transmit an experience. If you do, viewers will experience the moment much as you did.

Moments

The wow you just experienced and recorded is called a "moment." Moments are wonderful bits of reality, full of meaning. Moments often make the best television because, when used properly, they take advantage of our hardwiring, the way we experience the world. You will encounter moments during the course of shooting and gathering a story. Sometimes they happen right in front of you; other times they happen during an interview.

GREAT MOMENTS ARE ALMOST ALWAYS UNEXPECTED   Moments are often powerful, funny, poignant, and urgent precisely because you don't see them coming. For example, imagine you are interviewing a farmer about the tightening economics of small farms. He is being forced to sell his family's farm. He interrupts the interview to yell across the yard, "Sarah! Grab your daddy's saddle! Tomorrow they'll take everything not nailed to the barn floor." This is a moment. It helps you appreciate more about what is happening than whatever he was telling you about before the interruption.

ONE THOUGHT ABOUT FIELD TEAMWORK   If you're part of a team, capturing moments in the field requires the reporter/producer and photographer to work together. It means the reporter cannot barge into a situation, talking over the possible moments that would occur were he or she less disruptive. It means a reporter has to think and act like a good photographer—looking for powerful moments, sounds, and pictures. It means the photographer and soundperson have to think like storytellers. They need to be flexible, intuitive, and fast on their feet. They need to value moments more than perfectly lit or framed shots.

WRITING YOUR FIRST SENTENCE

Once you return from shooting your story in the field, if you have not already started writing (I recommend you begin writing early in the day whenever possible, even before your news gathering is complete), you have to sit down and write. The most daunting challenge in writing a short story for broadcast is often (no surprise here) the first sentence. Ideally, the first sentence should impart critical information, attract the listener, and reflect the direction or tone that you are about to take. It can act as a signpost—giving the viewer a sense of where the story is going, and how it might end. Sounds like a lot to accomplish in a first sentence, doesn't it? Frankly, figuring all this out before you start writing is often overwhelming. Want writer's block? Try making your first sentence perfect.

    If you have trouble getting started, here are two thoughts. The first is courtesy of a friend and Pulitzer Prize winner Howard Weaver of McClatchy Newspapers:

Lower your expectations: That's right. Even the best writers do it. When you're stuck trying to write something really good, sometimes it helps to risk writing something bad. Lighten up, demand less of yourself, and start writing. Writing will often get your creative juices flowing and lead to something better. At least it will get you going. This doesn't mean you should be lazy. It means that getting going is an important part of the process.

Another writer's advice for beating the first sentence block is a bit more colorful:

Just vomit: "Throw up" your immediate ideas on the page. Don't edit yourself before you start. Just get it out. Purge. Again, just writing something down will often get you going. Then, you'll be ready to begin considering how to tell the rest of your story.

THE THREE HORSES—STORYTELLING TOOLS FOR VIDEO STORIES

When it comes to writing for video, I believe there are three "great horses"—storytelling *tools* or engines that you must master if you want to tell powerful video stories. These horses are powerful. But before you "saddle up," try this exercise: Think of a great movie, or even a great novel, something you really loved. Can you remember the reasons you liked it so much? It probably had strong characters—people who interested you because of what you discovered about them or what they did. It probably had a strong plot line: a mystery, a drama, or a sequence of events that evolved and led to a satisfactory ending. The movie also likely surprised you in many ways: It took you someplace you were not expecting to go, things happened that you didn't anticipate, or people said things that you didn't see coming.

These elements are storytelling engines—tools that make story lines compelling and meaningful. I've found that it does not matter if your story is two minutes long or two hours, these horses remain important. I call them "horses" because I've found they have their own momentum—energy I can use while reporting or "telling" stories. The three great horses are simple: surprise, quest, and character. All three are different, but you can easily learn how to recognize them, capture them, and write to them.

FIRST HORSE: SURPRISE

At *Dateline NBC,* we called surprises "reveals." For example, I once wrote a story about a television anchor in California who was an alcoholic. Unable to quit drinking, his life dramatically unraveled—he lost his wife, his friends, and his health—all while being on the air every day. Eventually, he lost his job, too. We interviewed him, broke, bloated, and in denial, during the final stages of his decline. It was clear he wasn't going to make it. His liver was damaged, and his doctors said he had only weeks left to live. Several months after our interview, we received a phone call. A friend had found him on the floor of his empty apartment. I wrote the story something like this:

SOT: (*Charla, his friend talking*) "I hadn't heard from him for a couple of days. He didn't answer his phone. So I went to his place, opened the door. The first thing I saw was that small, dead Christmas tree in the corner. The heat was off. It was cold. And then I saw him in the middle of the floor."

LARSON NARRATION: Charla called 911. Paramedics rushed Dave to the hospital. Emergency room doctors fought to save his life. But after all the vodka, all the years of breakdowns, and broken promises, the former newsman...survived.

SOT: (*The anchor, now many months sober and a smiling picture of health*)
"Yeah, been sober six months now. I can't believe I made it."

The anchor's survival was a surprise. Everyone watching the story was expecting him to die. His survival and his appearance on camera produced a "wow." It was something I purposely held back while reporting our story, so the audience could appreciate how desperate his situation was before his collapse and enjoy the same sense of surprise and victory I experienced when I first saw the recovered alcoholic with his fresh, lean face—healthy and strong after months of sobriety. Imagine if I had just reported the facts. It would have been something like this: "A former newsman is fine and recovering tonight in a local hospital. A friend said he had been drinking too much." That may be an accurate report, but not much of a story.

Here's the Windup, and the Pitch

The key to writing for surprises is to remember that all surprises require a setup. You have to prepare your audience to expect one thing: only to be surprised by another. It is a lot like telling a joke. A joke first makes you think about one thing and then delivers an unexpected punch line. It is always done *in that order*. Think of the primitive childhood joke,

Question: "Why did the chicken cross the road?"
Answer: "To get to the other side."

The punch line always comes at the end. It is never, "Chickens get to the other side by crossing the road."

Likewise, a surprise is always delivered *at the very end* of a deliberate sentence, or sequence of sentences. To do this, you must first recognize the parts of the story that surprise you—a moment, a comment from an interview, a development—and then, set up your surprise with a deliberate sequence of fact. This will often require you to delay and hold back some information until the best stage has been set to deliver your surprise. This does not mean that you should mislead your audience on factual matters. It simply requires you to recognize the natural surprises that happen and allow them to exist in your storytelling. Warning: Reporters have difficulty holding back information. Storytellers seem to do it naturally.

The Audiences' Right Not to Know

Using surprise properly turns one journalism standard on its head. As journalists we know it is essential to our democracy that people be informed. So, we work to protect the "public's right to know." However, a storyteller changes this a little. A storyteller knows that it is the public's right *not* to know *until the best possible moment.*

Surprise and the Setup

I once wrote a story about a small town in which the mayor had a phony, prank parking meter. There were three surprises in the story:

1. There was only one parking meter in the entire town.
2. The meter was movable.
3. The person behind the joke was the mayor.

The mayor would take the parking meter up and down the street and "ticket" his friend's cars. But of course, I didn't tell the story that way; I told it like this:

NARRATION: The people of central Washington count on a few days being over 100 degrees every July. Wheat farmers out here count on 10 inches of rain every year.

SOT: (*SOUND OF WHEAT POURING INTO HOPPER*)

NARRATION: And there is a small town out here named Mansfield. Driving through town takes exactly...

SOT: (*SOUND ON ONE CAR WHOOSING PAST CAMERA*)

NARRATION: That long. Things are pretty predictable here, too.

SOT: "BREAD DOUGH WILL BE HERE THURSDAY."

NARRATION: Rick the grocer knows every customer. He knows every car on Main Street.

SOT: "THE BLUE PICKUP IS THE ZELLUMS'. ETHEL POOLE, SHE'S PROBABLY JUST ABOUT READY TO GO TO WORK IN CHELAN."

NARRATION: Lynn the café owner knows her customers so well she can start their orders before they arrive.

SOT: "HARRY BEARD, HE'S USUALLY A HOT CAKE AND BACON, OR FRIED ONE EGG HASHBROWNS AND TOAST, OR, TOM POOLE, WHICH IS A HAM AND CHEESE OMELET EVERY SATURDAY MORNING, LIKE CLOCKWORK."

NARRATION: That's why it kind of surprised everyone when a stranger from the big city showed up. (*Reveal meter here*) One...parking meter. The only meter in 7 thousand 200 square miles.

SOT: "JUST HAVIN' A LITTLE FUN."

NARRATION: Tom Snell, the county's road boss, bought the meter as a prank.

SOT: "IT COST ME 50 DOLLARS, BUT IT SITS HERE ON THE STREET EVER SINCE."

NARRATION: Tom knows most out-of-towners aren't dumb enough to fall for the parking meter. (*Car passes meter*)

SOT: "AW, HE'S GONNA TRY TO GO AROUND, AW SHOOT! YOU SEE THERE'S A TYPICAL RESPONSE."

NARRATION: But you see, they don't have to be. (*They roll meter down the sidewalk to the parked car*)

SOT: (*Rolling meter*) "I THINK WE GOT 'EM NOW."

NARRATION: This victim was from Canada.

SOT: "IT'S A WAY TO MAKE MONEY I GUESS; IT'S A SMALL TOWN."

NARRATION: And when there aren't a lot of visitors, Tom includes his friends. Friends like Harold Beard. *(Rolling meter)* That's Harold's truck over there. That's Harold.

SOT: "GIMME A TICKET HERE, FOR CRYING OUT LOUD. NOT SUPPOSED TO GET A TICKET IN THIS TOWN" *(Laughter)*.

NARRATION: The meter is not just Tom's joke. Shortly after breakfast we saw Rick the grocer nail Floyd Avenell's car.

SOT: *(Laughter)* "IT'S NOT LIGHT. BUT IT DOES GET MOVED QUITE FREQUENTLY." *(Flag in background)* **NAT SOT:** *(Rolling meter)*

SOT: "YEAH, I PUT IT IN FRONT OF THE MAYOR'S CAR. I PUT IT IN FRONT OF THE SHERIFF'S CAR. *(Snort)*

NARRATION: There goes Lydia, the lady who owns the tavern.

SOT: *(Rolling meter)* "IT'S KINDA FUN."

NARRATION: Now you'd think sooner or later someone would get sick of it all and complain about Tom's parking meter to the mayor.

SOT: "DON'T THINK IT WOULD DO THEM ANY GOOD." *(LARSON: "HOW'S THAT?")* "'CUZ I'M THE MAYOR."

NARRATION: So maybe small towns are predictable. But if you go to Mansfield, don't be surprised if they treat you … like they've known you all your life.

SOT: "EVERY TOWN'S GOT ITS WAY."

NARRATION: In fact, you can almost count on it.

SOT: "TIME EXPIRED. HOW 'BOUT AN I-OWE-YOU? YOU DON'T EVEN HAVE A PENNY? I DON'T! SEE, I'M A FARMER'S WIFE!"

NARRATION: John Larson,

SOT: "WHAT'S NEXT? I'M TRYING TO WORK ON A FIRE HYDRANT ON WHEELS."

NARRATION: KOMO News Four, Mansfield.

SOT: *(Laughter)*

Three Surprises and Three Setups

Notice how all three surprises in the previous story come at the end of a setup.

FIRST SURPRISE: THERE IS ONLY ONE METER. THE SETUP   NARRATION: That's why it kind of surprised everyone when a stranger from the big city showed up. *(Reveal meter here)* One … parking meter. The only meter in 7 thousand 200 square miles. (The viewer is expecting us to introduce a person here, not a parking meter.)

SECOND SURPRISE: THE METER IS MOVABLE. THE SETUP   *NARRATION:* Tom knows most out-of-towners aren't dumb enough to fall for the parking meter. *(Car passes meter)* SOT: "AW, HE'S GONNA TRY TO GO AROUND, AW SHOOT! YOU SEE

THERE'S A TYPICAL RESPONSE." NARRATION: But you see, they don't have to be. (*They roll meter down the sidewalk to the parked car*) (The viewer here is expecting the out-of-towner to successfully avoid the meter.)

THIRD SURPRISE: THE PERSON BEHIND THE JOKE WAS THE MAYOR. THE SETUP *NARRATION:* Now you'd think sooner or later someone would get sick of it all and complain about Tom's parking meter to the mayor. SOT: "DON'T THINK IT WOULD DO THEM ANY GOOD. (LARSON: "HOW'S THAT?") "'CUZ I'M THE MAYOR." (The viewer is expecting Tom to explain that people do complain to the mayor.)

Experience Surprise

Whenever possible, it is important to allow your audience to experience the surprise instead of just reporting the surprise to them. This means the best surprises are delivered by the *field video and audio*, not by a reporter's narrated track. Notice in the previous story that all three surprises *are never reported*, but are visually demonstrated.

I don't say, "In this entire town they have only one parking meter." Instead, I say, "That's why it kind of surprised everyone when a stranger from the big city showed up." Next, I let the video reveal the one parking meter.

For the surprise that the meter moves, I don't say, "The meter moves." Instead, I say, "But you see, they don't have to be." Then the video reveals for the first time that the meter moves.

Last, instead of saying "The man behind the prank is the mayor of the town" I write, "Now you'd think sooner or later someone would get sick of it all and complain about Tom's parking meter to the mayor." And then I let the interview reveal it with the SOT: "DON'T THINK IT WOULD DO THEM ANY GOOD." (LARSON: "HOW'S THAT?") "'CUZ I'M THE MAYOR."

Surprise Changes the Way You Gather News

Surprises are moments or wows that you don't expect. Once you start trying to capture surprises on camera you must be patient and wait for them. You also must be able to anticipate where the surprises might occur, and make sure your camera is rolling and your audio is strong. Last, you need to be very flexible. Surprises frequently don't happen where you think they will. A good storyteller becomes adept at rewriting stories to include unexpected surprises.

A Note about Rhythm

Notice how the writing in the parking meter story is often interrupted by natural sound and interviews. Almost every sentence is followed by a break for sound. Whereas every story does not require this many breaks, every good story has its own rhythm. Just like a song, a good narrated video story has a beat—a cadence of words and sentences that you can almost tap your foot to. Preachers know this: When a good preacher gets going, his or her congregation can often clap their hands to the rhythm of the preacher's delivery. Lawyers trying to sway a jury know it, too. The late Johnnie Cochran, famous lawyer in the OJ Simpson trial, kept repeating his message about the bloody glove, and how it didn't fit Simpson's hand: "If it doesn't fit, you must acquit. If it doesn't fit, you must acquit."

When you want your story to accelerate, and your viewers' attention to intensify, shorten your sentences and/or increase the regularity of your breaks for natural sound and sound bites. If you want to slow it down, do the opposite.

SECOND HORSE: QUEST

The second horse is "quest." It is a lot like plot, but simpler and more specific. Quest consists of "someone trying to get something done."

Example: Let's say you've been assigned to a story about a city councilman who changed his vote on a zoning ordinance, supporting a developer's plan to knock down some aging but popular retail stores. While you wait to interview the councilman, you notice his secretary's phone is ringing constantly, with many constituents complaining about the councilman's vote. The secretary explains, "The councilman is on the line; may I have your name and he'll get back to you." With each new call, the secretary writes out the details of the complaint, and then spikes the note on a rapidly growing stack of messages. She is clearly overwhelmed by the volume of phone calls. Finally, you get a chance to enter the councilman's office. He, initially on the phone, hangs up to do an interview with you.

A *straight news report* might write it this way:

NARRATION: Last night's city council cleared the way for BrightCity to develop L Street.

SOT: "BY A VOTE OF 6 TO 5 THE MOTION IS DEFEATED."

SOT: (*SOUND OF CROWD'S GASPS AND PROTESTS*)

NARRATION: More than 150 people, who turned out expecting to celebrate saving the popular businesses along L Street, were stunned.

SOT: "I CAN'T BELIEVE THEY DID THIS. AFTER ALL THE PROMISES, THEY JUST LET THE BRIGHTCITY DEVELOPERS HAVE THEIR WAY."

SOT: "IT WASN'T SUPPOSED TO GO LIKE THIS. EVERYONE IS SAYING HARDESTY SOLD US OUT."

NARRATION: Councilman Dave Hardesty had publically supported efforts to save the aging buildings and businesses along L Street, but last night he voted…

SOT: "NAY."

NARRATION: Today the councilman explained.

SOT: (COUNCILMAN *HARDESTY*) "AFTER CAREFUL CONSIDERATION, I NOW THINK EVERYONE WILL EVENTUALLY BENEFIT FROM BRIGHTCITY. L STREET NEEDS NEW IDEAS AND NEW LIFE."

NARRATION: Which means, work on the proposed BrightCity complex of 140 Condominiums, plus retail, will begin almost immediately.

SOT: (*DON SALESKY, BRIGHTCITY DEVELOPER*) "WE'RE DELIGHTED THE COUNCIL TOOK THE TIME TO STUDY THE ISSUES, AND UNDERSTAND HOW BRIGHTCITY WILL HELP THE ENTIRE AREA. WE'RE EXCITED."

NARRATION: L Street supporters promised to keep up the fight saying they will now take their campaign from the historic street . . . to the Courts. John Larson, NBC News, Spokane.

Storytelling Using Quest

There is nothing wrong with straight reporting, but it does not take advantage of the "pull" of a good story. Using storytelling quest, or "someone trying to get something done," completely changes whose "voice" carries the story. It requires you to focus at least some of your report on one person. For example, the previous report might be told like this:

SOT: (*ADMINISTRATIVE ASSISTANT DANA LEWIS*) "COUNCILMAN HARDESTY'S OFFICE."

NARRATION: 18 Years a receptionist, Dana Lewis thought she'd heard it all.

SOT: (*DANA LEWIS*) "YES, I UNDERSTAND YOU'RE UPSET."

NARRATION: But today,

SOT: (*DANA LEWIS ON PHONE*) "COUNCILMAN HARDESTY'S OFFICE."

NARRATION: This secretary needs a secretary.

SOT: (*DANA LEWIS*) "OF COURSE I'LL TELL HIM! WHY DO YOU THINK I'VE BEEN WRITING THIS DOWN?"

NARRATION: Her phone was already ringing with angry complaints when she walked in at 8.

SOT: (*DANA LEWIS*) "YES, I THINK HE KNOWS THAT, BUT AS I SAID, I WILL TELL HIM."

NARRATION: That was five hours ago,

SOT: (*PHONE RINGING*) "COUNCILMAN'S HARDESTY'S OFFICE; PLEASE HOLD. THIS IS UNREAL!"

NARRATION: Her boss, Councilman Dave Hardesty, last night changed his vote on the L Street project,

SOT: "NAY."

SOT: (*SOUND OF CROWD'S GASPS AND PROTESTS.*)

NARRATION: Angering almost everyone who came to watch.

SOT: "IT WASN'T SUPPOSED TO GO LIKE THIS. EVERYONE IS SAYING HARDESTY SOLD US OUT."

SOT: (*RING*) "WHAT'S YOUR NAME? MR. LINDSTROM? OKAY."

NARRATION: 107 Complaints—and she hasn't had lunch yet.

SOT: (*DANA LEWIS*) "YES, I'LL TELL THE COUNCILMAN."

NARRATION: We told him first.

LARSON: "Your secretary is going to need a raise or a vacation."

SOT: (*COUNCILMAN HARDESTY LAUGHING*) "YES, I GUESS SHE WILL. WE'LL JUST HAVE TO EDUCATE PEOPLE HOW GOOD THIS IS GOING TO BE. (*EDIT*) I NOW THINK EVERYONE WILL EVENTUALLY BENEFIT FROM BRIGHTCITY. L STREET NEEDS NEW IDEAS AND NEW LIFE."

SOT: (*PHONE RINGS*)

NARRATION: Supporters of saving L Street are already planning to sue the city, sue BrightCity, and sue Councilman Hardesty. But don't tell Dana; she's got her hands full.

SOT: (*PHONE RINGS*)

SOT: (*DANA LEWIS*) "YES . . . I'D BE HAPPY TO WRITE DOWN YOUR COMPLAINT."

NARRATION: John Larson, NBC News, Spokane.

Finding the Quest

Remember, quest is simply "someone trying to get something done." In the previous example, the secretary's quest is simple: "Dana the secretary is trying to answer the phones and write down all the complaints following last night's council vote." Most reporters would ignore the secretary. Storytellers would not. You can use Dana's experience to draw in the viewer and drive home the contentiousness of the vote. In the process, the secretary's quest shows us how the councilman is partially shielded from his actions, and we learn how a local democracy works.

If you look for them, small personal quests are often all around you. They are literally "in your way." A secretary answering calls, a janitor sweeping up after a demonstration, a police officer trying to call in the details of a tragic accident, a fire victim trying to find out if anyone has found her missing pet—all are quests worth consideration.

Ask yourself, could this small quest demonstrate my larger story in an interesting or powerful way? Can I use this quest to share other important facts of the story? If the answers are yes, try using it.

Quest Changes News Gathering

Once a storyteller decides to follow someone's quest, everything changes. The story's focus changes. What the reporter and photographer choose to photograph changes. Suddenly, recording a secretary's phone call may be more important than shooting an exterior of the council building. The interview questions change as well. Instead of asking the councilman why he voted the way he did, you're asking the secretary, "What time did you come into work? Was the phone ringing? Have you eaten lunch yet?"

THIRD HORSE: CHARACTER

My third horse is character. There are people in all good stories; the challenge is to find the right details about those people, their life, or their quest to make them meaningful and memorable. This is what I call finding character. Talking heads do not automatically have character; you need to find it. Sometimes, compelling video provides details that make someone memorable. Other times, it is a personal fact or a special quote that makes him or her memorable.

Telling Details

One of the most important lessons a journalist can learn is that building character into a story requires a search for powerful details. "Telling" details can be the contents of a wallet, a favorite nickname, an heirloom, a recurring dream, a child who passed away, the color of a car, anything. In order for details to be telling, they need to be symbolic of something larger: the quality of a life, the context of a struggle, the courage or fear of a character, and so on. How will you know if a detail is telling? It will strike you, move you emotionally, surprise you, or add depth and new dimension to the story.

For example, Chip Scanlan, a fine reporter, writer, and professor at the Poynter Institute in Florida, was once given an assignment to write about smoking and cancer for the *St. Petersburg Times*. He interviewed the widow of a cigarette smoker. Her name was Marie. Chip asked all the regular questions but kept listening for details that might bring Marie or her loss into clearer focus. If she told Chip that she missed her husband, Chip would ask deeper questions like, "When do you miss him most?" "Is there a time of day or night when it is especially difficult?" Eventually, he asked for a tour of Marie's house. As they stood in the master bedroom Marie said, "Would you believe it? At night, I sprinkle his aftershave on my pillow. Just to feel close to him."

This is a powerful detail. It says much about the wife, her love, and her loss. Somehow, it even tells us about her husband. Details like this, however, do not come easily. Chip was patient. As he tells it,

> **Scanlan:**   I interviewed Joe's widow, Marie, at her home in Fort Myers. We sat for a while on her couch, looking at scrapbooks while she told me the story of their lives together and his terminal illness.
>
> **Larson:**   What were some of the questions you may have asked that did not pay off with anything memorable?
>
> **Scanlan:**   I asked, "How has this affected you? What's your life like without him? What's it like to see someone go through what your husband endured?" These are all serviceable questions, but I don't think I was getting enough to help me answer my initial questions. At that point, I asked Marie if she'd give me a tour of her house. It changed the static nature of the interview; it gave me a chance to see details, hear stories behind them, which "showed" rather than "told."
>
> **Larson:**   What led to the aftershave comment?
>
> **Scanlan:**   Marie took me up into the bedroom she'd shared with her husband. It was immaculate. I spied a photo stuck in the mirror—one of those 3 × 2 inch casual shots. I noted it in my notebook. It was then that, unbidden, Marie said, "Would you believe it? At night, I sprinkle his aftershave on my pillow. Just to feel close to him."
>
> I was speechless. I couldn't believe she would tell a stranger such an intimate detail. I felt compelled to ask her if I could use it my story. Yes, she said. But the quote haunted me. I prided myself on being the kind of reporter that people would trust enough to share their lives, but to be honest, I also felt protective when they did so. After I drafted the story, I called Marie back, and once again asked if I could use the quote. Yes, she said. And then just before the story was ready to go to press, I called her a third time.

Notice that Scanlan immediately sensed the personal nature and power of this telling comment. Yet instead of rushing it to print, he asked her three times if she wanted him to withhold it. This not only tells you a lot about who Chip Scanlan is, but also something about the kind of people strong storytellers often are—thoughtful, caring, intuitive, engaged. People with powerful personal details trust such reporters more than they do reporters who seem to be "in it for themselves."

Bottom line: People fascinate me, and the trappings of their lives are windows into their inner lives, which is what I've always been after as a reporter and writer.

TIPS FOR WRITING STRONG STORIES

Physician, Heal Thyself

I hope you will have many good teachers. In writing, however, only one teacher will watch your every step and stay with you throughout your career—you. Journalism is a worldwide craft often practiced by people in small rooms with small desks. In other words, although your work will take you out into the world, you often might feel isolated when it comes to improving your craft. Reach outside your immediate environment. Seek out the exciting work of other journalists around the country and around the world. Educate yourself with examples you like. Stay enthused.

The "Rip It Off" School of Journalism

It sounds awful, but I first learned to write by ripping people off. I would read good writing and then try to steal it. Don't get me wrong: I didn't steal quotes or crib observations. I didn't plagiarize. (Plagiarism is a wonderfully efficient way to find a new career in the fast-food industry.) No, I'd notice *how* other people told their stories, and then try to use their techniques. I'd try to write like John McPhee of *The New Yorker* magazine one month. Another month, I'd try to write like John Hart of NBC News. I never wound up writing much like either of them, but I would try their use of detail, their sense of pace, their choice of subject, and I improved in the process. I made them my heroes.

Think Heroes: Bono, Mother Teresa, Tiger Woods

Great writing is like great music, political activism, or sport. It requires heroes.

Every good writer has heroes. Find yours. Find writers who make you curious, angry, sad, or laugh out loud. Then, figure out how they did it.

Years ago, I discovered the work of John McPhee. He had a powerful, intelligent curiosity. He would gather details, arrange them in a special order, and create a total effect that would be greater than the sum of the individual parts. I learned from McPhee how a well-chosen fact could be wonderful, humorous, and striking.

John Hart was an NBC News correspondent who had a way of using telling details as metaphors. He'd write international new stories full of powerful details. I remember his story of the violence in Northern Ireland between the Catholics and the Protestants. He chose to mention a teenaged girl who had been attacked. Her attackers, full of religious righteousness, had carved the girl's face with a knife. The scar, Hart observed, "was in the shape of the Cross."

Strong Stories Are the Work of Strong Storytellers

I was working in a small television station in Alaska and part of my first reporting job was to write down what happened on *NBC Nightly News* every night. The program had many strong writers and reporters back then: Tom Petit, Tom Brokaw, Ken Bodie, John Hart, Judy Woodruff, Roger Mudd. I noticed some reports were very professional, but not very interesting. I noticed other reports were professional *and* interesting—informative *and* moving. The same reporters, regardless of the subject, consistently did the best stories. It didn't matter if it was a story about the White House, a flood in the Midwest, a protest, or a riot—the best reporters moved from one subject to another and made it compelling. An assignment manager once told me, "There are no bad stories, only bad reporters." He was wrong. (I thought to myself, "There are no bad stories, only unimaginative assignment managers.") There are plenty of bad stories—pointless, unimportant, unworthy of our attention. However, the assignment manager was right about one thing: A strong reporter consistently tells powerful stories, whereas weak reporters do not.

Challenge Yourself

When I was a reporter in Seattle, I learned the highest broadcast journalism award was the Columbia–DuPont Baton—given to broadcast journalists around the world by Columbia University, the same institution behind the Pulitzer Prize. Only the best are recognized. So, I wrote to Columbia for a copy of that year's winners, explaining that I was "teaching a course on excellence in journalism."

A box of winning stories arrived around Christmas each year. I pored over them. I was teaching a course, but there was only one student enrolled—me. I cut out a picture of the Baton and hung it in my closet so I would see it every morning when I dressed. I'd say to myself, "Somewhere a reporter is doing work worthy of the DuPont. What can I do *today* to make it be me?" It took a few years, but eventually I won a DuPont for an investigation of the insurance industry. A few years later, I won another. But my long journey to the award ceremonies really began back in Seattle, opening that box of tapes each year and studying the finest work the world had to offer, all by myself.

At the awards ceremony in New York, I confessed my deception to the DuPont director, the woman whom I had written to years earlier and who had faithfully sent me the tapes each year. She laughed, her eyes lit up, and she said, "Obviously, the course was a complete success."

Concluding Thoughts

Always remember, reporting and storytelling require different tool sets. A reporter works on sources, gathering information and getting it right. A storyteller works on transmitting an experience in a powerful and meaningful way. When strong reporting and strong storytelling converge, the result is great journalism—work capable of both informing and moving its audience.

Like great reporting, great storytelling demands that we challenge ourselves and dig deep. We have to care about the individuals we encounter and listen for the deeper resonances of their stories. Storytellers must "show" their stories, instead of just "report" their stories. They must involve viewers with powerful pictures, sounds, and thoughts. To do this, all the tools of the medium—video cameras, microphones, writing, editing, and your own passion—must be engaged and in sync.

The payoff is twofold. You become the best journalist you can be, usually moving ahead of the less imaginative reporters working around you. More important, your work will help people care about their world and bring people together with meaningful information.

SUMMARY

The best stories and storytellers transmit experience. In a sense we are "tour guides," who take our audience by the hand and walk them into and through the story. Show them around; point out the pictures and sounds that matter most. Help them focus and understand what they are seeing. And then tell them deeper stories while they watch.

Writing a compelling story can be difficult. An even more daunting challenge can be writing the first sentence. If you have trouble starting your story, demand less of yourself and begin to write. Often the simple act of writing will lead you to something better. Get something down on the page, even if it fails to meet your standards. You can polish it later.

Powerful video stories require that you use effective storytelling tools, engines that make stories compelling and meaningful. Three of the most important tools are the three horses: surprise, quest, and character.

Surprises are the unexpected elements in a story, the U-turn that helps elevate a story from routine to exceptional. Surprises require a setup. You prepare the audience to expect one thing, only to deliver something different, always in that order—much like the unexpected punch line to a joke. You delay and hold back some information until the stage is set to deliver your surprise. Surprises can occur multiple times in stories, and the best are delivered by the field video and audio, rather than a reporter's narrated track. Reporters find it difficult to hold back information. Storytellers do it naturally.

Another important tool is quest. It is similar to plot in that it consists of "someone trying to get something done," often against opposition. Showing a person's effort to achieve a goal gives storytellers a way to draw in the viewer, to drive home the meaning and context of events. Quests can be something as small as a fire victim trying to find her missing pet, or a rancher trying to move horses away from an approaching wildfire. The key is to use even small quests to demonstrate the larger story in an interesting or powerful way.

A third important tool is character. All good stories involve people, so the challenge is to find the telling details about the people in your stories, their lives, or their dreams, goals, and hopes. Compelling video can help reveal character and make someone memorable. Even small things like an heirloom or the sound of a voice can be powerful details, provided they symbolize larger meaning, such as the influence of a grandparent, or the ways in which the blind "see" through sound. Other times, you might use a personal fact or a special quote to help illuminate character. You will know the detail is "telling" if it strikes you, moves you emotionally, surprises you, or adds depth and new dimension to the story.

As you learn to write as a storyteller, you will be the only teacher who will watch your every step and stay with you for your entire career. You can learn new writing approaches by seeking out the work of journalists whose writing you admire. Educate yourself by studying their examples and even imitating their style as you begin your writing career. This doesn't mean you should plagiarize, but that you should notice and practice *how* other people tell their stories, and then try to use their techniques. Find writing heroes; absorb and analyze their work as you begin to develop your own unique style.

No one ever perfects writing or storytelling. We only improve our skills and become better at our jobs through observation, practice, and long experience. It's fun and rewarding, even if it takes us the rest of our lives to master.

DISCUSSION

1. Why is it important to transmit a sense of experience in your video stories?
2. What is meant by the tour guide school of writing for video?
3. Why is writing the first sentence of your story so challenging? How does John Larson suggest you solve the problem?
4. John Larson speaks of the "three great horses"—the storytelling tools—which every storytelling reporter must master. Discuss the use of each tool from the perspective of (a) traditional journalism, as it is typically practiced in print media and (b) by a few notable storytellers in television and on the web. What qualities do these horses lend the storytelling process?
5. How do you set up surprises in stories?
6. Why do you delay surprises in stories?
7. Describe how storytelling reporters can use surprises, telling details, and memorable moments as little golden nuggets to keep the viewer interested as the story unfolds.
8. Some storytellers equate surprises in stories with the layers of an onion. Explain how you can use their insight in your own storytelling.
9. Why is it more important to let viewers experience the surprise in field video and audio instead of just reporting the surprise to them?
10. How does the search for surprises change the way you gather news?
11. Define *quest* and explain its role in the storytelling process.
12. Define and discuss the differences in writing and story structure between the straight news script in this chapter about BrightCity's L Street vote, and the script that emphasizes storytelling quest.
13. You can find people pursuing quest in many activities. Name ten newsworthy situations that involve quest and specify the nature of the quest in each instance.
14. Define *character* and explain why it's important to find the small, telling details about a person's character, life, or quest to make your stories and characters memorable.
15. Describe the steps a storyteller can take to create a lifelong system of continuing education as a writer.

EXERCISES

1. Obtain some of John Larson's stories (shot with photographer Mark Morache), which are available from www.nppa.org/professional_development/self-training_resources/AV_library/tv.html. View the stories and review Larson's and Moraches's advice regarding storytelling and teamwork. Write a two-page, double-spaced summation of your findings.
2. Select five newspaper stories. Read them closely to absorb important information about each story. Next, follow the advice for how to write a compelling lead sentence for each story you chose. First, review examples of straight news scripts and storytelling scripts in this chapter. Follow the advice to "lower your expectations" for your opening sentences and "throw up" your immediate ideas on the page rather than edit yourself before you start. Finally, write the most powerful lead sentences you can for each of the stories you chose.
3. In your everyday interactions with people, begin to recognize when you feel something about what they say or do. It may be the way an elderly widow wipes her kitchen table clean repeatedly, or how a person walks, or how he or she unself-consciously sings to himself or herself. Look for the larger meaning in these behaviors; how are they symbols you can incorporate in your stories to address larger issues?
4. Study the parking meter script in this chapter and view the story (see exercise 1). Identify the three surprises in the story and explain how each surprise is set up. In what way are the three surprises revealed through video? Interviews? Other audio? Reporter narration?

5. Watch a local television newscast. Identify how many stories do, or could, emphasize quest: someone trying to get something done. Describe what force or forces in each story oppose the story subject's efforts to accomplish a goal.

6. Write two stories about the same subject: (1) a straight news report; (2) the same subject but told as a story that emphasizes someone's quest for a goal. Review the city council story in this chapter before you begin.

7. Read the work of authors and journalists whose writing you admire. Make a list of telling details that appear in their writing and describe how the writers use these details as symbolism of something larger. Review the sections "The Third Horse: Character" and "Telling Details" before you begin.

8. Create a lifelong plan for ongoing education as a writer committed to developing and perfecting a unique and compelling storytelling style. Review the section "Physician, Heal Thyself" before you begin.

9. Describe in detail the tour guide philosophy of writing for video, as described in this chapter.

10. Watch a television newscast and read the first section of your local newspaper. For each medium, describe the stories that (a) moved you or made you laugh; (b) made you say "Wow!" In each instance, describe the story elements that influenced your reaction(s). Next, describe how you might share such moments with your audience in a video story.

11. Describe the qualities that define moments. How do moments differ from telling details?

11

Video Journalism
Storytelling on Your Own

—By John Larson
© 2012 John Larson

I didn't always work by myself. Often, I still don't, but I've learned first hand the challenges and advantages to shooting, writing, editing, and producing stories on my own. Some call it **Video Journalism**, or being a **One-Man Band** (**OMB**). Others call it Multimedia or **Backpack Journalism**. In truth, even a typical day requires more equipment that you can fit in a backpack (Figure 11.2). Whatever you call it, it means video storytelling by yourself.

THE BIG PICTURE

In news coverage or comparable endeavors, **crew size** varies from a single person to as many as a dozen. I've worked in small market, major market, public broadcasting, and network television. In small market television, I worked with a part-time videographer, who was also employed as a half-time used car salesman (I call this the "One and a Half Person Crew"). As a magazine correspondent for *Dateline NBC*, I worked with eight-person crews. Every step of the way, I tried to learn how the best people were doing things. By watching excellent videographers, I gained valuable insights about composition, sound, and editing. I studied how audio and lighting specialists did things, and why. When I began trying to do it all myself, I discovered I'd picked up more knowledge than I first realized.

SIZE MATTERS—BIGGER IS NOT ALWAYS BETTER

Wherever and however you work during your career, you can expect to work alone at times, and at other times with crews of varying sizes. The most common configurations for video journalists take several forms.

1. One-person crew (a single video journalist who shoots, writes, and edits)
2. **Two-person crews** (photographer and reporter) allow great flexibility and creativity. Assuming the photographer and reporter communicate well, and "work on the same page," they can produce powerful, creative stories in short turnaround times. Even working side-by-side, each person can apply individual strengths and creativity while working independently. They can move efficiently in the field, and change direction and focus as

FIGURE 11.1

John Larson, on assignment as a video journalist.

Copyright © 2012 John Larson

FIGURE 11.2

Gear for a video journalist can reach pack-mule proportions. Rarely will a backpack suffice.

Copyright © 2012 John Larson

the story changes, with little time for deliberation or setup. The photographer often edits the video, making sure to use the best elements.

3. **Three-person crews** (photographer, reporter, and sound person) usually mean an audio specialist is on board. This is especially helpful when more than one person is interviewed at a time, or when the environment presents audio challenges—wind, background noise, radio frequency interference. An ambitious audio person can help share almost every task—gather information, troubleshoot logistics, carry gear, and even meet prospective interviewees. The audio specialist also can "watch the cameraperson's back" when shooting in dangerous or fluid situations. Drawbacks to a three-person crew include the extra expense and less spontaneity. Adding a third person sometimes slows down the process.

4. **Four-person crews** usually add a producer or assistant producer in the field. Drawbacks include the added expense, and some loss of spontaneity—four people must now discuss every move.

5. **Six- to eight-person crews** are standard on two-camera interviews for network news magazine shows. Programs such as *60 Minutes* and *48 Hours* commonly use eight-person crews, and even larger teams in special

circumstances. Here, lighting is critical; a dozen lights are common. Set-up time for an interview averages around three hours. The benefit is that the video usually looks great—well lit, and color enriched. Mistakes are few. The audio is carefully monitored. If necessary, producers can help the correspondent research questions, and craft follow-up questions. The downside is that big crews diminish spontaneity, and seldom can react fast enough to capture the unexpected. I've watched helplessly as journalistically important moments occurred just off camera, while the eight-person crew—with all its lights, mics, and producers—could not react quickly enough to capture it (Figure 11.3.)

Six- to eight-person crews are standard on two-camera interviews for network news magazine shows. Here, lighting is critical; a dozen lights are common. Set-up benefit time for an interview averages around three hours. The is that the video usually looks great—well lit, and color enriched. Mistakes are few. The audio is carefully monitored. If necessary, producers can help the correspondent research questions, and craft follow-up questions. The downside is that big crews diminish spontaneity, and seldom can react fast enough to capture the unexpected. I've watched helplessly as journalistically important moments

FIGURE 11.3

At the network level, top-end sound equipment can generate audio quality that equals the realism and clarity of high definition video.

Copyright © 2012 Dustin Eddo

Big Events Call for Big Crews

Networks may send several crews to meet impending deadlines, or to cover disasters, international summits, or other one-time events of such magnitude that no single crew would suffice (Figure 11.4).

Crews covering a major event—a hurricane, earthquake, or a military invasion, for example—might work on more than one story at a time, with changing rosters, for multiple programs on their network. Such duties require smart, fit, adaptable, and travel-hardened professionals (Figure 11.5).

From one network to another, crews generally have similar configurations:

Director of photography (DP) (in charge of the camera and lighting crews)

Camerapersons (one or more videographers or cinematographers)

Sound Recordists (these individuals record interviews and other audio from multiple cameras. They also time code copies on DVD and transcriptions at the same time. They also act as assistants to the DP, helping with lighting and grip work).

Producer (This person coordinates and manages the project, assembles the crew, and works closely with the correspondent.) The producer on four-person crews may preinterview potential sources,

FIGURE 11.4
A CBS crew works on assignment to cover Brazil's booming economy.

Copyright © 2012 Dustin Eddo

FIGURE 11.5
Crews that travel internationally must be team players, and able to spend long periods away from home.

Copyright © 2012 Dustin Eddo

line up final interviews, gather information and file tape, feed video, make overseas travel arrangements, troubleshoot anything that gets in the way, and even shoot video in a pinch. Six- to eight-person crews commonly include an Associate Producer who can oversee logistics, and serve with equivalent authority in the producer's absence.

Associate Producer (This person conducts and/or oversees research, sometimes writes or edits scripts, assumes final authority in the producer's or correspondent's absence, and serves as a segment producer on complex stories.) Most of all, the assistant producer excels at multitasking, whether to help supervise crews; monitor expenditures; act to safeguard the crew and equipment; and when

things change or go wrong, ensure that air freight, catered meals, and hotel beds materialize when and where needed.

Correspondent (the reporter, or reporter-anchor)

Miscellaneous (experts in law, science, animal behavior, law enforcement, additional lighting or electrical personnel, among others and whenever necessary)

Depending on the country and the story, other crewmembers may be necessary:

A **local "fixer"**—often a respected local journalist, who speaks the language and has already developed excellent sources and contacts

Drivers

Security ■

occurred just off camera, while the eight-person crew—with all its lights, mics, and producers—could not react quickly enough to capture it (Figure 11.6).

BOTTOM LINE

In the end, the ideal crew size is whatever it takes to get the best job done. Your audiences seldom care how many people helped tell your story. They care most about, "How good is it?" They may recognize or prefer a given reporter, correspondent, or anchor on a story never or rarely aware of those behind the camera, and even then only when the credits roll.

FIGURE 11.6
Equipment requirements to produce top-quality video can diminish the big crews' ability to react quickly to breaking news events.

Copyright © 2012 Dustin Eddo

STARTING OUT, OVER OR UP

A prerequisite for every video journalist is to become an aggressive learner. If you're already good in one area, don't be afraid to learn something new. I began as a reporter and learned about camerawork and editing by watching other people on the job. I also studied network television news, which represented the best writing, storytelling, and editing at the time. But eventually, I had to take a course in *Final Cut Pro™* for video editing, and I hired a professional to help me become more proficient with my video camera. I still call friends to ask for help and advice.

If you're a reporter who wants to learn how to shoot and edit, or a photographer who'd like to become a writer and text editor, fear not. Thousands of people have already made the jump. It can be intimidating at first, but it can be rewarding, too.

SIX OVERLOOKED TOOLS FOR VIDEO JOURNALISTS

VJs do everything: produce, shoot, write, and edit. A hundred other tasks accompany those basic duties: preproducing, scheduling, traveling, finding locations, meeting people, filling the gas tank, getting directions, charging batteries, packing and unpacking equipment, updating software, preinterviewing, gathering information, fact-checking, and repairing broken equipment in the field. Over time, experience helps teach us how to work more efficiently, tell better stories, and still manage the other obligations. Through personal experience and by watching others, I've discovered six tools that VJs often overlook.

1. **Preproducing.** Educate yourself about your story before you begin to shoot. This process usually requires research and phone work. Learn everything you can. Google relentlessly. Read news articles. Call experts and people close to the story. "Preinterview" them. Ask questions you would ask in the field. Begin to outline the direction your story might take. Identify locations where you will need to shoot. Decide whom you will interview on camera and the topics you will cover with your interview subjects.

   Follow this with more sharply focused **pre-producing**: What responses will interviewees likely give to my questions? What information might I need to ask them as strong follow-up questions? When possible, decide not only what you need to shoot and who to interview on camera, but also what you DON'T need to shoot and whom you DON'T need to interview on camera. Ask yourself, "What would be the most powerful way to open this story, or close it? What video and sound might I want?"

2. **Focused Listening.** I try to sit down in the field and listen to people before I take out my camera and start shooting (Figure 11.7). This, of course, depends on how much time you have. In general, introducing yourself and listening closely is the best way to begin any interview, but it's difficult when you're carrying and setting up your own gear.

FIGURE 11.7

Correspondent John Larson prefers to talk and interact with the interviewee before he begins an on-camera interview. Both parties learn more about one another, while Larson gains valuable insights and information he otherwise might not discover.

Copyright © 2012 John Larson

FIGURE 11.8

Lisa Berglund, NPPA Photojournalist of the Year, moves in close to her subjects to gather powerful sound and pictures.

Copyright © 2012 Jon Warren/World Vision

FIGURE 11.9

Dave Delozier, KUSA-TV, Denver, earned recognition as National Video Journalist of the Year for his reporting, photography, editing, writing, and storytelling abilities.

Copyright © 2012 Dave Delozier

Be mindful that your interview subjects are sizing you up. They're trying to figure out how much you know, care, and whether they can trust you. It's surprising how quickly people can form an opinion of you, and how it can affect the interview. Whenever I can have a conversation with interviewees, the personal details they share often help me create more compelling stories. Ask them about their families, and why the story means so much to them. If you have the time, try to meet people and listen to them.

Lisa Berglund, named Photojournalist of the Year by the National Press Photographers Association (NPPA), often shoots her own stories in Africa (Figure 11.8). "Listening and having conversations is all part of being human while you're in the field," says Berglund. "You're trying to break down the barriers between people and just tell stories honestly and naturally."[1]

Dave Delozier (Figure 11.9), NPPA Video Journalist of the Year, says he always wears his headphones in the field; but when he sits down for an interview, he checks his sound and then takes his headphones off. "I don't wear headphones during my main sit-down interviews because I don't want my subjects to think about being recorded all the time," he says. "I just want to talk to them and listen normally."[2]

3. **Gather Great Sound** Gathering sound is well covered elsewhere in this book, but it deserves special mention here. Many VJs overlook good, clear, crisp sound. Don't. As soon as possible, pin a wireless mic on everyone you can. Wear your headphones, mindful of Dave Delozier's advice regarding sit-down interviews. Get your shotgun mic off your camera and close to whatever you are shooting. Listen to what is being said! "Get creative in your video," says Delozier, "but not in your sound—I want crisp sound, of their words and their feelings. Once I have that, I have the foundation."[3]

If you hear sound that would add meaning to your story, you can react to it like no one else: you can ask a question about it, shoot a good shot to illustrate the sound, follow with your camera what a person is pointing at during the interview, think of the line you will write to showcase a sound—or even its absence.

I once began a story about the bad economy with the words, "The first thing you notice at the Rayonier pulp mill is the silence." I stopped voice-over narration at that point to let the camera linger on the old mill's vast interior. A few spiderwebs and an old shoe occupied a dusty window casing; elsewhere machinery lay gutted, the mill now silent and forsaken. In an old break room, we found a deck of cards; a work glove whose sculpture reflected a working man's hand; and an old punch clock, still keeping time for employees long since departed. Silence served as metaphor to help symbolize larger issues—international competitors, market conditions, government policies, and environmental regulations— that led to layoffs that would further debilitate the area's already fragile economy.

"You have to do this every day," says Delozier. When you stop thinking about the process, that's when you can focus on storytelling. That's when great stories happen."[4]

Another way to stay ahead of the story is to listen. Greg Bledsoe, a Digital Journalist at KNSD in San Diego, CA, says, "Shoot with your ears. I constantly try to listen to what's going on around me. I may be pointing the camera in one direction, but my ears are scanning 360 degrees. While I'm getting one shot, my ears are already telling me where the next shot will be."[5] Other video journalists sometimes find stories by driving around with their car windows open, or by just sitting somewhere like the San Diego zoo and listening.[†]

FIGURE 11.10

A Danish painter helps a fellow in need by removing a stuck filter from video journalist John Larson's camera lens.

Copyright © 2012 John Larson

4. **Ask for Help.** Asking for help makes most journalists uncomfortable; it just feels unprofessional. Sometimes, though, VJs must ask for help. They have too much equipment; too many challenges; too many questions needing answers; too much to do in too little time, not to occasionally need help. It's okay to ask someone to help carry or fix something if you genuinely need help.

A Danish house painter once freed a stuck UV lens filter on my lens after everyone else failed (Figure 11.10). Another time, I asked a homeowner to help me off his roof. I felt it was too dangerous to try it on my own (Figure 11.11). When Lisa Berglund, a NPPA National Press Photographer of the Year, needed help, she asked an Ethiopian boy to carry her tripod (Figure 11.12). "He was so little, but he really wanted to help," Lisa said. "He couldn't carry it far, but it was fun for him and it helped me."[6]

Avoid crossing ethical lines by letting police or people involved in the story become part of your news gathering effort. But, when necessary, *Ask, and Ye Shall Receive.*

5. **Write in Your Head.** Writing in your head as you shoot is the VJ's single, greatest advantage. If someone else

---

[†]John DeTarsio used the power of sound to uncover an original story at the San Diego Zoo. Stumped for ideas about another Day-At-The-Zoo assignment, he sat down to think about alternatives. A few minutes later, he heard a guide who sounded more like a street performer, warming up his next tour group. He asked to ride along and shot a memorable story that helped viewers feel part of the tour.

normally shoots your video, you may already know how previewing and logging the video can generate new ideas. When you shoot your own video, these ideas not only occur *while* you're shooting, they can change *how* you shoot.

Whenever you see an exceptional moment in your viewfinder—a certain scene or powerful moment—immediately think of a line you might write about it. Change your shooting to reflect how you will phrase the line, and other lines you will write before and after it. In other words, let the video/audio inform your writing on the spot—react to it, and build on it.

6. **Let your writing inform how you shoot.** If you know you plan to write a line about how something happened, for example, write the line in your head, and then shoot video that illustrates that line perfectly. Remember, you "write" not only with words, but with the sounds you gather; the pictures you choose to take; the composition, moods, and silences; and the actions and behaviors that occur within your storytelling environment.

FIGURE 11.12

An Ethiopian boy carries a tripod to help VJ Lisa Berglund, on assignment in Ethiopia.

MINUTE BY MINUTE—ONE MAN BAND LESSONS LEARNED IN THE FIELD

PBS's *World Focus* sent me to Denmark in advance of the Global Climate Change Summit in Copenhagen. Usually, we would travel with three or four people—the correspondent (me), a producer, a cameraperson, and often a fourth person who could run audio, shoot an extra camera, and/or help with the difficult logistics of working in a foreign country. This time I traveled as a VJ, employing only a Danish friend who helped me with local knowledge and language. I shot, produced, wrote, and edited the stories myself. While I had already shot some video, this was the first time my video and editing would appear on a national broadcast.

A GUIDED TOUR: LESSONS LEARNED

Below you'll find a link to one of the five stories I shot in Denmark, called *Everyday Danes Profit from Wind Power*. If you first view the story on the web, and then go back through it, you can learn what I learned, and see what worked and what didn't work.

To view the story log on to www.youtube.com and search for "Everday Danes Profit from Wind Power"

FIGURE 11.13
You also can access the story by photographing this tag on your smartphone, using an app such as Mobiletag or Scanlife.

After you view the full story, go back to the beginning. You'll see a small timer somewhere on the screen. You can use this timer to scrub through the video, stop it, and replay segments as you reference the following comments regarding what I learned, what I did, and what I should have done.

Everyday Danes Profit from Wind Power

0:03 **Opening Shots (Good and Bad).** A wide opening shot is good, but even better with the sound of the waves. I walked to the water's edge to capture clean sound of the waves. The shot of tulips is off the tripod, and to my eye, too shaky. There was no reason I had to shoot it off the tripod.

0:08–0:23 **Writing an Open.** I began my story with a question, "What can one Danish art dealer, one Danish farmer, and two pigs tell us about how Denmark became a world leader in renewable wind power?" I rarely begin a story with a question, but here a question helped me introduce the three "characters" right away. The Rule of Threes even works in opening

FIGURE 11.14

John Larson, dressed in protective clothing and breathing gear, meets a friend at a Danish windmill painting facility. Larson is about to shoot in hazardous conditions while a painter spraypaints inside a partial section of windmill tower. The shots Larson made inside the tower section begin at 1:04 in the video story, *Everyday Danes Profit from Wind Power*, which you can access using the provided link or QR code.

Copyright © 2012 John Larson

sentences. I tried to invite viewers into the story with interesting sound and video right at the top, all while foreshadowing the story's ultimate theme: *Everyday people helped build the most successful wind power network in the world.* And, I liked the pigs.

0:23 **The Most Basic Sound.** Never forget to record sound of your most basic, important subject. If your story is about a vote, record sounds of voting— murmuring voices, the ratcheting of privacy curtains closing and opening. If it's about construction, record the sounds of construction. Because this story is about windmills, I needed the "whooshing" sounds of windmill blades.

0:25 **Allow Shots to Unfold.** Not all shots have to be quick. To me, the silhouette of the wind turbine is good, but I felt the sun creeping out from behind made it better.

0:57 **Remember to avoid autofocus.** The tight shot of the welder is out of focus. You can see that parts of the background are in focus. I didn't realize my autofocus was on, so the camera focused on the background, resulting in soft focus on the welder. Shoot in manual focus whenever you can. The same goes for auto-audio and auto-white balance. Try to stay in manual settings whenever possible.

1:06 **Matched Cuts Editing.** One of my favorite shots is of the painter. The raw video contained overlapping action, so I could match the action of his arm while cutting from the medium shot to the medium-wide shot. Then, I made sure the painter appeared in the last shot in the sequence, so I could dissolve from his white coveralls to the white windmill tower.

1:09—I arranged to meet the company vice president at the base of a windmill at the Copenhagen Convention Center. The VP was late. The mill was broken. Two guys were working on it, one of them way up on top. Still no VP, so I interviewed them. I knew it would be fun to "reveal" the worker on top of the mill, so I shot the tilt-to-the-top-of-the-mill shot. As I was shooting, a line occurred to me: "To get a sense of just how heady these times are for Vestas, we went straight to the top," so I shot the tilt-to-the-top-of-the-mill shot several times. I wanted the timing to match the line, revealing the worker at the end of the sentence. I wasn't very good with my tripod, so you can see it jiggle.

1:25 **Interesting Interviews/Telling Details.** Interviews can be interesting in many ways, including their physical location. Interviewing the worker atop the mill is visually more interesting to me than interviewing him at the bottom (but impossible without a wireless mic). His interview also is symbolic—a "telling detail." He represents the many new employees in the wind industry who have left traditional jobs to work in renewable energy. He's working on the mill that will soon power the Conference by itself.

1:52 **Shooting Stand-ups (Good and Bad).** On the good side, I waited for the best light during the last hour before sunset, the **"golden hour,"**[‡] to shoot the standup with the mills behind me. On the bad side, notice the fuzzy, overmodulated audio. I checked the audio level before I shot the standup, but I spoke more loudly when I actually shot it. You can sometimes boost low audio when you edit, but you can't do much to correct overmodulated audio.

For the standup, I asked my Danish friend to stand in for me while I framed the shot. If I'm alone, I record consecutive practice standups, each time checking the video until I have the desired framing. I also turn the viewfinder around, so I can locate myself in the frame while I shoot the standup. If you want, you can always set up a light stand extended to your height and focus on that. **Mark the shot**—where you will stand—with removable tape or an object such as your notebook. Be mindful that some tapes can damage fragile surfaces. Once the lens is focused, remove the light stand from view, and then step back into frame on your designated mark, and deliver your standup. If you plan to move during the shot—say into frame and out of frame, or walk around the corner into frame—you can **block the shot** by marking where to begin and end your movement.

2:04 **Repetition. Reprises**—repeating sentences and sound bites—are uncommon storytelling tools in news and corporate video, but they can be effective. Here, I reprise sound bites from the top of the story. You hear the farmer say,

---

[‡]Golden Hour refers to the rich, saturated light that occurs under clear skies during the first hour after sunrise and the last hour before sunset. See the Golden Hour Calculator with input for your region and time of year at http://www.b-roll.net/goldenhour/Alternatively, you can photograph the following tag with an app such as MobileTag or ScanLife on your smart phone.

Golden Hour Calculator

"I think it was too good, too good to tear down" at the beginning and at the end. A reprise helps reintroduce a character, and helps prevent confusion. It can also help emphasize central themes (Everyday people helped build the wind industry). A reprise is like a chorus in a song. Sometimes, repetition is a good thing.

2:14 **Natural Sound.** I remembered hearing the farmer's laughter on the wireless microphone as he walked to his windmill. It matched the sense of joy and accomplishment he shared when he told me how he outwitted investors and put up the mill himself. Here, natural sound supplies not only meaning but punctuation, in this case both to insert a little "exclamation mark" and to "underline" the farmer's sense of accomplishment.

2:31 **Bad framing.** Notice that my microphone is showing in the upper right hand of the shot. I did it again at 3:42. I didn't know yet that my camera "overscans"—meaning that it actually shoots a wider shot than I see in the viewfinder. I also didn't know yet that I could just zoom in a little more, or that during editing I could crop out the mistake in Final Cut Pro™.

3:00 **Shaky Out-zoom.** When you use a tripod to in-zoom, out-zoom, tilt, or pan, it's advisable to practice first, always with a good tripod. I had not practiced enough. This video was again shot during "Golden Hour" to give it that rich, saturated light.

3:54 **Bad Lighting.** Notice the poor exposure on the man sitting at his computer. The window behind him is too bright, requiring that I provide additional light to "fill," or supplement, the light on his face. I didn't take time to set up the light, and the shot suffered.

4:00–4:32 **Back-and-Forth Conversations.** This technique makes the story look as if two cameras were used to record one conversation. Actually, one camera was used to "match cut" between two similar conversations. During the interview, I noticed several answers that could be more specific. I wanted to ask those questions again. After the original interview, I set up the camera again, this time pointing at me, and re-asked the questions: e.g., "How much is your salary? It is all volunteer?" His answers were better the second time.

Reversal questions are common in one-camera shoots. Some journalists may wonder if the practice is ethical, but one test considers whether the VJ's actions would be acceptable under public scrutiny. Acceptable conduct requires that you only reask the same questions while still in the interviewee's presence, with the person's full understanding and consent; it means never to misrepresent the conversation, never to match a reversal question with a different answer, or to create a misleading or false context for the interview. Stay true to the conversation.

4:45–5:09 **Engage. Have Fun.** When I struggled with the Danish pronunciation of the Power Cooperative I was not intending to use it in my story (You'll notice that I did not mike myself). When logging the tape, I realized that my poor Danish was interesting and playful, so I wrote it into the story. Sometimes it's appropriate to interact and have fun with your interviewees. Even to share a beer from the camera's point of view. The "Skol!" toast wound up being the story's final closing sound.

FIGURE 11.15
John Larson asks on-camera questions of his subject during a "reinterview" to create reverse angle shots that can later be intercut to help improve the story's pace and permit matched-cut editing.

Copyright © 2012 John Larson

The Future of Video Journalists

Video journalists are playing an increasingly important role in gathering information around the world. Scandinavian countries like Norway and Denmark have used VJs with success for many years. In the United States, most broadcast news operations are replacing some two- and three-person crews with video journalists. They do it to save money or to increase the number of journalists gathering and producing stories in the field.

The results have been mixed. When companies use VJs only to cut costs, the product has suffered. Reporters usually can't shoot as well as gifted photographers. Photographers usually can't write and dig for information as well as gifted reporters. When VJs are asked to do the same amount of work each day that once required two or three people, the content usually suffers.

But, where companies use VJs to cover stories once considered too distant, complex, time-intensive, or expensive, the results can be outstanding. Sometimes, the VJ can travel overseas to shoot and tell the stories three-person crews rarely or never cover. At home, given adequate time, VJs enjoy a sense of ownership and control over stories that few other journalists can match.

Increasingly, some VJs become **Multimedia Journalists (MMJs)**. They not only shoot, write, and edit their stories, but they write stories for the web, blog, assemble computer slide shows, "Tweet" for Twitter, and write other content for social networking sites like Facebook. Multimedia journalists with such skills and creativity can play powerful roles in the emerging landscape of journalism, but with a caveat. All this takes time to learn. Even when you can do everything, you can't do everything all the time. Choose your strengths. Become proficient in one medium, and challenge yourself in others. I am stronger at storytelling, and less strong at editing. I need to work on editing. I also want to learn more about various forms of online storytelling. I will continue to explore and learn. You can, too.

SUMMARY

New technology and tight budgets have prompted television news, corporate video firms, and comparable organizations to reintroduce the so-called One-Man Band (OMB), a term for the individual men and women who have learned how to shoot, write, and edit video stories by themselves. Equivalent terms include Backpack Journalist, Video Journalist (VJ), All-Platform Journalist, and Solo Video Journalist.

Beyond shooting, writing, and editing stories, the video journalist also must conduct research, find good stories, set up interviews, find locations, maintain and repair equipment, and meet all deadlines—among dozens more duties in a typical week.

Networks, local stations, and other organizations use video journalists to cover stories otherwise too expensive or too impractical for larger crews, which can range from two- to eight-people or more, including producers, sound recordists, the correspondent, the Director of Photography (DP), and the DP's assistant. Network crews working abroad frequently add to that roster a respected local expert who speaks the native language fluently, drivers, and security personnel.

Six commonly overlooked tools can help the VJ produce interesting stories quickly. They include preproducing the story, or learning everything possible through research and phone work, talking with experts, and conducting "preinterviews" by phone to determine the story's most likely direction.

A second tool when time permits is to practice focused-listening. Before shooting the story, try to talk and interact with people in your stories before you begin your on-camera interviews. This approach helps the VJ and story subjects come to know one another better, and sometimes uncovers valuable insights and information otherwise unobtainable.

A third tool is to gather great storytelling sound, which serves as the other half of the image. Great sound conveys information, sense of place, feeling, experience, and emotion. Many VJs overlook the small sounds that can enhance the viewer's sense of "being there," and that inform the ear just as surely as images inform the eye.

Your greatest advantage lies in knowing where the story is headed. Work aggressively to capture good "shots" with the microphone. If you listen for sounds, anticipate the action, and think like a video editor as you shoot, you can react like no one else, whether it be to ask a question, illustrate the sound with a good shot, or "thought write" an accompanying line as you record a shot.

The fourth tool is a willingness to ask for help when you genuinely need it. You may have too much equipment to descend a ladder safely, or perhaps you can't carry all the gear to another location on your own. Most VJs must ask for help at times, and most will usually find someone willing to lend a hand.

The fifth tool is to practice "thought writing," or writing in your head as you shoot or log video. What you see and hear in the field influences what you will say in the story's voice-over script. You may change your shooting to reflect how you wish to phrase a line, or think of a line you might write. The goal is learning to let the video/audio inform your writing, on the spot, as you react to images and sound, and build on them.

The sixth tool is the opposite of thought writing. You write or think of a sentence or more of voice-over copy you want to use, and then shoot video/audio that will illustrate that line.

Thus, using these six tools, you "write" not only with words, but with the sounds you gather; the pictures you choose to take; the composition, moods, and silences; and the actions and behaviors that occur within your storytelling environment.

This chapter contains a section titled *A Guided Tour: Lessons Learned*, in which John Larson, former *Dateline NBC* correspondent, self-critiques a PBS story that he shot, produced, and reported in Denmark. Larson was on his first international assignment as a VJ. He provides access to this web story and a self-critique so that others may learn what he learned and to help show what worked and didn't work.

VJs play an important role in gathering information worldwide. They work in many countries, and some travel widely. In the United States, organizations have replaced some two- and three-person crews with VJs, whether to cut costs or to put more journalists in the field gathering and producing stories.

The results have been mixed when companies replace crews with VJs, while expecting one person to do the same work every day that once required two or three people. When companies use VJs to cover stories once thought too remote, expensive, or time-intensive, VJs can shoot and tell exceptional stories that most crews only rarely or never cover.

As technology becomes easier to use, more VJs also are becoming Multimedia Journalists (MMJs). They still report, write, shoot, and edit, but also write stories for the web, blog, "Tweet," and write content for social networking sites such as Facebook. Such skills and creativity can play powerful roles in the emerging landscape of journalism and comparable fields, but they take time to learn. Even if VJs or MMJs can do everything, seldom can they do everything all the time. A good approach, then, is to choose your strengths. First, become proficient in one medium, and then challenge yourself in others.

KEY TERMS

associate producer   184
backpack journalism   180
block the shot   191
camerapersons   182
correspondent   184
crew sizes   184
director of
   photography   182
drivers   184

four-person crews   181
golden hour   191
local "fixer,"   184
mark the shot   191
miscellaneous   184
multimedia journalist
   (MMJ)   193
one-man band (OMB)   180
preproducing   185

producer   182
reprises   191
security   184
six- to eight-person
   crews   181
sound recordist   182
three-person crews   181
two-person crews   180
video journalism   180

DISCUSSION

1. Discuss the primary reasons that television news stations and similar organizations have replaced some video field production crews with VJs who do everything alone.
2. Compare the advantages and disadvantages of respective crew sizes with those of the VJ working alone.
3. Assume you're counseling a midcareer professional—perhaps a photographer, video editor, or reporter. The person feels pressured to retool as a VJ who can do it all but is confused about where to begin. What advice would you give that person? What approach would you recommend? Explain how long the transition might take before the person is fully capable in all areas.
4. Assume a fully capable VJ comes to you, asking how to become a multimedia journalist. What would you tell that person? What skills should the person acquire? Explain how long it might take the person to become proficient in multimedia journalism.
5. Discuss the important contributions of storytelling sound in video stories, and explain the meaning of "sound is the other half of the image." Finally, provide an example of how you might record sound while shooting a story to use as the "other half of the image."
6. Explain what "Write in Your Head" means, provide an example, and explain how you might apply the concept while shooting video in the field.
7. Explain how a specific shot might inform your writing, even after you return to the edit bay.
8. Based on your existing knowledge gained from experience, readings, and observations, list at least five additional techniques and/or approaches that John Larson might have added to his story in an ideal world, given sufficient time and resources. Before you complete this exercise, reread the section in this chapter, "A Guided Tour: Lessons Learned" as you review John Larson's accompanying video story: *Everyday Danes Profit from Wind Power* at http://www.youtube.com/watch?v=dvTtt-tWoSY
9. Discuss your current or planned approach to shoot your own standup in the field without any help.
10. When, if ever, is it appropriate for a VJ to ask someone for help? In what situations might a request for help be inappropriate, if ever?
11. Discuss what you have learned at large to this point about VJs and their responsibilities—while working as a VJ yourself, interning or otherwise observing VJs at work, or in your own research and readings. Also, share your thoughts regarding appropriate attire and public conduct for VJs while on routine assignments, and while attending more formal or solemn events.
12. How do you see the future of the "one-man-band"? Is the practice here to stay? If so, in what situations and under what conditions? How likely is "burnout" among VJs? How can they avoid burnout? What are an organization's professional and humanitarian obligations to its VJs?

EXERCISES

1. Assume you're in charge of all video production at your operation, including budgeting and hiring. List and explain the minimum qualities you look for when you hire a VJ. Include education, experience, attitude, creativity, professional abilities, and minimum physical abilities.
2. List several situations where a large crew (or crews) would be necessary to cover a story in your region, and explain how you would deploy that crew (or crews).
3. Create a pocket field guide of the "Six Overlooked Tools for Video Journalists" that you can laminate and carry for reference while preproducing, reporting, writing, and shooting stories in the field.
4. Explain in detail why sound is such an important storytelling tool for VJs, and how audiences benefit when VJs go the extra mile to capture good sound.
5. Create a flowchart or time line that lists all education and proficiencies a person must acquire before becoming a competent VJ—and from that point forward a competent multimedia journalist.

6. List the main points John Larson makes in the section about what did not work in *Everyday Danes Profit from Wind Power*. Next, list additional techniques or approaches, which in an ideal world might have made the story even stronger.

7. Write a job description for an organization's human resource manual, outlining the duties, responsibilities, and expectations for a new VJ position your company soon will announce. Include educational requirements, work experience, probable work schedule, salary, and benefits including vacation time. Include any other requirements you wish, such as recommendation letters, need to pass a drug test and criminal background check, satisfactory driving record, valid driver's license and passport, supply own car, and be able to carry x pounds of gear for x distance.

8. Assume that you work, or soon will begin work as a VJ. Drawing upon personal experience, and your sense of what is fair and reasonable, write guidelines that will help your organization better appreciate VJs and the role they play, provide them proper working conditions, develop fair work schedules, and prevent burnout. Include an explanation of likely benefits to the organization should it adopt your recommendations.

9. Explain in detail how experience as a VJ might help you become a more efficient and professional crewmember at some point in your future. Next, explain in detail how working as a crewmember could help you become a better VJ.

10. Conduct sufficient online research to make an informed prediction about the future of video journalism. Include an assessment of technology's continuing impacts. Also address what VJs must do every day to attract ongoing audience patronage and loyalty, given today's unlimited content choices on numerous media platforms.

11. Assume you oversee the local branch of a national organization that specializes in video production, whether in news or an allied field. Upper management wants you to replace all two- and three-person crews with VJs in the coming year, claiming a VJ can produce just as many stories as a crew, allowing the company to save money on salaries, equipment, transportation, and benefits. Respond to upper management in a one-page memo, outlining specific reasons where you agree and/or disagree with this plan.

NOTES

1. Lisa Berglund, comments to John Larson, Detroit, October 2010.
2. Dave Delozier, comments to John Larson, Denver, CO, March 2010.
3. Ibid.
4. Dave Delozier, comments to John Larson, Denver, CO, February 2009.
5. Greg Bledsoe, KNSD-TV, in comments to John Larson, San Diego, CA, May 2010. For more insights, see Deborah Potter, "Shoot with Your Ears," *Newslab*, http://www.newslab.org/2009/09/11/shoot-with-your-ears/
6. Lisa Berglund, comments to John Larson, regarding tips and insights about video journalism, May 2010.

12

How to Improve Your Storytelling Ability

Audiences with many viewing choices expect certain standards from their favorite information sources. At the very least, they want their stories and storytellers to be interesting and appealing. Even when your intentions are noble but your work suffers, viewers can only judge what you put on the screen. In the end, nothing else matters. "The ability to appeal, whatever the subject matter, separates the successful creator from the artistic failure," writes filmmaker and author Edward Dmytryk in his book *On Film Editing*.[1] Survival and professional advancement depend on a commitment to produce stories with a style and substance that are consistently solid, unique, and appealing, even on days when you might willingly trade your job for a dead mouse.

SEEK GRADUAL IMPROVEMENT

As you work to make your stories ever more attractive and compelling, you may notice competitors who seem more capable than you. Perhaps they have more experience and confidence, or their stories just seem more inviting. While it's useful to study others' techniques, it's important to realize that you are in competition primarily with yourself to improve each new story you report.

Implicit in the process of self-improvement is the possibility of failure, a hazard that keeps some people from realizing big achievements in their careers. You can't fail if you don't try, after all, but neither can you succeed. "Don't be afraid to fail," advises KAKE's Larry Hatteberg. "You don't learn unless you fail."[2] An occasional failure can be seen as a virtue in the journalist's professional development, with each new success building on some past failure.

Improvement is a gradual process that creates its own frustrations. The trick, says NBC national correspondent Bob Dotson, is to go for the minor victories. "Don't try to hit a home run every time out, just get on first base every time at bat," says Dotson. "You find the right word, or write a phrase that works, or shoot a scene that tells the story."[3]

The commitment to slow, steady development can result in significant improvements over time. Dan Rather, long-time news anchor at CBS and now HDNet, suggests that what moves a career along is doing the routine things extraordinarily well time after time.

HAVE A STORY

Often, reporters and photojournalists confuse their accounts of events with stories. Routinely they identify the story subject, but not the story itself: "My story is about consumer spending." But as you will have discovered, a story **focus** or **commitment** is one of the storyteller's most potent tools. The focus statement provides a way to give the story life and help drive it forward.

Typically, in a team setting, the reporter is left to identify the story, although in reality that job should fall to everyone involved. Because you may see the story differently than the **assignment editor** or the person who accompanies you into the field, whether that person is the reporter or the photographer, remember to communicate your ideas to one another so that all agree on a single focus.

Even when you work alone in the field, if you can invest just two or three minutes to develop a focus statement, you can have a stronger story and spend less time in the field. Even when the action is moving quickly all around you, and it seems as if you must purely and simply react, force yourself to take time to think. Recognize that you must be flexible enough to change your story commitment if the event changes.

INVOLVE THE CAMERA

Viewers hunger for a sense of involvement in stories. Indeed the promise of a sense of first-person experience is one reason we turn to television and web video even for news.

The involved camera helps create the experiential illusion and thereby provides a way to help differentiate your reporting from the competition. Try to involve the camera more directly in the action—to place the viewer in the very heart of the story (Figure 12.1 a, b). When you involve the camera, you involve the viewer.

Look also for unique camera angles to help tell your story and to make it more visually memorable. Avoid extreme angles that could destroy the viewer's sense of direct involvement in the story.

SEQUENCES ADVANCE THE STORY

Sequential video produces a continuous, uninterrupted flow of action that tells much of the story, even without narration. A series of shots are edited together to create for viewers the illusion of continuity along a timeline from beginning to end. Pictures, sound bites, and natural sound communicate much of the information.

BOX 12.1   THE ESSENCE OF STORYTELLING

The essence of all storytelling is conflict. There is no very good story in the premise "He wanted her and he got her; the end." Conflict—the quest for a goal against opposition—keeps the story going.

The eighty-two-year-old woman who nurses heroin-addicted babies back to health is engaged in one of life's greatest conflicts: life and health over death and suffering. The runner who has lost his leg to cancer but rides across America in a wheelchair to raise money for athletes with physical disabilities illustrates his character under pressure. Because so many journalism stories are accounts of things gone wrong, conflict and struggle are inevitable components of television news. To ignore them is to ignore the nature not only of news, but life itself. ∎

FIGURE 12.1
When the camera is involved in the action, so is the audience.

A commonly used, but much less effective, alternative is called **illustrative video**. This reporting approach simply uses video that illustrates the script, roughly in the proportion of one scene per sentence of voice-over narration. It is similar to a series of unrelated slides or scenes with little regard for the order or rhythm or even for the meaning of individual shots working together. Illustrative video builds mostly around talk, and rarely tells a story along a timeline.

DON'T TRY TO SHOW ALL OF NEW ZEALAND

A frustration of every video reporter is the lack of airtime available to tell complex stories. "If only I had a couple more minutes," pleads the reporter. "You can have five more seconds if you'll give up a week of your summer vacation," the producer replies. At such times it is useful to remember the strong messages and nuances that can be communicated by a thirty-second or even a fifteen-second commercial. The best commercial messages are simple, yet powerful and memorable.

One approach in the face of insufficient airtime is to follow the maxim that "less is more." Photojournalist Larry Hatteberg has crystallized the concept in his advice, "Don't try to show all of New Zealand."[4] Hatteberg forged this conviction while on assignment to portray New Zealand in a four-part series. Confronted with showing the nation's overwhelming complexity in only four two-minute reports, Hatteberg dramatically narrowed his focus. He chose a sheep rancher, a street magician, a fishing boat captain, and a railroad engineer, and told his stories through them. Still, after viewing the stories, there is a sense that we have seen all of New Zealand after all, because the treatment is both wide-ranging and powerful. Hatteberg's approach mirrors the sentiments of John Grierson, the British documentary historian and filmmaker, who once observed that while newspapers can tell the story of the entire mail service, you must make a film about one single letter.

PURSUE YOUR INTEREST IN PEOPLE

It's important to care about the people in your stories. Caring simply means that you are interested in your subject and that you listen hard to what the person has to say (Figure 12.2). This does not mean you should become emotionally or personally involved. The key is to report honestly and with appropriate feeling. "[The story] has to come from the heart if it is going to work well. For in the end, I have to feel the story if I am going to reflect it with feeling," writes television journalist Tim Fisher.[5]

MOTIVATE VIEWERS TO WATCH

In helping viewers want to watch your stories, it is important to avoid telling them everything they need to know in the voice-over script. Rarely, in the newscast built on words, will you have to watch a story to understand it. Often, you can listen from the next room with little loss in meaning. This kind of television, of course, is radio with pictures and is neither involving nor engaging.

A more powerful reporting method is to help people watch through voice-over that invites the viewer to reengage with the screen constantly. It is a "This" versus "This tea ceremony" approach. If you read the next two sentences aloud, the distinction becomes clear: "Every hiker should carry one of these in his backpack" versus "Every hiker should carry a compass in his backpack." Only the first sentence invites viewers to watch the screen.

FIGURE 12.2
The strongest visual stories normally result when the journalist is interested in the subject and pays attention to what the person has to say.

DEVELOP VIDEO FLUENCY

In this word-oriented culture, the effort to express the story visually without stating it flatly, in words, is a trick easier said than done. For all its eloquence, the visual image receives short shrift among some journalists, even in the face of generations of film-makers who have proven the power of visual communication. "Very early . . . I discovered that viewers are more attentive to silent sequences than they are to dialogue scenes," writes filmmaker Edward Dmytryk. "When the screen talk[s], so d[oes] the viewer. Silent scenes command attention."[6]

The same realities persist today. *Time* magazine noted that after screenings of *Ryan's Daughter,* director David Lean was wounded by reviewers "who so often tend to listen to movies more intently than they look at them, thus missing much of [Lean's] special grace and subtlety."[7] Happily, film and television viewers learn more from visual information than critics insensitive to the larger meanings and experiences that visual fluency offers. Repeatedly we learn that the television viewer would rather see it than hear about it.

At one time such advice was sufficient. But today many newsrooms require journalists to report on multiple platforms. Throughout the day the reporter may employ desktop-based editing, create computer graphics, cut voice-over tracks, post a web article, stream video, record a news tease, appear on set for an anchor debrief, create a blog or podcast, even select still photos from video for web-based articles, and broadcast story updates to mobile phones.

Today, "journalists are expected to be multimedia utility players," says newspaper and magazine columnist Robert J. Samuelson. "Up to a point, this is valuable:

finding new ways to engage and inform. But it's also time consuming."[8] Newsroom software helps enable such versatility by letting the reporter write as little as a single story but publish in various formats—as web article, news script, mobile phone broadcast—to several different platforms.[9]

The key is to learn when to use specific tools to best communicate your message in the medium at hand. It is no longer a matter of spoken words and moving images, but rather of graphics, audio only, audio with video, still photography, the spoken word meant to be heard, the written word meant to be read, text messages, and the like.

Excuses

In the face of deadline pressure, budget restraints, and equipment breakdowns, virtually every video story is imperfect in some sense, and some are outright forgettable. As a memo at a television station in Texas reminds news personnel, "We have some decent stories that we are making average."[10] Inquire at any newsroom why a particular story failed, and you may encounter The Excuse—that tendency to blame anything but ourselves.

Some excuses, of course, are legitimate. They explain something beyond our control that went wrong. Other excuses masquerade for indifference and procrastination. Note that some of the most common excuses are admissions of failure and tell of stories seldom remembered:

- "It was a dumb assignment. The producer didn't know what he wanted."
- "I don't have enough time to do a good job. I have to cover six stories a day."
- "My equipment is no good."
- "I didn't have time to set up the camera on a tripod."
- "They don't pay me enough that I have to do everything around here."
- "You can't shoot sequences in spot news."
- "It's the photographer's job to take the pix. I don't feel I can suggest shots."
- "Audiences don't expect that level of quality."
- "It's not my job, that's up to the reporter."

Professionals leave such excuses to the competition. Ultimately, on every story, the choice comes down to a simple yes or no whenever you ask yourself, "Am I going to do my best job on this story or not?"

KNOW THE COMMUNITY

The smaller a community the more journalists you find who are on their way through town to a better job. At one time market hopping may have helped further careers, but tenure in the marketplace can offer great rewards. Organizations need employees who want to live in the community and are willing to stay long enough to learn something about it. No one who arrives in town and leaves eight months later can discover much about the community, and even two years is little enough time for a video journalist to learn about an area, its politics, and its people. Generally, assuming acceptable pay and working conditions, the longer video journalists can stay in an area the better. Tenure in the marketplace allows journalists to develop more recognition and acceptance among viewers and to report stories about the community with a depth and sensitivity not found in the work of reporters on their way through town.

In a sense you are a historian for the market area you serve. You tell the stories of the soldiers, the boat builders, the archaeologists, the miners, and the musicians of

BOX 12.2 COMMUNITY-ORIENTED JOURNALISM

Traditionally, journalists have struggled to make their accounts objective, but inherent in all stories is a point of view: the job of determining *which* point of view falls to the journalist. Will a particular news story be simply an account of an event or situation, or of how the event affected people and how they responded? Will Durant, the American educator and historian, typically addressed such questions from a philosopher's perspective:

"Civilization is a stream with banks. The stream is sometimes filled with blood from people killing, stealing, shouting and doing things historians usually record, while on the banks, unnoticed, people build homes, make love, raise children, sing songs, write poetry. The story of civilization is the story of what happened on the banks."

(Quoted in Jim Hicks, "Spry Old Team Does It Again," *Life* [October 18, 1963], 92) ■

your region. Someday, should you reach the network level, you still will tell similar stories from your travels, but share them with larger audiences.

CURIOSITY PAYS

Curiosity is a prerequisite if video journalists are to understand the market or the field they work in. One broadcast executive tells of a reporter who spent nearly eighteen months in town. A week and a half before she was to leave the state for another reporting job, she came to him to ask directions to the nearby mountains, which she had never visited. After a year and a half on the job, she had yet to explore the streets or to learn in which direction the freeways ran.

Cities and communities reveal themselves to explorers, so soon upon your arrival in town, come to know everything you can about street names, geographical oddities, regional pronunciations, community leaders, and Saturday night dances. Introduce yourself to the municipal court judge and walk along the riverfront. At restaurants, pass up the cheeseburger and sample the regional specialties like alligator tail or huckleberry pie. Attend or visit area churches and synagogues and take in a movie at the local drive-in. In short, immerse yourself in the area's history, culture, commerce, and religion, and your knowledge will lead you to become a more effective storyteller.

SEE BEYOND THE OBVIOUS

Every day, journalists reaffirm that viewers will never care more about a story than the reporter. If you can find a new way to cover the routine story, even those you have covered repeatedly over the years, then it will be more interesting and memorable for your audience.

"It's the Boy Scout motto, 'Be Prepared,'" says Art Donahue, whose awards include National Television News Photographer of the Year. "Make things look a little more interesting; try to think of everyday stories in a different way, not just as a standup and two talking heads on every story."[11] Donahue, a master at showing familiar subjects in a new light, once told the story of freeway traffic jams caused by a bridge under repair using only pictures and off-air sound recorded from truckers' CB radio chatter.

SHOW AUDIENCES WHAT THEY MISSED

Your obligation as a visual storyteller is to show viewers what they would have missed, even had they been eyewitnesses to the event. Search for unique story angles that other reporters may have overlooked in their rush to cover the story. While the competition is shooting the smoke and flames at the apartment house fire, look around you. Perhaps you will notice an elderly man next door trying to fight back the fire with a garden hose to save his modest home. The observant looking for a better story seem to encounter such "lucky breaks."

NBC correspondent Bob Dotson notes that after a tornado strikes, reporters seem to gravitate to the governor touring the area to ask how things look. But when Dotson covered the aftermath of a tornado in South Carolina, he found a man even more articulate than the governor. "'Well, it got my teeth, but it didn't get me," the

INTERNATIONAL VIDEO JOURNALISM

Mark Carlson, an Associated Press video journalist based in Brussels, Belgium, says his occupation as a journalist has produced the most rewarding experiences in his life (Figures 12.3 and 12.4). "I have found life to be a lot easier to understand when I listen to other people tell their stories," says Carlson. "I can't count how many times I've had someone lead me on a guided tour of their home after it has been destroyed by a natural disaster. Each time I walk through the ruins, I know that I'm not just telling a story, but sharing someone's life with the world. It is a most awesome responsibility..."[12] Below, Carlson's bio profiles his career from college to the present, and his advice on how to make it all work.

Bio (Excerpted)

I am a videographer, reporter, writer, video editor, producer, assignment editor, travel agent, and accountant for the AP. Video journalists have different responsibilities at different news organizations, but the job is the same everywhere, and it is for one person to do the work of two or three different people.

I began my career as a radio/television news broadcasting student at Southern Illinois University/Carbondale and worked there for WSIU-TV, a PBS affiliate, for four years. In my sophomore year, I also was hired at local ABC affiliate WSIL-TV as a part-time news/sports photographer and worked my way up to a one-man-band TV reporter.

I then moved on to WBIR, the NBC affiliate in Knoxville, TN, as a news/sports photographer. My next job was as a news photographer with the Fox affiliate WITI-TV in Milwaukee, WI.

After working in local TV news for nearly ten years, I began exploring jobs with broader news opportunities, and that's when I accepted the position of video journalist for the Associated Press based in Chicago. In 2010, I transferred to Brussels to cover the capital of Europe as a VJ for the AP.

I have covered the Fort Hood shootings, Gulf of Mexico oil spill, West Virginia coal mine explosion, Virginia Tech shootings, California wildfires, tropical storms, tornados, hurricanes, space shuttle launch, President Gerald Ford's funeral, the 2008 presidential election campaign in 18 states, President Obama's inauguration, Beijing and Vancouver Olympics, Super Bowls, World Series, Kentucky Derby, and Final Fours.

Whenever I go out into the field on an assignment, I am up against network TV crews with endless staff and resources. But that is not intimidating because I perform all of their jobs faster, cheaper, and more efficiently.

Everyone has limits on what they can and cannot do. The key to success is maximizing what you can do within those limits. Journalism is a business of competition. How does one person succeed when the competition is a crew of multiple people doing the same thing? Well, you have to figure out ways to force the competition to compete against your strengths.

—Mark Carlson ∎

FIGURE 12.3

Video Journalist Mark Carlson on assignment to cover the Beijing Olympics.

Copyright © 2012 Mark D. Carlson

FIGURE 12.4

Video Journalist Mark Carlson, covering the presidential campaign, appears on camera in addition to reporting, shooting, writing, and editing the story on his own.

Copyright © 2012 Mark D. Carlson

man said. And he reached down in the debris and held up his mud-covered dentures. "This guy crystallized it for me," says Dotson.[13]

HELP VIEWERS EXPERIENCE THE STORY AS YOU DID

Our hopes and dreams, our victories, failures, and despair, and our love, our loneliness, and faith, are woven within each of us from life's complex fabric. We swim in a sea of commonality. A decade into the new millennium, about a billion people worldwide watched[14] as rescuers pulled 33 trapped miners to safety following a mine collapse in Chile. One in every six or seven people on earth watched the unfolding story because we empathized with those miners. Their story addressed what we all feel in common about life, freedom, and wanting to see for ourselves how the story would end.

Any time you work on a news report, a reality program, or even an on-camera interview, try to stuff human experience into your work—a reconstruction of what it was like to be there. You can conduct interviews while your subjects remain focused on a familiar task in a familiar environment, perhaps talking to a tow truck driver about to repossess another luxury car in a down economy. At every turn, the key is to look for meaningful detail and capture it in images and sound that help illuminate the story subject's life, situation, passions, and struggles.

Even adding storytelling elements to straight news reports can make facts more interesting and compelling to watch and build loyalty toward those that offer such content. Those little extra details can elevate viewer experience and help viewers better understand, remember, and relate to story content.

Gary Reaves (Figure 12.5), as senior reporter at WFAA-TV, Dallas, told the story of a woman whose 13-year-old daughter died in a ski accident. The victim's mother hoped someday to meet the person who received her daughter's heart. One day on the

FIGURE 12.5

Gary Reaves, CBS News and WFAA, Dallas, looks for ways to help viewers relate to what they see in his stories.

Copyright © 2012 by Bernestine Singley

Internet she located the woman, a 40-year-old nurse whose heart began to fail after her second child's birth.

When the teen's mother and the heart recipient finally met and hugged one another, photojournalist Chris Mathis was recording video while reporter Gary Reaves stayed out of sight in an adjoining room. Later, back at WFAA, Reaves finished his script and handed it off to video editor Robert Hall, who created a visual and auditory narrative from that most human language of tears, hugs, and silences. On home screens, those moments conveyed a tangible sense of what each woman must be experiencing—grief and joy mingling in shared understanding for how one lost life could enable life in another. An equally poignant moment followed when the heart recipient, a nurse, handed the mother a stethoscope. Holding the scope to her ears, the mother listened to her late daughter's heart beating strong and steady in the nurse's chest.[15]

"On a story like that, I know from the beginning that the big payoff will come at the end. I'm trying from the first word to get viewers to the point that they feel like they are in the room with two people they care about," says Reaves. "At that point, I want to get out of the way, and let them experience it the same way I did. (Well, actually, I was in the next room peeking around the corner trying to stay out of the shot . . . but you get the point.)"[16]

ABC World News rebroadcast Reaves' report nationally to offer insights about organ donation from the viewpoints of the donor family and recipient.[17] Imagine the power of the medium whenever viewers, too, can hear that healthy heart beating away in a stranger's chest, or any other legitimate sound that helps viewers "see with their ears."

BOX 12.3 A CONVERSATION WITH GARY REAVES

How do you describe the difference between reporting and storytelling?

Reporting is gathering and confirming information, and working at it until you have all the essential facts.

Storytelling is how you convey that information and how you make it meaningful to your audience.

I want viewers to understand and remember my stories. But I also rewrite my video stories for the web. I find it more difficult to create images off a flat piece of paper—that video script I created to tell the story with video, audio, and where I position them. I have great admiration for anyone who can convert video and sound into a compelling print or web story and make it look easy.

Then in one sense, storytelling is choosing the elements that best convey that story. Say, for example, you cover city government. What elements might turn a dull news conference with the mayor into a story that viewers will talk about the next day?

At a news conference, while everybody else is recording what the mayor says, I might turn around and look for someone in the audience. Chances are my viewers can relate to the guy with the problem and how he talks, more than to the mayor who only speaks to the problem in calculated language. As the reporter and writer, I can still define the issue and why it matters, but I can convey its essence most powerfully through a guy who looks and talks more like our viewers.

Media observers have said that print media report first to the intellect, video first to the heart, meaning it affects viewers emotionally. Many journalists try to eliminate emotion from their stories, believing it somehow biases their work. When and how do you use emotion as an element in fair and accurate visual storytelling?

In some way all stories are about people, and all people respond in some way to significant events in their lives. It's not only anger or fear. It might be joy, grief, humor, cowardice, or disdain—any legitimate human emotion that fairly lends insight and meaning to my reporting.

Your story has to connect with viewers. Any reaction to the story is better than no reaction. I want my viewers to watch and understand, and somehow relate to what they see. Otherwise, they're only waiting for the next reporter's story, or turning away altogether.

—A Conversation with Gary Reaves[18]
CBS News, WFAA Dallas ■

ADAPT YOUR REPORTING TO STORY DEMANDS

Unthinking enslavement to pictures can be just as devastating as an unreasonable loyalty to words. Strong storytelling demands that the most effective communication methods be used from moment to moment. If pictures and natural sound can best tell the story, then use them. If the story can more effectively be told through a reporter, with graphics, or through silence, then shape the story accordingly.

REPORTING THE NONVISUAL STORY

Many of the stories you are assigned will be static and nonvisual, unless you can find a way to make them move. Into this category fall city council meetings, public hearings, empty fields to be used as major building sites, and vacant buildings that have just been designated as historical landmarks. To lend essential movement and interest to such reports, several approaches can help:

- Look for preshot video, file film, and old newsreels, which show the subject in action.
- Look for life and for things that move in the scene, be they rippling flags, flying birds, or people riding by on bicycles.
- Research the story so that you have a more complete idea of the story's visual potential.
- Try to humanize the story by focusing on people, people-related subjects, or symbols of people and how they live. (In the aftermath of a house fire, perhaps the close-up of a charred photo album can remind us that fire touched people like ourselves.)
- Find a hook for the nonvisual story. Try to relate this event to a larger event or to an existing interest or issue.
- Shoot and use sequences in your report: To see is to believe, but to see sequentially is to experience.
- Use art, models, or, if ethically warranted, recreations.
- Pick out the main issue and do a story on that.
- Use digital video effects (DVE), as CBS once used in the story of a man's death after a police dispatcher had refused to send an ambulance. Through the use of a squeeze zoom, a freeze frame of the victim's house was shown on one side of the screen; a still shot of the dispatcher was shown to the other side of the frame. A graphic artist connected the two images with renderings of transmitted signals as viewers listened to a recording of the fateful interchange.
- Work a reporter standup into the story, preferably as a sequence.
- Create imagery in the mind's eye through sound.
- Write to create imagery.
- Touch feelings through little surprises and moments of real-life drama.

- Use innovative lighting that helps define the story's mood and environment.
- Pitch reporting opportunities to people in the news—let them define and describe their environment, the event, and the moment.
- Shoot pictures that share experience.
- Challenge yourself. Improve your attitude. Remember that your audience will never care more about the story than you do.

PERSONAL APPEARANCE AND CONDUCT

Whenever you are in public, you not only represent the organization for which you work, in many ways you are the organization. How you conduct yourself and how you dress can influence not only how the community thinks of your station, but even the quality of your stories. "You can gain access to stories or be denied access, based on how you dress," says Rich Clarkson, former photographic director of *National Geographic.*[19]

Some TV stations and corporate or community organizations provide reporters and anchors with a wardrobe allowance because they believe personal appearance and station image matter. But aside from the typical jackets, caps, and golf shirts that display the company logo, photojournalists rarely receive such benefits. If the photographer ruins clothes covering a story, stations may pay the cleaning bills or replacement costs. If the station refuses to pay the cost, consider paying it yourself to maintain your own standards of appearance.

ETIQUETTE

Reporters around the country have made a name for themselves as pushy, rude, and aggressive. Deservedly or not, the public sometimes thinks of journalists as uncaring and unsympathetic. Competition and deadline pressures are partly to blame, but sometimes the problem can be a simple lack of sensitivity.

At funerals, or in similar stories that involve death or illness, first seek the family's permission before you shoot any video or conduct interviews. As you cover the story, conduct yourself according to the considerations you would expect from a reporter or photographer if this were your family. Dress appropriately for the occasion and try to shoot the story with a longer lens to remain as far away and inconspicuous as you can.

SHOOTING AND REPORTING SPOT NEWS

Covering **spot-news** or other events beyond your control is almost an art form in itself. The following discussion offers guidelines that can help you transform chaos into good storytelling.

Seconds Count

Timing can be everything when you cover spot news. Those first on the scene usually get the best video and the most awards for spot-news coverage. Early on, people are still excited (and exciting) and events are still happening.

Learn to Shoot by Instinct

Equipment familiarity is essential if you are to develop an instinct for shooting fast-moving events. The equipment should become such a natural extension of yourself that your reactions are automatic; you don't have to stop and think about it. Practice makes perfect. During lulls in the news day, practice rack-focusing from one object to another. Imagine shots. Think about how to cover stories, even when you're at home sitting in the easy chair. And learn to listen when the interviewee speaks so you'll know whether to move in for a close shot or pull back for a shot of the speaker's husband.

Be Ready

The Scout motto "Be prepared" is the first rule in shooting and reporting uncontrolled events. That means having batteries that are charged and connected to the camera, recording media loaded and cued, camera white-balanced, and the mind switched to "think." One photojournalist is said to have photographed five planes crashing, over the course of his career, because he's always ready.

Avoid "Sticks"

When you shoot spot news, tripods are impractical. Get off the tripod and shoot handheld, but remember the rules that affect handholding: Don't handhold on telephoto; to minimize shakiness, consider leaving the lens on wide angle; determine the near plane of focus for the lens you are using and don't go closer to your subjects than that distance.

Anticipate

Covering spot news means working ahead in your mind and asking what you will need to shoot next. Although no rehearsals are possible when you shoot spot news, you can try to understand in advance what is likely to happen or to imagine what may happen. "If you see something you like you've probably missed it," says freelance photographer Darrell Barton. "Don't think with the camera on, think before you turn it on."[20]

Shoot the Essentials First

Shoot the essentials first when you cover spot news; you can't go back and ask for retakes. As you shoot, edit in your head. Previsualize and shoot what you know you'll need. Think of three shots at a time: the shot you're taking, the shot you just took, and the shot you'll take next. Remember to shoot reactions. Pick up cutaways and other shots after the event.

Shoot Sequences

Shoot sequences, especially on spot news, or you'll wind up with a slide show. You can't always shoot spot news sequentially, but you can create the illusion of sequences by shooting one firefighter's face, another firefighter's hands, and yet another firefighter's feet. Or you can photograph a basketball player shooting the ball, then cut to a CU of a basketball photographed at another time during the game as it goes through the hoop. You also can "snap zoom" while you're shooting, as discussed in Chapter 2 (a long shot, for example, followed by an instant zoom to a medium shot or a close-up). During editing, the few frames of the snap zoom can be eliminated from the scene to create the illusion of a three- or four-shot sequence.

Tell a Story through People

Impose a theme on your story. Good spot-news coverage is partly a product of the journalist's ability to show the human effects of an event. And although you don't control the event, you can shoot the essential scenes and sounds that reflect the event in meaningful symbols. Look for shots that tell us how the event affected people: the charred luggage at a plane crash, improperly installed electrical wiring at a mobile home fire, or perhaps the photograph of a child now the subject of a mountain search and rescue.

Be Considerate of Authorities at the Scene

It's the old saying that you can catch more flies with honey than with vinegar. If an official won't let you into the scene of a spot-news event, try to talk your way in. Sometimes you can begin to shoot without permission—and continue to shoot—with a statement to the police/fire/military authorities as simple as, "Let me know if I get in your way." Such a statement implies you're willing to cooperate with those in charge, and sometimes that's all they need to hear. A word of warning: Don't be intimidated; don't be shooed away from the event too easily. Many of the best scenes may occur soon after you have been told to go home.

Be Considerate of People in Spot-News Events

Spot-news subjects, be they mine rescue workers or helicopter pilots, are under intense pressure and stress. They may be experiencing grief; they may be in physical shock. Learn to "read" the physical and psychological signs of stress and fatigue to know when it's best to stop pushing.

People in spot-news events are less aware of the camera than they would be in slower-moving stories. Often, the reporting crew is the last thing on the minds of victims caught up in tragedy or in emotional, stressful events. Sometimes they will remain unaware of your presence, until someone tells them days or months later that you covered the story. Still, to avoid upsetting people, don't crowd or otherwise violate their personal space, but do work to get good close-ups, and remember to treat people—and their privacy, dignity, and emotions—the way you would want to be treated in similar circumstances.

Play It Safe

You face risks each time you cover spot news. You may encounter downed power lines, smoke, dioxin, asbestos, PCBs, bare electrical wires, high water, toxic spills and chemicals, heat, fire, cold, high winds, explosions, falling walls, ice, and people with knives, guns, and explosives. And if those don't get you, you can even be run over by a parade float while you're shooting a cutaway of the onlookers.

Carry everything you will need to cover the story, because you may be unable to return to the vehicle or helicopter for spare recording media, a first aid kit, protective clothing, a change of clothes, food, or adequate lights for night shooting. Be prepared, and remember: No story is worth your life.

Don't Try to Be an Emotional Superperson

Some spot-news and similar events are so gruesome and unimaginable they can affect you more than you might realize or admit. Such conditions are no different than soldiers returning from the battlefield with posttraumatic stress disorder. So be conscious of your feelings, and if necessary, talk them out with somebody who understands what you've gone through. Otherwise, those experiences and memories could build up and someday overwhelm you.

Remember Good Taste

When you report spot news, show what is appropriate and nothing more. You may decide to show only a recent photo of a drowning victim rather than the covered body or a very long shot of a resuscitation effort rather than close shots. Some shots, such as a sequence of someone putting a gun into his mouth and pulling the trigger, should never make air. How does one know whether to record such footage? Some journalists make the shot, regardless of content, then decide later whether it should be aired, or else leave the decision to the producer, anchor, managing editor, or news director. Although the practice of "shoot now, decide later," often is valid, it can lead to charges of invasion of privacy and other legal entanglements (see Chapter 14, Law and the Video Journalist). Often, the best response in such situations is to follow the adage, "If you don't want it on air, don't shoot it." The competition may air shots you consciously chose not to make, but remember propriety and its role in helping you protect your credibility and the community's respect.

TOWARD A NEWS PHILOSOPHY

In the past, video reporters and storytellers have commonly defined their job as information gathering and delivery. "We deliver the information; it's up to the audience to understand," the reasoning went. Journalists could practice such elitism in the days when viewing options were limited. But today, audiences have gained control of the medium. Viewers with computers, smartphones, tablets, mobile satellite dishes, cable- and wireless-streaming TV and digital video recorders even control the program schedule. They decide whom they will watch, when, where, for how long, and on what platforms. When stories are powerful, compelling, and engaging, viewers may stick around to watch. They seldom watch dull, routine, or predictable stories. As always, the heart of captivating video remains the story, with true celebrity achieved only by mastering the visual communications process.

SUMMARY

The most successful journalists produce reports and stories that appeal to audiences, regardless of the story's subject matter. Improving storytelling ability is a gradual process of learning to do the routine things extraordinarily well time after time. Whereas some journalists seek perfection in their work, a more feasible alternative is to seek excellence.

Because storytellers need stories, a good approach is to summarize the story to be told in a simple, declarative sentence, which photojournalists call their commitment or focus statement. Once the focus or commitment is defined, the storyteller, even in journalism, must look for elements of opposition or conflict. Active conflict, such as a person's drive to overcome a handicap or fight illiteracy, helps illuminate the essence of individuals and even communities. Not every story contains conflict; some stories are merely accounts or announcements of events and fall outside this discussion.

As a photojournalist, avoid excuses. Audiences can judge your work only by what you put on the screen. Some excuses are legitimate, but they can too easily become alibis. Strong storytellers try to show familiar subjects in a new light. Some even succeed in showing viewers familiar with a subject what they have overlooked. In such endeavors, the more the camera is involved in the action, the more realistic the story will be.

Other devices to strengthen the storytelling effort include telling the story through people, the use of matched-action sequences, and narrowing story focus to a manageable level. As John Grierson, the British documentarian, observed, while newspapers can tell the story of the entire mail service, moving images are often at their best when they tell the story of a single letter.

Although words are crucial to the storytelling process, too many words can overwhelm a report. Use words, pictures, sounds, and silences sometimes by themselves, sometimes together—in whatever combinations best tell the story. Through such dedication, even so-called nonvisual stories can be made compelling and interesting.

Many of the same considerations apply to spot-news reporting, with the important proviso that reporters and photographers must anticipate fast-developing action and be extraordinarily conscious of personal safety. In the course of all conduct, television journalists are public figures. Their actions reflect not only on themselves, but also on their employers and their profession.

KEY TERMS

assignment editor 199	focus 199	sequential video 199
commitment 199	illustrative video 200	spot news 210

DISCUSSION

1. Discuss steps the photojournalist can take to make the style and substance of news stories more appealing while still preserving the story's fundamental accuracy and integrity.
2. What is the difference between excellence and perfection in the reporting process? Which of these options is the wiser pursuit?
3. Explain why it is important to identify the story you're reporting and to state it aloud, or at least sum up the story in your mind, before the reporting process begins.
4. Why is communication between the reporter and photographer so vital throughout the reporting process?
5. Discuss the role of conflict in storytelling and how the concept applies to television news stories.
6. When excuses become a habit, a way of life almost, they can erode the photojournalist's ability to produce work of consistent excellence. Identify the attitudes and personal practices that can help you avoid making excuses about your work.
7. Identify a half-dozen or more activities that can help you learn more about your community. Explain why those activities are important to help make you a better reporter, photographer, or storyteller.
8. What steps can you, as a photojournalist, take to show viewers what they might have missed, even had they been eyewitnesses to the story you're reporting?
9. Why is it important for the photojournalist to capture and transmit a sense of experience about the story being reported?
10. Discuss the approaches you can follow when you must tell complex stories briefly, yet with power.

11. Why is it important for you to care about the people in your stories, or at least to be interested in them? If you care too much about the people in your reports, can you remain detached and objective when reporting their stories?

12. Describe a good reporting method that can help make viewers watch stories by frequently inviting them to reengage with the television screen.

13. Discuss ways you can make so-called nonvisual stories more visually appealing and informative.

14. Photographers have to work in all manner of environments and weather extremes, so to what extent should they have to maintain a well-groomed, well-dressed appearance in public? As part of your answer, describe the proper attire that you believe a photographer or video journalist normally should wear on field assignment.

15. Describe effective reporting practices and considerations for personal safety when covering spot-news stories.

16. When all is said and done, what is the journalist's most important obligation in reporting the news?

EXERCISES

1. To help improve your ability to develop focus or commitment statements, choose a very simple object or phenomenon, such as a pumpkin, a Christmas tree ornament, or a spring breeze, and identify a focus statement that will help you generate a visual story about the subject. Example: "The spring breeze is a trash collector." Next, identify two or three main points you want to communicate about the subject and find visual proof for those main points. In a story centered on a car wash, for example, a main point might be, "Every time you clean something, you make something else dirty."

2. Find an ordinary subject and strive to make it more appealing through your lighting, audio, photography, or reporting.

3. Construct a television story that uses only pictures and sounds, but no voice-over narration, to tell a visual story complete with beginning, middle, and ending.

4. Study books, films, and compelling stories for the presence of conflict. Analyze the role of conflict in storytelling.

5. Take a fresh look at the community in which you live. Learn more about the area's history, culture, commerce, and religions. If you can do so safely, jog or take walks through areas of the community that are unfamiliar to you. Find a story to photograph and report based on your new awareness of some aspect of the community and its people.

6. Take a complex subject such as the issues that surround no-smoking ordinances and shoot two or three simple reports that illustrate the principle that "you can write an article about the mail service, but you must make a film about a single letter."

7. Write a script to accompany a story you have photographed and/or reported that constantly reengages viewers with the screen. Use phrases such as, "Be sure to include one of these in your backpack," rather than "Be sure to take a compass."

8. Choose a "nonvisual" story subject, such as a historic cabin or other building in your community that is open for public tours. Strive to make your photography and reporting about the subject powerful, compelling, and engaging.

9. Study spot-news stories for evidence of the video journalist's or reporting team's ability to tell such events through people. Note how often sequences are present in the spot-news stories you view. If sequences were absent, would they have been possible to photograph?

11. Interview police, fire, or sheriff's authorities and inquire about their greatest frustrations when working with video reporters and photographers.

12. Visit a federal, state, or local environmental safety official and learn more about toxic chemicals and other environmental hazards you can expect to encounter during spot-news coverage.

NOTES

1. Edward Dmytryk, *On Film Editing* (Stoneham, MA: Focal Press, 1984), 78.
2. Remarks at the NPPA TV News-Video Workshop, Norman, OK, March 17, 2003.
3. Interview with the author, Fort Collins, CO, April 26, 1981.
4. Larry Hatteberg, "People-Oriented photojournalism," a presentation at the NPPA TV News-Video Workshop, Norman, OK, March 18, 1986.
5. Tim Fisher, "Television Is a Trust," *News Photographer* (November 1984), 21.
6. Dmytryk, *On Film Editing*, 79.
7. Richard Schickel, "A Superb Passage to India," *Time* (December 31, 1984), 55.
8. Robert J. Samuelson, "Long Live the News Business," *Newsweek* (May 28, 2007), 40.
9. Glen Dickson, "Newsrooms Go Multiplatform," *Broadcasting & Cable*, March 26, 2007, www.broadcastingcable.com/.
10. A newsroom memo from Jim Prather, then news director, KRIS-TV, Corpus Christi, TX, January 1986.
11. Art Donahue, "Utilizing a Creative Eye for Everyday Assignments," a presentation at the NPPA TV News-Video Workshop, Norman, OK, March 21, 1986.
12. Mark Carlson, in e-mail comments and bio to the lead author, January 11, 2011.
13. Bob Dotson, 2003
14. MSNBC, cited by Joanne Ostrow, "Uplifting TV moment for viewers worldwide," Denver Post, October 14, 2010, http://www.denverpost.com/television/ci_16324297 (Downloaded October 14, 2010).
15. Gary Reaves, "Heartbeat brings joy to parents of Coppell donor," http://www.wfaa .com/news/taylors-gift-103409364.html (downloaded Oct 5, 2010).
16. Gary Reaves, written comments in an e-mail to the author, October 6, 2010.
17. http://abcnews.go.com/WNT/video/american-heart-mothers-heartbeat-transplant-donor-organ-diane-sawyer-gary-reeves-11714682 (downloaded October 5, 2010. Aired on ABC World News September 23, 2010. Video runs 2:24.).
18. Excerpts from a telephone conversation with the primary author, October 12, 2010.
19. Rich Clarkson, "TV News Photographers as Professionals—Some Believe You Have a Long Way to Go," a presentation at the NPPA TV News-Video Workshop, Norman, OK, March 21, 1986.
20. Darrell Barton, "Connects to Journalism Students at the University of Oklahoma," November 5, 2002.

CHAPTER

13

Live Shots and Remotes

—Luan Akin

Television and web audiences frequently become participants in the
reporting process, sometimes as knowledgeable about the developing
story as the field reporter. This chapter details the live reporting process,
tells how to organize and write the story in the field, and examines the
traits and abilities that help make television and web reporters "live
capable." (Figure 13.1)

I never will understand why I didn't spot the tornado myself. Denver's forecast on this
June day called for severe weather—heavy rain, lightning, hail, and possible tornadoes.
That meant the helicopter crew of pilot Mike Silva, photographer David Gregg, and I
would be chasing storms. Only this time, the storm found us.

As I drove to the airport, the cloud layer overhead clamped down on the city, growing
darker, lower, and more ominous. I caught up with Mike and David as they half-walked,
half-ran to the helicopter. I yelled to Mike that we needed to get in the air right away.
A funnel had been sighted over Denver. Without missing a beat—without even looking
up—Mike jerked his index finger and pointed to the sky. A towering funnel was dead
overhead.

It wasn't large by midwestern standards, but it was the biggest funnel our city had
seen in a long time. It turned out to be one of seven tornadoes that hammered Denver
that afternoon.

For the next four hours, we were part of a "live" marathon. Mike, David, and I did one
shot after another. We were live (from a respectful distance) as a twister snapped power lines
and ripped up huge trees, tossing them half a block away. When we weren't live, other CBS4
crews were. One team on the ground walked viewers through a neighborhood that had been
especially hard-hit. The photographer shot "off the shoulder" as the reporter stepped over

FIGURE 13.1

Luan Akin gained her reputation as a helicopter specialist and general assignment reporter for CBS4-TV, a Denver station owned and operated by CBS. She has originated hundreds of live remotes from virtually every location a news helicopter can fly to, whether high in the Rocky Mountains or even from a bird's-eye view of fierce storms above the high mountain plains. The pilot in this photo is Mike Silva.

downed tree limbs and the live truck engineer helped guide the long run of cable. Yet another crew was going live ten miles away, in a business district that had been torn apart. The shots went round-robin, intermixed with weather bulletins and live up-dates from the newsroom.

It was one of those times when all the teamwork and technology paid off. It was also one of the most grueling afternoons I've had in television. But it was one of the most rewarding, thanks to the challenge of "going live."

WHAT DOES IT TAKE TO "GO LIVE"?

All the general skills important in TV news are doubly important for successful "live" work. Among them are a well-developed vocabulary, good news sense, experience as a general assignment reporter, and strong interviewing skills. They all add up to the ability to tell a story clearly and accurately under what can be chaotic conditions (see Figure 13.2). But perhaps the single most important skill in a good live reporter is a knack for writing and talking conversationally. Many reporters make the job of going live much more difficult than it needs to be. They try so hard to look and sound serious and professional, and end up sounding stuffy and awkward.

If you're in the habit of writing conversationally, telling stories in a simple, straightforward style, you'll find it much easier to talk that way, too. Short sentences

FIGURE 13.2
Live reporting requires the ability to write and speak conversationally and to tell the story clearly and accurately under field conditions.

filled with everyday words can help your audience understand even the most complicated story.

SPOT NEWS

"Spot news" and "live shots"— they go together like ham 'n eggs. To less-experienced reporters, going live from the scene of a breaking news story can seem like trial by fire, but developing a system of your own can help tame the madness. It's a matter of knowing what to expect. We'll take it from the top.

Gather as You Go

The wheeler-dealers of the world are always telling us time is money. But if you're on your way to a spot-news story, time is information, or at least it should be. You can't afford to wait until you arrive on scene before you begin asking questions.

There are all kinds of information-gathering possibilities in the average news van. The two-way radio and mobile phone are good examples. Often, the assignment desk or someone else at news base hears about the story first and lets you know that all heck's breaking loose somewhere. Make good use of your mobile phone, but coordinate with your newsroom. Avoid duplicating calls to the same sources, such as police dispatchers. Stations that make a habit of that may find the dispatchers are less patient or cooperative during future emergencies.

Scanners can be especially helpful as you're racing to the scene of a breaking story. Lock out (eliminate from the scan) all frequencies except those carrying radio traffic relating to the story you're working on. Handle the information you hear on scanners carefully. Treat the information as fact only after you or someone in your newsroom has verified it. And always be careful to attribute what you're reporting to the appropriate source. My helicopter crew and I once were dispatched based on the following scanner traffic:

> "A DEAD HIPPOPOTAMUS HAS BEEN SPOTTED ON THE SHOULDER OF PEÑA BOULEVARD NEAR DENVER INTERNATIONAL AIRPORT . . ."

Clearly, this one required a bit of skepticism. Fortunately, as we flew toward the scene, what I reported was:

"POLICE SAY A MOTORIST CLAIMS THERE'S A DEAD HIPPOPOTAMUS ON THE SHOULDER OF PEÑA BOULEVARD NEAR DENVER INTERNATIONAL AIRPORT..."

It turned out to be a cow...apparently, a rather unattractive cow.

Don't forget to listen to "the competition" (competing radio or TV stations) as you head toward a spot-news story. You can bet they'll be listening to you. If you think you're on to something they haven't heard about yet, be careful how much you say on two-way.

TV and web reporters can monitor radio stations with the best news departments in their market. Updates or cut-ins from those stations can provide still more background information. Just remember that you or someone in your newsroom needs to confirm that information before you use it.

Immediacy versus Information

Once on scene, one of the first issues to deal with is obvious: When is your newsroom expecting you to go live? If the story involves a threat or major inconvenience to the public, news reporters are obligated to get the information out as quickly as possible. But what if the situation is less urgent? Newcomers to news might assume it's standard procedure to spend several minutes at the scene gathering vast amounts of information before the first live report. Not necessarily.

Sometimes uncertainty is the price of instant news. The news business is especially competitive. There can be lots of pressure to be first with a breaking story. That's when you may have to fall back on the adage: "Go with what you have."

By the time radio reporters reach a breaking news story, they may have already gone live over the two-way radio or a mobile phone. TV helicopter crews face the same challenge—heading toward a scene and going live at the same time with little information. Reporters with TV ground crews may be expected to jump out of their car

---

BOX 13.1   LIVE/REPORTER INTROS

One of the first things a reporter should do at the "top" or beginning of a live shot is clarify the location of the scene. Some stories might require only a general description of the location:

"WE'RE HERE NEAR THE BASE OF SUGARLOAF MOUNTAIN WHERE FIREFIGHTERS SAY THEY'RE GETTING THE UPPER HAND ON THIS WILDFIRE . . ."

If a newsworthy element of the story involves a specific location, the reporter should make that location clear.

"WE'RE ON LOST ANGEL DRIVE NEAR THE SUMMIT OF SUGARLOAF MOUNTAIN. FIREFIGHTERS NOW TELL US THE WILDFIRE HAS DESTROYED EVERY HOME ALONG THIS HALF-MILE ROAD."

If a specific location is newsworthy, it's important to make sure the audience is told just where that location is. Any crossroll (video run within a live shot) the reporter is using also will need graphics. If the scene of the live shot is the same location as the first video in the crossroll, there may be no need to repeat the locator graphic. If there's room for confusion, don't hesitate to list the location twice. ■

and step up to the camera, ready to present whatever information has been gathered en route to the scene. Reporters should have the right to postpone a live shot if for any reason they don't trust the information they've been given. But don't assume you need to have every detail down pat before a live shot is justified.

In fast-breaking stories, where initial information is thin and there's pressure to go live right away, let these two simple rules of thumb be your guide:

GUIDELINE #1: TELL THE AUDIENCE WHAT YOU KNOW   It sounds obvious, but you'd be surprised how easy it is to overlook information right in front of you.

- Where are you? Use a specific address only if it's pertinent to the story. Otherwise, use a junction or landmark that viewers or listeners will recognize.
- What's happened? Perhaps a body's been found. Or a building's on fire. Or a child appears to have fallen through thin ice. At the very least, you should be able to explain what type of call or alarm brought emergency crews to the scene.
- What can you see from your vantage point? Clearly, radio reporters routinely have to help their listeners visualize the scene. But even with the added benefit of live pictures, TV reporters need to remember that viewers will see only what the camera can shoot.
- Describe the broader picture outside that TV frame: the effect of freezing weather on firefighting equipment, or a traffic jam caused by police cars blocking access to a murder scene. Just be careful what conclusions you draw from those observations. In the chaos of a rapidly unfolding story, it's easy to add 2 + 2 and get 5.
- Be careful to qualify what you say, especially when the information is sketchy. Make liberal use of terms such as "still unclear," "at this time…," and "unconfirmed reports."

GUIDELINE #2: TELL THE AUDIENCE WHAT YOU DON'T KNOW   More precisely, acknowledge questions the audience might have that you simply can't answer . . . yet. But be sure to tell them you're trying to get the answers, and then get them:

"NO WORD SO FAR ON HOW THIS FIRE BEGAN OR WHETHER ANYONE MAY BE TRAPPED INSIDE…"

or

"FOR NOW, THERE'S NO INDICATION WHERE THE CHILD'S PARENTS WERE WHEN THE LITTLE BOY WANDERED OFF AND FELL THROUGH THE ICE…"

Acknowledging unanswered questions is far better than having your audience assume you've overlooked important parts of the story.

Hit the Ground Running

If the spot-news story is slightly less chaotic than the scenes described, then hopefully you've arrived with several questions already answered. For example, is there a command post, and if so, where? In larger towns and cities, many police and fire departments are becoming increasingly sophisticated in their dealings with the media. During emergencies, these agencies will often establish a **command post**, an on-scene headquarters, and have a designated **PIO** or Public Information Officer available there. That person's duties include gathering information for news reporters.

An effective PIO is especially important when the media is kept at a distance—outside a roped-off murder scene or at a dangerous fire. If they're willing, PIOs can help clear the way for better access to a story, arranging to help TV photographers move in briefly for closer pictures of the scene. The command post is often the best place to send TV microwave or satellite trucks, at least in the early stages of a breaking story. That will put the TV crew closest to the PIO, a vital source of information.

Remember that the command post, indeed, the general scene of the spot-news event, may not be the only scene your station needs to cover. Try to determine what other locations are important to the story, locations that another news crew should check out. Examples would be a hospital where the injured are being taken or a staging area where people have been told they can wait for an "all clear."

Although PIOs can be valuable, no self-respecting reporter will be satisfied with only the "official" information such a spokesperson provides. Be on the lookout for other sources of information: neighbors who might have known the murder victim, an angler who may have seen the now-missing child playing near the water's edge.

Look for People "Once Removed"

In the next section we'll talk about live interviews with people such as eyewitnesses and bystanders. For now, just remember to pay attention not only to the obvious players in the story, whether the emergency command personnel or the immediate victims of a crime, but also to the people "once removed." They may be the men and women actually fighting the fire or the neighbors who used to babysit for the children who have apparently died in that fire. If time permits, and the people are willing, record an interview. It's a lot safer than assuming you'll be able to find them later.

TELEVISION LIVE SHOT FORMATS

Creativity as much as technology limits the "look" of TV live shots, even spot-news live shots where the pace is fast and furious. Live reports can be broadcast in several formats, but often, if time permits, you can enhance the live shot's production value by combining parts and pieces of different formats. The point isn't to set a new world record on the number of roll cues needed within one ninety-second live shot. The goal is to use different elements to communicate more information more effectively. Just as an entire newscast needs to be produced with attention to production techniques and pacing, live shots should have a "finished" look, too.

"Blue Eyes," "Naked Live," or "Thumb Suckers"

As unappealing as they may sound, these TV slang terms all refer to remotes that have no **crossroll**, no video or interviews within the shot. It's just the reporter and his or her imagination. So let's put that imagination to work. One of the best reasons to go live is to make the viewer an eyewitness to a story as it unfolds. If the scene has a lot of different elements, why not take the viewers on a tour?

Say you're doing a live shot on a winter storm that's dumped two feet of snow on the city. Don't just stand there! Ask the photographer to shoot off the shoulder if necessary. Make sure the photographer understands what you plan to do, and which direction you'll be going so you'll be framed properly in the shot. Then walk around in this knee-deep snow, live. Dig through what appears to be a snowdrift and uncover a mailbox. Measure the snow depth. Give the viewers the feeling they're right there, standing in the snow next to you.

Wireless lavaliere microphones are ideal for this kind of walking shot, but even a lavaliere hardwired to the truck will work. Lavs leave your hands free to handle your notes, or gesture and refer to the scene around you. You might also want to use a hand prop, something pertinent to the scene, that helps put the story into better perspective. Just don't get carried away; it's important to get to the video quickly. Remember, pacing within a live shot is just as important as pacing within the overall newscast.

As long as noise levels permit, lavalieres are usually better than stick mikes for all TV live reports. One clear exception is remotes with live interviews, which takes us to our next topic.

Live Interviews

If you like a good challenge, you'll love live interviews at the scene of a breaking news story. Live "Q and A" with officials will generally go one of two ways:

1. Either they're comfortable dealing with the press and know they should give fairly short, straightforward answers, or
2. They lapse into "officialese," and talk about "extricating" people instead of freeing them, or "extinguishing the blaze" instead of putting out the fire.

Try to talk with the person first, well before you're both in front of a live camera or microphone. Get a sense of what to expect, and whether a live interview would help your coverage or hurt it. Give the person an idea of how much time you have for the live interview, and in general, what subjects you plan to cover. During the interview itself, listen carefully to their answers. Don't be so focused on your next question that you miss an important detail worth pursuing.

If your live interview is with an eyewitness or bystander, be especially careful. You could have a loose cannon in your midst and not know it until it's too late. And there's always the chance the most talkative person off camera will freeze or revert to one-word answers as soon as the live shot begins.

Avoid using lavaliere microphones during live interviews. When you're holding the mike, you have more control over what happens. You may want to record the interview for use later. Discuss your plans with your photographer, too, so he or she can zoom in for tighter shots if time allows.

Say the person's name and relationship to the story at the beginning and end of the live interview. And don't forget to give that same information to your producer so a **key** (words on graphics electronically inserted into the video scene) can be ordered to superimpose the person's name at the bottom of the screen during the live shot. If you want your photographer to remain wide, on a **two shot** (a shot that shows two people in the frame), tell your producer whether the person's name and title should be superimposed screen right or left.

Live/VTR VO/Live (Live/Voice-Over-Video/Live)

At last! Let's get some video into this live shot! With a little planning, it's amazing how quickly video shot at the scene of a breaking news story can be "turned around" and appear as crossroll just minutes later. One trick is for photographers to "edit in the camera." Shoot the basics: wide, medium, tight—clean, simple shots that can be microwaved or streamed back to news base and edited in the same order they were shot.

The use of crossroll comes at a price. It means the reporter's job just became more complicated. Now, the producer is going to need specific cues: three- or four-word phrases that indicate when the reporter wants the video crossroll to start and stop. The "roll cue" is the cue to start the video. The "cue back to remote" is the cue for the director to switch back to the remote camera, that is, the camera shooting the live shot.

Be precise with your roll cues. If you get sloppy or paraphrase them, the producer and director might miss them, and the crossroll may never run. To make sure you don't forget the cue or change it accidentally, write it down if necessary so you can refer to it during the live shot. If your intro includes detailed facts or figures, write those down, too. Otherwise, try to avoid reading your intro. It can drain the energy and immediacy right out of the shot.

Reference Video in the Live Shot

One of the first rules of writing for television news is to "reference your video." Make sure what you're saying complements what the viewers are seeing. That can be tough if you're voicing over video you can't see. If you don't have a TV monitor at your live location, or for any reason you can't see the crossroll, keep your references general. If you want to make specific references to certain shots, you'll need to relay editing instructions based on the script you plan to read.

For example, editing instructions for crossroll at a serious apartment fire might go something like this:

> "OFF THE TOP, GIVE ME EIGHT SECONDS OF THE BEST FLAME FOOTAGE. FOLLOW THAT WITH SIX SECONDS OF FIRE TRUCKS ROLLING ONTO THE SCENE. NEXT, GIVE ME SIX SECONDS OF THE VICTIM BEING LOADED INTO THE AMBULANCE, THEN EIGHT SECONDS OF THE CROWD WATCHING. CLOSE OUT WITH AT LEAST TEN MORE SECONDS OF VARIOUS SHOTS OF THE BURNING BUILDING."

It's a rough outline, but it lets you reference several different visual elements in your crossroll even when you cannot see the video. If the video rolls on cue, you're in business.

Live/VTR VO/SOT/VTR VO/Live (Live/Voice-Over-Video/Sound on Tape/Voice Over/Live)

Ah, the plot thickens! The live shot becomes more complicated, but hopefully more interesting with **SOT** (sound on tape, disc, or hard drive). It may be part of an interview shot earlier with an eyewitness or an official. Or it may be **nats**, natural sound, perhaps a police officer shouting instructions or demonstrators chanting. Natural SOT could even be nonverbal, such as the countdown and explosion at a building demolition.

Let's say you're going live from the scene of a small-plane crash. You've interviewed an eyewitness to the crash, and you want part of that interview, a sound bite, used as crossroll. The editors back at base will need to know what video you want for the voice over going into the bite: general shots of the crash scene, or something more specific, perhaps an ambulance pulling away, then close-up shots of the wreckage. Some stations will edit the VO/SOT/VO onto one tape or other video source. Some stations will use two sources. The advantages of each method are discussed in Chapter 8, Video Script Formats.

Either way, the editors will need to know how much video to lay down before and after the bite, and which bite to use. It's up to the reporter to supply that information. Assuming time is tight, don't feed significantly more video or sound than you'll need for crossroll. Streamline the process for the editors as much as possible.

Make sure the SOT serves a purpose, and don't forget pacing. Don't take an otherwise high-energy live report and bring it to a screeching halt with a forty-five second sound bite that puts your audience to sleep. Remember, most TV live shots will run from one to two and a half minutes long, including crossroll. Make good use of your time.

Cues for crossroll that includes SOT are the same as cues for voice-over crossroll. Make your roll cue and your cue back to remote clear and specific. Be sure not to duplicate the wording for your cues in other parts of your script. If the video starts or stops at the wrong time, it can be hard to make a graceful recovery.

When necessary, crossroll can consist of SOT alone, with no voice over before or after. In other words, Live/SOT/Live. It's generally not pretty, and you should have a reason for doing it. But if it's important to convey certain information, and if the person giving that information can't or won't give a live interview, SOT alone is an option.

Live/VTR SOT PKG/Live (Live/Video Package/Live)

Thankfully, having to feed back all the elements needed to package a news story isn't as common as it once was. Most satellite trucks and many news vans include editing facilities (Figure 13.3). They are, in effect, extensions of the studio, sometimes requiring the reporter to become reporter/director/producer. Smartphones and tablets with editing capability and a wireless connection can get the job done in a pinch.

By the time a video journalist or news crew gathers enough material to package a story, editing in the field can proceed much as it would at base. If the distance between the scene of the story and the station isn't that far, the piece can be edited back at the station.

Still, for one reason or another, a reporter may sometimes need to feed a narration track and video for an editor to cut back at the station. As the reporter, you can do several things to make that process easier and more efficient.

NARRATION

Once your package script is written, your narration can be fed back live or prerecorded and fed back with the video. When the editor at the station is ready to record the feed, send the track first. Remember, the editor will most likely be working without a written script. By sending the track first, the editor can listen to the track as it's being fed, and become familiar with the story. Once the track's in and the video feed begins, the editor can watch for the people and events you've included in the script.

As you cut the narration, refer to each portion of track between sound bites as "section 1, section 2 . . ." That will help give you a way of referring to the script when it's time to give editing instructions. And just as you do when you record in the audio booth at the station, give a clear 3-2-1 countdown before you begin each section of track.

Note an important exception to the argument that the narration track should be fed first. If time is running out and you have a photographer, the video can be fed in while you're writing the script. Doing two things at once helps ensure that your package makes its slot.

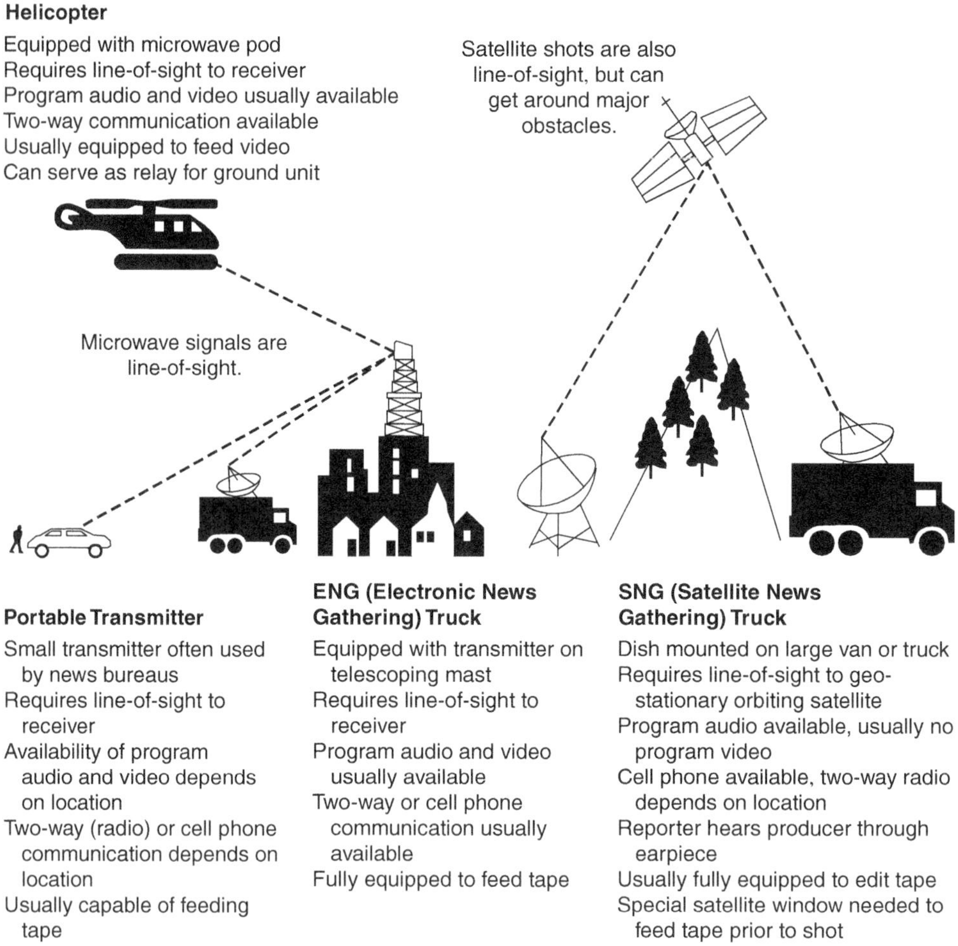

Helicopter

Equipped with microwave pod
Requires line-of-sight to receiver
Program audio and video usually available
Two-way communication available
Usually equipped to feed video
Can serve as relay for ground unit

Satellite shots are also
line-of-sight, but can
get around major
obstacles.

Microwave signals are
line-of-sight.

Portable Transmitter

Small transmitter often used
  by news bureaus
Requires line-of-sight to
  receiver
Availability of program
  audio and video depends
  on location
Two-way (radio) or cell phone
  communication depends on
  location
Usually capable of feeding
  tape

**ENG (Electronic News
Gathering) Truck**

Equipped with transmitter on
  telescoping mast
Requires line-of-sight to
  receiver
Program audio and video
  usually available
Two-way or cell phone
  communication usually
  available
Fully equipped to feed tape

**SNG (Satellite News
Gathering) Truck**

Dish mounted on large van or truck
Requires line-of-sight to geo-
  stationary orbiting satellite
Program audio available, usually no
  program video
Cell phone available, two-way radio
  depends on location
Reporter hears producer through
  earpiece
Usually fully equipped to edit tape
Special satellite window needed to
  feed tape prior to shot

FIGURE 13.3

The method of transmitting the microwave signal to the station affects how the reporter
works in the field. The ability to communicate with the station, and the reporter's access to
"air" or "program" audio and video, can simplify or greatly complicate a live shot.

Sound Bites

Before you feed or record your narration track, make sure you've written within
your script the in-cues and out-cues of the sound bites you plan to use. Then, after
a clean pause in your narration, read the cues as well, giving the speaker's full
name and title for keys or **CGs** (words electronically produced on a computerized
"character generator" and superimposed over a scene). You might even describe
the person so the editor can find the bite more easily. The same guidelines apply to
any natural sound breaks you've called for. Explain within breaks in your narration
which "nats" you want and where they can be found. Don't make the editor's job
harder than it has to be.

Video

You want to make sure the editor has enough video to make the piece look as good as possible, but not so much it overwhelms the editor. Just because your photographer has shot three tapes doesn't mean all three tapes need to be fed for your package.

If possible, talk with the editor on two-way radio or cell phone as the video is being fed. You can describe the scene and the players as you go. Try to point out people and places that require careful referencing (e.g., criminal suspects or the exterior of a home where someone's been found murdered). Saying the right thing over the wrong picture can be disastrous.

If it's impossible to talk to the editor, additional editing instructions can be recorded at the end of the narration track. Again, be as specific as necessary to make sure referencing within the package will be correct.

HELICOPTER LIVE SHOTS

Any live shot format that will work on the ground will work from a helicopter, though some are more cumbersome than others. Shooting, narrating, and feeding an entire package from a helicopter would be awkward, but it's certainly possible. The one exception is the "walking" live shot discussed previously.

When technology allows, live interviews from helicopters can be effective. The interviewee may be on the ground, at a scene where aerials add to the story. For example, a reporter in a helicopter could use audio patched through a cell phone or a two-way radio to interview a firefighter on the line of a forest fire. This technique can also be used when two reporters are covering the same story. The producer can have them "toss" live to one another, air to ground, for example. A news source can also be interviewed live as he or she views the scene from the air. The questions could come from a reporter who's also aboard the helicopter, from a reporter at the scene on the ground, or even from an anchor on set.

During any live shot, it's important to keep in mind the transition between the live shot background and the first video at the top of the crossroll. It can be confusing if the scenes look too similar. This is especially true with helicopter live shots if the photographer is shooting out the window and the crossroll begins with another aerial. Avoid that if possible. At the very least, warn the producer, and ask for a dissolve or another effect to help distinguish between the live remote shot and the video prerecorded.

Because of their mobility, helicopters can often get to the scene of a breaking news story long before a ground crew arrives. Even if aerials are of no value in covering the story, the producer may ask the helicopter crew to go live with whatever tidbits of information are available. In effect, the helicopter crew is simply breaking the story. The challenge for the reporter is to make the aerial perspective of the scene as meaningful as possible, emphasize that a news crew is en route on the ground, and tell audiences that more information should be available shortly.

LIVE IN THE NEWSROOM

With television's emphasis on having a live look, some stations originate entire newscasts from a set in their newsroom. Even more common is a "news desk" in the newsroom, an alternative to the set in the studio. A news desk live shot is an option when producers want a reporter to present a story live but don't have a feasible live location, or don't have the time or technology to make the remote work.

Live shots from the newsroom also may be the best way to bring a late-breaking national story home to local viewers. An example would be a major plane crash in another part of the country. Live updates from the newsroom can be aired throughout the local news show. **Phoners**, live telephone interviews with eyewitnesses or officials on scene, can be dramatic and informative. The phoners can serve as the next best thing until video of the scene is available. The telephone interviews can also run over video that's already in house, with the local anchor or reporter at the news desk asking questions related to the scenes that are showing.

Phoners and their video counterpart, "Skype" interviews, can be an easy way out of investing the time and energy needed to go live at the scene of the story. But they can also be an effective and legitimate way to maintain or reinforce a reporter's identification with a particular story. Crossroll options for a newsroom live shot are the same as for any remote shot.

LIVE GRAPHICS

Stations have different guidelines governing the use of graphics (keys and CGs) during remote broadcasts. But it's standard procedure at many stations to maintain a small "live" graphic in the upper left-hand corner of the picture. Because the graphic may remain on-screen throughout the report, photographers must frame live shots so the graphic doesn't obscure important action. That action might look cluttered and confusing with the word *live* keyed over it.

Remember, the name and title of people being interviewed live should also be relayed to news base. If the live interview will be on a two-shot, make sure the graphics operator knows who will be on which side of the screen.

LIVE/ANCHOR INTROS

The sense of immediacy surrounding a live shot begins with the anchor's introduction or toss. Ideally, the reporter in the field will have written the intro and dictated it to the news base. The most obvious reason for having the reporter write the anchor's intro is accuracy. The reporter, after all, is on the scene. For the most part, writers, producers, and anchors back in the newsroom are getting a distilled version of what's going on. That can leave too much room for error.

When the reporter writes the anchor's intro, it's easier to coordinate information. The flow between the point where the anchor leaves off and the reporter begins is built in, or should be, so the toss from the studio to the field becomes stronger.

Anchor: Some business owners along South Broadway are fuming tonight…angry that city hall has scheduled extensive road construction during the last two weeks of the Christmas shopping season.

Newsfour's Kathy Walsh is live in that shopping district with more on why the store owners there are so mad.

Reporter: BILL, I'M STANDING AT BROADWAY AND CEDAR. BARRICADES LIKE THIS CLOSE THE TWO RIGHT-HAND LANES OF BROADWAY FOR NEARLY HALF A MILE. THAT'S SIX BLOCKS OF STORES…AND DOZENS OF STORE OWNERS…WHO SAY THEIR CUSTOMERS CAN'T FIND A PLACE TO PARK.

The anchor's intro flows logically and smoothly into the reporter's intro. The reporter could strengthen her presentation further by using a wireless mike, walking around the barricades, as the photographer pulls out to a wider shot to show the extent of construction.

Realistically, reporters often don't have time to stop and write an intro for the anchor. The best approach then is for the reporter to suggest information for an intro. That way there can still be a strong transition from the news set to the remote. Reporters who haven't written the anchor's intro, and certainly those who haven't even suggested an intro, should make a point to find out what has been written before the live shot begins. Surprises are one of the last things you want in live television.

The anchor's introduction to a live shot is like a well-written intro to any TV story. It needs to establish why the audience should care about the information coming up. But the purpose for the intro doesn't end there. When anchors are setting up a toss to a live report, they should make it clear why the story is being presented live. Is the situation changing and evolving? Do unanswered questions require the reporter's continued presence at the scene? Such references in the anchor's intro will add to the sense of urgency about the story. (We'll discuss the debate about "live for the sake of live" shortly.)

A few final points about anchor intros to live shots: They should be brief, but substantive (i.e., no vague references to "some sort of police problem somewhere in the city"). On the other hand, if the anchor's going to use all the information available about a breaking news story, the reporter on scene without anything to add can look pretty foolish.

And should the anchor toss to the reporter in the field with a question? Some news directors discourage it. Still, a tightly written intro followed by a simple, direct question can be a clean and effective transition. But questions that aren't well delivered or that sound "canned" can be deadly. If a question is included as part of the anchor's intro, it's vital the reporter knows the question, so the response can be accurate and natural.

REPORTER CLOSE

Like a well-produced story, a well-produced live shot should have a beginning, middle, and end. A strong close to a live shot will play off the final shots and sound in the crossroll. The reporter's live close should "tie up" the story. If appropriate, refer to the next likely event or development. And remember, there's a big difference between assuring the audience (and the anchor) that you'll be following the story, and promising an update. Refer to a follow-up live shot only if the show's producer has agreed to make room for one.

Most newsrooms avoid having the reporter give his or her own sign-off at the end of the live shot. That's usually left to the anchor. The cleanest, simplest way for the reporter to toss back to the anchor is to use the anchor's first name somewhere in the reporter's final sentence.

ANCHOR CLOSE

Whether the anchor asks the reporter a question at the end of a live shot is usually a function of how much spare time the newscast contains. If the producer wants "Q and A" to wrap up the shot, it's best to have the reporter suggest a question. That doesn't mean the question has to be scripted. Like questions going into a live shot, questions coming out of a live shot can sound phony.

Some anchors seem to feel the reporter at a breaking news story is duty-bound to answer any question the anchor comes up with. Realistically, it doesn't work that way.

Even reasonable questions sometimes don't have timely answers. That means reporters have to learn how to say "I don't know," but say it gracefully. If it's a good question, say so, and perhaps acknowledge that you've been wondering the same thing. Then explain why the information isn't available yet.

If it's a stupid question, answer with as much tact as you can muster. It might be tempting to respond otherwise, but it wouldn't be professional.

WHY GO LIVE?

One of the most obvious reasons to go live is simple: timing. A significant spot-news story is breaking and the only way to cover it during the regular newscast is with a live shot. A truck and crew are dispatched and the live shot is scheduled into the show. But many stories that don't qualify as spot news still deserve live coverage.

Ongoing events that can change rapidly often make good stories for live shots. Jury deliberations in a big murder case or a train wreck are but two examples. The wreck would initially be handled as spot news, but the live crews are kept on scene to cover the story as it unfolds: the search for victims, removing the mangled cars, reopening the track, and the on-scene investigation into what went wrong.

Perhaps the greatest strength of live coverage is that it enhances what television already does best: make the audience an eyewitness to the news. Live coverage can "bring a story home," even if it's happening halfway around the world.

Remotes (live reports from the field) can enhance much smaller stories, too. Take a strike, for example. A picket line can be a strong visual backdrop for a live shot (though it quickly becomes clichéd). A reporter can use a picket to represent the larger story, then personalize the dispute and bring it to life with crossroll profiling one of the workers on the picket line. How is the strike affecting that worker's family? Do the striker's young children understand what's going on? How long can the worker afford to hold out?

WHY NOT GO LIVE?

It's easier to determine when we should go live than when we shouldn't. The benefits of live coverage of major breaking stories are obvious. Knowing when not to go live is a more subtle matter.

Newsmakers are increasingly savvy about orchestrating live coverage. Routinely, politicians, union officials, and leaders of special interest groups make announcements or hold demonstrations during regularly scheduled newscasts. Or they create a well-timed "dog and pony show," making a nonevent especially visual in hopes of luring live TV coverage. Some of these stories warrant live coverage, but many do not. News producers may be especially vulnerable on weekends when they often have to struggle to fill their shows.

There are no handy rules to determine whether going live with a scheduled event is playing into the newsmakers' hands. It comes down to a matter of public interest. How much do your viewers care about this story? If the interest is there, then live coverage is probably justified. When timing is the problem, there's always the option of sending a live truck to feed back video of the event without going live at the scene with a reporter. It gets the story in the show, without giving the event more "play" than it deserves.

What about those shots that are clearly "live for the sake of live"? We see reporters all the time at remote locations leading into stories that an anchor on set could just as easily have introduced. Night after night, even at the network level, we see correspondents reporting live from their desks, telling us about the latest goings-on at the Pentagon or the White House. The network reporters' live introductions and closes are often just one sentence long, hardly so weighty the anchor couldn't have said as much. So why go live with these stories? Astute producers know how to make such live shots work.

Above all, they know the best live reporting occurs when live shots help make viewers eyewitnesses to an event. Something happening that can be *seen* to be happening.

Some of the worst live reporting occurs when reporters stand in the dark during a newscast and show some video shot hours earlier. Poor examples: a reporter stands before city hall and reports on a zoning board decision made hours earlier; or a reporter stands in darkness at the scene of a mattress fire extinguished hours earlier.

In all live shots, the reporter must link viewers to the story. Even when standing in the dark, far removed in time from an event, the reporter must still bridge the distance between the scene and the viewer. How? By providing a logical reason for taking viewers to the scene: "What you can't see here tonight are the hundreds of votive candles still burning inside Christ Church Cathedral, or the dozens of faithful still inside praying for peace, following Cincinnati's largest peace rally in a generation."

In another example, the reporter might show baseball ticket stubs discarded in front of a stadium where the home team lost hours earlier: "At one o'clock this afternoon, these tickets represented hopes and dreams for the team's faithful. Tonight, they litter the stadium grounds, the refuse of a failed season."

Another goal is to give viewers a sense of confidence in what the reporter is saying. A correspondent becomes a familiar face, explaining time and again what the Pentagon is up to. If the audience becomes familiar with a station's reporting staff, and sees them routinely in live shots and standups, viewers may relate better to those reporters and listen more closely to what they say. Presumably, they may even be more likely to tune in. You may have the greatest story of all time, but it's not worth much if no one's watching.

LIVE PHONERS

There will be times when a station can't send a reporter to cover a story live. Perhaps there aren't enough people or the story's too far away. This is the time to reach for your videophone or even a regular telephone.

If the story is especially important, live telephone interviews are an option. Phoners that have been recorded are a bit safer, but they may also lose some of their drama. Some reporters try to avoid phoners with officials like dispatchers, for example, who haven't actually been to the scene of a breaking story. But most emergency crews have mobile phones in their cars. If dispatch will give you the phone number for one of the units on scene, you have a good shot at live coverage, using someone else's video- or mobile phone.

LIVE TEASES

You have to snag viewers before you can inform them. In the best of worlds, you'll have compelling video that will grab the audience like a 300-pound linebacker. But always you need to snag viewers, and that's where teases come in.

Live teases delivered from live remote locations let you pique interest and keep your audience hanging in there through brief breaks in programming. As with all teases, remember the cardinal rule: Never promise more than you can deliver. If you hint at high drama or significant developments that don't exist, viewers will come to distrust you. Your teases will lose their impact, and you may lose your audience.

Mechanics of a Live Tease

You can master the basic logistics that make live teases work without much experience. Once you have the mechanics down, you can concentrate on showcasing tease content, certainly the more creative and challenging part of the job.

Teases within an overall newscast generally promote three to five stories. A standard format might include a couple of video teases voiced over by the anchors, a live tease or two from reporters in the field, followed by quick references to upcoming weather or sports stories.

If your live shot includes a tease, make sure you know what comes immediately before your tease. If the item just before you is a scripted tease delivered by an anchor, ask for the specific words that will serve as your cue. If *you* follow another live tease, the producer may not have a scripted phrase to give you. Just be sure you know what story and reporter come before you, and listen for the obvious break. Either way, be looking at the camera, not the field monitor, from the moment your shot is "hot." Establish strong eye contact immediately.

Plan for noise. If your live location makes it difficult for you to hear your cue, ask your producer to give a "go" to your photographer when your camera's hot. Make sure your photographer knows that cue is coming, and is ready to give you a clear visual signal to begin.

Clarify with your producer whether a specific toss is needed at the end of your tease. Should you simply complete your tease and stop talking or pitch to another reporter or anchor?

Content of Live Teases

Like all teases in television, live teases should hint at a story's content but stop well short of revealing the story itself. Your goal is to raise a question in the viewer's mind during the tease, and then to answer that question in your live shot that follows. That doesn't mean teases should be delivered in the form of a question. Once in a while, questions are okay if they're compelling: "How does it feel to fall two-thousand feet from an airplane and live to tell about it? We have a live report, next." Inane questions, though, annoy viewers: "How could getting a simple haircut kill you? Find out after the break." A better practice is to begin your tease almost like a compelling lead to a news story.

Example #1

"There's a new store in town that can help you look like a million bucks…without spending a dime. I'm Tom Russell. We'll take you there live."

This tease lets viewers form the obvious questions, "What store and where is it?" As an added bonus, it promises the viewer a benefit: The viewer will learn how to look great while saving money. The tease and story content compel, engage, and benefit viewers. They realize from the tease they'll miss something important if they don't watch. By contrast, the following story tease offers fewer reasons to stay tuned.

Example #2

> "Where can you get a really good deal on clothes in Denver? I'm Tom Russell. I'll have a live report."

Ho hum. Pretty boring. Not much energy. The phrase "live report" is accurate, but not very exciting. Guess I'll head to bed.

Incorporate Your Surroundings in the Tease

Whenever you report live from the field, show your surroundings. Use what viewers can see in the background, or as you move through the background, to energize the story. In our story about the new clothing store, maybe we can show two hundred customers waiting in line on opening day.

Motivate Movement in the Tease

Movement in a tease can help make the story come to life, but the movement has to make sense. Just like your scripts and ad-libs, your movement and delivery need to be crisp and conversational. Any movement should be natural, too. If it feels awkward or forced, odds are it will look that way.

Check out all the reporters who do the "walk to nowhere" in **standups**, and you'll get the idea. Simply walking from point A to point B in a standup for no reason except to add movement makes little sense. Walking from point A, where a runaway truck swerved to avoid kids in a crosswalk, to point B, where the truck overturned, looks natural and helps viewers better understand the story.

Tease length is more a matter of common sense than rules. On average, good, tight teases will run from five to ten seconds. Much shorter, and you risk the old "World ends. Film at 11" caricature. Much longer, and the show's pace will drag. These are guidelines, obviously, and not rules etched in stone.

Begin now to watch other newscasts and reporters with a critical eye and ear, and figure out what works best and why. Experiment. Add your own signature. Follow your own sensibilities and instincts, and soon you'll develop an effective style that others will try to emulate.

SOME PARTING ADVICE

Many of the guidelines that will help make your stories more effective are equally important when you go live. Be conversational. Tell the story naturally, in the sort of clean, simple style you'd use if you were talking to a friend. Reporters should also make the live introductions and closes that wrap around their packages smooth and natural.

Try using newspaper stories to practice ad-libbing live shots. Jot down notes from a story that might have made a good remote. Use those notes to practice telling that story live, without a script. Challenge yourself further and imagine what the overall scene of that story would have been like. Describe those surroundings if it adds to the story. Remember, TV viewers can see only what's within the camera frame, and sometimes must depend on the picture the reporter paints in their imagination.

Credibility isn't just a matter of sounding as if you know what you're talking about. You also have to look like you know what you're talking about. In other words, dress appropriately. It's distracting to see a reporter in a three-piece suit and Italian shoes going live from a muddy wheat field that's been flattened by hail. To some viewers, that reporter will look so foolish that the story's point is lost. That doesn't mean you need to invest in bib overalls and a straw hat. Just don't clash with your live background.

The same guideline applies for reporters covering bad weather. If you're not dressed for the part, your message may not get through. Most reporters who do a lot of live shots keep spare clothing handy. It just makes sense.

A FINAL THOUGHT

One of the best tips for any reporter is to be human—in your approach to a story, in the way you write it, and in any live work surrounding that story. If you're curious about something, odds are your audience will be curious, too. If grotesque or tragic events at a spot-news story shock you, it's okay to let some of that show. You have to be professional and keep a certain distance between yourself and the events you cover. But there's such a thing as being so emotionally objective the story becomes sterile. At that point, many in the audience may begin to wonder why the story matters, whether you care about it, or why they should care.

SUMMARY

All the general communication skills important in radio and television news are doubly important for successful live reports. Such skills include a well-rounded vocabulary, good news judgment, solid reporting experience, and strong interviewing skills. Of all these skills, the most important remains a knack for writing and talking conversationally.

Specialists in live reporting gather information even while en route to the scene. The average news car or van allows journalists to monitor police, fire, and civil defense frequencies; communicate with the newsroom; and often, speak with news sources via a mobile phone.

You may have to go on air upon arrival, with no opportunity to gather information beyond what you collected en route to the scene. In such situations, follow two rules of thumb: (1) tell the audience what you know, and (2) tell them what you don't know. In all cases, qualify what you say, especially when the information is sketchy, using such terms as "still unclear at this time" and "unconfirmed reports."

Hit the ground running when you arrive on scene. Look for a command post and public information officer, or PIO, who can help clear the way for better access to a story. Also search for other locations and ways to report the story so your report will contain more than the "official" information such a spokesperson provides.

If you feed raw material back to the station, narration can be fed live or prerecorded and fed back with the field video. Because the editor may have to work without a written script, try to send the voice track first. This lets the editor listen to the track as it's being fed and become familiar with the story.

Almost any live shot that will work on the ground will work from a helicopter. You can do virtually anything but the "walking" live shot from a helicopter, including shooting, narrating, and feeding an entire package.

The sense of immediacy surrounding live shots begins with the anchor's introduction or toss. Ideally, because the reporter in the field knows most about the story, the reporter will write the intro and dictate it to base. This approach also strengthens the flow of the toss from studio to the field. If the reporter lacks time to write an anchor intro, another approach is to suggest information for an intro.

The reporter's live close should "tie up" the story. If appropriate, refer to the next likely development. Remind the audience and the anchor you'll be following the story, but promise a follow-up live shot only if the show's producer has agreed to make room for one.

Whether through coverage of spot or breaking news, or by updating the news as it unfolds, live reports make audiences an eyewitness to the news. Although the benefits of live coverage are obvious, knowing when not to go live is a more subtle matter. If the story doesn't warrant live coverage, video of the event can be fed back without going live at the scene with a reporter.

Whenever you report live from the field, dress appropriately for the environment. Whether in the field with news sources, or on screen as a television reporter, you have to look and sound like you know what you're talking about. The goal in every instance is to avoid distractions, so that you can keep news sources and audiences focused on story content. Most of all, be professional, but also be human in your reports—in the way you approach the story, in the way you write it, and in any live work surrounding that story.

KEY TERMS

blue eyes   222
CGs   226
command post   221
crossroll   222
key   223

naked live   222
nats   224
phoners   228
PIO   221
remotes   230

scanners   219
SOT   224
standups   233
thumb suckers   222
two shot   223

EXERCISES

1. Assess the general writing, reporting, and communication skills you possess to conduct successful live reports for radio or television news. As part of your assessment, determine to what extent you have a well-developed vocabulary, good news judgment, adequate reporting experience, and strong interviewing skills. Also, make an honest assessment of your writing and speaking skills, especially your ability to write and speak fluently and conversationally under pressure. Develop a multiphase plan to strengthen skills or abilities you feel deficient in, and establish a regular schedule to practice writing and speaking under pressure.

2. Practice gathering information "on the run." Take notes as you listen to a breaking story on a radio or television newscast. Study your notes briefly, then step before a radio microphone or television camera and record a practice live shot. Replay the recording and analyze your performance.

3. Monitor live reports on your favorite radio news station. Analyze those qualities that make live reports on your favorite station so effective. Prepare a two-page report, double-spaced, and discuss your findings in class.

4. For practice, ask a friend to shoot video in at least three locations as you locate yourself at the beginning of a live shot. At each location, alternatively provide a description of the location, a specific description of a junction or landmark that viewers or listeners in your area would recognize, and finally the locations' exact address if available. If help is unavailable, set up the camera and record yourself.

5. For practice, record the introduction to a live report, using background notes from a newspaper or web article or a television news story. Include as much of the following information as possible in forty seconds or less: your location, what's happened, what you can see from your vantage point, and the "broader picture" that exists outside the TV frame. Qualify your information as necessary, and use terms such as "still unclear," "at this time," and "unconfirmed reports" as warranted.

6. Record the live close to a practice report, this time telling your imaginary audience what you don't know. End the close with a toss back to the studio anchor, including as part of your last line the anchor's first name.

7. Interview a Public Information Officer at a police or fire department about his or her dealings with media representatives, protocols the PIO follows during emergencies, how the command post operates, and the procedures and guidelines reporters are expected to follow. Submit a report of not more than five double-spaced pages and discuss your findings in class.

8. Record yourself delivering a :50 to :60 "thumb sucker" to camera. Play back the result and analyze your performance. Note especially the sense of urgency you communicate, how fluid and extemporaneous you sound, and your ability to develop and maintain eye contact with the audience.

9. Using your own or donated footage, produce a practice live/SOT/live report not to exceed 1:20. Play back the result and analyze your performance.

10. Using your own or donated footage, produce a live/VTR/live report. As part of your script, note the roll cue and cue back to remote for the crossroll.

11. Using the newspaper as a reference source, write a practice live report that includes editing instructions for crossroll on a spot-news story. For guidance, see pages 219–220.

12. Using your own or donated footage, produce a live/VO/SOT/live report, including all necessary roll cues for the producer. Record your own live intro and close.

13. Write the script for a spot-news package, using any source of information you wish. Prerecord all voice-over narration as though it were to be fed live back to the station. Refer to each portion of track between sound bites as "section 1, section 2..." and give a clear 3-2-1 countdown before you begin each section of track.

14. Record a practice live report from a real or imaginary newsroom. This can be a late-breaking story or one or more live updates from the newsroom.

15. Based on any of the live intros you have written for any of the exercises above, write anchor intros that flow smoothly from the anchor to your own report. Keep the anchor intro brief but specific. For additional practice, record the anchor intro on tape and use it to introduce your own live intro.

16. Ad-lib a reporter close that includes a smooth toss back to the anchor. Reference the final shots and sound in the crossroll as you tie up the story. If appropriate, refer to the next likely event or development and assure the audience, if appropriate, that you'll be following the story. Include the anchor's first name as part of the last line in your close.

17. Practice preparing and delivering three versions each of a radio voicer, a radio news wrap, and if practical, a live interview in which you report and update a spot-news story over time in the field, including interviews with significant sources.

CHAPTER

14

Law and the Digital Journalist

Journalists make ethical and legal judgments every day that hinge on familiarity with First Amendment guarantees of *freedom of press and speech*, Fourth Amendment guarantees of the individual's *right to privacy*, and Sixth Amendment guarantees of the *right to a public trial by an impartial jury*. Many legal transgressions occur in the field as journalists *gather* and *report* the news. Journalists unfamiliar with state and federal statutes that govern news coverage remain vulnerable to anyone willing to seek compensation or other advantage through the courts. People can sue for anything, and some news sources may use their apparent command of the law to censor, influence, or otherwise profit from news reports and their timing.

The **Internet** raises further legal questions. Who owns the rights to published or "repurposed" material? Should journalists observe a print or a broadcast legal model, or both, when using the Internet? If a site defames an individual or institution, who is responsible? Is it the original author, the online service, and/or the journalist who quoted the information?

Some business ventures buy up blanket copyrights to the output from newspapers and other publishers, and then troll web sites and social media for material that has been reposted without their permission. "Media companies' assets are very much their copyrights," says Steve Gibson, the CEO of Righthaven, a copyright trolling firm. "These companies need to understand and appreciate that those assets have value more than merely the present advertising revenues."[1] Gibson believes infringements occur by the millions, if not billions.[2]

Such companies prosecute even private, obviously innocent violators, and frequently collect monetary damages. Law firms also troll the Internet in much the same way, looking for libelous reports against their clients, whether corporate or individual.[3] As technology and media platforms influence how electronic journalists gather and report the news, courts struggle to answer ever-changing questions and issues.

This chapter discusses legal questions that journalists face routinely and offers guidelines to help journalists know when to seek advice. A generous application of fairness can help eliminate the need for some routine legal advice, but the guiding rule should always be "If in doubt, seek help" In no way should any part of this chapter be considered as actual legal advice or as a substitute for appropriate legal counsel.

GATHERING THE NEWS

The First Amendment usually protects the right to speak and publish, but it does not automatically protect the right to gather news. Even so, the courts have generally held that if journalists are to report news they must also have the right to gather it. As a rule when gathering news, journalists may go anywhere a person can go without special permission—so long as their equipment doesn't get in the way. Although journalists may attend a theater opening, a political rally, or a courtroom trial, they almost never can light, photograph, record, or transmit live pictures of these same events without first obtaining special permission. When it comes to gathering the news, nowhere in the **law** are reporters and photojournalists more likely to cost their stations money than in matters of libel (defamation) and invasion of privacy.

LIBEL

Libel (defined in the courts as malicious defamation) is the use of factual information (as opposed to opinion) that holds someone in hatred or contempt, subjects the person to ridicule, or otherwise lowers esteem for the individual. Property, businesses, and institutions can also be libeled. **Defamation** can occur as soon as you communicate a false statement of fact to a third party, even if you never broadcast the statement. Although oral defamation might qualify as **slander**, in television news it's considered libel, even if the alleged defamation is made orally.

Know the Statement Is True

Because libel is a statement of information that constitutes defamation (as opposed to a statement of opinion), an excellent protection against liability is to have good reason to believe a statement is true. Few journalists can know with certainty that a statement is false. For the most part, journalists can only know what they see in documents or hear from sources. If a reporter uses evaluative judgment words, such as, "probably," "in most people's opinion," or "any sane person can see," those words would probably fall under the heading of opinion, which cannot be false in the same sense that a statement of fact can be false. Fortunately, for journalists to be liable for defamation, they must normally know a statement is false or be aware that it is probably false. Such latitude offers a heady measure of legal protection.

In some states a common test for defamation is negligence. In other words, courts look for evidence that the journalist used "due care" in evaluating the truth of a defamatory statement. To protect yourself against charges of negligence, always adopt a higher standard than the law sets. Ask yourself, "Do I believe the statement to be true?" This is a much easier and more practical question to ask than, "Do I believe the statement to be false?"

Another test is to ask, "Whom am I talking about? Might what I report in some way lower our esteem for that person?" In applying such a test, it's important to remember that most substantive news is derogatory to someone. Still, if you can answer yes to the question "Does this look and feel authentic?" you'll probably be safe even if the statement later proves to be false. As yet another safeguard, ask yourself, "Does the public have a right to know this?" Perhaps the information addresses some aspect of public business, for example, or comes from sworn testimony or from subpoenaed information that is part of the court record.

Evaluate Sources to Eliminate Malice

Whenever someone makes derogatory statements about another person, try to evaluate the person's motives. Was he just fired? Is he bitter? Perhaps you interview a woman whose sister has been beaten to death, and the woman tells you, "Her husband was a no-good bum. He beat her for years." In that moment, you are helpless to know whether the statement is true or false.

Only if the statement is made during a live broadcast, and only if you used due care to stop it, might you escape liability should the broader standards of defamation be applied. In the previous example, the woman could make the statement; you could say what the woman told you; you could make the statement without attribution; but in all three instances the court would typically consider your responsibility for the allegation to be the same. Later you might be able to establish the woman's malice, but if you air the allegation without first evaluating your source, the court may ask whether there was something further you should have done—and there usually is—to establish the source's motives.

Note the distinction between the two concepts of malice applied in this discussion. An older, common-law version of malice applies in establishing the malice of the news source. Because of the 1964 U.S. Supreme Court ruling in *New York Times v. Sullivan,* however, a second concept of malice applies to the journalist. This newer concept, called "actual malice," or the Sullivan Rule, as later modified, results from the Court's opinion that "Constitutional guarantees require, we think, a federal rule that prohibits a public official from recovering damages for a defamatory falsehood relating to his official conduct unless he proves that the statement was made with 'actual malice'—that is, with knowledge that it was false or with reckless disregard of whether it was false or not."[4]

The ruling applies to public figures or to persons who have voluntarily placed themselves in the public view. The issue of actual malice as it applies to private plaintiffs is left to state law. Some states allow reporters to repeat charges they suspect are false. Other states require that reporters investigate such charges before they repeat them.[5] You can study a fascinating array of up-to-the-minute free speech, copyright, and invasion of privacy decisions by entering such terms in your Internet browser as you encounter them while reading this chapter. A good starting point is the College Media Adviser's site at http://www.collegemedia.org/. Other resources are noted throughout this chapter and within the endnotes.

Assume the Highest Standard

Actions for libel can be brought in any state in which a station's signal is received. A Pennsylvania resident libeled by a New York station could bring suit in his home state, for example, although Pennsylvania courts normally would use the libel standards that apply in New York. This offers some protection against individuals who might otherwise sue in the state with the most favorable chances for settlement. Consequently, attorneys generally advise that you assume the standard for your own state, or preferably an even higher standard.

Use Caution When Dealing with Police

Any time police serve as your primary source for potentially defamatory statements, or any time you're tempted to publish information obtained from the police radio, use caution. A street cop may tell you on the record, "This looks like it could be a gangland drug-related shooting," but to protect yourself check further; otherwise, simply through inference, you could be defaming an innocent person. In one libel action, a reporter aired police-supplied photographs of alleged "thieves and burglars" at a flea market. One of the persons clearly identified in the photographs had no police record and sued for libel. A court ordered the police to pay a penalty for libel.

INVASION OF PRIVACY

The Fourth Amendment to the Constitution protects the individual's right to privacy, including the "right of the people to be secure in their persons, houses, papers, and effects." As defined in the courts, **invasion of privacy** is any act of intrusion that occurs without an individual's consent, including trespass and publication of embarrassing facts (even if true), and that violates an individual's reasonable expectation of the right to privacy (Figure 14.1).

As the concept affects journalists, it has parallels with libel law, but note the distinction about truth. Libel is actionable only if the report is false. Invasion of privacy can be actionable even if the report is true. Exceptions occur if the information is already part of the public record or if the report concerns activities that occurred in public. Such information is privileged, even though it might be false, provided it is reported completely and as accurately as it was made available to the journalist.

In gathering television news, one of the most common forms of invasion of privacy is **trespass**. Trespass occurs when you enter someone's property or premises illegally.

FIGURE 14.1

The Fourth Amendment to the Constitution guarantees the individual's right to privacy. Violations of state or federal privacy laws can lead to a journalist being charged with invasion of privacy, trespass, eavesdropping, and unauthorized surveillance.

Often, trespass is inadvertent. Someone with apparent authority gives you permission to enter the scene of a news event; later, someone with greater authority tells you to leave and threatens you with a lawsuit. What are the damages for walking into a person's home and invading privacy? The answer can be anything from one dollar in actual damages to clean the carpet you soiled, to punitive damages that are anyone's guess for causing "emotional distress."

DEFAMATION

An area of great danger to journalists is unsuspecting defamation, which often occurs when pictures or video are used to carry most of the reporting load. Each of the following examples conceivably might lead to claims of an alleged invasion of privacy called *publicizing in a false light.*

- The camera shows a reporter on a crowded street corner, then pans over to show a hapless passerby as the reporter says, "Tax cheats cost the government billions every year."
- Voice-over narration discusses the problem of overweight Americans while the television screen shows generic cover footage of women walking along a street. The women, through "guilt by illustration," are implicated as being overweight.
- Reporter voice-over narration says, "Drug dealers are using their profits to buy huge homes like these." The narration is unwittingly married with generic cover footage that shows the home of a respected commodities exchange executive. A lawsuit follows.
- Several young women walk along a street against voice-over narration that charges that the area being shown is full of prostitutes. The women, not surprisingly, sue the station.

The use of **generic video**, which some attorneys call "inadvertent cutaways," is a dangerous journalistic practice that leads to libel and invasion of privacy suits. When suits are filed against reporters who shoot a street scene, then use it generically for two years to illustrate scripts about prostitutes, thieves, and tax evaders, judges are likely to say, "When you were talking about the mad rapist, you could be understood to have been talking about the person you showed on the screen. Let's let the jury decide."

USE OF THE WORD *ALLEGED*

A time-honored way to handle criminal cases is to remember the adage, "No charges, no name." In criminal cases, a person's identity should be withheld until charges are filed. At the point charges are filed, the word *alleged* can be one of the reporter's most important legal protections. This is because how much you can say (and sometimes show) about anyone associated with a crime or a criminal depends on the level of that person's involvement.

There are at least three critical levels to consider:

1. Material witnesses: Some people are brought in as material witnesses, nothing more.
2. Suspects: Other individuals are brought in as suspects, or material witnesses may become suspects.
3. Arraignment: Only at arraignment does actual "alleging" begin; at this point someone charged with murder becomes an *alleged* killer.

In a sense, even someone *convicted* of murder remains an alleged killer. The jury may say he was the killer, but the journalist can never know with absolute certainty. Although the conventional wisdom in many newsrooms holds that the word *alleged* is useless under the law, it may help establish the journalist's "state of mind" toward the suspect when the story was reported.

APPARENT AUTHORITY

Technically, you are liable for trespass if you're in the wrong place at the wrong time. Typically, however, courts determine a journalist's guilt or innocence based on **apparent authority**. The following examples illustrate some of the everyday challenges journalists are likely to encounter.

Fatal Fire

You seek permission to shoot video of a fatal fire at a retirement facility. The angle on your story is that many of these facilities in your area may not be fireproof. The manager is on duty and tells you, "Go on in." The fire chief, at your request, later also grants you access to enter the facility. You shoot video until the fire is almost out, but as you prepare to leave, the facility's owner arrives. The fire chief has long since left, but the owner tells you to leave immediately. The moment the owner tells you to leave, you must leave, but the most immediate question is whether you're liable for trespass for having entered the facility in the first place.

Courts generally answer this question based on apparent authority. If someone on the scene says, "I own or lease this property; come on in," and you have no reason to doubt that person's authority, it's normally safe to enter the premises. If you can't find the owner or manager and the fire chief gives you permission to enter, you may still enter the premises. However, once inside, you might still be liable for trespass or invasion of privacy if, for example, you inadvertently shoot into a private room and show an elderly resident in an embarrassing situation.

Assuming you do not invade anyone's privacy, it's probably safe to air any footage you shot while you had apparent authority to shoot, that is, from the facility's manager or from the fire chief. If the owner (the last person to arrive at the scene) tells you not to use any footage you've shot, even under the fire chief's apparent authority, it's probably still safe to air anything shot before the owner's arrival. In this example, if anyone were to be sued, it probably would be the fire chief. If in doubt, consult your station attorney.

Day Care Center

You receive permission from a city building inspector to enter a day care center that has been cited for safety violations. The city building inspector is the apparent authority, although you must leave if the manager or owner (either of whom have greater authority than the building inspector) tells you to leave.

Landlord–Tenant Dispute

You're covering a landlord–tenant group dispute. You normally may enter someone's private apartment at that person's invitation, even if the landlord tells you to leave, because in many states tenancy rights give the individual greater apparent authority than the landlord. You also may stand on public property to photograph the apartment complex and you may be able to stand on a common area of the apartment grounds and shoot video, again with a tenant's permission.

Entering a Restaurant

You learn that your state health department may close a local restaurant if unsanitary conditions aren't corrected. As part of your report, you enter the restaurant with cameras rolling, walk to the manager, and begin to ask questions. The restaurant is open to the public, you reason, so anyone can come in. A further question is whether you're liable for what you shoot before the manager tells you to leave.

In this example, the concept of limited invitation also applies. The courts have held that in the case of restaurants (or even car dealerships), the public has a **limited invitation** (see *LeMistral, Inc. v. Columbia Broadcasting System,* 402 N.Y.S.2d 815, 817. N.Y. App. Div. 1978). The public is welcome to come in to eat at a restaurant, or buy cars at a dealership, but not to come in and shoot video. Such practices in your state may therefore fall under the heading of invasion of privacy.

Often, private homes, businesses, and institutions can assume quasi-public status because of some event. Generally, you can shoot anything your eyes can see, if you have permission to shoot in the first place. Be aware, however, that examples are simply that. Check state laws to be certain where you stand and where you can stand. In one incident, reporting crews from two television stations sought permission to enter leased land to photograph horses that were said to be starving. The crews obtained permission from the landowner but not from the individuals who had leased the land. In this case, the overriding question was whether the reporters had reasonable belief that the owner had apparent authority, an answer that will vary from one state to the next.

TECHNOLOGY

Technology has created other opportunities for trespass. The news helicopter is but one example. In numerous states, property lines are considered to extend from the boundaries of the property to the heavens. Technically, any time a helicopter or airplane flies over someone's property it may be trespassing. Practically, however, the damages of such an act are minimal—unless, of course, a news helicopter hovers for too long above a burning home and fans the flames.

As a rule, journalists have been able to record anything they could see, even with a telephoto lens and a shotgun mike, but the rules may change as more photographers acquire 1,000-mm lenses and ever-more-sensitive microphones. Although it's true no one has yet determined the maximum focal length you can use to record a news event, it's equally true that some judge, somewhere, will also ask whether subjects of the long lenses and shotgun and parabolic mikes had a reasonable expectation of privacy.

Hidden Microphones

If someone stands unclothed before an open living room window in a crowded city, that individual might be expected to know someone could be lurking in the distance with a telephoto lens. But if that individual is holding a private conversation inside the home, that same person should have a reasonable expectation to privacy, which extends to protection from "snooper" microphones or even from normal shotgun mikes, which can pick up hushed conversation from great distances.

Shotgun Microphones

In some states, intrusion with shotgun mikes can constitute eavesdropping, a transgression governed by state and federal statutes. Hence, the recording of a restaurant conversation that could be overheard passively by any third party might constitute intrusion because of the patron's reasonable expectation of privacy while dining.

However, you may get by with airing portions of the district attorney's comments you recorded at opening night of a new theater presentation, even if the DA said he didn't like the play and even though you recorded his comments without his knowledge and as a third party to his conversation.

Obviously, the use of concealed microphones for any purpose should be undertaken with great care in order to avoid lawsuits for intrusion. And no journalist should plant a microphone in a flowerpot or make secret recordings of any kind without first checking with the station attorney.

TELEPHONE RECORDINGS

Telephone recordings have great potential to cause legal problems because they can so easily be misused to invade someone's privacy. Recordings do help ensure exact quotes, and they are commonly used as the electronic equivalent of a reporter's notes (something to consider should you ever be subpoenaed), but sometimes their use can backfire (Figure 14.2).

FIGURE 14.2
Even routine telephone use can lead to lawsuits for invasion of privacy. No recordings or broadcasts of a conversation can be made unless the source is so advised.

To prevent problems, it's mandatory that you always advise the person on the other end that you intend to record a conversation, regardless of who initiates the call. Federal Communications Commission (FCC) rule 47 C.F.R.S73.1206 governs the broadcast of live and recorded telephone conversations. *Before* recording a telephone conversation for a future broadcast or broadcasting a telephone call simultaneously with its occurrence (live), journalists must inform any party to the call of their intent to broadcast the conversation. It is not sufficient to give notice just before the broadcast of a recorded call. An exception exists when the party is aware, or may be presumed to be aware, that the conversation is being or likely will be broadcast, as in the call placed to a broadcast program that features call-in telephone conversations.

Even if you intend to record the conversation only for your records, you should advise the person, preferably before the conversation begins. For maximum protection, record not only your statement of intent, but also the other person's verbal consent. If you intend to use excerpts of the conversation on air, you should advise the person before the primary conversation begins—again, as near the start of the call as possible.

Surveillance in States with One-Party Consent

Title III of the Omnibus Crime Control and Safe Streets Act of 1968 regulates recorded conversations. The act allows law enforcement agents to conduct electronic surveillance, provided a judge has reviewed the plan and agrees. In many states and under federal law, an exception can be made for the reporter, provided the reporter doesn't intend to damage an individual's reputation falsely or to violate someone's privacy without newsworthy justification. Generally, under such laws, it is legal to monitor telephone calls or make surveillance recordings when one party to the conversation knows what is happening.

Hidden Voice Recorders

Although using a hidden voice recorder where a person has a reasonable expectation of privacy may not violate federal law, in some states the practice might add to a plaintiff's claim for invasion of privacy or trespass. In states with one-party consent and under federal law, a person acting in the reporter's place may be able to record a conversation without the reporter's presence, provided the person who carries the recorder understands what is happening. To be safe, always check with legal counsel.

Two-Party Consent

Twelve states with "two-party consent" require that all parties to conversations, even if more than two, give their consent if the conversations are recorded. Those states are California, Connecticut, Delaware, Florida, Illinois, Massachusetts, Maryland, Montana, Nevada, New Hampshire, Pennsylvania, and Washington. Unless consent is obtained from all parties, severe criminal penalties are possible. Reporters who wish to record conversations in two-party consent states should seek knowledgeable counsel to avoid the possibility of severe criminal penalties. For the most recent list of one- and two-party consent states, see The Reporters Committee for Freedom of the Press (RCFP) web site at www.rcfp.org, or write or call RCFP, 1101 Wilson Blvd., Suite 1100, Arlington, VA 22209, 800-336-4243 or 703-807-2100.[6]

Juvenile News Sources

With some exceptions, a child is defined as anyone under the age of eighteen years. Normally, you can use juvenile names and pictures if you obtain them legally—and if the identities are already part of the public record. But to be on the safe side it's always wise to consult your state law for the exceptions.

Children's right to privacy is protected from the streets to the home to the courtroom. When a reporter wishes to interview a child on a public street, there is no guarantee of the child's legal consent to talk unless the person is at least eighteen years of age. The same caution extends to news coverage in schools. Because of the principle of limited invitation, a school principal may legally refuse a reporting crew the right to take pictures or to conduct interviews with children in the school unless the crew first obtains parental permission. Reporters are also routinely excluded from juvenile trials.

From one state to another, juvenile law varies. A juvenile charged with murder, habitual crime, or other felony may forfeit his or her right to privacy. Occasionally, stations may jointly decide not to air a child's identity, even though the child's name has been legally obtained and can legally be broadcast. When the choices are difficult and competition a factor, a guiding principle is to ask, "What does the public need to know?" and "Does the public have a right to know this child's identity?"

SUBPOENAS AND SHIELD LAWS

A reporter's notes, outtakes, and sources are normally protected because it is generally held that no one has the right to determine a reporter's editorial judgment. In a number of states, this protection is formally extended through **shield laws**. However, members of the legal community may ask a judge or jury to rule otherwise. The mildest form of **subpoena** or court order to produce documents or other information is for an on-air recording; the most severe is for a reporter's notes or the names of sources.

A reporter must never tell anyone the identities of secret sources or of the content of notes or outtakes. Once you've revealed such knowledge, you forfeit your right to withhold the same information from the courts. If your attorney or news director asks whether you have source material, you may answer that you have the material, but never divulge the contents. Attorneys and news directors are the ones paid to say, in court, "Yes, there is material, but we're not producing it."

In protecting sources, the key is never to promise a source complete confidentiality unless you're willing to go to jail indefinitely.

ACCESS LAWS

Whereas shield laws allow the journalist to protect confidential sources under certain circumstances, *access* or *sunshine laws* protect the journalist's right of access to judicial, legislative, and executive records, extraordinary school board and city council proceedings, and the like, which otherwise might be kept off limits to the public. Such open meeting and open records laws may apply to state government but not to local government.

Journalists are routinely excluded from closed sessions of sensitive personnel and legal matters at all levels of government, although some officials may invoke such exclusionary rules to bar journalists from meetings that should remain open to the public. Legal counsel may be necessary to gain permission to attend such meetings or even to learn of actions taken during meetings that should have been conducted in public.

COURTROOM TELEVISION

Because the Sixth Amendment to the Constitution guarantees defendants in criminal cases the right to a *public* trial, television journalists have fought for decades to bring television cameras into the courtroom. "We have watched wars live on television," the argument goes, "so perhaps it's time that American news viewers are able to see what happens in American courtrooms." Slowly, in state courts at least, they are winning the battle.

The Role of Cameras in the Courtroom

For years, media observers have argued that televised trials help ensure that public trials are indeed public and that they subject judges and other public officials to greater public scrutiny.[7] Edward Estlow, as president of the E. W. Scripps Company, said, "A trial committed to videotape is a trial more accurately reported because the cameras create a record that both newspaper and broadcast representatives can then consult in order to verify their reportage."[8]

Journalists believe cameras in the courtroom help audiences better understand the judicial process (Figure 14.3). "Legal experts say that people watching the action on television are getting a glimpse of the excitement of trial work performed by articulate, competent, and hard-working attorneys," observed Harriet Chiang, as legal affairs writer for the *San Francisco Chronicle*.[9] But Chiang and other legal

FIGURE 14.3

The Sixth Amendment to the Constitution guarantees the individual's right to a speedy and public trial by an impartial jury. The issue of free press–fair trial involves such considerations as shield laws, subpoenas, and television in the courtroom.

experts note that both sides may become preoccupied with publicity rather than the quest for justice, engaging in "sand-lot style" lawyering.[10]

When cameras are allowed in the courtroom, still more concerns must be answered. If the camera is within the jury's view, will jurors be influenced as to what the reporter and photographer feel is the most newsworthy or most significant testimony? Will undercover police be publicly identified should they be called to the witness stand? Will journalists use the camera to cover only the most sensational trials or to record only the most sensational testimony (i.e., the star witness breaking down on the witness stand)? What if the rape victim's name is inadvertently spoken, or her face shown, during a courtroom broadcast? What if a prisoner is called to testify, then later faces retribution from prison cellmates? What if perspiration on the judge's bald head is unsightly? What if the prosecutor can't match the defense attorney's performance? What if…?

Most States Allow Courtroom Media Coverage

Some form of extended media coverage, meaning coverage by television, radio, or still photography, is permitted in forty-eight states, with a majority allowing cameras in a criminal trial. Consent of the presiding judge is usually required, and many states require advance written application for permission. Nearly all states prohibit coverage in cases that involve juveniles, victims of sex crimes, domestic relations cases, and trials that involve trade secrets. Coverage of jurors normally is either prohibited or restricted, to prevent juror identification. To stay abreast of changes in your state, or for a comprehensive summary of TV cameras in state courts, see http://www.rtdna .org/pages/best-practices/freedom-of-information.php.

Television Cameras Banned in Federal Courts

After a three-year experiment in six U.S. district courts and two appeals courts, the Judicial Conference of the United States ruled in late 1994 to ban television cameras in federal courtrooms. "[The] basic concern was the potential impact on jurors and witnesses; potential distraction of witnesses; and whether jurors were made nervous by any fear of possible harm," said David Sellers, a spokesperson for the twenty-seven-member panel of judges that issued the ruling.[11]

The experiment had allowed coverage of civil proceedings in the district courts of Indiana, Massachusetts, Michigan, New York, Pennsylvania, and Washington, and in federal appeals courts in New York City and San Francisco.[12] Criminal trials were excluded from coverage, and during the first two years of the experiment, media covered only a handful of civil cases. Judges repeatedly cautioned against media apathy, warning journalists the experiment might fail unless they increased coverage of federal court proceedings.[13] Still, the ban surprised many observers who fully believed the experiment had been a success.

In September 2010, the Judicial Conference of the United States, the policy-making arm of the federal courts, approved a pilot project lasting up to three years that permits cameras in some federal district courts. Court employees must set up and operate the cameras. The program permits coverage only of civil cases. It continues the rules that have banned cameras from federal criminal trials since 1946.

The conference also allows appeals courts to permit camera access. U.S. Appeals Courts in New York City (2nd Cir.) and San Francisco (9th Cir.) continue the practice.[14]

You can find continually updated information on the status of *cameras in federal courts* at the Radio Television Digital News Association (RTDNA) web site

at http://www.rtdna.org/ or the United States Courts web site at http://www
.uscourts.gov/; and for *state courts* at http://www.rtdna.org/pages/media_items
/cameras-in-the-court-a-state-by-state-guide55.php?g=45?id=55.

Standards for Courtroom Coverage

Gradually, judges, attorneys, and journalists establish the standards that answer
such questions. Today's journalists normally operate with one television pool
camera (and one still camera for combined newspaper and news service coverage. With **pool coverage**, a single camera is set up at a stationary point in the
courtroom (Figure 14.4), and its signal is fed live to the station, to video recorders
just outside the courtroom, or to a central receiving location elsewhere within
the courthouse. All stations that wish to cover the trial are provided access to the
video signal from the courtroom camera, a method designed to create the least distraction. Sound can be supplied simply by tapping into the public address system
found in most courtrooms.

Cameras normally are excluded from pretrial hearings in criminal cases, from
voir dire (a preliminary examination to establish a prospective juror's competence
and suitability), and from proceedings in the judge's chambers. Depending on the
state and the judge, cameras may be allowed at other proceedings such as trial
hearings, sentencing, resentencing, and the like (Figure 14.5).

In many states, the judge is the absolute authority when it comes to cameras in the
courtroom. Each judge handles the procedures differently. Some judges will not allow zooms or camera movement. Others will allow zooms, but not pans—so as not

FIGURE 14.4

Pool coverage minimizes disruptions in the courtroom by using a single camera to feed
signals to all stations that wish to cover the proceedings.

FIGURE 14.5

Television hardware and its sometimes-intrusive nature have caused resistance to cameras in the courtroom. In the future, less distracting technology may lead to more video trial coverage.

to distract the jury with camera movement. The judge may require the photographer and reporter to wear a coat and tie or other suitable dress. Some judges require that once set up, the photographer and reporter remain in the courtroom—even though the next three days of testimony may not make a newsworthy story—so jurors won't be influenced by the reporter and photographer's judgment about the most newsworthy or most significant testimony. At any point in the trial, a judge may terminate coverage if it hinders the judicial process or appears to jeopardize an individual's right to a fair trial.

Where new courtroom facilities are under construction, spaces to conceal the television camera are an ordinary part of courtroom blueprints. Two-way windows at the back of the courtroom conceal the camera so no one in the courtroom is aware of its presence. If cameras cannot be seen it is more difficult for them to influence the trial's outcome, though it is possible, especially if courtroom participants know the proceedings are being televised. However, almost without exception, the camera's presence is quickly forgotten, becoming as common a fixture as the gavel or the witness stand.[15]

Some Do's and Don'ts

When a broadcast news organization wishes to originate trial coverage, the first step is to submit a written request for camera coverage to the judge at least twenty-four hours in advance. If the judge denies access, the judge's word is final: There usually is no appeal process. If the judge allows trial coverage, rules will almost certainly be imposed—undoubtedly similar to those that follow.[16] You can find specific regulations for any state regarding cameras in the courtrooms and how to gain approval for media coverage, at the National Center for State Courts web site, http://www.ncsc .org/information-and-resources/browse-by-state.aspx This site also lists Court Media Centers, where you can access news releases, recent orders and opinions, alerts, cases of interest, and other useful information.

Cameras in the Courtroom

Do's:

- Do pool all TV and audio coverage.
- Do use only one operator for TV coverage using only one camera set in one location.
- Do dress and conduct yourself in a manner consistent with the dignity and decorum of the courtroom.
- Do use the existing court audio system for sound recording if technically feasible.

Don'ts:

- Don't leave media identification on cameras or clothes.
- Don't take close-ups of jury members.
- Don't use auxiliary TV lights.
- Don't take audio recordings of attorney–client conversations or conferences held at the bench.
- Don't change tape or disk drives while court is in session.
- Don't use portable voice recorders.
- Don't ask the judge to referee a media dispute, such as over pooling.

After the Verdict Is In

Once the verdict is in and the jury has been dismissed, courthouse reporters traditionally have been free to question jurors about the verdict, their secret deliberations, and why they voted as they did. Still, individuals called to jury duty remain private citizens, and today some courts extend the right to privacy to jurors as they return to everyday life. In re Express - News Corp., 695 F.2d 807 (5th Cir, 1982) the 5th U.S. Circuit Court of Appeals ruled that "jurors, even after completing their duty, are entitled to privacy and to protection against harassment."

Should attorneys appeal the verdict in a televised trial, their first request may be for video recordings of the trial. The stations' own rules should apply in governing whether to honor the request. Some stations might supply whatever footage has been aired, but no outtakes. Other stations might supply nothing at all—even in the face of a subpoena. The reasoning is that if pool coverage is allowed, bar associations, watchdog groups, and attorneys can record the trial themselves, unless coverage is limited to news organizations as it sometimes is.

THE DIGITAL MILLENNIUM COPYRIGHT ACT OF 1998[17]

The Digital Millennium Copyright Act (DMCA) is the outgrowth of a 1997 Supreme Court decision that gives the Internet the same free speech protections as print media. The Internet is the first electronic medium afforded such protections (opposed to news programs broadcast over public airwaves, for example) because it's easy to access and has so many voices, many of them unedited.[18]

Copyright Defined

The United States Copyright Office defines **copyright** as "a form of protection provided by [U.S. law] (title 17, U. S. Code) to the authors of 'original works of authorship,' including literary, dramatic, musical, artistic, and certain other intellectual works. This protection is available to both published and unpublished works."

If you own the copyright, you can do whatever you want with the work, whether it's an audio recording, a book manuscript, video or video script, an original photo, video story or publication, slideshow, drawing, artwork, poem, or sheet music. You can duplicate your original work; rent, lease, or sell it; put it on the Internet; or otherwise show or display it publically. You are protected when the work is created and "fixed in a physical form." You also can transfer ownership to someone else.

Duration of Copyright

Copyright protection typically extends for the author's life plus an additional 70 years beyond the author's death. If two or more authors created the work, copyright continues for 70 years after the last surviving author dies. Exceptions to copyright eligibility include, in the copyright offices' exact language, the following[19]:

- "Works that have not been fixed in a tangible form of expression (for example, choreographic works that have not been notated or recorded, or improvisational speeches or performances that have not been written or recorded)
- "Titles, names, short phrases, and slogans; familiar symbols or designs; mere variations of typographic ornamentation, lettering, or coloring; mere listings of ingredients or contents
- "Ideas, procedures, methods, systems, processes, concepts, principles, discoveries, or devices, as distinguished from a description, explanation, or illustration
- "Works consisting entirely of information that is common property and containing no original authorship (for example: standard calendars, height and weight charts, tape measures and rulers, and lists or tables taken from public documents or other common sources)."

Copyright Notice

Beginning March 1, 1989, you are not required to register or publish anything you created in order to establish copyright.[20] Such copyright is conferred automatically. Note, however, that registration *is* necessary if you were to sue someone for using your work without permission. Legal protection is greatest when you register your work within 90 days after first publication, rather than after you discover someone is using your work without permission.

Without registration, you may be able to recover only actual damages—which are usually tough to prove—and/or what profits the defendant(s) realized from infringing your work. Timely registration may also help you recover significant statutory damages and attorney fees.

Registration Proves You Own the Work

Registration provides a public record of proof that you own the work, and that your copyright is valid. A formal copyright notice identifies you, the year of first publication, and tells the public your work is protected by copyright.[21]

How to Register Copyright[22]

If you place a formal copyright notice on "visually perceptible" works such as video, scripts, graphics, or magazine articles, the notice must contain three elements:

- Either the symbol ©, the word Copyright, or the abbreviation Copr.
- The year the work was first published. (Exceptions occur when the picture, graphic, or even a sculpture is reproduced on jewelry, stationary, postcards, or similar items.)
- The name or an abbreviation that identifies the owner.

Thus, any of the following forms of copyright notice would suffice:

© 2012 Hans Jensen
Copyright 2012 Hans Jensen
Copr. 2012 Hans Jensen

Notice of copyright on sound recordings uses the symbol "P" in a circle (the designation for phonorecord, i. e., ℗ *2012 Wowza Records Inc.*) rather than the copyright symbol ©.

You can register your work at http://www.copyright.gov/eco/index.html, either electronically or using paper forms. See www.copyright.gov for information regarding your specific work and the number of copies to submit. You can download the most common copyright forms at http://www.copyright.gov/forms/formco2d.pdf

(You also can access either site to register online or by mail. Simply photograph the appropriate tag below on your smartphone, using an app such as Mobiletag or Scanlife.)

FIGURE 14.6A
Register Copyright Online

FIGURE 14.6B
Register Copyright by Mail

What You Own

If you (or an organization) wanted to hold a yard or tag sale to sell or give away some books, old newspapers, magazines, CDs, DVDs, film reels, phonograph records, and VHS tapes, you could. While you don't own the content (it's copyrighted), you do own the recording media (printed materials, DVDs, and video cassettes). Moreover, the publisher or other creator has already received a payment or royalty for every item you wish to sell.

Under the DMCA, it's a different story with content you download from the Internet. You could not sell that downloaded content, whether you bought an e-book novel or e-textbook, a Netflix movie streamed to your computer or TV, a digital copy of a *Chicago Tribune* or *Time* article, or copies of music from iTunes or Amazon. com. That's because *such items are copies of the original.* Just as you can't copy and distribute entire books, DVDs, CDs, magazines, newspapers, video or cassette tapes, and phonograph records in physical form, neither can you copy and distribute them in digital form.

Nothing on the Internet, other than a live webcast, is in its original physical form. While it's true that physical media are rarely available in their original form either, *the issue is whether the content originator is fairly compensated for copies downloaded from the Internet.* Anyone who copies and distributes digital media illegally deprives artists, writers, musicians, and other copyright holders of lawful income.

FAIR USE

The doctrine of **fair use** provides a defense against copyright infringement. As a television reporter, web journalist, or video journalist, you may wish to show, quote, or otherwise display part of someone else's work. You might quote part of an article or a book, for example, or show clips from a theatrical film as part of your critique of a copyrighted work. You might include a photo or two in your report from a touring exhibit. Copyright law allows publication of representative examples, or "fair use" of such materials, without permission from the copyright owner, provided you credit the work and its author(s). The "Fair Use" doctrine assumes that the public and the copyright owner potentially benefit from such limited but "enhanced" publication.

Section 107 of the United States Copyright Law extends "fair comment and criticism" to "news reporting, teaching, scholarship, and research." Still, how do you know whether a particular use is fair? Section 107 sets out four factors to help you decide[23]:

1. the purpose and character of the use, including whether such use is of commercial nature or is for nonprofit educational purposes
2. the nature of the copyrighted work
3. amount and substantiality of the portion used in relation to the copyrighted work as a whole
4. the effect of the use upon the potential market for or value of the copyrighted work.

In the words of Section 107, "…distinction between 'fair use' and infringement may be unclear and not easily defined. No specific number of words, lines, or notes that may safely be taken without permission. General guides for brevity, or how much work you can fairly copy without permission. Acknowledging the source of the copyrighted material does not substitute for obtaining permission."[24]

If you were to innocently include more content than fair use would allow in a story, you could put yourself, your employer, its owners, and its web host at risk. Whenever you're in doubt, even in private or semi-public communication, hesitate. You can't always know what to do regarding copyright and fair use, but you can always ask for legal guidance. As the Knight Citizen News Network notes, "Newspapers, magazines, and broadcast networks typically have their own lawyers. But citizen media outlets, bloggers, social network members and other Internet users generally don't have lawyers on standby."[25] Beyond such guidance lies yet another backup plan: "If in doubt, you must leave it out."

GENERAL FAIR USE GUIDELINES FOR EDUCATION AND PUBLISHING

Definitions for fair use vary, but the educational and publishing communities have generally agreed on guidelines from the Report of the House Committee on the Judiciary (H.R. 94-1476). Guidelines appear on numerous university web sites. You can find a representative example at the University of Pittsburg[26]:

Prose:
A complete article, story, or essay of less than 2,500 words

OR

An excerpt from any prose work of not more than 1,000 words or 10 percent of the work, whichever is less, but not less than 500 words

Illustration:
One chart, graph, diagram, drawing, cartoon, or picture per book or per periodical issue ■

Internet Service Providers

Section 512 protects the Internet Service Provider (ISP) from liability if it simply serves as a "passive conduit" for illegal or copyrighted content that a client or other user uploads. Protections vary according to the type of service the ISP offers. If it provides storage for caches, web hosting, or hyperlinking, then it must comply with a provision called "notice and take-down."[27] This provision requires that any online service provider must take down infringing material when the copyright owner gives notice of its presence on the provider's service.[28, 29]

Plagiarism

The doctrine of fair use has an evil twin called **plagiarism**, the act of representing someone else's work as your own. Anyone who appropriates copyrighted material without identifying the source is guilty of plagiarism. Stealing another's work is as simple as copying and pasting material off the Internet. It represents an ethical and moral lapse and can lead to litigation. Even unintentional plagiarism can get you fired. Telling the boss you acted innocently probably won't help much.[30]

You can avoid plagiarism if you simply attribute other people's work. No matter the source, attribute the material, whether you quote something from a book or a newspaper article, show a video clip or a web page, use a line from a song, or even use a direct or paraphrased quote from a conversation with another person. Also remember to attribute the source of ideas, opinions, and claims that others originate.

Even content that appears to reside in the public domain may have copyright protection. This includes e-mail, postings to social sites, and stories derived from or based on an existing work. You must also cite information that has passed out of copyright and that now exists in the public domain.

It's unnecessary to attribute common knowledge, such as the medical consensus that smoking is dangerous, or the popularity of gambling in Atlantic City and Las Vegas.

Chip Scanlan at the Poynter Institute offers a handy guide to help you avoid plagiarism at http://www.poynter.org/uncategorized/3323/the-first-peril-fabrication/

(To access Scanlan's guide, you can photograph the QR code in Figure 14.7 with your smartphone, using an app such as Mobiletag or Scanlife.)

| FIGURE 14.7

Obtain Rights When Necessary

Universities commonly notify faculty, staff, and students to first obtain the rights to use copyrighted material that exceeds fair use guidelines. You can find information about *protecting yourself* at many university web sites, including, for example, Indiana University.[31]

You can access information about *obtaining permission to use copyrighted works*, including the following works, at web sites such as the U.S. Copyright Office (Circular 22),[32] the Poynter Institute,[33] the University of California,[34] and eHow.com.[35]

- Works in Print
- Online Works
- Musical Works
- Images/Pictures
- Motion Pictures
- Software
- Syndicated Cartoons
- Syndicated Editorials
- Religious Works

Government Publications[36]

As a rule, works produced by the United States government have no copyright protection. Title 17 of the United States Code (17 USC § 105) states, "Copyright protection under this title is not available for any work of the United States Government, but the United States Government is not precluded from receiving and holding copyrights transferred to it by assignment, bequest, or otherwise."[37] (Note that all works without copyright must still be attributed.) The government has no obligation to make *all* works publically available, and it can deny access to even non-copyrighted works for reasons of national security, export control, and patent applications.

Sometimes the federal government acquires ownership of copyrighted works, which continue to retain their original copyright protection. The government does own copyright to the work, however, if an independent contractor assigns copyright back to the government. Hence, government works, such as public service announcements, sometimes carry copyright notice.[38]

Outside contractors may own copyright to the work they produce for the federal government, so it can be difficult to know which documents are in the "public domain" and which are not. Furthermore, the government doesn't have to give notice that its works carry no U.S. copyright, and it or its agencies may still copyright the works in other countries.[39, 40]

Freedom of Information Requests

If you believe your local, state, or federal government is withholding information in the public interest, but that would cause no harm other than to those who would deny its publication, you can file to see the document under Freedom of Information for disclosure of government information.

The Reporters Committee for Freedom of the Press offers the *Federal Government Guide* to open records and meetings laws, how to file requests for documents and records, and typical response times at http://www.rcfp.org/fogg/index.php

RCFP also offers the *State Open Government Guide* regarding open records and meetings laws in your state, and how to request such information, at http://www.rcfp.org/ogg/index.php

See also a state-to-state guide for access to government data at "Access to Electronic Records, http://www.rcfp.org/elecaccess/.

Municipal regulations, such as access to city council records, will be handled locally. Consult your local government for that information.

Using Information from Government Web Sites

Government web sites are not subject to copyright protection in the United States, provided government employees created the work as part of their official duties.[41] The rules change if a contractor develops or maintains a government web site. Then, any qualifying work the contractor created has copyright protection. Copyrighted work that others own but post to a government site carries similar protection.[42]

State and Local Government Copyright

Note that guidance up to this point refers only to the United States government and provisions of Title 17 of the United States Code. Assume that nothing covered herein applies when it comes to state and local governments. These entities often claim copyright to works they create, and they can demand, prohibit, or even restrict copyright on the works their agencies produce.[43] Your best protection is knowing how your state and local governments approach copyright practices, or at least know where to look on short notice.

Works Made for Hire

Your employer owns the copyright should you create or prepare a work as an employee, through you, the author. Neither would you own copyright if you signed a contract to create a "work for hire," nor would you own copyright for your contributions to a collective work, motion picture, or audio recording.[44]

In the case of works made for hire, and for anonymous and pseudonymous works ("unless the author's identity is revealed in Copyright Office records"), the duration of copyright extends for the shorter of 95 years from publication or 120 years from creation.[45, 46]

You will avoid copyright issues if you respect every creative individual's contributions through fair and accurate attribution, and if necessary, by seeking permission to use that person's copyrighted material.

A Legal Perspective

Questions about the law and its interpretations confront every journalist, frequently under the pressures and deadlines of field reporting. Whereas legal counsel may not be immediately available, every journalist can rely on a powerful ally called common sense. The answer to many legal questions is a product of nothing more than a sense of good judgment, fairness, taste, and a concern for the dignity—and privacy—of others. Treat others as you would expect to be treated in the same situation and, above all, remember: When in doubt, consult an authority—either station or legal.

SUMMARY

Self-interest requires that journalists stay abreast of laws that apply to the reporting process. Although the act of reporting the news can lead to legal challenges, many legal transgressions occur in the field during the process of gathering the news. Even when journalists are on solid legal ground, defending against lawsuits can be costly and time-consuming and tends to make reporters overly cautious in covering subsequent stories.

Two of the most important areas of concern to journalists are libel and invasion of privacy. Libel is the use of factual information, as opposed to opinion, that holds someone in hatred or contempt, subjects the person to ridicule, or otherwise lowers our esteem for the individual. Invasion of privacy is any act of intrusion, including trespass and publication of embarrassing facts, even if true, that violates an individual's reasonable expectation of a right to privacy.

Normally, to be liable for defamation, journalists must know that a statement is false or be aware it probably is false. An excellent protection against libel, therefore, is to have good reason to broadcast only statements you believe to be true, and to use due care in evaluating the truth of defamatory information. Another problem area is unsuspecting defamation, which can occur when generic or file video is used to illustrate a script that carries most of the reporting load.

One of the most common forms of invasion of privacy is trespass. The guiding rule is to obtain permission to enter any private or semiprivate area before you shoot, not afterward. Often, trespass is inadvertent and occurs because someone with apparent authority, perhaps a police officer or fire official, gives the photojournalist permission to shoot. Generally, the footage can be aired up to the point that someone with greater authority, perhaps the building owner, arrives and tells the photographer to leave.

The principle of limited invitation prohibits journalists from freely entering quasi-public businesses and institutions, such as restaurants and supermarkets, to report and take pictures.

Technology has created new opportunities for trespass and eavesdropping. Telephoto lenses and tiny microphones that can pick up hushed conversations from great distances are but two examples. In no case should you attempt to use concealed microphones or cameras, or make secret recordings without first obtaining competent legal counsel.

Telephone recordings can easily be used to invade an individual's privacy. Always advise the person on the other end that you intend to record the conversation, even if you intend to record it only for your records.

Some states require that both parties to conversations give their consent if the conversations are to be recorded. In other states a person acting in the reporter's place may be able to record a conversation, provided the person who carries the recorder understands what is happening.

Courts are extra sensitive about protecting children's rights to privacy. Be especially cautious about broadcasting children's names, pictures, or other information that would allow them to be identified, even when such information already is part of the public record.

Shield laws help protect the reporter's confidential sources, conversations, notes, and outtakes, but attorneys routinely try to subpoena such information. For maximum protection, tell no one the identities of secret sources or of the content of notes or outtakes. Once you reveal such knowledge, even to your supervisor, you forfeit your right to withhold the same information from the courts. When protecting sources, never promise a source complete confidentiality unless you're willing to go to jail indefinitely.

Whereas shield laws allow the journalist to protect confidential sources under certain circumstances, access or sunshine laws protect the journalist's ability to inspect records and other vital information that otherwise might be kept off-limits to the public.

Although most states allow television cameras and microphones into trial courts, permission normally is granted at the sole discretion of the trial judge, who may also require the defendant's or the attorney's consent. To help preserve the right to televise courtroom trials, reporters and photographers are obliged to dress appropriately to the courtroom environment, and they must strive to create the fewest distractions possible and follow the judge's rules and instructions to the letter.

Copyright is conferred automatically on works created after March 1, 1989. Neither publication nor copyright registration is required. Registration is required if you sue someone for using your work without permission. Legal protection is greatest if you register a work within 90 days of first publication, an action that could help you recover not only actual damages but significant statutory damages and attorney fees.

Fair use allows publication of representative samples of work, such as a quote, a video scene, a book passage, or one or two photos from a touring exhibit, without obtaining the copyright owner's permission, although what constitutes "fair use" is open to debate. Some firms that buy up others' copyrights troll the Internet, hoping to reach lucrative settlements even for innocent infringements.

Generally, United States publications carry no copyright, although such works may still be copyrighted in other countries, and some publications may be withheld for reasons of national security, patent applications, and export control. The federal government does own the copyright to some donated works and whenever an independent contractor assigns copyright back to the government. Whether a work is copyrighted or not, it must be attributed.

Copyright for works that employees create belongs to the employer, or by virtue of a freelance contract to create a "work for hire." You would not own copyright for contributions to a collective work, motion picture, or audio recording.

Plagiarism is the act of representing someone else's work as your own. To avoid the problem, seek permission to use the work, and be certain to attribute it. Otherwise, follow fair use guidelines and always attribute.

In all matters regarding law and the gathering and reporting of news, the best guide to the proper course of action is to be found in good judgment, fairness, taste, and a concern for the dignity and privacy of others. Beyond these considerations, remember the adage "When in doubt, seek help."

KEY TERMS

apparent authority   242
copyright   252
defamation   238
fair use   254
generic video   241
Internet   237

invasion of privacy   240
law   238
libel   238
limited invitation   243
plagiarism   255
pool coverage   249

shield laws   246
slander   238
subpoena   246
trespass   240

DISCUSSION

1. At what point during the reporting process must journalists be concerned about considerations of law? Explain your answer.
2. Discuss the potential chilling effect that litigation or the threat of litigation can have on video content. Provide an example or two as part of your response.
3. What right, if any, does the journalist have to gather the news?
4. Explain the customary definition of libel as it applies to digital journalists. Is it possible to "visually libel" a person with the video camera or through a television graphic?
5. What actions on the part of video journalists might constitute invasion of privacy?
6. What steps can the journalist take to avoid libel suits?
7. What are the most important actions a journalist can take to protect against charges of negligence in libel suits?
8. Discuss the Sullivan Rule as it applies to public figures or persons who have voluntarily placed themselves in the public view.
9. Why is it important to use caution when using police information as the main source of potentially defamatory statements?
10. Discuss the potentially dangerous journalistic practice of using generic video, also known as inadvertent cutaways, which can lead to libel and invasion of privacy suits. Suggest alternatives that can help the journalist avoid unsuspecting defamation or "guilt by illustration."
11. Discuss the principle of apparent authority as it applies to invasion of privacy.
12. Explain the role of technology in creating new opportunities for trespass and invasion of privacy.
13. Even routine telephone use can lead to lawsuits for invasion of privacy. Describe steps the journalist can take to avoid legal problems, especially when making telephone recordings.
14. What precautions are essential for the journalist to observe in reporting news that involves children or juveniles?
15. Although shield laws may help the journalist protect a source's identity, that right can easily be forfeited. Explain how.
16. Discuss sunshine laws and the degree of protection they typically afford journalists and the public.
17. Discuss your views about the role of television in the courtroom. To what extent do you believe journalists should have an unqualified right to record and report courtroom trials? How do you respond to the Judicial Conference of the United States ruling in late 1994 to ban television cameras in federal courtrooms?
18. What standards of conduct and dress should the photojournalist observe when photographing courtroom trials?
19. What considerations should govern a journalist's relationship with jurors both during and after the trial?
20. When is it legal to use other people's music, images, and words without their permission under the doctrine of fair use?
21. Discuss common limitations on what constitutes acceptable length or duration of material cited or used under provisions of fair use.

EXERCISES

1. Invite a television news director, general manager, or public relations manager to discuss steps the organization routinely takes to avoid libel suits and other legal challenges. A number of stations conduct ongoing legal seminars to help news employees stay sensitive to legal issues and aware of changes in the law. Some stations may allow you to attend such seminars.

2. Seek to identify and interview a newspaper or television reporter whose story has resulted in litigation.

3. You can request personal copies of pocket-sized legal references from many state bar, press, and broadcast associations. Such references commonly cover libel and invasion of privacy laws (including trespass and eavesdropping), and state laws that help protect the journalist's right of access to public records.

4. Attend a trial where television cameras are allowed in the courtroom and observe the procedures that reporters and photographers follow.

5. Watch television or cable newscasts for the use of generic video or inadvertent cutaways that might potentially lead to libel or invasion of privacy suits.

6. Write a short letter to an imaginary trial judge requesting permission to shoot video at an upcoming criminal trial. Attempt to anticipate and answer whatever objections a judge might have to your request.

7. Suggest reporter guidelines for recognizing where the limitations of "fair use" become "infringement of copyright."

NOTES

1. David Kravets. "Newspaper Chain's New Business Plan: Copyright Suits," Wired.com, published July 22, 2010, http://www.wired.com/threatlevel/2010/07/copyright-trolling-for-dollars/ (accessed January 3, 2011).

2. Ibid.

3. Ibid.

4. U.S. Supreme Court, New York Times Co. v. Sullivan, 376 U.S. 254 (1964), No. 39, Argued January 6, 1964, Decided March 9, 1964. For full text see http://supreme.justia.com/us/376/254/case.html

5. Jim Redmond, Frederick Shook, Dan Lattimore, and Laurie Lattimore-Volkman, *The Broadcast News Process*, 7th ed. (Englewood, CO: Morton, 2005).

6. http://www.rcfp.org/taping/quick.html and http://defend-yourself-go-pro-se.blogspot.com/2011/05/can-we-tape-or-record.html

7. "Shop Talk at Thirty: A Case for Courtroom Cameras," *RTNDA Digest*, as reprinted with permission from *Editor & Publisher*, from a speech delivered May 18, 1984, by Edward Estlow, president of the E. W. Scripps Company, before the Judicial Conference of the Sixth U.S. Circuit, 3.

8. Ibid.

9. Harriet Chiang, "Ito's Snakepit," *San Francisco Chronicle* (February 12, 1995), 1.

10. Ibid.

11. "TV Cameras Barred from Federal Courts," *San Francisco Examiner*, September 22, 1994, A-11.

12. "Out of Order," *Denver Post*, September 22, 1994, 18-A.

13. Tony Mauro, "Use It or Lose It," *RTNDA Communicator* (August 1993), 9.

14. "Judicial Conference allows cameras in federal district courts," The Reporters Committee for Freedom of the Press, September 15, 2010, http://www.rcfp.org/newsitems/index.php?i=11558 (accessed January 13, 2011).

15. Radio-Television News Directors Association Legal Seminar, "Broadcast Coverage of the Courts," Denver, CO, June 2, 1984.

16. Excerpted from "Cameras in Colorado Courtrooms," (Aurora, CO: Colorado Broadcasters Association), 1983, and "Expanded media coverage of court proceedings," Media Alert, Colorado Courts, ensuing from Colorado Supreme Court Rules, Chapter 38, Rule 2, Media

Coverage of Court Proceedings, effective July 1, 2010, http://www.courts
.state.co.us/userfiles/file/Media/Cameras%202010%20update.pdf (accessed January
3, 2011).

17. Digital Millennium Copyright Act of 1998, http://www.copyright.gov/legislation
/dmca.pdf (accessed January 13, 2011).

18. You can download a summary copy of *The Digital Millennium Copyright Act Of 1998*
from the U.S. Copyright Office at http://www.copyright.gov/legislation/dmca.pdf

19. "Copyright Basics," U.S. Copyright Office, http://www.copyright.gov/circs/circ1.pdf
(accessed January 11, 2011).

20. Ibid.

21. Susan Montgomery, John Welch, and Tom Hemnes, Vol. 9, No. 1, "United States: Benefits
of timely copyright registration," International Bar Association Committee L News
Newsletter of the Intellectual Property and Entertainment Law; Committee of the Section
on Business Law, http://www.foleyhoag.com/newscenter/publications
/general/benefits-of-timely-copyright-registration.aspx (accessed January 11, 2011).

22. "Copyright Basics, U.S. Copyright Office, http://www.copyright.gov/circs/circ01.pdf
(accessed January 13, 2011).

23. "Limitations on exclusive rights: Fair use: § 107," *Copyright Law of the United States of
America* Circular 92, http://www.copyright.gov/title17/92chap1.html

24. "Copyright – Fair Use", U.S. Copyright Office, http://www.copyright.gov/fls/fl102
.html (accessed January 11, 2011).

25. "Top 10 Rules for Limiting Legal Risk," Knight Citizen News Network, an initiative of
J-Lab: The Institute for Interactive Journalism (accessed January 11, 2011).

26. See "Copyright Information: FAQ," University Library System Digital Library, University
of Pittsburg, at http://www.library.pitt.edu/guides/copyright/faqanswers.html

27. "Protecting Internet Platforms for Expression and Innovation," Center for Democracy and
Technology, May 3, 2010 (accessed January 11, 2010).

28. "Protecting Internet Platforms for Expression and Innovation (Sec. 2: "EU and U.S. Policies
Protect Intermediaries from Liability"), Center for Democracy and Technology, http://
www.cdt.org/policy/protecting-internet-platforms-expression-and-innovation (accessed
January 11, 2011).

29. "Copyright Law Meets the World Wide Web," http://www.acm.org/crossroads
/xrds2-2/weblaw.html (accessed January 11, 2011).

30. Susan Kinzie, "An Education in the Dangers of Online Research," *Washington Post*, http://
www.washingtonpost.com/wp-dyn/content/article/2008/08/09/AR2008080901453.html
(accessed January 11, 2011).

31. See http://filesharing.iu.edu/protect

32. See http://www.copyright.gov/circs/circ22.pdf

33. See http://www.poynter.org/uncategorized/775/copyright-issues-and-answers/

34. See http://www.universityofcalifornia.edu/copyright/permission.html

35. See http://www.ehow.com/how_18035_permission-copyrighted-material.html

36. "Frequently Asked Questions About Copyright: Issues Affecting the U.S. Government
(Section 3.0 U.S. Government Works," CENDI (the Commerce, Energy, NASA, Defense
Information Managers Group), http://www.cendi.gov/publications/04-8copyright.html
(accessed January 12, 2011).

37. "17 U.S.C. § 105. Subject matter of copyright: United States Government works,"
*Copyright Law of the United States of America and Related Laws Contained in Title 17
of the United States Code, Circular 92*, U. S. Copyright Office, http://www
.copyright.gov/title17/92chap1.html#105 (accessed January 12, 2011).

38. "Can the government copyright its works? (3.6)," Copyright Law, The [Stason] Ultimate
Learn and Resource Center, http://stason.org/TULARC/business/copyright/3-6-Can-the-
government-copyright-its-works.html (accessed January 12, 2011).

39. "Freedom of Information Act Guide," U.S. Department of Justice, http://www.justice
.gov/oip/foi-act.htm (accessed January 12, 2011).

40. "Frequently Asked Questions About Copyright: Issues Affecting the U.S. Government," CENDI Copyright Task Group, http://www.cendi.gov/publications/04-8copyright.html#317 (accessed January 12, 2011).

41. Ibid, (3.1.9)

42. 17 U.S.C. § 201 (D), Copyright Law of the United States of America and Related Laws Contained in Title 17 of the *United States Code* Circular 92, Chapter 2, http://www .copyright.gov/title17/92chap2.html (accessed January 12, 2011).

43. CENDI, op cit, (3.2.3)

44. See http://www.copyright.gov/title17/92chap1.html

45. "Copyright Basics."

46. "Works Made for Hire Under the 1976 Copyright Act," *Circular 9*, United States Copyright Office, http://www.publishers.org/main/Copyright/attachments /RPAC_powerpoints_1.pdf (accessed January 11, 2011).

15

Journalistic Ethics

Numerous journalists make unethical decisions during their careers, sometimes further diminishing public trust and confidence in the profession. Some journalists use deception to expose deception, citing occasions when it may be both necessary and ethical to break the law to expose a larger wrongdoing—to obtain false identities, for example, to show how easily false documents can be obtained. Others might practice misrepresentation to gather evidence of nursing home fraud, for example, by posing as a patient's relative. Still other journalists, equally committed to serving the public good, may leap from concealed areas with cameras rolling to ambush unsuspecting adversaries. Later they may march with those same cameras, unannounced, into offices, businesses, and other private property.

The defense for such practices can be persuasive. "How else could we prove fraudulent practices at the cancer clinic unless we posed as cancer patients ourselves?" they ask. "If I hadn't sneaked a look at documents in the DA's office, our community might never have learned of prostitution kickbacks to local police," another maintains. "Television is a visual medium; how else can we demonstrate the national problem of illegally obtained passports unless we misrepresent the identities of crew and misrepresent the reasons we're shooting this footage?"

DEFINITION OF ETHICS

As such discussion implies, law and ethics are intertwined. Often, unethical activities also are illegal. Breaking and entering, theft, trespass, and intentional libel are but a few examples. However, ethics is a branch of philosophy, not of law, and the distinction between the two is clear. Whereas laws are rules of living and conduct enforced by an external authority (usually by means of penalties), **ethics** are the rules of living and conduct that you impose on yourself, or that your profession strongly suggests you should impose on yourself, and few enforceable penalties exist. At its core, ethics include your own determination of what is fair, truthful, accurate, compassionate, and responsible conduct.

EFFECTS OF COMPETITION

Many ethical problems that reporters encounter come from knowing the competition is in head-to-head combat—and pushing hard (Figure 15.1). In their zeal to be first with the best story, some reporters overstep the boundaries that define ethical behavior. Every few years a reporter gains national notoriety for faking news stories or plagiarizing the work of other reporters. Other reporters trample lawns, snoop in mailboxes, misrepresent their identities, speak falsehoods to reticent news sources to force responses, stage news events, and generally conduct themselves unprofessionally. The public takes note of such transgressions and, over time, journalists and their profession lose credibility because of it.

In the 1980s a third of U.S. citizens believed news reports were often inaccurate. In 2000 that number jumped to almost two-thirds of those polled, primarily because of the post-presidential election controversy in Florida that year. Gallup Poll interviews since then find that nearly 60 percent of those interviewed rated news stories as "often inaccurate," with 36 percent rating them "accurate."[1] A CBS News/New York Times Poll conducted in 2006 found that only about half the respondents said they trusted the media "most of the time," whereas more than a third said they believe news media tell the truth "only some of the time."[2] Again in a 2010 Gallup survey on media use and evaluation, only 12 percent of respondents said they had a great deal of trust in newspapers, television and radio news, while 57 percent said they trusted those media not very much or not at all.[3] *Confidence* in newspapers and television news has reached near record lows, with only 1 in 4 Americans having "a great deal or quite a lot" of confidence in those media.[4] The journalist's most valuable asset is

FIGURE 15.1

The pressures of competition to be first with the best story can significantly influence the journalist's ethical and professional conduct. *Copyright © 2012 Scott Rensberger*

not simply the headline-making story, but credibility itself. If the audience does not find the journalism profession credible, little else matters.

SITUATIONAL ETHICS

One story after another invites the reporter and photojournalist to redefine ethical conduct. The practice of judging a situation based on the good that will likely come from a particular course of action is called **situational ethics**. As a philosophical theory, situational ethics can either help or harm the journalist. Will coverage of a suicide attempt illuminate the helplessness of unemployment, or is the journalist's first obligation to save the person's life? Is it the photographer's duty to rescue victims from an overturned school bus or to shoot footage of the rescue for a story addressing the larger issue of school bus safety? The answers to such questions inevitably vary according to the story, its treatment, and the journalist covering the story.

Given that journalists as a class adhere to no universally accepted code of ethics, who then regulates the journalist's conduct and establishes the norms for competence and ethical behavior? Traditionally, individuals and institutions throughout most levels of society have searched for methods to force journalists to conduct themselves ethically and to license them, if necessary, to achieve that objective.

LICENSING

The call to license journalists might even sound reasonable. Before doctors or lawyers can practice their professions, they must complete rigorous study, demonstrate their competence before peers, and be licensed in the state in which they practice. By contrast, anyone can become a journalist by assigning oneself the title; no license or formal review of competence is required. Yet journalists remain as accountable to their clients as lawyers and doctors, and their ethical behavior must be equally above reproach. Why, then, should journalists not have to meet the same standards as other professionals?

In the United States, a predominant attitude has been that journalists cannot be licensed, because to do so would be to license their ideas. Only journalists who disseminated an approved doctrine might qualify for licenses. If a journalist's point of view differs from that of a review board, who can reasonably say such difference constitutes "incompetence"?

Because every administration and special interest group wants to cast itself in the most favorable light, and wants its views heard above all others, concepts like "competence" and "official doctrine" vary according to who is in power. If licensing were imposed, whose versions of truth should be used as the foundations on which to license journalists? Republicans? Democrats? Socialists? Protestants? Muslims? Jews? White supremacists? Abortion rights advocates? Right-to-life advocates? Hunting groups? Environmentalists? Conservative courts? Liberal courts? The most reasonable answer would seem to advocate the responsible dissemination of all ideas. Ultimately, the engine that drives a democracy is precisely the freedom to debate and to adopt and promote differing philosophies and points of view.

CONTRACT WITH THE PUBLIC

In the end, a far more powerful review board than any public agency or congressional law governs journalistic conduct in the United States. Each hour of each day, this same entity—the public—extends and renews the journalist's license to operate, by virtue of its patronage. David Halberstam, former *New York Times* correspondent who received the Pulitzer Prize for his Vietnam War reporting, once likened the journalist's press card to a social credit card that is subject to periodic renewal. While this social credit card is not a formal document, it represents an extension of trust that viewers can withdraw at will and without advance notice. Even when the public overlooks a journalist's indiscretions, there remains a group of peers, employers, and even advertisers who can bring powerful sanctions against that journalist.

As the CBS reporter Edward R. Murrow once observed, "to be believable, [journalists] must be credible." Today, as suspicions of malpractice increase, magazine and newspaper advertisements ask why reporters don't at least practice the Code of Ethics of the Society of Professional Journalists (Sigma Delta Chi), a code outsiders sometimes view as a rough equivalent of the Hippocratic Oath for physicians. However, no code of ethics could answer every dilemma the journalist faces in covering the news.

AT ISSUE: IMAGE MANIPULATION

Photographs have the kind of authority over imagination today, which the printed word had yesterday, and the spoken word before that. They seem utterly real. They come, we imagine, directly to us without human meddling, and they are the most effortless food for the mind conceivable.

Walter Lippman
Public Opinion

Cultural values may have led earlier generations to believe in the inherent fairness and accuracy of reality-based video. Sometimes this category includes content on sites such as YouTube, Facebook, and *The Daily Show with Jon Stewart*. Such sites feature content ranging from comedy to satire, commentary, drama, personal perspectives, and political entertainment. They may turn to riveting and accurate news reporting and analysis from time to time, provided it builds ratings or enhances their brand. In the main, however, their primary emphasis is on peer-to-peer communication, advertising, entertainment, satire and comedy.

Note the distinction between reality-based video and reality-based programming. Today's so-called reality programs may stage events; direct participants to perform certain activities; or imply through word, deed and omission that what you're watching is reality. Such programs may feature ordinary people in supposedly unscripted situations, but their primary emphasis is on entertainment and sensationalism.

By contrast, legitimate video *news organizations and comparable outlets* strive to present accurate, fair and impartial news content. They place primary emphasis on reporting, packaging and disseminating accurate visual reports *and stories* of news, public affairs, and extended formats such as investigative specials and documentaries.

We expect news organizations, then, never to omit essential information and to avoid all fraudulence, manipulation, deception, and misrepresentation. Their obligation is to fairly reconstruct or represent what actually happened, or to fairly portray the person or issue in question. This may require alerting viewers they're watching a staged or reenacted event, but that it fairly and accurately depicts what happened.

Not all communication is true, of course. Reporters make mistakes, misunderstand what they see and hear, omit vital facts or main points, trust inaccurate information they've confirmed with multiple sources, or accept at face value what police and political sources tell them. Producers, assignment editors and news directors sometimes influence story angles and content via personal bias, reliance upon assumptions or amended facts, or their inability to keep up with what's happening in the field.

What to Do?

Despite our best intentions, technology sometimes outwits us. High definition television brings viewers face to face with people's physical imperfections. With clarity roughly six times greater than analog television,[5] high-def cameras magnify everything from acne scars to wrinkles, bags under the eyes, and poor makeup jobs. High-def studio lighting and adjustments in make-up help hide those imperfections for news anchors, but without similar lighting adjustments in the field an anchor, reporter or virtually anyone else can suddenly appear ten years older.[6] Field lighting thus takes on greater importance than ever.

BOX 15.1 CLASSIC VIEWS OF ETHICAL NEWS PHOTOGRAPHY IN JOURNALISM

"Journalism," says *Toledo Blade* ombudsman Jack Lessenberry, "is supposed to show the world as it is, not as we would like it to be. That is perfectly understood by anyone who gets into the business. To do otherwise is to lie not only to your boss, but to your market--the public you serve.[7]

"Multimedia journalism demands that you learn how to gather and edit audio and video content, and write web-based articles, create podcasts, and sometimes produce blogs. Such multi-tasking invites journalists to create troublesome shortcuts," says Rich Beckman, 'new journalism educator' and Knight Chair in Visual Journalism at the University of Miami. "We need ambient sound, but lack the time to record it on location. Why not just use stock sound available on-line or from the station's audio library, or transfer an audio track from one soccer game and use it in another? The point is, "borrowed" sound never amounts to actual content recorded at the source. It never existed until you created it. It is an inaccurate representation."[8]

The same considerations apply to digitally altered still photographs and video. While such editing may make an image, whether still or moving, more esthetically pleasing, it still amounts to falsification, writes Donald R. Winslow, editor of *Photographer Magazine*. Purists may argue that composition, exposure, even the photographic angle itself amount to editorial manipulation, thus impacting viewer perceptions of content and meaning. Audiences need to know they are watching reconstructions of actual events, rather than recreations embellished to create greater viewer appeal. For such reasons, respectable media organizations avoid image manipulation.[9]

"It's never okay to digitally alter news photographs, even for the supposed purpose of 'good taste,'" says *News Photographer* editor Donald Winslow.[10]

Make Your Case About Digital Manipulation

In the main, either an employer provides ethical guidelines to follow, or else you must decide for yourself what is right or wrong. The following questions can help you define, perhaps challenge, your ethical viewpoints regarding digital manipulation. As you answer each question, please assume your mandate is to present accurate, fair and impartial news content at all times.

1. It's often said, "Perception is reality." How do you define the differences?
2. Consider the different meanings of "reality" and "perception," and "a reality." To what extent do the terms represent any similarities?
3. Do you believe it's possible to capture what really happened with a single still or video camera, or even several cameras? Please explain your viewpoint.
4. In your experience, is it reasonable to assume every photographer will photograph or otherwise document the same event from the same

locations, angles, focal length lens settings, camera settings, composition, time, or lighting conditions? If yes, please explain why you so believe. If you believe such an outcome is statistically impossible, explain how such differences in approach might impact the viewer's perception of reality.

5. Do you believe you have or will encounter situations in your own life where you must earn and keep the public trust? If yes, please list five representative situations that might require your most ethical conduct while gathering, photographing, writing and editing the content in question.

6. As a professional in a competitive media environment, is it possible to capture reality, or only to reconstruct a reasonable characterization of how you saw and photographed something?

7. If two photographers cover the same event or issue, what might prevent audiences from coming away with the same perceptions of what happened or was considered? Could a still or video editor, graphic artist, or even a writer, similarly impact meanings through choice of words, artwork or typography? Explain how or why not.

8. Are not images much the same as words whose meanings people perceive subjectively, according to their own teaching, prior experience and emotional makeup?

9. To what extent does the still camera capture "truth"—that is, can a single photo capture an accurate, representative portrayal of reality—whether of a subject, event, or issue—in a single photograph? Explain either how that might be possible, or why it's impossible. Provide an image that proves your point.

10. Is it possible to lie about or misrepresent reality with a still camera? With a video camera? Please explain your viewpoint.

11. Assume you're the manager at a newspaper, magazine or web production facility. The photo editor asks you to rule on a photo showing a winsome woman with facial blemishes. *"They create too many distractions,"* says the photo editor. *"You'd never notice her blemishes in person, but they dominate the photo."* Do you tell editor

to leave the photo as is, or to remove the blemishes with software? You might either decide, *"Leave the photo as is,"* or *"Let's make her look the same as she does in real life. That should harm no one."* As manager, what do you tell the photo editor, and how do you justify your decision to her?

12. As a photographer, explain how you could manipulate viewer feelings (emotional responses) with a still or video camera. Further, explain how you could influence viewer feelings by manipulating images or video using software.

13. Do you believe images or video can ever convey the same meaning as words? Why or why not?

14. Is one picture ever worth a thousand words? If no, why not? If yes, how so?

15. Is one word ever worth a thousand pictures? Please explain your viewpoint.

16. It's said that images most often report to the heart, while the printed word reports first to the intellect. Do you believe that a viewer's emotional reaction originates from something in the images you recorded, or in how you recorded them—or both? Explain your reasoning.

17. To what extent do you believe it's acceptable for a legitimate news organization to manipulate a still image using Adobe Photoshop™ or InDesign™? How about manipulating video in Final Cut Pro™; Avid™; or Adobe Premiere™, or similar software?

18. Is a still photograph more accurate if you eliminate distractions that occurred naturally or unavoidably in the still photo you will show viewers? Assume, for example, you want to show a high school scoreboard but eliminate some tennis shoes that belong to students standing behind the scoreboard? Your editor says 'change nothing.' How do you make a case that it's fair to eliminate unnecessary distractions, whether in writing or in images? Contrast your answer with the notion that journalists omit much of what they observe in written reports. Are not their omissions made to reinforce clarity? In what ways is the written report different from editing a photo to enhance clarity or eliminate distractions and the non-essential?

19. Do you believe it's acceptable to use software to change the exposure or contrast in a photo?

20. Back to the scoreboard: what will you say and do if the same editor who told you not to eliminate legs and feet, now wants you to enhance the same shot's exposure and contrast so viewers can see minute but important detail that otherwise would remain invisible? What if the winning coach could see game time remaining, but the losing coach couldn't see the scoreboard against the sun's glare? If the story hinges on the losing coach's inability to see the scoreboard, what should the image show? If the story hinges on the winning coach's advantage, what should the image show? Which best represents "reality" or what actually happened?

21. Composition sometimes is defined as showing viewers what you want them to see. Is it acceptable to recompose a shot with your camera while in the field?

22. Is it ever acceptable to crop or recompose a shot with software after you return from the field?

23. Is it acceptable while in the field to soften contrast or color if you only use lens filters or change exposure? How about using software after you return from the field? What do you say if a team member or superior demands that your still photo or video is "too harsh—make it look like it really was just before dawn"?

24. Long focal length lenses, wide apertures, and long distances between a subject and your camera can result in backgrounds that appear out of focus. Should you ever use a certain focal length lens, or perhaps change distance between the camera and subject to place viewer attention where you want it within the frame? To sharpen focus or soften it? Is it acceptable to use software to manipulate depth of field in the image after you return from the field? Why or why not? Under what conditions, if any?

25. Is composing a shot or scene in the field with the zoom lens more ethical than recomposing or cropping it with computer software? If so, in what way?

26. Zooming in no way replicates how viewers see an event. The human eye never zooms. Is a zoom therefore ethically permissible in video shots? Why or why not?

27. The human eye cannot pan a scene like a video camera does. The eye looks here, then there, and forms a composite of all the "shots" it takes. Is a panning movement therefore ethically prohibited? Why or why not?

28. Assume that a person photographed under indoor fluorescent light shows up on screen with a greenish skin tone. Later in a video story or photo spread, a different person photographed under incandescent light appears orangish-yellow. In both cases, the photographer forgot about color balance. Is it ethically warranted to digitally manipulate these shots to more accurately portray a person as they appear in real life? Please explain your position. Does your answer conflict with anything you've said elsewhere in this section?

29. A renowned media ethicist conducts an ethics workshop at your organization. During the presentation, he shows two video network news stories, both identical except for one difference. The original photographer produced both videos, using the same equipment, with the same settings and composition, and edited them identically. The first video tells the story on a sunny day; the second video shows the story on a rainy, fog-shrouded day. Viewers saw only one story, not both. In your view, does one version distort the "truth" more than another? Could viewers watch either video and come away with the same understanding and sense of place? **A)** Please explain why or why not. (Note: You may have read elsewhere that the heart of most good stories lies in how story subjects react to situations that confront them. **B)** Could both stories convey the journalist's identical message and focus, or would the weather—and changes in mood and subject reaction—alter what viewers remember about the story and the central character? ■

CASE STUDIES IN ETHICAL DILEMMAS

With few opportunities to define ethical standards under the pressure of deadlines and instant reporting, journalists must establish solid editorial and ethical philosophies before those dilemmas arise. The following situations are offered to help the reporter and photojournalist accomplish that objective. They encompass such situations as trespass, illegal surveillance, and invasion of privacy. As in most ethical deliberations, there are few answers, mostly questions.

As you consider the following ethical situations,[11] you might want to know that professional journalists were divided in roughly equal numbers about whether to proceed in such circumstances or to avoid becoming involved. Panels that addressed these issues convened at the NPPA Television News-Video Workshop. Panel members included news directors, photographers, and reporters. Videos of the first four panels are available from the National Press Photographers Association, 3200 Croasdaile Drive, Suite 306, Durham, NC 27705. Also, see http://nppa.org/. The legal principles raised here are addressed in Chapter 14, Law and the Digital Journalist. *You'll find a discussion of each situation at the end of this chapter.* For more case studies, see http://journalism.indiana.edu/resources/ethics/

Trespass

Case 1. Safety officials have condemned an abandoned, privately owned building and posted it as unfit for human habitation. The owner has constructed a fence to keep out transients and children who might otherwise enter. "No trespassing" signs are prominently posted.

Last evening a child died and two others were injured when a stairway collapsed inside the building. A community citizens group says the building is one of dozens that pose such dangers. You are assigned to shoot video and a reporter standup inside the building. You can't locate the owner to obtain permission to enter the building, but police suggest they might look the other way should you decide to trespass. Will you enter the building illegally or stay out?

Case 2. You are researching an investigative report about a palm reader who is said to con elderly people out of their life savings. You visit the palm reader at her place of business and she tells you to get lost. Later you decide to visit her at her residence. A "No trespassing" sign is posted on the front gate of the fence around her property. Will you go up to her house and knock on the door? Will you jump the fence if the gate is locked?

Surveillance Photography

The palm reader regularly invites elderly people to her residence, where you believe she conducts many of her con operations. One night you notice she has left the curtains open and the shades up, and you can see her sitting at a table with people who appear to be clients. Will you stand on the street and photograph the woman's activities through the open window? Will you try to obtain sound with a shotgun or parabolic microphone?

Hostage Coverage

Case 1. An emotionally disturbed man holds hostages inside a sleazy bar. He says he'll kill one of the hostages unless he can broadcast a message to his wife. Police ask you to loan them your video camera so two of their officers can pose as a reporter–photographer crew to gain entry to the bar. You don't have time to contact the assignment desk or news director for advice. What will you decide?

Case 2. A distraught father holds his children hostage in a private home. Through the window, he can see your camera. He opens the door and shouts that he'll kill himself unless you leave the area. Unknown to the man, police plan to rush the house in about fifteen minutes, and your assignment editor has told you not to miss the action. Do you retreat? When police rush the house, do you follow right behind them to photograph this dramatic, if unpredictable and possibly dangerous, moment?

Entrapment

To show how easy it is for minors to buy liquor, you send a seventeen-year-old minor into a couple of liquor stores, record video of the purchases through the store windows with a long lens from a van across the street, then walk into both stores, camera rolling, to interview the clerks. The clerks protest that you are guilty of entrapment and ambush journalism. How do you reply?

Invasion of Privacy

You wish to document a historic medical procedure in which your cameras would peer inside the patient's body. The patient is too ill to respond to your request. The doctors will give their approval, provided the patient's family doesn't object. You tell the family your audience has the right to see this moment of history unfolding. The family says, "Sorry, but we don't want our relative to become a sideshow for TV news people. Permission denied." What should you (and your station) do next?

Violence

Case 1. You cover a demonstration that turns violent. Four persons are injured. Your camera is rolling as a demonstrator steps into the frame, shoots, and kills a police dog. Police club some demonstrators. Elsewhere, demonstrators threaten police officers with baseball bats. Will you show this violence on the evening news to give the audience an accurate portrayal of the event?

Case 2. You're photographing a federal informer as he walks along a courthouse hallway between two marshals. Suddenly a man steps from a telephone booth and shoots the informer dead. You capture the event on video. Will you show the scene of the killing on tonight's news? If your competition shows it?

Protecting Confidential Sources

You're preparing a story on a radical terrorist group. You promise not to reveal sources or confidential information when you first talk with the terrorist leader. Later he tells you the group has lost control of one of its members who plans to bomb the federal court building tomorrow night. Will you go to the police or FBI with your information?

Breaking and Entering

You're producing a half-hour special on drug use in your city and have learned the address of a drug dealer. You go to the house, but no one answers when you knock on the door. You then notice that a window is open. You determine the house is vacant. Will you climb inside to check out the place or will you not enter the house?

Destroying Police Evidence

A person has been stabbed to death in a hotel. You arrive with your camera just as police arrive. The detective, an old acquaintance, tells you to go in, shoot your video, and leave before crime lab technicians arrive. He says if you don't act now, the technicians won't let you in for fear you might disturb evidence, perhaps even destroy clues to the murderer's identity. The detective doesn't seem all that worried that your presence inside the room might destroy evidence. Do you shoot the murder scene or not enter the room at all?

Televising Executions

Your state has approved your right to televise live broadcasts of executions. Your news director believes the public is ready for live broadcasts, but he wants to record the execution for broadcast during the late evening news for the event's "deterrent value." The general manager also has endorsed a delayed broadcast of the execution, citing her belief that if a society endorses capital punishment, then citizens should see the consequences. What do you say—and do?

Covering Suicide Attempts

Case 1. You're en route to work when your assignment editor calls you about a woman who's threatened to jump from a bridge with her one-year-old child in her arms unless her estranged husband returns immediately and makes up his arrears in alimony. You're one of the first people on the scene. When you arrive, the mother makes a further demand that your station broadcast a live appeal from her to her husband. A woman who identifies herself as the distraught woman's mother runs up to her daughter, clutches her, and says to you, "Put down that damn camera and help me grab her!" Do you put down your camera, or do you continue to record video?

Case 2. A man who is emotionally disturbed has perched himself atop an office building and says he plans to jump to his death because his protracted unemployment has made it impossible for him to provide for his family. He's telephoned your station and competing stations to advise newsrooms of his planned suicide. Do you cover the event?

Illegally Obtained Information

You're at the district attorney's office. He leaves the room to find some information you've requested. While you wait, you notice an interesting file folder lying open on his desk. Do you look at the top page? The top three or four pages? Do you make notes if the information appears to be of interest? If the file folder is closed, would you open it, especially if you believe it could provide information important to a story you're doing?

Yielding Editorial Control of News Content

A truck carrying nuclear warheads overturns on a highway in your area. The defense department prohibits any photographers at the area on grounds of safety and national security. Defense department officials say they will escort reporters into the area and permit them to photograph selected views of the accident, on condition they submit all video recordings for defense department screening before they are aired. Should you agree to these conditions to obtain footage?

Cooperating with Police

Inside an office building, now surrounded by a SWAT team, an armed man has shot out several windows and asked for a live television interview so he can broadcast his message to the public. Officers say that unless they can impersonate your crew, they may have to storm the building with resulting injury or loss of life. They promise you can air any of the footage they manage to record. If you hand over your credentials and camera to the police, will you air any footage or interviews the police manage to shoot? If you don't hand over your camera, would you use video the police later shot with their own camera?

Private Lives of Public Officials

What will you do if you are the first to confirm information that a prominent individual, perhaps a state senator, is having an affair? Has been diagnosed as having a serious but not life-threatening illness? Is undergoing psychiatric counseling for marital difficulties? Is showing early signs of senility in everyday conduct, which, although not evident to the public, is readily apparent to a loyal staff? Is an alcoholic or abuses other drugs? Is gay or lesbian?

Misrepresentation

Case 1. You are sitting in a bar where you happen to engage in a conversation with the new city attorney. The attorney thinks you're just another person at the bar and begins to open up, pouring out information that would make a great story. At this point, do you tell the attorney you're a journalist or do you hide the fact?

Case 2. You're investigating the death of a person who has died under mysterious circumstances. Relatives won't talk, but someone in the newsroom suggests you obtain information from the victim's relatives by posing as a coroner's assistant. Will you act on this suggestion?

Accepting Favors

Few news operations allow their journalists to accept favors from news sources. In the past such favors have included free airline, sporting event, and concert tickets; books; meals; magazine subscriptions; taxi fares; and limousine service. Freebies are dangerous precisely because of their intent: to obligate journalists to news sources in the hope of at least some coverage or more favorable coverage.

Today the general wisdom is that if the public pays, so does the journalist. If the story is newsworthy, the station can afford to cover it. Most journalists would agree that it is permissible to accept something as insignificant in value as a cup of coffee or an hors d'oeuvre at a charity ball that is equally free to the public.

Reporting in Context

The television camera is notorious for its ability to isolate events from the larger environments in which they exist. The camera, focusing naturally on the drama and the spontaneous evolution of a news event, can turn the reality of a few flooded streets into the illusion of a flood-ravaged city. It can make the angry faces of a few hundred protesters seem like a mob of thousands, or the towering flames of an apartment house fire seem like a reenactment of the burning of Atlanta.

No news report makes its journey into the minds of all viewers intact, and the potential for misunderstanding increases when events are reported out of context.

The next time protesters chain themselves to a railroad track to keep trains from carrying nuclear warheads through an urban area, it may be appropriate to contrast the protester's viewpoint with the majority opinion of the rest of the city's residents. Although it is important to show the event, and to provide a vicarious experience of what happened, it is equally important to place the story in perspective.

REVERSE-ANGLE QUESTIONS

As in all questions of ethics, the overriding precaution is to do nothing that would unjustifiably inflict damage on others or that anyone could misperceive and later use to damage the journalist's credibility. The advice applies to the practice of shooting reverse-angle questions after the interviewee has left the scene. Perhaps the reporter has phrased the question ineptly and wishes to restate it more articulately, this time on camera, or perhaps the reverse-angle question will be employed as an editing device to condense the interview with no loss of visual continuity.

To preserve one's journalistic integrity, reverse-angle questions must be asked while the interviewee is still present. The reporter may wish to give the interviewee a simple explanation of the need for such a shot. Otherwise, accusations may surface that the interview was edited out of context or that the interviewee was made to appear to say things he or she never said and does not believe.

STAGED NEWS EVENTS

Occasionally you may need to stage an event to be photographed. In fact, numerous news events are staged. Interviews and news conferences are among those events in which the time, location, and even the content and context are determined in advance (Figure 15.2). This form of staging is normally acceptable because it's so apparent to the viewer. The audience recognizes that no one can force interviewees to answer questions against their will, although unethical reporters have been known to coach persons to answer interview questions with predetermined answers. When we stage unfairly, we create something that did not exist. It would not have happened in our absence. When we stage fairly, we recreate what already existed—what would have happened even in our absence.

Not every instance of staging needs to be identified. No breach of ethics should occur if you ask subjects to perform some action common to their everyday routine that, even in your absence, they would normally perform anyway. You might, for example, wish to ask a person to come through the door to her office again, so you can reshoot the scene from a more appropriate angle. Perhaps an artist is not working in her studio the day you wish to shoot. No loss of public confidence should result if you ask the artist to sit down in the studio and paint for a few minutes, so you can shoot some video for your story. It is perhaps less ethical to tell the artist where to sit, how to sit, or what to paint, or to rearrange any part of the studio or any other environment to create a more pleasing composition for your own shots.

REENACTMENTS

Reenactment also is occasionally permissible. Perhaps you want to show how psychiatrists treat child abuse victims, but don't wish to interrupt therapy or invade the actual victim's privacy. Use reenactments sparingly, and anytime you do reenact an

FIGURE 15.2
News conferences are one example of stories that are staged in the sense that the time, location, and even the general content and context of the event are determined in advance.

event, tell your audience. They will respect your candor, and their belief in what you show and tell them will increase.

Another example of reenactment, potentially far more damaging to the reporter's credibility, is illustrated in the following scenario:

Reporting crews from three television stations have just arrived to interview a presidential candidate's state campaign manager the morning after the candidate's victory in the New Hampshire primary.

While the crews are still setting up but not yet rolling, they hear the campaign manager tell someone on the telephone, "I think we're going to take this state as easily as we took New Hampshire." All three stations miss the bite, but start rolling in hopes they can capture a similar statement before the campaign manager hangs up.

The conversation continues, but now the campaign manager is voicing a series of "uh huh's" into the telephone. Finally, one reporter hands the campaign manager a note that reads, "Talk about New Hampshire."

Finally, the campaign manager tells the person on the other end of the telephone, "Some reporters here want me to talk to you about New Hampshire," and he proceeds to talk about the previous day's primary victory. That night, some of the stations air the comments as if they were made during a spontaneous telephone conversation.

Of the numerous questions that surround such reporting methods, two are paramount. First, should the reporter have prompted the campaign manager to restate his original comments? Second, should reporters from the other stations have aired those comments as if they originated spontaneously? Does the note differ in its intent, had another journalist prompted the campaign manager verbally, using the same words?

Beyond the general subject, does the note suggest in any way what the campaign manager should say?

Some reporters would air the comments. Others would avoid airing them altogether. Still others answer the first two questions by asking a third: Would the audience have approved if it could have peered over the reporter's shoulder as he handed the campaign manager that note?

FILE VIDEO

Always identify file video to prevent any possibility that viewers believe the old video is current. Many stations label such video "File," "File Video," or "Library Footage" and often include the date it first aired. Often, you may have only a few crucial seconds of video to illustrate a story that advances over time (stale footage showing the aftermath of an airline crash as the investigation advances over weeks, months, or even years, for example, or perhaps old footage of a murder suspect walking to court as the trial, sentencing, and appeal processes run their course). Ideally, use such file video sparingly and try to advance it over time to avoid endless repetition.

MATERIAL PROVIDED BY OUTSIDE SOURCES

Equally important is the need to identify all video that comes from any source outside your newsroom. Normally, the origin of network and news syndication stories is self-evident. In everything from mike flags, screen graphics, and reporter signoffs, the authorship and logos of network and syndication services receive obvious and prominent treatment. The biggest problem occurs with video news releases and footage from businesses, public relations firms, government agencies, and other special interest groups. Such stories arrive at the station free of cost, and reduced budgets make their use tempting. Stations frequently produce their own stories from such footage, updating and localizing the material as warranted, and may use their own reporters and anchors to voice such stories from the studio.[12] Unless stations identify the source, audiences have no way to know the story may represent a special interest point of view.

TOWARD AN INDIVIDUAL CODE OF ETHICS

Ethics can be thought of as promoting fair play, even for those individuals and institutions we dislike. Often the best response to a news situation is detachment, the hallmark on which objective reporting is founded. But ethical reporting is more than the simple transmission of facts and truth, and it is more than fairness and accuracy. It is also the dedication to good taste and to a regard for human dignity and life. Not infrequently, ethical reporting is possible only when the journalist has made a much broader ethical commitment to be sensitive in reporting how others live, believe, and behave.[13] Sensitivity and compassion are not frequently mentioned as journalistic virtues or as prerequisites for employment, but they are qualities the public can rightfully demand from a profession often noted, and occasionally disdained, for its cynicism.

As you develop a personal code of ethics, you may wish to consider the following guidelines. They form the basis for many individual codes of ethics in journalism:

■ Broadcast only information that you know to be accurate, fair, and complete.
■ Tell your audience what you don't know.

- If you make a mistake, tell your audience.
- Respect the privacy of others.
- Do nothing to misrepresent your identity.
- Whenever you disclose information that damages a person's reputation, disclose the source.
- Leave the making of secret recordings to authorized officials.
- Respect the right of all individuals to a fair trial.
- Promise confidentiality to a source only if you are willing to be jailed to protect the source.
- Pay for your own meals, travel, special events tickets, books, music, personal items, and services.
- Accept only gifts, admissions, and services that are free of obligation and equally available to the public.
- Avoid outside employment or other activities that might damage your ability to report fairly or might appear to influence your ability to be fair.
- Avoid making endorsements of products or institutions.
- Guard against arrogance and bad taste in your reports.
- Stay out of bushes and dark doorways.
- Never break a law to expose a wrong.

Many news organizations also encourage employees to follow the guidelines in the Radio Television Digital News Association (**RTDNA**) and National Press Photographers Association (**NPPA**) codes of ethics.

BOX 15.2 CODE OF ETHICS AND PROFESSIONAL CONDUCT

Radio Television Digital News Association

The Radio Television Digital News Association, wishing to foster the highest professional standards of electronic journalism, promote public understanding of and confidence in electronic journalism, and strengthen principles of journalistic freedom to gather and disseminate information, establishes this Code of Ethics and Professional Conduct.

Preamble

Professional electronic journalists should operate as trustees of the public, seek the truth, report it fairly and with integrity and independence, and stand accountable for their actions.

Public Trust

Professional electronic journalists should recognize that their first obligation is to the public.
    Professional electronic journalists should:

- Understand that any commitment other than service to the public undermines trust and credibility.

- Recognize that service in the public interest creates an obligation to reflect the diversity of the community and guard against oversimplification of issues or events.
- Provide a full range of information to enable the public to make enlightened decisions.
- Fight to ensure that the public's business is conducted in public.

Truth

Professional electronic journalists should pursue truth aggressively and present the news accurately, in context, and as completely as possible.
    Professional electronic journalists should:

- Continuously seek the truth.
- Resist distortions that obscure the importance of events.
- Clearly disclose the origin of information and label all material provided by outsiders.

Professional electronic journalists should not:

- Report anything known to be false.
- Manipulate images or sounds in any way that is misleading.
- Plagiarize.
- Present images or sounds that are reenacted without informing the public.

Fairness

Professional electronic journalists should present the news fairly and impartially, placing primary value on significance and relevance.

Professional electronic journalists should:

- Treat all subjects of news coverage with respect and dignity, showing particular compassion to victims of crime or tragedy.
- Exercise special care when children are involved in a story and give children greater privacy protection than adults.
- Seek to understand the diversity of their community and inform the public without bias or stereotype.
- Present a diversity of expressions, opinions, and ideas in context.
- Present analytical reporting based on professional perspective, not personal bias.
- Respect the right to a fair trial.

Integrity

Professional electronic journalists should present the news with integrity and decency, avoiding real or perceived conflicts of interest, and respect the dignity and intelligence of the audience as well as the subjects of news.

Professional electronic journalists should:

- Identify sources whenever possible. Confidential sources should be used only when it is clearly in the public interest to gather or convey important information or when a person providing information might be harmed. Journalists should keep all commitments to protect a confidential source.
- Clearly label opinion and commentary.
- Guard against extended coverage of events or individuals that fails to significantly advance a story, place the event in context, or add to the public knowledge.

- Refrain from contacting participants in violent situations while the situation is in progress.
- Use technological tools with skill and thoughtfulness, avoiding techniques that skew facts, distort reality, or sensationalize events.
- Use surreptitious newsgathering techniques, including hidden cameras or microphones, only if there is no other way to obtain stories of significant public importance and only if the technique is explained to the audience.
- Disseminate the private transmissions of other news organizations only with permission.

Professional electronic journalists should not:

- Pay news sources who have a vested interest in a story.
- Accept gifts, favors, or compensation from those who might seek to influence coverage.
- Engage in activities that may compromise their integrity or independence.

Independence

Professional electronic journalists should defend the independence of all journalists from those seeking influence or control over news content.

Professional electronic journalists should:

- Gather and report news without fear or favor, and vigorously resist undue influence from any outside forces, including advertisers, sources, story subjects, powerful individuals, and special interest groups.
- Resist those who would seek to buy or politically influence news content or who would seek to intimidate those who gather and disseminate the news.
- Determine news content solely through editorial judgment and not as the result of outside influence.
- Resist any self-interest or peer pressure that might erode journalistic duty and service to the public.
- Recognize that sponsorship of the news will not be used in any way to determine, restrict, or manipulate content.
- Refuse to allow the interests of ownership or management to influence news judgment and content inappropriately.

- Defend the rights of the free press for all journalists, recognizing that any professional or government licensing of journalists is a violation of that freedom.

Accountability

Professional electronic journalists should recognize that they are accountable for their actions to the public, the profession, and themselves.

Professional electronic journalists should:

- Actively encourage adherence to these standards by all journalists and their employers.
- Respond to public concerns. Investigate complaints and correct errors promptly and with as much prominence as the original report.
- Explain journalistic processes to the public, especially when practices spark questions or controversy.
- Recognize that professional electronic journalists are duty-bound to conduct themselves ethically.

- Refrain from ordering or encouraging courses of action that would force employees to commit an unethical act.
- Carefully listen to employees who raise ethical objections and create environments in which such objections and discussions are encouraged.
- Seek support for and provide opportunities to train employees in ethical decision-making.

In meeting its responsibility to the profession of electronic journalism, RTNDA has created this code to identify important issues, to serve as a guide for its members, to facilitate self-scrutiny, and to shape future debate.

Source: Adopted at RTNDA 2000 in Minneapolis, MN, September 14, 2000. Reprinted by permission of the Radio-Television News Directors Association (renamed in 2009 as the Radio Television Digital News Association (**RTDNA**).

BOX 15.3   CODE OF ETHICS

National Press Photographers Association

Preamble

The National Press Photographers Association, a professional society that promotes the highest standards in photojournalism, acknowledges concern for every person's need both to be fully informed about public events and to be recognized as part of the world in which we live.

Photojournalists operate as trustees of the public. Our primary role is to report visually on the significant events and on the varied viewpoints in our common world. Our primary goal is the faithful and comprehensive depiction of the subject at hand. As photojournalists, we have the responsibility to document society and to preserve its history through images.

Photographic and video images can reveal great truths, expose wrongdoing and neglect, inspire hope and understanding and connect people around the globe through the language of visual understanding. Photographs can also cause great harm if they are callously intrusive or are manipulated.

This code is intended to promote the highest quality in all forms of photojournalism and to strengthen public confidence in the profession. It is also meant to serve as an educational tool both for those who practice and for those who appreciate photojournalism. To that end, The National Press Photographers Association sets forth the following Code of Ethics:

Code of Ethics

Photojournalists and those who manage visual news productions are accountable for upholding the following standards in their daily work:

1. Be accurate and comprehensive in the representation of subjects.
2. Resist being manipulated by staged photo opportunities.
3. Be complete and provide context when photographing or recording subjects. Avoid stereotyping individuals and groups. Recognize and work to avoid presenting one's own biases in the work.

4. Treat all subjects with respect and dignity. Give special consideration to vulnerable subjects and compassion to victims of crime or tragedy. Intrude on private moments of grief only when the public has an overriding and justifiable need to see.

5. While photographing subjects do not intentionally contribute to, alter, or seek to alter or influence events.

6. Editing should maintain the integrity of the photographic images' content and context. Do not manipulate images or add or alter sound in any way that can mislead viewers or misrepresent subjects.

7. Do not pay sources or subjects or reward them materially for information or participation.

8. Do not accept gifts, favors, or compensation from those who might seek to influence coverage.

9. Do not intentionally sabotage the efforts of other journalists.

Ideally, photojournalists should:

1. Strive to ensure that the public's business is conducted in public. Defend the rights of access for all journalists.

2. Think proactively, as a student of psychology, sociology, politics and art to develop a unique vision and presentation. Work with a voracious appetite for current events and contemporary visual media.

3. Strive for total and unrestricted access to subjects, recommend alternatives to shallow or rushed opportunities, seek a diversity of viewpoints, and work to show unpopular or unnoticed points of view.

4. Avoid political, civic, and business involvements or other employment that compromise or give the appearance of compromising one's own journalistic independence.

5. Strive to be unobtrusive and humble in dealing with subjects.

6. Respect the integrity of the photographic moment.

7. Strive by example and influence to maintain the spirit and high standards expressed in this code. When confronted with situations in which the proper action is not clear, seek the counsel of those who exhibit the highest standards of the profession. Photojournalists should continuously study their craft and the ethics that guide it.

Source: Reprinted by permission of the National Press Photographers Association (NPPA).

SUMMARY

Ethics are rules of living and conduct that you impose on yourself or those your profession strongly suggests you should follow. Laws, by contrast, are rules of living and conduct that are enforced by an external authority, usually by means of penalties.

The pressures of competition tempt some journalists to commit unethical practices. Sooner or later, however, such acts end up reflecting unfavorably on the profession at large. Other problems can result when journalists practice situational ethics, the practice of determining what to do from one situation to the next on the basis of the good that will likely result from a particular course of action.

In the absence of a universally accepted code of ethics, it falls to the individual journalist to determine what is good and bad, right and wrong, fair and unfair. Given the indiscretions of some journalists, ranging from accepting favors and staging news to trespass and entrapment, some groups and individuals would seek to impose their own notions of ethical behavior on journalists and to license them. However, ideas, unlike pharmaceuticals and vending machines, are difficult to license.

In the end, the public extends to journalists somewhat the equivalent of a license to operate through its trust and patronage. Without these fundamental components in place, no journalist can be heard.

KEY TERMS

ethics   264
NPPA   278

RTDNA   278
situational ethics   266

DISCUSSION

1. Describe the essential differences between ethics and law.
2. Based on your observations of news coverage and promotion, discuss how competitive pressures can influence the journalist's ethical decisions.
3. Discuss what role situational ethics should play in your professional career.
4. Describe from personal observation any reporting practices with which you disagree.
5. Discuss your views about the wisdom of licensing journalists to (a) certify journalistic competency and (b) help ensure fairness in reporting.
6. In the absence of review boards and licensing boards for journalists, what other forces exist to help ensure that the journalist reports fairly and competently?
7. Under what circumstances, if any, are reenactments of stories ethically defensible?
8. Should a journalist refuse all gifts or just those above a certain value (ten dollars and higher? twenty-five dollars and up?)? What about a cup of coffee at a restaurant? A drink at a bar? A meal? A movie ticket?
9. Under what circumstances is it acceptable for a journalist to hold another paying job, say as a speechwriter for a public relations company or as a video editor for an industrial telecommunications company?
10. As a journalist, when is it permissible for you to accept pay from a special interest group for a speech you make? To shoot video for a paid political spot?
11. When is it acceptable for you to publish information about a public official that you learned secondhand because your spouse or friend works in close association with that public official?
12. Under what circumstances, if any, is secret recording ethical?

EXERCISES

1. Respond to your choice of any five of the ethical conflict situations that begin on page 271 of this chapter, and defend your answers.
2. Choose five individuals to play the roles of (1) assignment editor, (2) news director, (3) person in the news, (4) photographer, and (5) reporter. Ask penetrating questions to prompt the various individuals to respond to the ethical conflict situations beginning on page 271 and lead them to defend their responses.
3. Invite working journalists, perhaps a reporter–photographer team from a local station, to describe how they would react to the ethical conflict situations outlined in this chapter.
4. Make a list of favors you would accept without reservation from news sources and those you would refuse to accept under any circumstances. Explain your decisions.
5. Construct a personal code of journalistic ethics that you will follow as a working professional.

DISCUSSION OF ETHICAL CONFLICT SITUATIONS

Following are discussions of possible scenarios in response to the ethical conflict situations posed on pages 271–275. Your answers may vary, and you can expect a spirited defense of differing points of view whether you raise these issues in class discussion or with working professionals. In the end, there is no "right" answer, unless the response you advocate runs counter to humanitarian considerations; would harm an individual's safety, reputation, or mental well-being; results in the breaking of a law; or runs contrary to your station's ethical guidelines.

Trespass

Case 1. Discussion. You could be guilty of trespassing unless you obtain permission to enter the building. If you are unable to locate the owner, ask a police officer to give you permission to enter the building. If you are later challenged, you can at least cite your decision to act based on "apparent authority."

Case 2. Even with a "No trespassing" sign on the front gate, there would seem to be little harm in knocking on the woman's door. You have virtually no other way to announce your presence. If the gate is locked and you jump the fence, however, you may be guilty of trespassing.

Surveillance Photography

If the palm reader leaves her curtains open and her shades up, she might be expected to know that someone might attempt to take a picture. If you attempt to record sound with a shotgun or parabolic mike, however, the judge might rule that the palm reader had a reasonable expectation to privacy in her private conversations, even though her windows were open.

Hostage Coverage

Case 1. In this instance, the police have chosen to misrepresent their identity. If you hand over your camera, you have chosen only to lend the police a camera. If the man holding hostages calls your station to confirm that the individuals with your camera are station employees, not police, serious harm could result to the hostages, especially if the assignment desk or news director is uninformed of your decision.

Case 2. In the first instance, retreat. Don't endanger the man's life or his children's lives. In the second instance, when police do rush the house, your decision to follow immediately behind the police involves your own safety. No story is worth your life.

Entrapment

You have asked a minor to break the law by purchasing liquor, a common example of breaking the law to expose a wrongdoing. This job may better be left to police. You can then record the purchase through the window with a long lens from a van parked across the street, because generally you can photograph anything that you can see from a public location. The tactic of walking, unannounced, into the liquor store with camera rolling is less ethical. Ambush journalism gives interview subjects no time to collect their thoughts or to respond to questions in a rational, thoughtful way.

Invasion of Privacy

Honor the family's wishes. Wait for another day and another time when you do have permission. If you are convinced your cause is right, state your case once again, gently.

Violence

Case 1. The violence is the most eloquent statement you have to communicate the essence of this story. To edit it out would be to portray the demonstration as far more benign than it was. Be cautious, however, to avoid showing activities that would violate ordinary sensibilities and good taste.

Case 2. Some stations air such footage, others convert it to a still-frame graphic or substitute a still photograph obtained from a newspaper photographer. Some viewers will expect to see the actual footage; other viewers will be outraged if you show it. The judgment call is yours.

Protecting Confidential Sources

The first step could be for you to plead with your source to inform the police or FBI himself. Otherwise, you might notify the police anonymously, without naming your source or his group, although such action would violate your promise not to reveal confidential information. You might also wish to inform your source of your decision to call police. If you fail to tell police, your decision could result in property damage and injury or death to innocent persons.

Breaking and Entering

Stay outside. Call police. Cover the action if they decide to enter the premises.

Destroying Police Evidence

You are better off staying outside. Murder trials can be lost over allegations of destruction of evidence.

Televising Executions

If viewers are given sufficient warning and time to prepare for a delayed broadcast, then they can choose to watch or tune away from the broadcast as they wish. Unsuspecting viewers, however, may still tune into the delayed broadcast. To broadcast the execution live might capitalize on the event more nearly for sensational or shock value, because an understanding of capital punishment and its deterrent value is far more complex than watching a person being put to death on live television.

Covering Suicide Attempts

Case 1. Delay the woman by calling the station. Do what you can to help save her and her child. Human decency and compassion take precedence over this story.

Case 2. Do not cover the story. If you do, you will be subject to this form of modified "hostage taking" for months to come. Anyone with a message could threaten suicide and expect you to come running.

Illegally Obtained Information

Keep your eyes where they belong. Curiosity might kill the cat in this case, especially if the DA has planted the folder for your benefit anyway. Even if the information was accurate, it would be illegally or at least unethically obtained.

Yielding Editorial Control of News Content

Air the footage, provided you tell viewers how it was obtained. Later, you may want to do a follow-up story to show the potential consequences of moving hazardous materials through populated areas.

Cooperating with Police

Air the footage and interviews, provided you inform your audience how the footage was obtained.

Private Lives of Public Officials

If the official's situation affects his or her ability to conduct the office, report it. Otherwise, let the information remain private. If the competition reports information that you believe should be kept private, refrain from reporting it. Most members of your audience will respect your decision.

Misrepresentation

Case 1. Inform the city attorney of your identity when he first begins to take you into his confidence.

Case 2. The misrepresentation of a journalist's identity may lead viewers to discredit the honor and integrity of all journalists. Don't pose as the coroner's assistant.

NOTES

1. Mark Gillespie, "Public Remains Skeptical of News Media," a Gallup organization article, May 30, 2003, www.realnews247.com/gallup_public_ remains_skeptical_of_news_media. htm (accessed June 8, 2007).
2. "CBS News/New York Times Poll. Jan. 20–25, 2006," www.pollingreport.com/media.htm (accessed June 8, 2007).
3. Gallup, "Media Use and Evaluation," http://www.gallup.com/poll/1663/media-use-evaluation. aspx (accessed December 28, 2010).
4. Gallup, "In U.S., Confidence in Newspapers, TV News Remains a Rarity," August 13, 2010, http://www.gallup.com/poll/142133/Confidence-Newspapers-News-Remains-Rarity .aspx (accessed December 28 2010).
5. Diane Holloway, "That's Harsh: Hi-def TV is changing our views of the stars," Cox News Services, 29 March 2007.
6. Ibid.
7. Donald R. Winslow, "Truth Will Out: Allen Detrich & The Toledo Blade," *News Photographer*, (May 2007), 51.
8. Rich Beckman, "Those Who Put Us At Risk," News Photographer, (May 2007), 14–15.
9. Donald R. Winslow, "Truth Will Out: Allen Detrich & The Toledo Blade," *News Photographer*, (May 2007), 43–53.
10. Ibid, 12
11. Excerpted from a panel participation seminar, "Situation Ethics for the TV News Photographer," presented by Dr. Carl C. Monk, then dean of Washburn University School of Law (Topeka, KS), at the National Press Photographers 24th Annual Television News-Video Workshop, Norman, OK, March 22, 1984, and drawing on discussions among professional journalists in similar sessions held at the workshop since then.
12. Jim Redmond, Frederick Shook, Dan Lattimore, and Laurie Lattimore-Volkmann, *The Broadcast News Process*, 7th ed. (Englewood, CO: Morton, 2005).
13. Gene Goodwin, "The Ethics of Compassion," *The Quill* (November 1983), 38–40.

Shooting Video
The Basics

Photographers take pictures. Photojournalists tell stories with their cameras. In fact, the best photojournalists use the camera much as the writer uses a computer keyboard—to report observations and tell stories. In essence, the camera is a writing and reporting instrument, an extension not so much of the outer eye as of the inner, mind's eye. What you see, think, and feel about people and events you often can share with other people through your camera.

Photography is among the most technical of the creative arts. To capture mood, action, and meaning properly and place emphasis where you want it demands that you be not only creatively adept, but technically proficient. Accordingly, it is important not only that you know yourself, your shot, and your story, but your equipment.

THE CAMERA

In some respects the electronic camera is similar to a film camera, but with an important difference (Figure A.1). The digital camera features the **charge-coupled device (CCD)**, a solid-state chip, the size of a thumbnail or smaller, that converts reflected light directly to electrical signals. The camera circuitry translates these impulses into strings of 1s and 0s for each frame of video. This digital information is decoded into a broadcast quality video signal that can be fed to a television monitor, recorded onto a hard drive or other recording medium, or routed to live transmission equipment. Because of their reduced size and weight, many solid state cameras are easier to transport and use under difficult field conditions.

The Camera Viewfinder

A black-and-white or color image of the scene also is reproduced in the camera viewfinder, itself a tiny television screen. The scene in the viewfinder is the same image as that recorded, streamed, or beamed live to home viewers. After a story is shot, it can be played back through the camera viewfinder. In this manner, the photographer can "field check" the video and be certain the scenes were properly recorded.

FIGURE A.1
The video camera creates images by converting light rays to electrical video signals that can be fed to a video recorder, hard drive, flash memory, disk, or to live transmission equipment, in effect making possible the direct observation of history.

White Balance

Professionals white-balance the camera before they cover a story, and thereafter each time the light source changes. **White balance** is the adjustment of camera circuitry to reproduce pure whites under the light source at hand. When the camera is properly white-balanced, there is said to be an absence of color "at white." Many cameras will adjust white balance automatically, although auto settings rarely produce ideal color. Most professionals white balance their own shots manually by showing the camera a white card or other white object in the scene and pressing a button. Most cameras also offer factory-preset white balances for indoor and outdoor light. Presets will work in a pinch, when important shots would otherwise be missed on fast-breaking events.

Video Formats

Over the years, video formats have included the Sony DVCAM, MiniDV Beta, Beta SP, and Digital Betacam; the Panasonic digital video (DVC and DVCPRO) and older to ancient M-II, D-3, and D-4 formats; three-quarter-inch, 4-mm, 8-mm, 19-mm, one-quarter-inch, one-inch, and two-inch video; Super VHS (S-VHS); Hi-Band 8 mm (Hi-8), and yet other digital video formats from manufacturers such as Sony, Canon, and JVC.

Of these options, **digital** video's more affordable price and features have made it a clear favorite in today's newsgathering operations and with cable and corporate producers. Even the smallest, handheld digital video cameras produce broadcast-quality images and offer other features such as high-quality audio and shutter speeds from 1/5 second to 1/15,000 second, a range useful for everything from low-light exposures to slow-motion and stop-action photography. At the mid- to high-end, digital video cameras shoot high-definition images and store still photographs on a hard disk drive or flash memory simultaneously while recording video (capturing still photos for on-screen graphics, for example). Some digital "still" cameras also can record high-def video and audio. As an added bonus, some digital recording media are small enough that a photographer can carry several hours of video in a coat pocket. Briefcase-sized digital laptop editors provide unparalleled ease of editing virtually anywhere. Some smartphones offer basic video and editing capability. The web site at www.digital journalist.org provides periodic updates on digital technology, including advances in digital video field acquisition, the process of recording video on cameras equipped with hard disk drives, optical disks, and memory sticks.

THE LENS

The lens gathers and focuses light and controls the amount of light that enters the camera. Professional lenses contain a series of convex and concave elements. They offer both auto and manual focus. If, while a shot is being made, the focus point shifts from one subject to another, the effect is called a **rack focus**. Gradually, sharp focus is transferred from an object in the foreground to a more distant object, or vice versa. Like most such techniques, the rack focus is least effective when it calls attention to itself.

Macro Lenses

Lenses on video cameras commonly allow **macro-focusing**, to reproduce larger-than-life images. This feature lets you magnify very small objects, such as printed material from a court document or newspaper, so viewers can see the object clearly. (Figure A.2).

The Zoom Lens

The most common "glass" on video cameras is the variable focal length or **zoom lens** (Figure A.3). This lens provides continuously variable focal-length settings from wide angle to telephoto. With its ability to provide various focal settings through such representative ranges as 12–120 mm or 25–250 mm, the zoom lens provides the equivalent of several focal length lenses in one. Because focal length is continuously variable, the photographer also can more precisely "crop" or compose scenes to eliminate undesirable elements within the frame.

FIGURE A.2

Macro lenses permit the photojournalist to record larger-than-life images, a feature that is especially convenient for magnifying small objects.

The zoom lens allows for infinitely variable composition throughout the full range of its focal-length settings. Many photographers abuse this lens, however, by choosing to zoom indiscriminately.

Originally, the zoom lens was invented to keep the picture from going to black as camera operators rotated their fixed-lens turrets during live studio broadcasts. The problem was especially acute in broadcasts that originated in single-camera studios. Home audiences saw momentary screen blackouts every time the camera operator rotated the turret to rack up a different lens.

HOW TO FOCUS THE ZOOM LENS   To focus the lens, zoom all the way in to a close-up on your subject. Focus the lens. Now zoom back out to the composition you want. Everything within the range of your zoom will be in focus. If you zoom in and are able to obtain a clean focus but then lose focus when you zoom back out, the lens may have a back focus problem that will require service.

Lens Focal Length

Lens **focal length** (Figure A.4) is determined by measuring the distance from the optical center or **node** of the lens to the film plane, in the case of film cameras, or the front surface of the target or CCD chip in video cameras. The **optical center** is the point inside the lens where light rays first bend as they are directed or brought to bear on the film plane or target during the focusing process. Seldom does the physical length of the lens housing accurately represent the lens's focal length.

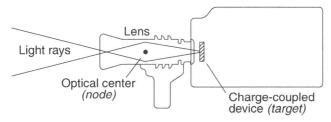

FIGURE A.4

Lens focal length is determined by measuring the distance from the optical center, or node, of the lens to the film plane or front surface of the CCD. The physical length of the lens housing is seldom an accurate expression of focal length.

Focal length determines the image size of the subject and the angle of view. Each time the focal length is doubled, the subject's image size doubles. If the focal length is cut in half, so is the subject's image size. Whereas a normal lens might provide a 45-degree angle of view, a wide-angle lens might produce more than a 90-degree angle of view.

Lens Perspective

"Normal" lens perspective is equivalent to the human eye's view of the world. The sizes of objects in relation to one another at certain distances are approximately equal to how the human eye sees things.

From one format to another, manufacturers determine normal lens perspective for that format by measuring the diagonal size of the film negative or target. Thus, in some video cameras, "normal focal length" might be 25 mm. Others might require a lens setting of approximately 12 mm in focal length, whereas in the 35-mm still camera, normal perspective results from lenses of 45 mm to approximately 55 mm in focal length.

WIDE-ANGLE LENSES   Lenses shorter than the focal length required to yield normal perspective are called **wide-angle lenses**. These lenses yield smaller subject size and tend to emphasize subject matter in the foreground. Compared to normal and long lenses, wide-angle lenses also yield apparent greater depth of field, defined as the area of the scene that appears to be in sharp focus.

LONG OR TELEPHOTO LENSES   Lenses or zoom lens settings greater than the focal length required to yield normal perspective are called **long** or **telephoto lenses**. Technically, all telephoto lenses are long lenses, although not all long lenses are telephoto lenses. Telephoto lenses qualify for the title because they are physically shorter than their focal length. Long lenses magnify image size and emphasize subject matter in the background. Most viewers are familiar with the tendency of long lenses to foreshorten distance, so that objects both far and near within the scene appear to be bunched up and shoved together, in an effect called *compression*. Long lenses also produce more shallow depth of field than normal and wide-angle lenses.

Lens Aperture (F/Stops)

Every camera requires an exact amount of light to produce perfect exposure. The amount of light required varies from one camera to the next depending on which CCD chip the camera uses. But from one application to another with a particular camera, the amount of light required to produce perfect exposure is always the same, regardless of whether the subject is photographed in the dark of night or on the brightest ski slope.

To control the amount of light entering the camera under varying light conditions, the lens is equipped with an adjustable **aperture**. Similar in function to the **iris** of the human eye, the aperture can be varied in size according to the prevailing light. The various aperture settings are expressed in **f/stops**, such as f/1.8, f/8, or f/22.

F/Stops Are Fractions

The f/stop number is a fraction, determined by comparing the effective diameter of the lens against its focal length. Because the f-number is a fraction, the higher the f/stop number, the smaller the aperture size. Thus, f/22 is a smaller aperture opening than f/1.4 (Figure A.5).

Each successive aperture either halves or doubles the amount of light entering the camera. At a setting of f/8, the lens admits only half the amount of light that it

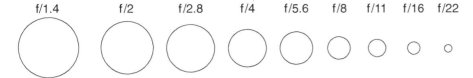

| f/1.4 | f/2 | f/2.8 | f/4 | f/5.6 | f/8 | f/11 | f/16 | f/22 |

FIGURE A.5

F/stop numbers represent fractions. Hence, the larger the f number, the smaller the aperture.

does when set to f/5.6. An aperture set to f/16 admits twice as much light as at f/22, whereas f/11 admits four times as much light as f/22. Thus, at the far end of the scale, f/1.2 admits 256 times more light than f/22.

As the aperture is made smaller, the photographer is said to "close down" or "stop down" the aperture. As the aperture size is made larger, the photographer is said to "open up" the aperture.

The most commonly encountered "whole" f/stop numbers are f/1.2, 2, 2.8, 4, 5.6, 8, 11, 16, and 22. For research, military, and related applications, some lenses are available with f/stop numbers that extend to 32, 45, and 64.

T/Stop

The f/stop is a theoretical value that assumes the lens is passing all the light available to it. A more accurate lens aperture setting is the **t/stop**, which takes into account the number of lens elements, lens coatings, and other light-absorbing properties of the lens elements and housing. If the lens is calibrated in t/stops, the letter *t* may appear on the lens housing next to the aperture numbers. Typically, the difference between the two values is about one-half f/stop.

Aperture Size Influences Depth of Field

Aperture size also affects **depth of field** (DOF), defined as the area within a scene that appears to be in focus. The smaller the aperture, the greater the apparent DOF (Figure A.6). The larger the aperture, the more shallow the DOF.

Aperture size affects depth of field because of its effect on light rays entering the lens. Because the camera can focus on only one plane or point in space at a time, only objects at that one distance from the camera can be in true focus. To one degree or another, every object at any other distance is rendered out of focus.

Razor-crisp focus results from pinpoints of light that strike the film plane or target surface. If the light rays are out of focus, they register not as pinpoints of light but as circles of light called **circles of confusion**. If the circles of confusion are small enough, the subject may appear sharp enough to be in focus. If the circles of confusion are extraordinarily large, however, the object will be reproduced in fuzzy or soft focus. Small apertures produce smaller circles of confusion, and thus greater apparent depth of field.

Other Factors That Affect Depth of Field

In addition to aperture size, depth of field also is determined by lens focal length and distance from subject. Wide-angle lenses produce greater apparent depth of field than long lenses, and depth of field increases as a lens is focused on objects further from the camera. Conversely, depth of field diminishes as the lens focuses on objects closer to the camera.

FIGURE A.6

Depth of field is an expression of the area within a scene that appears to be in focus. The left example illustrates shallow depth of field; the right illustrates **great depth of field**.

Focal length affects depth of field because of its influence on aperture size. Assuming all other factors remain equal, each time the lens housing doubles in length, only half the original amount of light is passed. To compensate for the light loss, the aperture size must be doubled. Thus, if the effective diameter of a 12-mm lens at f/8 is 2 mm, the effective diameter of a 25-mm lens at f/8 must be approximately 4 mm. Doubling the focal length of the 25-mm lens to 50 mm would result in an effective diameter at f/8 of approximately 8 mm. Because aperture size controls the size of circles of confusion, out-of-focus objects within the scene are more obviously out of focus when photographed with the 50-mm or 25-mm lenses than with the 12-mm lens.

You can see for yourself how the camera's distance from the subject affects depth of field. Hold an object very close to your eye, then without changing focus become aware of the surroundings behind the object. If you maintain your focus on the object, the background will appear to be out of focus.

Depth of Field

Most commonly, about one-third of the total range of depth of field occurs in front of the subject or focus point, and two-thirds behind the subject. Assume the lens is focused on a subject 45 feet from the camera, and that the total range of depth of field is 60 feet. In this example, the range of acceptable focus or depth of field would begin 20 feet in front of the subject (one-third of 60 feet) and extend to 40 feet behind the subject (two-thirds of 60 feet).

The near plane of acceptable focus would therefore begin at approximately 25 feet in front of the camera and extend to approximately 85 feet from the camera. ■

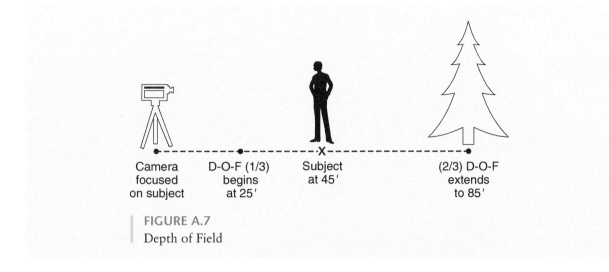

FIGURE A.7
Depth of Field

Now move the object further away from your eye and notice how depth of field increases. If you were to focus on the object several hundred feet away, the entire range of your view would appear to be in focus.

HOW TO OBTAIN MAXIMUM DEPTH OF FIELD   Depth of field increases in a scene whenever the following conditions are met, whether separately or in combination. Thus, **maximum depth of field** results whenever all the conditions are met:

- small aperture setting (i.e., f/22)
- short focal-length lens (wide angle)
- camera focused on objects far from it

HOW TO OBTAIN SHALLOW DEPTH OF FIELD   **Shallow depth of field** is desirable for artistic effect or when the photojournalist wishes to confine the viewer's attention to foreground subjects by throwing the background out of focus. Depth of field in a scene becomes shallower when the following conditions are met, whether separately or in combination. The minimum depth of field results when all the conditions are met:

- large aperture setting (i.e., f/2.8 or smaller)
- long focal-length lens (telephoto)
- camera focused on objects very near to it

Even in bright light, larger aperture settings are possible if the photographer uses neutral density filters to reduce the amount of light entering the lens (see Chapter 5, "The Magic of Light and Lighting").

Avoid Automatic Lens Settings

The video camera "sees" the scene in terms of the standard **gray scale** that is familiar to black-and-white photographers. At one end of the scale, represented by a value of 10, is pure white. At the other end of the scale, represented by a value of 0, is black. In between are the various shades of gray, ranging from light to very dark gray.

Objects within the scene are reproduced as various shades of white, gray, and black. The camera's color circuitry combines with the black-and-white picture to produce a color image. If you turn down the color on a television set, you can see the underlying black and white image.

If a scene is made up mostly of white and black tones, it is reproduced as a high-**contrast** image. If the scene is made up mostly of objects that yield medium gray tones, it will be reproduced as a low-contrast image (Figure A.8). In determining exposure, the camera's automatic exposure circuitry samples all the white, black, and gray areas in the scene, then calculates exposure based on an average of all the values represented. High-contrast scenes most easily fool the camera, such as when you photograph someone against a window, the sky, or a white wall. Images with such high-contrast ratios also typically sacrifice sharpness and subtle detail. The camera normally produces its most accurate exposure and fineness of detail when objects within the scene tend toward the middle of the gray scale.

Because the automatic circuitry adjusts constantly to changing light conditions, it can produce an undesirable "bloom" or surge in exposure whenever moving objects within the scene pass in front of backgrounds with differing shades of contrast. Exposure surge would occur in the following shots if the camera were left on the automatic exposure setting:

- a child rides a tricycle past a white picket fence interspersed with dark, ornamental bushes
- a woman doing sit-ups moves into and out of the frame in front of a light-colored wall
- bright sunlight methodically appears and disappears in the gaps between freight cars as a train roars past a railroad crossing

FIGURE A.8

Variations between the brightest and darkest objects dictate the degree of contrast in a scene. Variations between bright and dark objects in low-contrast images (left) are far less pronounced than in high-contrast scenes (right).

In each instance, the automatic circuitry will struggle first to reduce exposure, then to increase exposure to accommodate the changing light intensities. You can avoid problems by keeping the camera on manual exposure while you shoot.

Be Careful with That Camera

Whenever you're in the field, always remember Peterson's law: "Murphy was an optimist." If anything can go wrong in the world of television, it will. Leave your camera on the tripod, walk away for a moment, and be certain that fate will conspire, somehow, to tip it over: a wind gust, a puppy chasing cats, a clumsy passerby, whatever it takes to bring down that camera. Forget to lock down the tripod head, walk over to adjust the mike on your interviewee, and return to discover your $3,000 lens now dangles from a torqued camera body. It happens.

SUMMARY

Today it is possible to photograph technically high-quality images with little or no technical knowledge. Automatic focus, exposure, white balance, and simplified camera operation make this possible. But without an understanding of the basic processes involved in creating visual imagery, the photographer forfeits some supervision over content. Less achievable are the subtle distinctions in imagery that can be used to enhance the viewer's ability to experience the complex interrelations of nuance, mood, and meaning in stories.

The video camera somewhat duplicates the function of the human eye. The camera converts light rays to electrical signals that can be transmitted to home viewers or recorded on digital media for later broadcast. The camera lens gathers and focuses light, whereas the lens aperture or iris allows for precise exposure control. Lenses are available either in fixed focal lengths or, most commonly, as zoom lenses with continuously variable focal lengths. Changes in focal length allow the photographer to vary emphasis on subject matter by changing perspective and depth of field.

Although entirely adequate stories can be shot with virtually no understanding of the camera, photojournalists who aspire to excellence soon discover that mastery without understanding is unlikely.

KEY TERMS

aperture   290
charge-coupled device
   (CCD)   286
circles of confusion   291
contrast   294
depth of field (DOF)   291
digital   287
focal length   289

f/stops   290
gray scale   293
great depth of field   292
iris   290
long or telephoto lens   290
macro-focusing   288
maximum depth of
   field   292

node   289
optical center   289
rack focus   288
shallow depth of field   293
t/stop   291
white balance   287
wide-angle lens   290
zoom lens   288

DISCUSSION

1. Define the term *white balance* and explain why it is important.
2. In general terms, explain how video signals from the camera are recorded onto video.
3. List and describe the primary functions of the camera lens.
4. List the distinguishing features of the zoom lens and discuss its strengths and weaknesses.

5. Explain how focal length affects lens perspective, image size, and depth of field.
6. Explain the relationship between lens aperture size and f/stop number.
7. Describe steps the photographer can take to achieve shallow depth of field and great depth of field.
8. Explain why duplicate copies of digital recordings show very little loss in quality.

EXERCISES

1. Practice handholding the camera until you can hold it rock steady.
2. Using a television field camera or home video camera, white-balance the camera for sunlight and, without further adjustment, record one scene under fluorescent light, a second scene indoors under artificial quartz lights, and a third scene outdoors under normal sunlight. Now repeat the process, but this time balance the camera for artificial quartz light. Play back the scenes and compare the camera's response to varying degrees of color temperature.
3. Study the aperture on a camera lens as you change f/stop settings. Notice the relationship between large aperture sizes and small f/stop numbers and vice versa.
4. Position a subject in front of a window or other source of strong illumination. Allow the camera metering system to determine proper exposure. Notice how the subject tends to silhouette unless supplementary light is added to the front of the subject.
5. Allow camera circuitry to determine the proper exposure in a scene, then purposefully underexpose and overexpose the scene by one-half f/stop, next by one full f/stop, and finally by two full f/stops. Identify each stage of over- or underexposure by speaking into the camera microphone as you record the shots on video, or else use a small slate in the scene on which you have written +1/2 stop, +1 stop, etc. Notice the effect of over- and underexposure on colors and contrasts within the scene.
6. Without changing camera position, shoot a wide-angle shot of a subject, then a telephoto shot of the same subject. Notice the effect of focal-length setting on image size, depth of field, and emphasis on subject matter.
7. Shoot a subject in silhouette against a window, the sky, or other bright light source. Record the scene using the camera's automatic exposure meter. Next, switch the camera to manual exposure setting and record the scene two more times: first, so the subject is correctly exposed; second, so the background is correctly exposed. Play back the video and compare the three shots you have made, paying particular attention to variations in exposure, color reproduction, and fineness of detail between the respective scenes.
8. To become more familiar with the perspective produced at various lens focal settings, first shoot a series of shots with the camera in a fixed position. Make five individual shots, without zooming the lens during any individual shot, at the following or similar focal lengths: 15 mm, 30 mm, 50 mm, 75 mm, and 100 mm. Now, set and keep the focal length at normal perspective for the camera you are using and make five more shots, this time beginning at least 100 feet from a subject and then physically moving the camera ten footsteps closer each time you make a shot. Compare the lack of real change in perspective when the camera is left in one position and the true change in perspective that results when you physically move the camera.
9. Focus the camera on a scene in which a number of highlights are visible. Purposefully but gradually throw the scene out of focus and notice how elements within the scene are reproduced as ever-larger circles of confusion.
10. To become more familiar with the influences that affect depth of field, attach the camera to a tripod in a fixed location and shoot five shots of a subject at the following or similar focal lengths: 15 mm, 30 mm, 50 mm, 75 mm, and 100 mm. Do not move the camera between shots. Next, set the lens on the widest focal-length setting and make five more shots, this time physically moving the camera so that each shot is made approximately equidistant from the previous shot. Repeat the process, this time with the lens set on a long or telephoto length setting. Notice how depth of field decreases the closer the camera is to the subject and the longer the focal-length setting becomes.

Improving Performance in Field Reporting

Day after day, the video journalist's job description includes producing compelling and informative standups. The good news is that except for smell, on-camera presentations incorporate most aspects of human communication. When you master these principles, you will be more comfortable in front of the camera and microphone, more appealing to your managers and viewers, and perceived as a more polished and professional reporter. Ultimately, such qualities will make you a better and more marketable journalist and a better communicator every time you interact with others.

DEVELOP QUALITIES THAT MAKE YOU INTERESTING AND INTERESTED

One of the most difficult questions to answer about yourself is, "What makes me interesting?" Part of the answer lies in your appearance and physique. Perhaps you are tall and have freckles. Maybe you drag out the vowels in your words and clip your consonants. Maybe you scowl or blink too much or always wear a friendly smile. How you dress will make a difference. Where you grew up, and with whom, also matter, as do your personal beliefs and convictions, your education, your value system, and your life experiences. In a word, you are unique. That is the first quality that makes you interesting.

To be interesting, you also must be interested. To learn to care more intensely about every story that you report, you can use a model that Barry Nash, a Dallas-based talent development consultant, shares with field reporters and news anchors throughout the country. "Ask of every story you report whether the community wins or loses with this event," says Nash.[1] Using this approach, every story is about winning or losing. To some extent then, every story is about communicating that win or loss.

REASONS FOR STANDUPS

"Why do standups?"

"Why must we?"

"Do I have to?"

BOX B.1   AD-LIB YOUR STANDUPS

You generally appear most natural on camera when you ad-lib your standups, rather than memorize them, because you will deliver them with appropriate thoughtfulness, emphasis, and pausing. Because most standups are but two or three sentences, write the two or three main points on a 3-by-5 card for security and ad-lib the material. Sometimes you may want to memorize the script or use notes with complicated or unavoidably exact information, such as official or potentially libelous information. Otherwise, when you memorize, you may sound like you're reading aloud from a script. Why read something to your viewers when you can just as easily be conversational?

How to Prove Close Knowledge

Sometimes on-camera reporters ask, "How do I prove authority and credibility if I don't talk loudly or speak sternly?" Content drives everything you do, including your best performances. LOUD, S-T-E-R-N, and fast count for next to nothing in standups, unless they arise naturally from content. Simply speak with good energy as you would in a normal conversation in which the other person is 3 to 5 feet away from you. A better way to prove your close knowledge on-camera is to understand the topic, think through what it means, and then deliver your standup ad-lib with conversational emphasis and

pausing. Natural emphasis and pausing occur instinctively when we speak with authority and close knowledge. That same state of grace helps you naturally achieve appropriate levels of energy, emotion, pitch, pace, and volume in your delivery.

Often, you will speak into a lavaliere microphone, which lies on your chest. The resulting audio sounds so intimate it's like letting your collective audience place its ear on your chest. Even if you speak into a hand-held microphone, it will be close to your mouth (about 10 inches or so), which means you can still speak at conversational volume. Sometimes you may see the camera in the distance and think you must shout to be heard, but remember: the lavaliere mic is on your chest or the hand-held mic is but 10 inches from your mouth. There's no need to shout.

Avoid Rushed Delivery

Additionally, you will want to avoid rushing your delivery. Sometimes, given time restraints, you may feel tempted to "overwrite" so you can stuff as many facts as possible into your standup and voice-over copy. The result resembles trying to stuff 10 pounds of facts into a 5-pound bag. You delivered the facts all right, but no one remembers what you said. Furthermore, folks who talk too fast lose credibility. ■

You hear such questions now and again at newsrooms around the country. Some journalists hate standups. Others embrace them as a chance to appear on television at every opportunity, sometimes on multiple occasions within a story without justification. The main reason we do standups, of course, is to communicate information in visual, compelling ways through a one-to-one relationship with viewers or on-set anchors.

Sometimes you can just stand and talk through the facts, but so could the anchor back at the station. Audiences almost universally regard anchors as the best informed and most knowledgeable about the stories they present. Audiences assume that anchors make the most money and have the greatest experience, and they can see for themselves that anchors occupy the most coveted chairs on the set. Therefore, viewers usually prefer that anchors deliver all the news all the time, except when a reporter can report more powerfully or tell a better story. Otherwise, why would a station pay you for reporting what audiences believe their favorite anchor or personality can do better?

Why does the newsroom send you into the field? To report and show things in ways no one back at the station could manage. Or, to confirm, update, or add new information and perspectives the anchor and producer cannot access from the studio.

Standups enhance otherwise nonvisual stories. At other times, in the absence of appropriate visuals, they may offer the best way to communicate. Standups also help establish the reporter's credibility. Reporters who have been first-person, on-site observers can be assumed to know more about the story than those who get their facts from third-party sources without ever having set foot in the field. Without your standups, viewers may assume the anchors do most of the field reporting.

Even the people who sign your paychecks need to be reminded occasionally who's out there on the "front line." At contract renewal time, recognition of you and of your work is vital. Whereas not every story needs a standup, many stories and almost every career can benefit from standups incorporated judiciously into the reporting process.

Keep Your Attention on the Story

Look for ways to show something or do something during the standup, and thereby transfer focus from your performance to the camera. It's natural to wonder, "How do I look?" "Is my hair okay?" "Are my earrings too bold?" or "How can this sweater look so good in real life, yet so hideous on TV?" Always remember, the reporter is never the story, nor is your standup a fashion show or statement.

Cosmetically, your appearance and wardrobe are like the music in a film—audiences should never leave a theater humming the soundtrack or turn away from your story to talk about that gosh-awful tie or blouse. If they do, the music—your "music"—has become a distraction. The same principle applies to your wardrobe and cosmetics.

Give Yourself Something to Do

Even in field settings, some reporters may not sound or appear natural, comfortable, and relaxed. The problem may worsen during on-set appearances in the studio or whenever reporters cut voice-overs in the audio booth. To solve such problems, it may help to give yourself something to do or explain when you are on camera or in front of the microphone. This approach can help you transfer focus from yourself back onto the story and relieve your anxiety by giving your natural tension somewhere to go. Your on-camera appearance and narration tracks will thus be more comfortable and natural.

When you show or do something on camera, you can often provide visual proof of one or more of the story's main points. This creates a range of justifiable uses for standups, and a motive for reporters to plan informative and compelling ones. Happily, reporters can be interesting people in people stories and reports, too.

Justifiable Reasons for Standups

1. To show viewers what you look like—why remain anonymous?
2. To prove to viewers you were on location and therefore know more about the story than the audience or the anchor otherwise could.
3. As a bridge between unrelated segments of your story.
4. To comment on physical experiences in the environment.
5. To show viewers something the anchor can't. For example, a location reporter says, his breath visible as he talks, "Search and rescue teams believe the boy could have survived overnight if he found adequate shelter and stayed put, out of the wind."

6. To confirm a viewer's reaction to news content through your own reactions. For example, describing the growing courthouse suspense as a murder suspect awaits sentencing.
7. To justify your presence in the story by showing or explaining something to viewers that otherwise could not have been shown.

Five Common Standups[2]

Following are the five most common types of standups, those in which you show or demonstrate something. These are in addition to the "standupper," in which a person simply stands before the camera and talks. Even then, be aware of your body. Natural gestures help animate your upper body and make you more interesting to watch. When you're less active, hold your arms naturally at your side. Angle your body toward the camera, rather than confront your audience straight on and perhaps come across as somewhat adversarial.

Various newsrooms may use slightly different terminology for the following standups, but the concepts are the same.

1. Reference or location standup
2. Reveal or transition standup
3. Prop standup
4. Demonstration standup
5. Effects standup

Reference or Location Standup

Reporters use the reference or location standup to create a tie-in between the story subject and the background. In such standups, reporters stand in front of the courthouse and talk about the trial under way inside or the sentence about to be handed down. Words may not match the video.

In a live shot, the reporter might stand outside the mine entrance where miners are trapped deep underground. This location may be your best or only option on short notice. At least it proves you're at the scene, with the unspoken implication that you should know more than someone far removed. In such standups, it's good to acknowledge the background, even to turn your back to the camera as you do, to show viewers where to look—and to tell viewers what you see offscreen that would be interesting or important to them.

Reveal or Transition Standup

Beyond the simple reference standup is the reveal or transition standup. Here, the reporter might be standing on a beach as the standup begins, telling viewers that high bacteria levels make swimming unsafe. The reporter now moves out of frame and into a new frame to finish the standup by a "Beach Closed Until Further Notice" sign. The reporter also could walk the few steps from where the standup began over to the sign.

Movement can help make the story come to life, but the movement has to make sense. Just like your scripts and ad-libs, your movement and delivery need to be crisp and conversational. Any movement should be natural, too. If it feels awkward or forced, odds are it will look that way.

Check out all the reporters who do the "walk to nowhere" in standups, and you'll get the idea. Walking from Point A to Point B in a standup for no reason except to add movement makes little sense. Walking from Point A, where a runaway truck swerved to avoid kids in a crosswalk, to Point B, where the truck overturned, looks natural and helps viewers better understand the story. Standups must come across as natural, honest, and spontaneous—just as if you were showing someone in real life something important.

Prop Standup

The prop standup is just as simple as the reveal standup. The reporter holds something and shows it to viewers, often as part of a long shot, medium shot, close-up, matched-action sequence. The object you show offers proof of a story's main point. Examples are:

1. "Golf-ball-sized hail fell across the Fenimore farm." (Show a handful of golf-ball-sized hail)
2. "The complaint is only two pages long, but it calls for $2 million in damages." (Hold up, and look at, a copy of the legal complaint)
3. "Authorities say this baseball may be worth $1.5 million." (Show the baseball and look at it in your hand)

Avoid using prop standups if real people in the news could show the object more effectively. Perhaps the defense counsel can show the legal complaint to camera, Farmer Fenimore can show us the golf-ball-sized hail, or the person who caught the 756th home run can show us the ball himself. Again, another cardinal rule is: The reporter is never the story.

Demonstration Standup

Work to make every standup a visual story and commit yourself physically and mentally to selling that story. Where appropriate, strive to be physically and actively involved in its telling, a technique called the performance or **demonstration standup** (Figure B.1). The standup activity can be something as simple as a reporter pointing out the rusted bolts and flaking paint on an old bridge for a story on highway safety. Or it can be something as complex as huffing and puffing your way up a steep mountain road to illustrate the difficulty of reaching a recluse in a story about the healing power of solitude.

When you do standups, allow yourself to look at the environment, to interact with it, and even to turn your back to the camera as appropriate. In a feature story, if you have followed itinerant farmworkers on their rounds for most of a long, hot, grueling day, perhaps it will be appropriate for you to do a "sit-down" standup as you remove your hat and conclude for the audience that no one would work such long hours for such low pay if other employment were available.

To demonstrate the difficulty of balancing the federal budget, ABC senior political correspondent Jonathan Karl borrowed an idea from computer programmer Mathias Shapiro, who specializes in visualizing complex information. You can find examples of Shapiro's work at YouTube.com.

Using $100 in pennies (10,000 pennies), Karl covered a large conference table with 2,000 stacks of five pennies—each stack representing $2 billion in government spending, each penny thus worth $400 million. He divided the table of pennies into pie-like slices to illustrate defense spending and entitlements such as social security and Medicare; interest on government debt; and discretionary spending.

FIGURE B.1

Reporters can give themselves something to do when they are on camera as a way to transfer focus from themselves to the story they are telling. The technique is called a demonstration or performance standup. In this standup, the reporter shows a community book depository.

In the 1:34 standup, Karl shows that to date, Congress and the President have been willing to address only one slice of the pie representing discretionary spending, and even then proposed cuts in community action programs amount to one-third of a cent, which he represents by cutting off a third of a penny.

To watch the video, see http://www.mediaite.com/tv/abc-reporter-attempts-to-explain-the-budget-with-100-in-pennies/

Avoid melodrama in demonstration standups. The point is to communicate meaning, and to have a good time doing it. Make your time on camera relaxed, natural, and easy to watch, and use every action to help illustrate the story.

A good way to evaluate your standups is to ask yourself two questions: "Did my audience enjoy watching it?" and "Did I enjoy doing it?" When standups are most successful, the answer to both questions is *yes*. Another way to determine whether your standups are working is to look at them without sound. If you look like someone we'd like to watch, even with the sound off, your standup probably works.

Regardless of the activity you give yourself in demonstration standups, the cardinal advice against staging still applies: Your presence should never change the story. If, in your standup, you operate the controls on a ham radio and speak to the eyewitness of a volcanic eruption in Alaska, then your activities as a reporter have become the story. The story has been altered because the event is no longer what it would have been in your absence. On the other hand, no harm should result if you merely pause to shake the loose railing on a rusty old bridge as a way to show how fragile and dangerous the bridge has become.

Provided the reporter has the viewers' best interests at heart and is not simply posturing on camera, demonstration standups can be most interesting and educational for viewers. They also can advance a reporter's career. Using the medium to its fullest potential is a guaranteed way to build credibility and prove close knowledge. It also honors the adage that "content drives all performance."

Effects Standups

Some reporters use effects standups—computer-generated graphic and visual effects—to demonstrate otherwise abstract information. An effects standup might show the statistical chance of winning the lottery or what has to happen for shuttle astronauts to reenter the atmosphere safely.

For a standup in Houston, reporter Charles Hadlock began his standup showing black and white film of the two main actors driving along in the old TV show *Route 66*. Hadlock then dissolved into a color shot in which he drove a similar Chevy Corvette up to an old service station sitting alongside the abandoned highway, commenting as he sat in the driver's seat, "Buzz and Todd took a wrong turn in 1964, and were never seen again. I don't suppose they ever made it to Conway, Texas, but if they did, they probably stopped here. We stopped here to see Cecil and Zelma Walker." A sound bite with Zelma Walker follows.

Effects standups require creativity and time to plan, but they give reporters a way to show what most viewers could not otherwise know or see for themselves.

SEEK REACTION

Some folks may fear their reactions will impose an editorial bias on content, even lead viewers in how to think about content. But when you react legitimately to content, you come across as honest, natural, and thoughtful. Once again, audiences expect to see legitimate reactions from professional communicators.

The main reason we tell anybody anything is to elicit a response, to see how the other person will react. Yet, when you present information to the television camera, the lens gives you no reaction. To improve your performance in front of the camera, begin to treat the lens as if it were a person. Use whatever device works best for you. Maybe you tape a picture of your best friend to the camera lens and talk to that one person. Perhaps you imagine someone in the viewing audience and speak through the lens to that one individual. Whatever you do, believe that someone is there to react to you and to your story.

The key to eliciting audience reaction is simple: Learn to predict in your mind's eye how the audience is going to react to you and to your story. Remember that anchors and on-camera reporters lead audience reaction by demonstrating how they want the audience to react. If you want viewers to smile, for example, you must smile. If you say, "We're glad you could join us," then visually you have to prove to your audience that you really are glad for their presence, especially through your facial expressions.

COMMUNICATE WHAT YOU FEEL ABOUT THE STORY

Much of the energy in your reporting comes from what you feel about the story, both from the standpoint of your emotions and your sensory experiences. Expressing your *emotional experience* is valid, so long as you report honestly and with appropriate feeling. However, *extreme emotion* is unwarranted. It would be inappropriate, for example, to show extreme emotion, such as crying or anger, when reporting a story in which someone you know has died or been seriously injured.

From the standpoint of *sensory experience,* what you feel can be more important than what you do in reporting that story. "The important thing is the feeling, the experience of the moment," says Nash, "and the sensory experience is vital." To communicate that vital sense of experience to your audience, you must first understand the event in all its dimensions. Imagine for a moment that you have been assigned to report the outcome of a hockey game. Ask the following questions of yourself for this exercise—and for every story you cover.

1. **What do I SEE?** Perhaps you see tons of fans yelling, sweating, drinking, and cursing. You see the spray of powder as skate blades knife across the ice. You see the rhythm of the skaters and the grimaces on their faces. You see the scoreboard, and you see the puck skitter across the ice before it glances off a goalpost.

2. **What do I HEAR?** Now you hear the echo of the public address system, the crash and grunts of players. The crowd screams and there are occasional obscenities. "PEANUTS, get your red hot PEANUTS," a vendor in the crowd yells. "That son of a bitch!" the coach yells, and in the background music with a heavy beat blares through speakers.

3. **What do I SMELL?** Waves of scent wash over us from the beer, the player's sweat, and the popcorn. The air smells cold and crisp. The aftershave on the fellow next to you shouts for your attention. On the other side of you, a woman's perfume lingers.

4. **What do I FEEL?** Now, almost subconsciously, you become aware that your face is cold and you feel goose bumps on your arms. You feel adrenalin pumping through your body and you are flushed with excitement. Beneath your coat you feel, for the most part, cozy and warm.

5. **What do I TASTE?** You taste the afterbite and maltiness of the beer. There is the sharp, acid taste of the mustard on your hot dog and the crunchy, toasted flavor of the almonds in your chocolate bar.

DELIVERING FROM THE STUDIO

As an anchor or anytime you appear *on set* as a reporter, you will face two immediate problems:

1. if you are an anchor, making sense of other people's writing
2. sounding spontaneous and conversational when you read copy, even your own

To overcome these problems you will have to understand the story, know how to draw on your energy, and learn to talk to the audience with your whole self.

Words are your first ally, because the way words are built helps convey their meaning. Just for a moment, say the words *bowling ball* aloud. Roll the sounds around in your mouth, and as you say them aloud, throw the ball down an imaginary bowling alley. Notice how "heavy" the words sound when compared, for example, to the words *Ping-Pong ball.* Now say *Ping-Pong ball* aloud and toss it lightly as you "hold" it in your hand.

Having gone through this exercise, were you now to stand before a camera and say these words aloud, you could make your audience feel the difference because you've given your words some thought. You've felt the meaning of the words before you tried to communicate them. There is no right or wrong way to deliver words to an audience, only degrees of commitment and involvement in how you report stories that can distinguish you from your competition.

PUT EXPERIENCE INTO YOUR REPORTS

When you understand the experiences of a moment or an event, you can use words and actions to communicate what the pictures don't. It is a technique that NBC correspondent Bob Dotson has called "writing to the corners" of the picture. It is a descriptive form of reporting, sensual and tactile, which transcends two-dimensional imagery. "You could smell the storm's path before you could see it," Dotson once wrote in describing the path of a hurricane that had snapped tall pine trees and released their resinous fragrance.[3] Writing to the corners of the picture can help improve any story with static images or shots of aftermath.

When you set out to make your reporting experiential, create accurate mental pictures and experiences and speak to your audience of those moments. Try to make your story a report of what we see, hear, smell, taste, and touch. Largely your excellence as a video journalist lies in your ability to capture the moment and to communicate the texture of that moment, for when viewers experience an event they are more likely to understand and remember it.

MULTIDIMENSIONAL REPORTING

So often, reporters concern themselves more with how they look and sound in front of the camera than with how well they understand the story. However, the secret to being great lies in how effectively you communicate the story through **multidimensional reporting**. This means that you communicate with every reporting tool available—the camera, the microphone, the spoken word, the video editing process, and even by portraying the actions and behaviors of news subjects as warranted.

Audiences become interested in the story when they see you think about the story, interpret, and react to it. If viewers don't see your interest, they may wonder whether you like people, your job, or even if they can trust what you say. So, be *visually aggressive.* Use your body to communicate your interest and enthusiasm for the story and your audience. If you have reason to be sitting on-camera in a report or interview, sit on the edge of your chair and incline toward the camera with your body. Gesture with your hands when appropriate (see Figure B.2 A & B), and react in suitable ways, especially with facial expressions.

MARKING COPY

Whenever we speak, our natural inclination is to emphasize contrasts and new ideas. When we emphasize a word, we imply a contrast. We subdue old and less important ideas by deemphasizing them in our delivery. One of the quickest ways to improve your voice performance, then, is to go through your copy and underline the *ideas that contrast* ("angry crowd"—"did not react"; "human labor"—"machine-made goods"), as well as new *ideas.*

Some other considerations:[4]

- Never stress pronouns, unless they're used for contrast. EXAMPLE: "They voted for *you,* not *him.*"
- Don't stress any word you can eliminate without changing the meaning. EXAMPLE: "The course you recommend leads to *progress,* but the policy he sanctions leads to *disaster.*"
- When an adjective modifies a noun, it's often more reasonable to stress the adjective. EXAMPLE: "It was the *smallest* turnout in the county's *history.*"

FIGURE B.2 A & B
Handheld microphones can impede the reporter's ability to gesture and interact spontaneously with the story subject or environment. More natural and spontaneous standups can result when the reporter uses an inconspicuous lavaliere microphone, ideally in combination with a wireless transmitter-receiver system.

- Seldom stress anything in a parenthetical expression. EXAMPLE: "He was (said the chair) the last to leave the meeting."
- When you read a construction that contains a preposition with a personal pronoun for its object, stress the word before the preposition, perhaps stress the preposition, and subdue the pronoun. EXAMPLE: "A night in jail will be *good* for him."

Some exceptions:

- When the pronoun is followed by a restrictive modifier. EXAMPLE: "They *sent* for *him* before the votes had been counted."
- When the object of the pronoun is compound. EXAMPLE: "We have reporters standing by *here* and *there.*
- Normally you would not stress when the word immediately preceding the preposition is a personal pronoun or some other word. EXAMPLE: "Take it *with* you."
- Stress verbs infrequently.

As a rule, try not to let either your momentum or your inflection drop when reading copy. When either flags, so does audience attention. As you read copy, let your voice stay up and keep it up until you've completed your thought. Regardless of your inflection, pitch, or volume, the key is to maintain your energy through the ends of thoughts and sentences.

LEARN HOW TO RELAX

To communicate effectively on camera, you must feel comfortable and relaxed. You must relish everything you do and say, and not rush the delivery. Pause now for a moment and reestablish an awareness of your body. If your muscles are tense, relax. Tense muscles tell your brain, "Hey, I'm really tense," and your on-camera performance will suffer.

Pause also to become aware of how you breathe. One secret to performance success is to let your tummy pooch. Breathe with your diaphragm instead of your chest. You may notice that you tend to breathe differently when you sleep and after you first awake than during the rest of the day. If you do, begin work to establish more effective breathing patterns that will help you relax.

DEVELOP CONVERSATIONAL DELIVERY

Whether you are before a field or studio camera or sitting at a microphone in an audio booth, one of your primary obligations is to establish an intimate connection with your audience. Television can place the reporter visually closer to an audience than the reporter could approach in real life. "Television puts you as close to your audience as if you were kissing them with their eyes open," says Barry Nash. When you are that close to an audience, your voice will have to be close to an ideal level in conversational delivery, a process made easier if you follow three rules of thumb:

- The pitch of your voice goes up when you tense, so strive to relax.
- The pitch of your voice goes up as volume increases, so lower the volume of your delivery.
- The message we communicate has to do with how we think about others, not with how we think about ourselves. Think about the meaning of your words and the story's content, rather than what you look and sound like on camera.

To help reporters keep vocal pitch at conversational levels, voice coaches often have them read a real script into the microphone. As the practice session begins, the voice coach advises using a lower volume to keep pitch at conversational levels. As script delivery progresses, the voice coach may urge, "Softer, still softer, down-down-down" or may even recommend that the reporter read the script in a half or full whisper. Whispering serves two purposes in this exercise: First, it emphasizes the need to lower volume in order to lower pitch; second, it helps to reveal the nature of intimacy. We sometimes tend to pay more attention to people who whisper than to those who shout.

Another valuable exercise is to practice standup delivery at varying distances from the field camera. The farther you are from the camera, the greater the danger that you'll try to yell to it. This is true even when the field mike is clipped to your lapel. When yelling occurs, up goes tension, up goes pitch, and out goes intimacy. The problem occurs in part because we are "talking to the camera," not to the audience. Outside, you may have to yell if there's a bulldozer at work behind you, but in that case the environment will tell you what to do.

In standups, just as when you write voice over, remember to keep it conversational and to incorporate moments of silence or "white space." You can be silent if you're doing something meaningful. If you taste a new food, it is acceptable to taste, savor, swallow, react, and then speak.

To communicate intimately with your audience, keep your focus off yourself. The messages we communicate have to do not with how we think about ourselves, but with how we think about others. If you wish to make an audience laugh, it will work better to tell yourself "I'm going to make the audience laugh" than to say, "This is funny." The goal is to have a relationship with the unseen audience and to elicit a response.

YOUR APPEARANCE

Although it may seem that set design, clothing, cosmetics, hairstyles, and accessories have little to do with journalism, they mimic problems that confront print journalists in newspaper layout, design, and format. If newspaper layout is sloppy, confusing, or unattractive, it can damage the story's very message. On television, the story is just as vulnerable to errors in personal appearance.

Even the length and style of your hair will influence how the audience perceives you. Generally, women can dress the part of the professional, which means choosing clothing that is both feminine and elegant—blouses and silks, for example, and clothing with softer lines. Mindful of prevailing hair styles, younger women may want to ask their stylists how to achieve a more mature, credible look.

Avoid Distractions in Wardrobe and Accessories

In television the cardinal rule is to focus attention on your face, not on your clothes or accessories (Figure B.3). Accessories for men and women reporters should be subdued so as not to draw the viewer's attention away from the face. If eyeglasses are a problem, consider substituting contact lenses. Remember that the camera comes so close to you that sometimes all you have to communicate is what's in your eyes. Eyeglasses

FIGURE B.3

Dressing appropriately from one story environment to the next is a good way for reporters to enhance their credibility. In all on-camera appearances, an important consideration is to choose clothing and accessories that will help keep attention on the face.

add another filter to distract the audience and yet another barrier through which you must project yourself.

Whenever you appear on camera, dress appropriately for the story. This advice is important to all television reporters, male or female, because if viewers worry about your tie or scarf, they will miss the story. If you report from a recycling plant, you may want to loosen your neckwear and hold your jacket over your arm or shoulder, or ditch it altogether. If you report from the ski slopes, trade your wool coat for a ski jacket. On skid row, a silk business suit may be out of place, both because it doesn't fit in and because it may psychologically distance you from your news sources.

Colors and Cut Matter

This same advice applies when you conduct interviews: Dress to reinforce your credibility. If the moment is relaxed and informal, your demeanor and the way you dress should help reinforce a sense of informality, so take off your coat and roll up your sleeves. If the story is investigative and confrontational, professional clothing in darker tones may help reinforce the sense of your story. If the setting is a hospital lab, you may want to wear a lab coat so that you don't look out of place.

Whatever you do, dress to avoid "disappearing into the background." If the background of trash against which you appear at the landfill is bland and brown, a jacket of the same tone will do you no favors. Similar problems arise if you wear "cool" colors for an appearance on a "cool" set. If you know in advance what colors are present, you can dress to create at least some contrast between you and the background. Remember, too, to consider textures when you dress. Some texture in clothing helps create visual interest.

FIELD LIGHTING FOR HDTV

High-definition television brings viewers face to face with people's physical imperfections. With a clarity roughly six times greater than analog television[5] high-def cameras magnify everything from acne scars to wrinkles, bags under the eyes, and poor makeup jobs. High-def studio lighting and adjustments in makeup help hide those imperfections for news anchors, but without similar lighting adjustments in the field an anchor, reporter or virtually anyone else can suddenly appear 10 years older.[6] Field lighting thus takes on greater importance than ever.

LET THE AUDIENCE KNOW YOU AS A FRIEND

Over time, viewers will evaluate you the same way they evaluate their best friends. When we first meet strangers at parties, part of our evaluation is based on their appearance. If you were asked to talk about your best friend, you could describe your friend's voice, dress, manner, and speech patterns. You could tell us something about your friend's birthplace and background and his or her age and approximate income. All these things we come to know about people we like. And all these things help make each of us unique.

Your individuality, then, is one of your greatest strengths in a medium that communicates through people. To really succeed, you must risk letting the audience come to know you as a friend. To do that you will have to let the things that make you unique come through. Such a task takes time and can hardly occur if you are a "market hopper" who moves from one job to another every year or so. The

BOX B.2   TALENT GROWTH MODEL

The Talent Growth Model
Stair Steps Toward Audience Appreciation for an On-Air News Talent

Levels 1 and 2:
The audience decides whether you have these qualities.

Level 5:
Persona
friendly, warm. comfortable, **community asset, charisma**

Level 4:
Journalistic Skill
probes, digs, investigative, credible, **expertise**, knowledgeable, credentials

Level 3:
Style Development
professionalism, naturalness, authoritative, credibility, **interaction**

Level 2:
Reading Skill
diction, delivery, clarity, speed smoothness, **interpretation**

Level 1:
Cosmetics
dress, make-up, voice quality, gestures, mannerisms, **body language**

Levels 3, 4 and 5:
You demonstrate these attributes by proving and revealing your personality and professionalism

The Talent Growth Model represents the process on-air personalities undergo in developing a relationship with the viewing audience. Many anchors are unable to establish more than a surface relationship with viewers. It takes time, dedication to the process, and patience to achieve the ultimate relationship with viewers.

The Talent Growth Model is divided into five phases of growth, each phase evolving and expanding from the other.

- Viewers first notice appearance. The audience reacts to the on-air person visually (Level 1). What does he or she look like? Included here are such things as hair, make-up, clothing and overall appearance. When the viewer accepts the anchor or reporter visually, he or she is ready to move on to the next level.
- Next, viewers listen. The developing anchor or reporter works to improve delivery (Level 2). Is the voice pleasant and easy to listen to, with no

apparent impediments? It is important to read copy smoothly, using conversational pacing, vocal variety and inflection, appropriate volume, and good diction.

The anchor or reporter needs to sound relaxed, comfortable, and friendly.

- "S/he's so professional." Being comfortable and confident in his/her role epitomizes what a professional should be (Level 3). The anchor or reporter looks and acts like a journalist and can be seen to do 'journalistic' activities. Viewers accept the person's apparent authority in the absence of contrary actions. The viewer also perceives talent to have an exciting job, and finds it off-putting if the anchor seems bored or uninvolved. Many anchors never progress beyond this point. Those who themselves road blocked at Level 3 often exit the profession.
- Being involved in community activities reinforces success. (Level 3 and 4) Making personal appearances, doing public speaking engagements, and

letting the audience see the anchor as a "real person" participating in "real life" activities is essential in continuing the growth of the relationship.

- Respected Journalist. Despite all the remarks within the industry about pretty or handsome "blow-dried talking heads," viewers appreciate responsible, capable journalists. At Level 4, the anchor or reporter has earned true authority, having served the community long and well. Level 4 talent show insight and can analyze complex issues in understandable ways. S/he must appear knowledgeable about current events in the community and country. Doing important stories and series, being seen as a working journalist, helps. A fine anchor or well recognized and respected reporter can reach this level.
- The chosen few. A few anchors manage to reach Level 5. They become Community Assets. The anchor has reached this level when viewers see him/her as a trusted friend who is invited into

their homes each evening. Viewers turn to this person because they depend on him/her to help them get through the day and make their lives better. Longevity in a market is a major factor in reaching this phase, and it definitely takes time to get to this level. At this stage, viewers are forgiving of the less-than-perfect qualities that block an anchor's growth in the beginning stages.

The Anchor Growth Model represents how the anchor develops this relationship. Whether he/she is able to implement the ideas depends on self-motivation, effort, and a strong desire to succeed in the business. However, even such dedication does not guarantee hitting the bull's-eye. To be seen as the trusted friend – an asset to the community – often depends upon a charismatic bond between an anchor and the viewer.

Graphic © 2011 Laura Schaub Designs. Used with permission. Research findings and text used with permission, courtesy Bill Taylor, NuFuture.TV, January 2011.

community in which you work is equally special; it, too, will require some time to reveal itself and for you to come to know it. Tenure in the marketplace, up to two years even in small markets, is thus important if you are to build this special relationship with the community—and it with you. Soon your reporting will take on added depth and show evidence of close, authoritative knowledge about the people, issues, and events in your community.

IMPACT HOW PEOPLE PERCEIVE YOUR INTERVIEW SOURCES

Body language, whether purposeful or inadvertent, influences how viewers perceive the people you interview. If you "open up" the interview, both visually and physically, the interview will appear to be more casual and relaxed. If, through body language, you communicate your friendship for and concern about the news source, your audience will more likely feel a sense of friendship and concern toward the person.

As a rule, interviews carry a more "adversarial" tone when the following visual elements are present:

- Reporter and interviewee wear coats and ties or other business attire.
- Something physical separates the news source from the reporter. The object may be as obvious as an office desk or something as seemingly innocent as a handheld stick mike.
- Physical distance is great between reporter and interviewer.

- Interviewee appears to be "trapped" or "pinned" behind a desk in a corner or against a wall, with nowhere to go.
- Reporter and interviewer face each other squarely, almost head-on.

Conversely, reporters and interviewees appear to be more relaxed and friendly when the opposite visual elements are present:

- Reporter and/or interviewee take off coats or at least unbutton them.
- Reporter sits beside the interviewee with nothing between them, not even a stick mike.
- Physical distance between reporter and interviewer is comfortably close.
- Interview is taken outside where the visual message is a sense of freedom, a clear impression that the interviewee has agreed to the interview of his or her own free will.
- Reporter angles in toward the other person, rather than facing the individual straight on in a confrontational manner.

Influencing how the audience perceives a news source may seem to smack of bias and staging, but in television or any form of human expression, there is no such thing as a neutral transaction. If an interviewee is kind at heart, honest, and friendly, no purpose will be served by inadvertently communicating an opposite impression. Unlike with newspapers, people interact with television. No matter how hard we strive to be objective and unbiased, it is well to remember that in television news, and in all human communication, even no action is a reaction.

Rather than failing to react, the key to being objective is to cover all sides of an issue with equal energy. Aggressively pursue all sides of the story so that your delivery remains committed and energetic throughout coverage of all the issues. If the story is about taxes going up, you may observe that it's great news for folks who live on the east side of town where new schools are needed, but bad news on the west side where elderly people need that money to pay their medical bills.

POSTURE MATTERS

Your posture—how you hold your body—is obvious to the audience and will affect how viewers perceive you and your reporting ability. Often, you can improve your posture by concentrating on how you hold your head and shoulders: Stand, run, and walk as if a string attached to the very crown of your head is lifting you—almost as if you were a puppet. This technique helps you keep your chin down and in, helps make the crown of your head go up, and helps prevent the appearance of "leading" with your head as if you're about to fall forward when you walk. Remember, too, to keep your shoulders down and rounded. You should feel relaxed and natural whenever you are on camera, and your appearance should reflect that feeling. Study the appearance of reporters you respect; often, you will discover that their posture is impeccable.

SPLIT-FOCUS PRESENTATION

Throughout your on-set interaction with an anchor, the audience normally will look at whichever of you is speaking. While the anchor talks, you should also look at the anchor. When you speak, the anchor should look at you. As you speak, remember to divide your attention between the anchor and the audience, a practice known as **split-focus presentation**, which helps make the audience part of your conversation. This technique is vastly preferable to the method in which both anchor and reporter resolutely face the camera and take turns speaking without ever turning their heads to acknowledge one another.

THE ANCHOR DEBRIEF

Going into your report, the anchor normally will set up your story with a brief remark or two, then turn toward you and comment briefly so that the two of you can interact. When you finish interacting with the anchor on set, be looking at the camera as you begin your introduction to the story. After your report has aired, you will need to return control of the show to the anchor. When transitioning back to the anchor as you finish your presentation, look at the anchor. At this point the anchor normally will ask a follow-up question or two, a form of debriefing that serves to reestablish the anchor's command of the show. This interchange is known as the **anchor debrief**.

Most often, you will be expected to have a question for the anchor to ask when you come out of a story back to the set. In formulating your questions, remember that good anchors will want to ask questions that represent the viewers' interests as well as the community's perspective. Ideally, you will take time to discuss your anticipated responses briefly with the anchor prior to airtime.

WHEN YOU ARE BEFORE THE CAMERA

Anytime you are before the camera, whether in the studio or the field, your work will demonstrate to your viewers the extent to which you are well groomed, conversational, professional, and incisive. Resolve, therefore, to develop a consistent and recognizable visual style and prove that you are a good journalist who knows what your audience needs to know about the stories you report. As *Time* columnist Hugh Sidey observed, "Journalists were originally created to enlighten, not to threaten; to inform, not to perform; to know, not to show."[7]

Ask questions, process information, show that you are a team player, and prove that you care about the community in which you work. Finally, show us that you care about us as viewers and, yes, even that you like us. If you do all these things, you may become the person in your market that viewers most often seek out as their most authoritative and likable news source.

HOW REPORTERS EVOLVE INTO ANCHORS

For most reporters the dream of becoming an anchor remains just that, although reporters who aim their careers can sometimes evolve into anchors. If management thinks of you primarily as a reporter, your aspirations may come to nothing, so the first trick is to give yourself opportunities to demonstrate your anchor potential. This can most easily be accomplished by producing stories that need on-set or split screen follow-up and amplification. Whenever practical, suggest to the producer that your story justifies putting you on-set to discuss it with newscast anchors. Further, anchors can react to the story and prove their own close knowledge about the topic. When you make it on-set or split screen, your performance will be crucial, so follow the pros' advice:

- Hone in on the anchor with your eyes and ears.
- Listen intently.
- Gesture appropriately, perhaps with a pencil, and even tap on the desk to make your point.
- Be natural and energetic.
- Be interested and interesting.
- Remember to focus on something outside yourself rather than your performance, and to enjoy what you're doing.

SUMMARY

Video journalists often communicate certain story elements through the reporter's on-camera performances in the field. Routinely, the most effective and memorable standups occur when performance originates as a natural outgrowth of story content. To be interesting on camera, the reporter must be interested—in stories, in the subjects of stories, and in the community and its residents—and be photographed in such a way that home viewers see the interest.

Most communication attempts to elicit a response. Yet the camera and microphone never respond to the journalist. Some good ways to seek a response are to treat the lens as if it were a person, imagine that you're talking to a friend, and/or envision in your mind's eye how the audience will react to you and your story.

Video journalists further enhance the story by capturing related sensory experiences—the sights, sounds, smells, tastes, and textures—and to fill in with words and actions what the pictures don't communicate. Audiences become more interested in the story when they see you think, react, or otherwise do something interesting on camera. Also try to capture the reporter's honest reactions during field interviews and other appropriate moments.

Reporters can use body language to communicate interest and enthusiasm for the story and the audience. To be more visually aggressive, the reporter can sit on the edge of the chair or other object, lean forward toward the camera or interview subject, make hand gestures, and alter facial expressions as appropriate. Note that gestures are more spontaneous and easy to make with a lavaliere microphone than while holding a hand mike (Figure B.2).

Effective performance depends on thorough knowledge of the story and its subjects. You can improve voice delivery by studying and practicing with words and by giving their sounds and meaning some thought. The way words are built helps to convey their meaning: "For years, citrus growers have likened the tang of Texas grapefruit juice to the crisp smack of an ocean wave." For natural voice delivery, emphasize contrasts and new ideas, and mark copy accordingly.

Whereas it's important to relax on camera, it's also important to project a sense of energy. Proper breathing and vocal techniques can help the reporter achieve energetic yet conversational delivery. A valuable exercise is to practice standup delivery at varying distances from the field camera. The goal is to overcome any tendency to yell to the camera, even when it is some distance away. When yelling occurs, tension and vocal pitch increase, while intimate connection with the audience decreases.

Even in standups it is acceptable for the reporter to stop talking occasionally in order to do something meaningful, such as show a padlocked gate or taste and savor a food. Demonstration standups, in which the reporter has an activity to perform while on camera, can help the reporter appear more natural and relaxed. However, no story should be altered by a reporter's presence in a standup.

Beyond their ability to enhance otherwise nonvisual stories, standups help establish the reporter's credibility and remind viewers who does the actual field reporting. Viewers might otherwise mistakenly credit anchors for originating many of the reports they see. Reporters and photographers can work as a team to help make standups visually reinforce the story to be told.

It is important for the reporter to dress appropriately for the story and to dress to keep attention on the face rather than on clothing, hair, or jewelry. Accessories should be subdued, and the reporter may want to avoid eyeglasses altogether. To succeed as an on-air reporter, you must allow the audience to come to know you as a friend and see the qualities that make you special.

Some reporters may evolve into anchors more quickly by producing stories that need on-set or split screen follow-up and amplification. When practical, suggest to the producer that you should appear on-set to discuss your report or related issues with the anchor. Techniques for interaction with the anchor include split-focus presentation and the anchor debrief.

Finally, photographers and reporters should strive to understand the people who watch reports. You are better qualified to serve audiences when you know their needs, interests, concerns, and aspirations. Likewise, tenure in the marketplace serves most reporters well. After serving for years as a trusted friend in the community, most reporters are welcomed as authoritative and likable sources for relevant yet interesting stories.

KEY TERMS

anchor debrief   313
demonstration standup   301

multidimensional
reporting   305

split-focus presentation   313

NOTES

1. Barry Nash is a professional talent consultant. A majority of remarks in this chapter are derived from his work with students at Colorado State University and with professional talent in markets of all sizes throughout the country. He is a partner in The Coaching Company, Dallas, TX (www.coachingcompany.com).
2. Greg Luft, unpublished manuscript shared with the principal author, Colorado State University, circa 2001.
3. *NBC Nightly News*, March 29, 1984. Reporters still "borrow" this line. The principal author has heard it parroted in Texas, Maryland, Louisiana, and Colorado.
4. The "Guide to Marking Copy" used as a general reference for this chapter was provided courtesy of Barry Nash, The Coaching Company, Dallas, TX.
5. Hugh Sidey, "The Mick Jaggers of Journalism," *Time* (October 5, 1987), 28.
6. Ibid
7. Diane Holloway, "That's Harsh: Hi-def TV is changing our views of the stars," Cox News Services, 29 March 2007.

The Assignment Editor and Producer

Architects of the Newscast

Digital technology has demonstrated for the past decade that constant change is here to stay. Appendix C provides valuable information and perspectives for video reporters and storytellers who work, or plan to work, in television news.

Those who work in arenas beyond television news may discover useful insights throughout this appendix as well, such as Internet Reporting, Toward a News Philosophy, Planning Ahead, and Incorporating a Sense of Community. You also may encounter still other useful or interesting information to apply in your own work.

At the most successful news operations, an astutely defined news philosophy serves as the underpinning of a daily operational guide. This philosophy shapes collective staff judgment about what is news, how it is to be covered, by whom, and how it is to be packaged and showcased. It is a philosophy born of a genuine understanding of the community, and it serves inevitably to help make the assignment editor and producer partners in building the daily newscast. Because both the assignment editor and producer are such key players in deciding the station's destiny, their partnership is essential.

THE ASSIGNMENT EDITOR

The assignment editor's job is to cover everything that happens, a responsibility some broadcasters consider the toughest job in the news department (Figure C.1). Many assignment editors have held previous jobs as reporters or producers, but whatever their background they often share a certain psychological profile and temperament. At minimum, every day these folks have to

- read newspapers
- monitor competitors and web postings
- monitor police, fire, sheriff, and emergency radio transmissions
- maintain close communication with the news director and producer
- know the reporters' egos, peculiarities, writing styles, and internal clocks
- know who can work with police, who has great interpersonal skills

- nurture the best general assignment reporters, the true prizes of the newsroom
- know whose stories are working, whose stories are failing
- help producers find the f-l-o-w in stories and transitions
- know what stories and story treatments will appeal to viewers
- know what stories are important to the community
- know what stories justify live reports
- follow breaking news, faster and better than the competition
- communicate with the promotion department
- know what stories need updates
- identify relevant feature stories
- based on current research, know what kinds of stories viewers are least likely to watch
- realize how the producer and reporter's writing complement the anchor's job of introducing stories
- know how to make any story more compelling, more understandable
- know which anchors would do the best job of introducing specific stories
- know how to make stories more instant and interesting, while preserving accuracy, polish, and professionalism
- protect time for research and constant updating
- excel in outperforming the competition, the driving force in every newsroom
- define relevant news—the news people want to know
- know how to improve what anchors and reporters do
- establish commonality with the audience
- stop smoking
- drink enough water
- spend enough time with family and other loved ones
- have a life outside the newsroom
- develop an informed, healthy mind
- get enough exercise and rest

The assignment editor also assigns crews, answers the phone, checks the news services, sorts and reads the mail, reads scripts of previous newscasts, keeps a news file, develops story ideas and sometimes helps write the stories, makes and adjusts schedules, helps organize the newsroom, and negotiates conflicts between staff members. Assignment editors read everything, always looking for another story, another angle, and they bear the greatest responsibility should the station miss a story. In a real sense, the assignment editor is a copartner, along with the producer, in helping shape the station's destiny (Figure C.1).

ASSIGNMENT EDITORS HELP CONCEPTUALIZE THE PACKAGE

Most reporters have worked with an assignment editor who sends crews to everything. Some assignment editors may think of packages and even newscasts as holes to fill. They tend to treat reporters and photographers as folks who bring home the fill dirt.

FIGURE C.1 A&B

An assignment editor schedules the day's stories and assigns reporting crews to cover them. Breaking news is assigned as it happens.

In actuality, only news that is important and interesting to the viewer needs to be covered. Such a simple axiom demands that the assignment editor be a good judge of what is truly newsworthy and interesting, and to know the community's pulse. A decision about which stories should be covered also can be shared with other newsroom employees (Figure C.2). Effective newsrooms often use a beat system in which reporters share more news coverage responsibilities with the desk; this encourages more enterprise reporting and follow-up.

Because assignment editors are in effect the "first reporter" on many stories, they, too, share a responsibility in helping determine the focus statement for many of the stories they assign. Although it may be too early to make a theme statement at the time a story is first assigned, the opportunity certainly exists for those stories on which planning and research are well under way.

FIGURE C.2

As a new shift begins, reporting crews consult with their assignment editor about the day's field assignments.

The Futures File in an Organized Newsroom

One device that helps assignment editors know which news to cover is the **futures file**. This file is a collection of story ideas, notes, and news releases about upcoming events. The futures file contains information about predictable news, so it helps create better newsroom organization. Better organization in turn can help reporters anticipate stories and how best to cover them rather than simply react to them.

The News Planner

Reporters usually receive story assignments the same day their stories will air. Reporters who may originate from three to six stories a day have little time to unearth sources or conduct in-depth research. But in some newsrooms, assignment editors and news planners try to plan story coverage far in advance to give reporters lead-time to develop stronger stories. The job of news planners is to think ahead, research stories, and generate story ideas not only for next week's newscasts but also for series that may be aired in coming months. Reporters work on these advance assignments as time permits throughout the news day, in addition to their daily reporting assignments.

Stringers

Even on slow news days when nothing seems to be happening, the station is likely to be awash in a sea of news, with access to material from sources as diverse as its own field reporters, feeds via satellite, network and local microwave sources, cooperating regional stations, news syndications, and the like. Problems may arise, however, in covering fast-breaking news in nearby local communities, unless the assignment editor has access to a news stringer network that is already in place.

Stringers are private individuals who agree to photograph breaking news for average payments of twenty-five to fifty dollars per story. Stringers may receive a telephone call from the assignment editor to cover a story, or they may cover a story "on spec" with payment forthcoming only if the story is used.

Internet Reporting

For virtually instant reporting, newsrooms may often rely on **Internet reporting**. Citizens with video phones that incorporate Internet access can record still and moving images at spot-news events, stream video to the station, or talk live with reporters and anchors. Such "improv" news footage may sometimes look unpolished and amateurish, yet transmit a gritty, first-person realism that makes for compelling television. Stations commonly solicit eyewitness video on their web sites.[1]

THE PRODUCER

Every day the newscast starts out as a blank page. If you think of the newscast as a house that must be built from the foundation up every day, then the producer can be thought of as its architect. As stories filter back from the field throughout the news day, as scripts are written, and as editors assemble VO/SOTs (voice-over/sound on tape) and packages, the producer works to structure and define the newscast. The job is an amalgam of deadlines and creative decisions. And occasionally there are opportunities to impact the newscast in ways that can help shape the station's destiny (Figure C.3).

FIGURE C.3
News personnel, including news anchors, show producers, and assignment editors, interact during a daily budget meeting to help plan the day's news coverage and determine probable lead stories of the day.

TOWARD A NEWS PHILOSOPHY

Unless viewers are involved in the newscast, they are vulnerable to raids from the competition. Yet night after night across the country, multitudes of viewers are served a kind of news hash, a mishmash of good news/bad news/irrelevant-dull-pointless news. The problem tends to be especially acute in the smaller markets, where viewers are in a sense sacrificial audiences who must either submit themselves to the available fare or go without. At the most proficient news operations, news is presented with an identifiable style. News treatment at these stations imparts relevancy to the day's events. Stories and production values build and hold audience interest. Audiences leave these newscasts feeling a sense of connection not only with the station and its anchors and reporters, but with the information itself.

The station's news philosophy and how it positions itself against competitors can help build market dominance. The station's philosophy becomes a tangible force over time as station management and staff begin to ask and answer of themselves: "What are we all about? How do we want people to think of us? What do we stand for?" Such questions help the station determine its image, its values, and its edicts.

Incorporating a Sense of Community

Communities are made up of people—their dreams, triumphs, and struggles. To understand a community, you must be part of it. One way to be more in touch with viewers and their needs and interests is by developing a broad foundation of first-person knowledge. This means activities as simple as taking time during days off to drive to various areas of the community, visit a café for a cup of coffee, or walk through a new residential area. Extending that same principle, broadcast journalists can be encouraged to involve themselves in community events and civic affairs, whatever their scope. Perhaps one day each month can be devoted to charitable or volunteer activities or to pay a visit to the local senior retirement facility. Whatever activities you choose, the payoff is greater understanding of and empathy with viewers who look to your station for an accurate portrayal of the happenings and life within their community—from a station whose employees are themselves contributing and involved members of the community.

Winning Stations Care about Their Communities

Care about your community, and it will show. Fail to care about your community, and every viewer will know. With that motto apparently in mind, WUSA-TV, Minneapolis–St. Paul, changed its station call letters to KARE-TV.

In a real sense, viewers help dictate the definition of news. Every night, viewers come to the station's newscast with certain expectations. They expect to be informed about the truly interesting and significant happenings of the day. They expect to encounter a certain range of experiences and for a while to inhabit certain emotional territories. They seek an identifiable presence in the show's primary and secondary talent (anchors and reporters), and they look to these people—people they have learned they can trust—for help in understanding the day's news. Most important, they look for interest and relevancy in exchange for the half hour or more of life they will invest in the station's newscast.

The Good News–Bad News Syndrome

Journalism has evolved as a profession that addresses "things gone wrong," with emphasis on issues and problems that need to be addressed and solved. Yet among the most important roles of journalism, as Walter Lippman has argued, is that of showing us the way. The world is gray, neither all good nor all bad. Typically, audiences want their newscasts to reflect a similar balance of content, made up neither of all good news nor all bad, but news that fairly represents what is happening in the viewer's many worlds.

Given that understanding of audience needs and interests, it is useful to examine the typical half-hour newscast. Look at each story and each element of production and rank it for emotional weight according to whether it can be categorized as "plus," "zero," or "minus." Determine for each component in the newscast—be it the story, standup, anchor reaction, or graphic, whether you feel positive, neutral, or negative toward it. As you rank stories in the news lineup, you may discover a long string of "bad news" stories, a common occurrence at stations where a news philosophy is absent or only vaguely operable. Some newscasts may go heavy on bad news for most of the hour, with a good news kicker at the end.

Placed in proper perspective, even so-called bad news can sometimes be converted from a minus to a zero, or even to a plus. Arguably, then, news is drawing the line. There is no such thing as good news or bad news, no such thing even as hard or soft news. "There is simply news and how you treat it," says Bill Brown, consultant and managing partner of The Coaching Company, Dallas. "It's whether you report fairly, with balance and perspective, and how you clue in your viewers."[2]

Brown cites as an example a story in which a woman's body was found years after her murder. Some stations in the market chose to emphasize the agony and tragedy of the event; other stations emphasized family members who expressed relief that they could now get on with their lives. In stories about Mexico City earthquakes, some stories of necessity dealt with the great loss of life and related tragedies. Other stories, however, dealt with the renewal of life expressed in accounts of the city's efforts to establish makeshift nurseries to accommodate the hundreds of newborn babies who arrived during the earthquakes. Such balance and perspective may help a station achieve dominant position in the ratings far more easily than when stations consider journalism to be predominantly accounts of "bad news."

Sources of News

As a station strives to initiate a better balance of content, staffers can find it useful to examine how news stories (and ideas for stories) originate. In the case of journalists, the observation that applies to the rest of humanity is operable: Most people seek the easiest solution to a task. The most obvious stories, therefore, are those that present themselves, and the easiest stories are those that take the least thought and are the most accessible to cover. This is one reason stations within a market tend to report the same stories and the same general types of stories. Stations that foster reporter enterprise and story ownership can rise above such imitative approaches, to produce stories that are more relevant, original, and interesting.

Two types of news routinely offer the accessibility journalists must rely on if they are to meet incessant daily deadlines. The first type includes both spot news, and the more predictable happenings such as public hearings, trials, and news conferences that can be scheduled and covered as developing stories. Information about spot news events is available around the clock to any station with police and fire scanners and to assignment editors and reporters who have cultivated their connections with local dispatchers and law enforcement agencies (Figure C.4).

The second common type of news source is the person who represents a special interest. In one way or another, this person seeks to promote a particular point of view or otherwise capitalize on public exposure of a deed or message. In this category are press secretaries, public relations practitioners, publicity agents, branches of the U.S. military, a university research project or fund-raising effort, a candidate for mayor, and a nuclear power plant just down the road. Typically, special interest sources schedule events and news conferences at times and locations as convenient for the reporter as possible. These sources try to provide events that are both visual and timely and can be pegged naturally to "real" news events. Some firms go so far as to provide the visuals themselves and sometimes even preshot and edited packages with well-written scripts that a station's reporter can voice as his or her own. These "video press releases" imitate local news formats; often they are aired "as is" at smaller stations, with no way for viewers to know the originator was someone with a product, service, or point of view to promote.

Given the deadline pressures assignment editors and producers face, it's small wonder that many newscasts tend to be event driven, a phenomenon that Bill Taylor of NuFuture. TV calls "clutch and brake" news. The newscast is filled with one event after another, with little sense of connection between stories or sections within the newscast or of the themes that may be present among the day's stories. One way to break out of the syndrome is to begin to look for the meaning behind events and situations and to generate interpretive stories even when there is no event per se.

FIGURE C.4
An assignment editor contacts sources and tracks crew locations during coverage of a breaking news story.

Story Follow-Up

In reality, few stories just happen and fade away. They keep going. Audiences have an extraordinary hunger for follow-up, and they look to stations to keep track of all the things that they, as viewers, can't keep up with. This means that a key element of reporter survival is story ownership and initiative. At most stations, many more stories contain valuable follow-up potential than actually receive it.

Nowhere must reporters wait for someone to assign them a story. In fact, the best reporters try to establish story ownership and to update their reports whenever new developments warrant.

Some news operations require that reporters generate a certain number of enterprise ideas each week and insist that reporters maintain a file on every story they report and follow up on them periodically. As a bonus, reporters who find themselves dissatisfied with assignments no longer have to always follow other people's story ideas.

Photographers have an equivalent responsibility to become involved in story development and follow-up. As journalists themselves, photographers can originate stories, set up interviews, and schedule reporters to help cover the news.

Determine Your News Philosophy

The destiny of any newscast hinges as much on the producer's news philosophy as it does on news judgment. If the producer has a valid news philosophy and community orientation, the newscast will typically represent a more palatable range and treatment of the day's news. The news will reflect more emphasis on people and less emphasis on institutions. The producer may even begin to deemphasize the next event/next event, clutch/brake syndrome and produce the newscast more as though it were a half-hour news package with a definable theme, logical transitions, and a logical beginning, middle, and end. Perhaps best of all, the newscast will begin to have a distinctly identifiable look. One look at this newscast and most viewers will know instantly which station they are watching.

Viewer Mood

Throughout the newscast, viewer mood must be at the forefront of the producer's mind. Typically, stories carry an "emotional charge" of plus, zero, or minus, so most producers try to avoid strings of any given type of story within the newscast, just as they strive to avoid "Ping-Pong" story order, which results in a rapidly alternating series of good news/bad news/good news stories. Few viewers enjoy an unending litany of negative stories. Conversely, if the story lineup Ping-Pongs back and forth between positive and negative stories, viewers may be unable to change their own moods so quickly, not to mention anchors who must ride an emotional roller coaster that requires smiles one instant and doleful faces the next.

As the person in charge of the ebb and flow of viewer mood, be mindful that a story's emotional charge can be altered, based both on your news philosophy and on your commitment to stories and newscasts that provide balance and perspective. At the very least, try to make the final story in every segment an upbeat one. This technique helps the audience place viewing experiences in a positive or at least neutral frame of mind and helps them be more receptive to stay tuned through the commercial breaks. Additionally, if the range of viewer emotions is predominantly negative, some viewers may tend to blame the anchors or the newscast itself rather than accept responsibility for their own feelings.

Monitor Story Count in Each Segment

Occasionally, one story is allowed to stand alone in a segment, but this practice can shortchange both the segment itself and the viewers at home. Pace falls off, commercials bunch up, and suddenly the lone story seems somehow gratuitous. The problem is especially acute in newscasts in which a franchise report is isolated as the sole story within a segment. The franchise might be a consumer report or health watch segment that airs every week at a scheduled time. Often these reports are treated as the "odd man out"; they're stuffed where they least clutter up the newscast lineup.

The key is to integrate franchises so that scheduled news stories flow naturally into them. If Dr. Johnson's syndicated report covers ways to avoid skin cancer, the producer can precede the report with something as simple as reader copy on a cancer-related story from the news services. A line or two of copy can then be used as a transition to the skin cancer report: "Despite breakthroughs in some forms of cancer treatment, skin cancer is a more serious threat than ever. Dr. Richard Johnson tells how we can reduce risks in our everyday lives."

Another goal is to end stories and segments with content that's "talkable"; in other words, for the anchors to join in as appropriate on the last moment of stories and segments. At the end of a cooking segment in the noon newscast, the technique can be something as simple as one anchor saying to the other, "That looks good. I'm glad it's lunchtime," followed by the co-anchor's acknowledgment, "Me too." The idea is to reach closure on stories and to close out segments with a definitive gesture that indicates "the end of this section is at hand."

Closure is important because we need to see anchors confirm the reactions we have as viewers. If anchors fail to acknowledge stories and packages, or to cleanly end each segment, viewers may see the anchors as callous, humorless, insensitive, unthoughtful, or disengaged. Because anchors show viewers how to react through their own reactions, some acknowledgment of stories is essential—even if the reaction is nothing more than a tilt of the head or a nonplussed expression.

Work with the Anchors

Depending on such factors as market size and the magnitude of the egos involved, producers can sometimes impact the look of the newscast by working more closely with anchors and reporters. Anchors can't react candidly or confidently to stories they haven't seen, for example, so a bit of grounding about the package the anchor won't have time to preview may result in a more spontaneous newscast. A moment or two spent on story setup can help to eliminate anchor uncertainty on the air. Or perhaps the producer can suggest that the anchor use simple, on-set props to better tell the story. Into this category fall such techniques as having an on-set anchor show how realistic today's fake credit cards look, even when held next to the real thing.

The dual or tandem anchor format can slow a show's pace if interaction becomes ponderous or if both anchors insist on "owning" the story. It helps if interaction between anchors remains friendly but precise and if story setups are kept to a minimum. Even the little half-beat hesitations that occur when the anchor comes back on air and waits to be cued or to affirm on-air status can be eliminated by using a floor director who gives the anchors tight, crisp air cues. More spontaneous interaction can result if the technical director is given permission to do live edits from one camera to the next during anchor interplay in the studio.

Within the news operation, reporter and anchor education also is important as the station strives to help employees focus and refocus on station goals and news philosophies, which can lead to improved newscast content and appearance.

TEASES

Most producers either write or assign the teases that are meant to tantalize viewers into staying tuned for the news to come: "Next, advice from the experts on the safest suntan of all. We'll have that story when we return, and more about the cheapest ways to travel this summer, wherever you're headed." Just as a newspaper headline reflects the essence of a print story, the broadcast tease tells us a tantalizing tidbit about the story to come, but doesn't give it away: "Someday all the medication you need may come in a glass of milk." This tease, which aired on CBS4 News, Denver, promoted a story that told viewers that scientists have genetically altered milk to produce a human heart drug.

Teases should reveal just enough about the story to keep viewers tuned in, but not so much information as to render the upcoming story unnecessary. "Tease the teasable reasons to watch a show," says NuFuture.TV's Bill Taylor. "Keep telling late night viewers why it's important to stay tuned, and remember to include, not exclude, the audience," says Taylor.[3]

When you write teases, try to find a way to communicate a sense that all viewers will need to know about/be interested in/benefit from/be entertained by this next story. Often, it is possible to sell people who appear in the stories you are teasing and let them sell the stories. Even in teases the saying holds that if you can sell the person, the person will sell the story.

Fulfill the Promise of the Tease

Night after night, year after year, it is imperative for the package to fulfill the promise of the tease. Viewers quickly grow tired of unkept promises. The same principle applies to the story lead-in. Avoid generic teases and lead-ins. The more specific, engaging, and compelling you can make them, the better.

HELP MAKE THE STATION A REGIONAL FORCE

To build larger audiences, a station may seek to establish itself as the one that does the best job covering regional news. Even stations that work zealously to cover regional news over the years may still be identified as serving primarily the community in which they physically reside. In either case, the producer can help the station achieve greater recognition as a regional force in covering news over a wide area.

One way to help establish a reputation for regional coverage is to "regionalize" the open to the newscast. The idea is to prove to viewers that you're covering their area. As warranted, stories from particular viewing areas can be featured in newsbreaks and teases. Besides the mention of other towns in headline stories, town names can be mentioned in weather and sports. In fact, the more mention of town names in weather, the better.

To project a more regional presence, newscast opens can also contain visuals of identifiable personalities, sports teams, architecture, and geography. Obviously, however, the station cannot become a regional force unless it makes a comprehensive effort to cover news of the region. That means the news operation must pay attention to communities whenever something happens in them.

Viewers receive most major stations in their state of residence, regardless of their location. For this reason, many stations incorporate state coverage under their umbrella of "regional" coverage. Stations routinely establish "bureaus" in outlying areas that use video journalists, or sometimes a resident reporter and photographer. Resident statehouse reporters are commonplace.

Some reporters may contend that a given event in an outlying community isn't "news" because of its narrow focus or limited appeal. But narrow story focus does not automatically exclude a wide audience. When the reporter develops a story with the viewer's interests in mind, everyone wins. Producers also can remind reporters that audiences will never care more about a story than the reporter, and that the only thing that makes a story dull is a dull reporter.

Producers also can lean on reporters to use the phone, and can use it themselves, to universalize the story. "If false alarms or bridge safety are a problem in one community, pick up the phone and find out if similar problems exist in other communities—including your own," says NuFuture.TV's Bill Taylor.[4] If you remember to follow up on more angles than just "the" story, and insist on more follow-up from your reporters, you may soon be airing background stories on how false alarms are investigated, or why money in the road and bridge fund is collecting interest instead of being spent on bridge repairs.

IMPROVE AUDIO-VIDEO LINKAGE

Viewers are the clear winners when script content matches the pictures on the screen—that ideal marriage of words and pictures known throughout the industry as audio-video *linkage,* or *referencing.* Producers and reporters alike have an obligation to monitor linkage within all stories in the newscast and to make the linkage as consistently on target as possible. This goal can be accomplished by following two simple rules. The first rule is: "Write the pictures first." The second rule is: "Don't talk about it unless you show it: See dog, say dog."

VISUALS

Often the producer has little control over visuals that are returned from the field. The producer can exercise control, however, over which visuals make air. One consideration is to avoid video stories that begin with shots of a blank wall rather than "visual leads," or images that instantly and more obviously communicate the story to come. If the story is about child abuse, for example, little purpose is served in opening the story with a shot of the courthouse wall.

Another visual pet peeve of producers is **BOPSA**, or "bunch of people sitting around." Reporters and photojournalists who are at a loss for more meaningful visuals to tell the story frequently bring home lots of BOPSA. Members of their audience with remote controls just as frequently tune out of the newscast at the appearance of BOPSA. Producers also can work with reporters to avoid going "head-to-head" from standups or interviews at the end of packages when the camera cuts back to an anchor on set. If the shot of the person seen in the last shot of the package (the head) is nearly identical in registration with the studio shot of the anchor (the other head), the show can look or feel awkward.

FRESHEN FILE VIDEO

In overseeing a newscast's visual appearance, producers should try to avoid constant reruns of file video. Often, the station may have only a few seconds of video showing a murder suspect walking to court, or of the shootout in which a prison escapee was killed, so the shot tends to be used cover and over ad nauseam as story updates are aired. Among the offenders in this category are file shots of the lamentable space shuttle explosion, shots of navy frigates under missile attack in the Persian Gulf, and stale footage showing the aftermath of airline crashes as the investigations advance over weeks, months, or even years. The solution is to use file video sparingly and to update file video so that audiences are exposed to somewhat fresher images as time progresses (Figure C.5).

USE TALKING HEADS WITH PURPOSE

Another way to improve the newscast's look and reduce viewer confusion is to reexamine how talking heads are used. Viewers often see sound bites in which a person can be seen talking while the reporter's voice continues at full volume but with sound from the bite barely audible. Each night viewers by the tens of thousands struggle to make out what the person is saying, while the reporter's voice-over narrative makes such understanding impossible.

To correct the problem, the producer can insist on eliminating all competing sound when bites are on-screen and establish a policy that anchors and reporters never talk over video of talking heads. Allowing speakers to be heard is simply a matter of courtesy and common sense. If a person can be seen talking on-screen, he or she also should be heard. If the talking head imparts information more effectively than any other means, then it should be used.

FIGURE C.5
File video provides a valuable resource to illuminate otherwise nonvisual stories. Care should be taken to use such video sparingly, update it whenever possible, and identify it in the broadcast as file footage, with a super.

The most gratuitous use of talking heads occurs when they are used to illustrate a sentence of voice-over copy in which the person's name is mentioned, or as the mandatory sound bite within a package because nothing better is available. If the sound bite lends nothing other than a visual ID of the person mentioned in the script, then perhaps it can be converted to a still-frame graphic in a window alongside the anchor, or even be eliminated.

WEATHER AND SPORTS

Weather and sports provide unusual challenges for the producer because often these sections of the newscast are treated as little "islands" somehow separate and distinct from the main show. Frequently, weather and sports talent act as their own producers and may not even be accountable to the news producer. Such autonomous identity can produce a "hands-off-my-show" mentality and a sense of "us–them" rather than the more desirable "us–us" view in which everyone contributes to help achieve common goals.

At the very least, the producer can negotiate to keep emphasis on the weather in perspective. On days when severe weather has struck or is imminent, it may be appropriate to lead the newscast with weather-related stories and to bring the weather anchor on set to report weather developments that constitute hard news. At other times when there are only a few, thin, scattered clouds and another week of temperatures in the mid-70s to report, the weather may be shortened to make room for more important breaking news.

Audiences are usually most interested in local temperatures, current conditions, and an immediate forecast that covers weather for the next couple of days. Such information usually can be communicated in two to two and a half minutes.

Sports anchors also are accountable for the time they devote to sports. The justification can be based on the amount of interesting and significant sports news available that day. Some news operations even require that the sports department justify its selection of stories in the sportscast, just as news must justify its selection. The goal is to keep the sportscast pace moving and its content relevant to general viewer interests.

Because of network coverage, local stations are almost forced to compete with an industry look in sports, except when using viewer-supplied video. Viewers accustomed to the professional polish and pace of network sportscasts have come to expect similar use of pictures and comparable pacing in local sports coverage. To compete more effectively, stations can make greater use of video and create more compelling sportscasts by concentrating more on the people angle in their stories.

Although sports is about winning and losing, and about scoreboards and won-and-lost columns, the most interesting sports (and news) has always been about the small human dramas inherent in athletic competition. Audiences still want to know who won the game, but if the sportscast is to appeal to the widest possible audience it must put less emphasis on scoreboards and more emphasis on storytelling and human drama.

Producers and assignment editors are journalists, and in a real sense they are reporters. Often the assignment editor is the first reporter on a story, sometimes the primary reporter. Just as important is the role of the producer, who must place stories within the context of the newscast, suggest graphics that will better tell the story, and help orchestrate that overwhelmingly complex information assembly line called the newsroom. Many are called to try their hands at these sometimes perplexing occupations, but only the best qualify to be chosen.

SUMMARY

Successful news organizations operate by news philosophies that reflect understanding of the communities they serve. This community understanding serves inevitably to make the assignment editor and producer partners in building the daily newscast.

The assignment editor monitors the news day, helps conceptualize news packages, and schedules and assigns reporting crews to cover stories. The producer is the architect of the newscast who helps determine story selection, the news lineup, and the use of various production elements within the newscast.

Both the producer and assignment editor may help write newscasts. At some stations, a news planner assists the assignment editor by generating ideas for stories and series and by conducting research and helping plan story coverage. Private individuals called stringers may be paid to shoot stories in outlying areas that would otherwise be difficult or impossible to cover.

At face value, journalism would seem to be mostly accounts of "bad news." Often, however, news is neither good nor bad, but simply a reflection of how it's treated. Most viewers want a balance of news that fairly represents what is happening in the viewer's many areas of interest and concern. Some bad news stories that start out with a negative emotional weight can be reasonably and fairly converted to a neutral or even a positive emotional charge. Of great importance is the need for assignment editors and producers to avoid long strings of negative or bad news stories.

Historically, newscasts have been built on a foundation of spot-news stories and information from special interest groups, including business, governments, and other public and private institutions. Such stories are relatively easy to identify and cover. But of at least equal importance in building a community newscast are enterprise stories, which result in a sense of story ownership and the need for follow-up on the part of both reporters and photographers. No one must wait for the assignment editor to assign a story.

As the station proves its worth to the community, management may seek to build larger audiences by establishing the station as a regional force. At such times, it is incumbent upon electronic journalists to universalize stories from outlying regions and relate them to the interests and concerns of viewers from the more immediate viewing areas.

Also important is the need to integrate sports into the newscast, rather than allow it to remain an island unto itself.

Communication between the assignment editor and producer is vital, as is their willingness to maintain communication with all members of the reporting team, including anchors, photographers, and reporters.

KEY TERMS
BOPSA   327
futures file   319   Internet reporting   319

DISCUSSION

1. Describe the typical duties of an assignment editor and discuss the assignment editor's role in the reporting process.
2. Describe the job of the news planner and contrast it with the duties of the assignment editor.
3. Describe the duties of the newscast producer and discuss the producer's role in the reporting process.
4. Define a personal news philosophy that incorporates a sense of responsiveness to the needs of the community in which you reside.
5. In what sense do viewers help dictate the definitions of news at their favorite stations?
6. Discuss the philosophy that contends there is no such thing as good news or bad news, but simply news and how you treat it.
7. Describe and provide an example of how the content of a story with an emotional weight of minus can be converted to an emotional weight of zero or even plus. Is the change of emphasis in your example ethically and professionally valid?
8. List and describe the most common sources of news. Contrast the impact of traditional news sources on news content with stories that originate by virtue of reporter enterprise.
9. Discuss the importance of story follow-up and story ownership as the concepts relate to television photographers and reporters.
10. Enumerate the most important considerations influencing news content, treatment, and story lineup in the typical newscast.
11. To what extent should news anchors interact with reporters and photographers and be considered as members of the reporting team? To what extent should anchors adhere to the concept that "all performance follows content"?
12. What is the role of the news tease in attracting and holding news viewers? Provide at least two examples of visual news teases that a photojournalist could originate for stories being shot in the field and that could be aired without the need for reporter or anchor voice-over narration (such as a shot of sheriff's officers breaking down the door to enter a suspected illegal gambling casino just outside the city limits).
13. How can the photographer and reporter help make their television station a more regional force?

14. How can producers, reporters, and photographers work together to eliminate "wallpaper video" and achieve more precise audio-video linkage?

15. In your role as a photojournalist, describe steps you can take to freshen or update file video of one-time news events in which only a few seconds of video could originally be photographed.

16. Discuss the steps a station might take to better integrate the sports and weather departments into the daily news operation, rather than allow them to remain as islands unto themselves. Why is such integration important?

EXERCISES

1. Invite a television assignment editor and newscast producer to class to discuss their respective duties.

2. Arrange to visit a television station to observe activities on the assignment desk. It may be possible for you to arrange a weekend visit, when the assignment editor may have more time to spend with you.

3. If you have access to a broadcast-quality camera or to a good-quality home video camera, contact your local station about appointment as a news stringer.

4. Interview community leaders and television viewers in your community to identify what they feel are the most important problems and issues in the community. Determine the extent to which these same individuals believe that local media, especially television news operations, are partners in the problem-solving process.

5. Conduct exercise 4, but instead of interviewing community leaders and television viewers, talk with local news directors, assignment editors, and producers. Further, ask them to describe their news philosophies and attitudes about the community.

6. Interview a random but representative selection of ten or more television viewers in your community and ask them what they expect of their favorite newscasts, and the extent to which they expect the station to become involved in the community.

7. Write a position statement no longer than three double-spaced, typewritten pages outlining the news philosophy that you recommend a station to follow. Define your views of how station employees should think of their obligation to the community. Determine an identifiable style and mood for the daily newscast, and identify proper values for news treatments, production, and promotion activities that will help attract, hold, and properly inform news viewers.

8. Test the concept that "there is no good news or bad news, but only news and how you treat it." Using a "bad news" or otherwise negative newspaper or television story as your starting point, try to fairly and accurately convert story emphasis to an emotional weight of zero (neutral) or even plus (positive).

9. List ten enterprise stories that you could assign yourself or another reporter or photographer today without having to wait for an assignment from the assignment editor.

10. Consult back issues of your local newspaper to find a story that was reported several weeks or months ago, and do a follow-up story on your own.

11. View a local television newscast to determine (a) the content and number of stories in each of the news segments between commercials and (b) the approximate emotional weight of each story (minus, zero, or plus). List each story and its emotional weight in a table for easy comparison.

12. Be alert for news teases that may appear "on the half hour" during daytime and evening prime-time hours. Record or write down, verbatim, any teases you hear. After you have watched the stories on the late evening newscast, rewrite the original teases to improve them. In each instance, include both the original tease and your rewrite.

13. Record an off-air story from a television newscast. Identify a shot or short sequence that could be used on the air as a visual tease, or else go out and shoot a visual tease that would have worked for the story that aired. Consider choosing a noncontroversial story, and avoid imposing on any of the subjects who appeared in the original report if you decide to retrace a story.

14. Watch your favorite television newscast for a week and assess the extent to which the station attempts to project a regional presence. List any devices the station uses to project itself as a regional force.
15. Record and study a local newscast to determine how precisely the audio-video linkage is controlled in stories. Also be on the alert for the use of stale or outdated file video. If you encounter obviously out-of-date video, think of ways to freshen the images.
16. View a sportscast and describe in two or three double-spaced, typewritten pages the steps that could be taken to improve the cast. Include observations about such considerations as length of the cast, individual story length, story count, graphics, production values, effective storytelling methods, emphasis on scores versus people, coverage of major and minor sports, use of visuals, quality of writing, and the sports anchor and reporters.

NOTES

1. *Joanne Ostrow, "Old Media Grounded Va. Tech Story," Denver Post*, April 21, 2007.
2. Bill Brown, "How to Survive as a Reporter," a presentation at Colorado State University, March 23, 1987.
3. Bill Taylor, comments at a television news workshop, Columbia, SC, June 14, 2003, and amplified in e-mail correspondence with the principal author, June 28, 2007 and August 19, 2010.
4. Ibid.

GLOSSARY

Aerial Shot   Shot taken from a camera mounted in an airplane, helicopter, or similar conveyance. (The Visual Grammar of Motion Picture Photography)

All-platform journalist   A person who works alone to report, write, shoot, and edit video reports and stories, whether for news, the web, or any other platform or field of employment. (Introduction, Video Journalism: Storytelling on Your Own).

Analog   The video output of nondigital cameras and tape decks that convert or store light rays to electrical signals rather than 1's and 0's. A quality loss occurs with every generation. (The Visual Grammar of Motion Picture Photography)

Anchor Debrief   The question-and-answer period between an anchor and on-set reporter immediately after the reporter's story has aired. (Improving Performance in Field Reporting—Appendix B)

Aperture   An adjustable iris inside the camera lens that controls how much light enters the camera. (Shooting Video: The Basics—Appendix A)

Apparent Authority   The authority of an individual that can be reasonably assumed to be sufficient for a reporter to enter someone's premises or other property, as in the case of permission from a police officer to enter an apartment in the building owner's absence. (Law and the Digital Journalist)

Aspect Ratio   The ratio of width to height in a television image. (The Visual Grammar of Motion Picture Photography)

Assignment editor   Selects, develops, and plans reporting assignments, whether news events or feature stories, to be covered by reporters. (How to Improve Your Storytelling Ability)

Axis Line   An imaginary straight line projected from the tip of the camera lens through the center of the subject and beyond. If the photographer shoots on both sides of the axis line, false reverses in the action may result. (The Visual Grammar of Motion Picture Photography)

Backlight   A light placed opposite the key light and shined down on the subject from behind. Also called a "rim light." (Writing with Light)

Backpack journalist   A person who works alone to report, write, shoot, and edit video reports and stories, whether for news, the web, or any other platform or field of employment. (Introduction, Video Journalism: Storytelling on Your Own)

Backpack reporter   A person who works alone to report, write, shoot, and edit video reports and stories, whether for news, the web, or any other platform or field of

employment. (Introduction, Video Journalism: Storytelling on Your Own)

Barndoors   The hinged metal doors used on light heads to block or direct light. (Writing with Light)

Bidirectional   A microphone pickup pattern in which sound is picked up in front and back, but not to the sides of the microphone. (The Sound Track)

Blue Eye   A live television report that consists solely of a reporter talking on camera from a remote location, without supporting video or prerecorded interviews. *See also* "Naked Live" and "Thumb Sucker." (Live Shots and Remotes)

BOPSA   A term used to describe boring scenes normally shot at meetings and luncheons that show a "bunch of people sitting around." (The Assignment Editor and Producer)

Bounce Light   Light is reflected off a surface to make it appear more soft and natural. (Writing with Light)

Broadlighting   The lighting pattern that results when the key light illuminates the side of the subject's face closest to camera. (Writing with Light)

Butterfly Light   A variation of top lighting in which the main light is placed high and slightly in front of the subject, resulting in a butterfly-shaped shadow beneath the subject's nose. Also called "glamour lighting." (Writing with Light)

CG   Character generator, a computer device that electronically produces words to be superimposed over a live or recorded image. (Live Shots and Remotes)

Charge-Coupled Device (CCD)   A solid-state chip that converts reflected light directly to electrical signals. (Shooting Television News: The Basics)

Circles of Confusion   Light rays that register as overlapping circles of light on the film planc or targct surface, rather than as pinpoints of light that produce crisp focus. (Shooting Television News: The Basics)

Close   The closing shot of the story; the ending toward which the rest of the story builds. (Video Script Formats; Writing the Package; Live Shots and Remotes)

Close-Up (CU)   A shot that fills the screen with the subject or with only a portion of the subject, as for example the face of a person or the full screen shot of a wrist watch. (Telling the Visual Story; The Visual Grammar of Motion Picture Photography)

Cold Cut   A cut in which an outgoing shot and its accompanying sound end simultaneously, only to be replaced at the splice line by new picture with new sound. The effect can destroy a story's otherwise smooth, fluid pace. (Video Editing: The Invisible Art)

Color Temperature   An expression of the proportion of red to blue light that the light source radiates. As color temperature increases, the light becomes progressively more bluish. (Writing with Light)

Combination Shot Camera follows action until a new moving subject enters frame, then picks up the new subject and follows it. (The Visual Grammar of Motion Picture Photography)

Command Post A temporary headquarters established at the scene of emergencies to control the flow of information, and to help reporters and photographers obtain access to the scene. (Live Shots and Remotes)

Commitment A declarative sentence that identifies the story to be told. The journalistic equivalent of the terms *theme, story line, premise,* or *point of view* as commonly used in literature and theater. *See also* "Focus." (Telling the Visual Story; Writing the Package; How to Improve Your Storytelling Ability)

Composition The placement and emphasis of visual elements on the screen. (The Visual Grammar of Motion Picture Photography; Video Editing: The Invisible Art)

Contrast The proportion of white tones in a scene in relationship to black or gray tones. High contrast results when objects in a scene are white and black, with few intermediate gray tones. Low contrast results when objects in scenes are white on white, black on black, or mostly medium gray. (Shooting Television News: The Basics)

Cookies Opaque panels with cutouts that create patterns of light and shadow on backgrounds. *See also* "Flags." (Writing with Light)

Crossroll Prerecorded video or interviews that roll on air following the reporter's live, on-camera introduction in a remote field report. (Video Script Formats; Live Shots and Remotes)

Cut The point in edited video at which audience attention is transferred instantly from one image to the next. *See also* "Edit Point." (Video Editing: The Invisible Art)

Cutaway A shot of some part of the peripheral action, such as a clock on the wall or football fans in a stadium, that can be used to divert the viewer's eye momentarily from the main action. Commonly used as an editorial device to help eliminate jump cuts or to condense time. *See also* "Motivated Cutaway." (The Visual Grammar of Motion Picture Photography; Video Editing: The Invisible Art)

Cut-In Shot A shot such as a close-up or insert that emphasizes particular elements of the action in a master shot. (The Visual Grammar of Motion Picture Photography)

Cutting at Rest Editing together scenes of matched action at points in which the action has momentarily stopped. (Video Editing: The Invisible Art)

Cutting on Action Cutting out of a scene as the action progresses and continuing the action without interruption at the start of the incoming scene. (Video Editing: The Invisible Art)

Decibel (dB) A measure of sound intensity that corresponds roughly to the minimum change in sound level that the human ear can detect. (The Sound Track)

Defamation Any statement that damages a person's name, reputation, or character. (Law and the Digital Journalist)

Demonstration Standup The reporter addresses the field camera while engaging in an activity that helps visually prove and reinforce the story being reported. (Improving Performance in Field Reporting—Appendix B)

Depth of Field (DOF) The range of acceptable focus in a scene. Normally, about one-third of the total range of depth of field occurs in front of the subject or focus point, and two-thirds behind the subject. (Shooting Television News: The Basics)

Digital Information is recorded on video, disk drive, computer, or other medium as a series of 1's and 0's. No quality loss occurs during duplication. (The Visual Grammar of Motion Picture Photography)

Digital Manipulation The practice of altering original still, video, or motion picture images by cropping, adding, removing, changing, substituting, or otherwise manipulating elements within the image or scene. (Journalistic Ethics)

Digitize The process of transferring pictures from tape to disk, where they reside in final form as digital data. (Video Editing: The Invisible Art)

Dissolve A scene optically fades to black on top of another scene, which optically fades from black to full exposure. The effect is a melting of one scene into the next. (The Visual Grammar of Motion Picture Photography; Video Editing: The Invisible Art)

Distancing The feeling that a news happening is remote or even unreal, which can overcome photographers as they watch events unfold in the camera viewfinder. (Shooting Video in the Field)

Distortion Any signal that unintentionally sounds or appears different on output from a transmission or recording device than it did on input. (The Sound Track)

Dolly Shot A shot made from a camera mounted on a wheeled conveyance that is moved either toward the subject or away from it. See also "Tracking Shot." (The Visual Grammar of Motion Picture Photography)

Double-System Film Editing A process in which film scenes and multiple sound tracks are manipulated independently of one another, in full synchronization. (Video Editing: The Invisible Art)

Dropouts Temporary interruptions in transmitted or recorded sound or picture. (The Sound Track)

Dynamic Microphone A rugged, handheld microphone often used in news applications. (The Sound Track)

Editing The editing of video and its attendant sound is the "conscious and deliberate guidance of viewer thoughts and associations." The editor strives both to create illusion and to reconstruct reality, as well as to guide viewers' emotional responses. (Telling the Visual Story; Video Editing: The Invisible Art)

Editing in the Camera   The practice of shooting sequences and overlapping action in generally the same order in which they are to be aired. (Shooting Video in the Field; Live Shots and Remotes)

Edit Point   The point at which one shot is surrendered and a new shot begins. *See also* "Cut." (Video Editing: The Invisible Art)

Electronic journalist   A person who works alone to report, write, shoot, and edit video reports and stories, whether for news, the web, or any other platform or field of employment. (Introduction, Video Journalism: Storytelling on Your Own)

Electronic reporter   A journalist using digital media, or a person who works alone to report, write, shoot, and edit video reports and stories, whether for news, the web, or any other platform or field of employment. (Introduction, Video Journalism: Storytelling on Your Own)

Establishing Shot   Used to introduce viewers to the story's locale or to the story itself. (The Visual Grammar of Motion Picture Photography)

Ethics   A philosophy of what is right and acceptable as it governs the rules of living and conduct that impact on professional deportment. (Journalistic Ethics)

Exterior Shot   A shot made outdoors. (The Visual Grammar of Motion Picture Photography)

Eyewash   Pictures whose meaning has little to do with the main point of the story being reported. *See also* "Wallpaper Video" and "Generic Video." (Introduction)

Fade   The scene fades to black (fade-out) or fades from black to full exposure (fade-in). (Video Editing: The Invisible Art)

False Reverse   A subject moving in one screen direction is seen in the next shot to be moving in the opposite direction. (The Visual Grammar of Motion Picture Photography; Video Editing: The Invisible Art; Shooting Video in the Field)

Feather   A technique used in zooming and panning shots, in which the artificial camera movement begins almost imperceptibly and builds to the intended speed, then slows and again ends almost imperceptibly. The technique reduces audience distraction by eliminating the abrupt and obvious beginning and ending of artificial camera movement. (The Visual Grammar of Motion Picture Photography)

Fill Light   A secondary light source set to produce illumination approximately one-fourth to one-half as intense as the key light. (Writing with Light)

Filmic Time   The representation of time in motion picture media as an elastic commodity. In television and film, time can be compressed or expanded far beyond the constraints of real time, which is inelastic. (Video Editing: The Invisible Art)

Filter   A colored glass or optical gel used in photography to control exposure, contrast, or color temperature. (Writing with Light)

Filter Factor   A measure of the amount of light that is lost when a filter is used in photography. Each factor of 2 cuts the original amount of light in half. (Writing with Light)

Flags   Opaque panels used to block light from certain areas. *See also* "Cookies." (Writing with Light)

Flash Cut   Brief fragments of shots are cut to exact rhythm against a musical beat or sound. Also called "rapid montage cutting," (Video Editing: The Invisible Art)

Flat Light   A flat, uninteresting light with little sense of depth or modeling which results when the primary light is mounted on the camera or very near it. (Writing with Light)

Focal Length   The designation of a camera lens and its angle of view as determined by measuring the distance from the optical center of the lens to the front surface of the CCD chip in television cameras. (Shooting Television News: The Basics)

Focus (of the story)   A simple, vivid, declarative sentence expressing the heart, the soul, of the story as it will be on air. *See also* "Commitment." (Telling the Visual Story; Writing the Package)

F/Stop   An aperture setting expressed as a fraction. (Shooting Television News: The Basics)

Futures File   A collection of story ideas, notes, and news releases about upcoming events. (The Assignment Editor and Producer: Architects of the Newscast—Appendix C)

Generic Video   Visuals from file video or similar source originally shot for one purpose, then later used haphazardly to "illustrate" a script. Often the pictures are inappropriate to the message being communicated. (Law and the Digital Journalist)

Gray Scale   A printed scale of contrast values ranging from black, through the various shades of gray, to pure white. (Shooting Television News: The Basics)

Great Depth of Field   The term used when a scene appears to be in focus from quite near the camera to and including the background. See also "Maximum Depth of Field" and "Shallow Depth of Field." (Shooting Television News: The Basics)

Gyro-Lens   A lens that electronically compensates for unintentional camera motion and vibration to produce a smoother, steadier shot. The lens is especially useful to smooth out aerial shots and handheld shots made on long-focal-length settings. (Shooting Television News: The Basics)

Hatchet Light   Side light that appears to "split" the subject's face in half. (Writing with Light)

Head-On Shot   Action in the shot moves directly toward camera. (The Visual Grammar of Motion Picture Photography; Video Editing: The Invisible Art)

Heat   The emotional or intellectual intensity often present in the most spontaneous and believable sound bites. (Shooting Video in the Field)

Hertz (Hz)   A unit of frequency expressed as one cycle per second. *See also* "Kilohertz." (The Sound Track)

High-Angle Shot   A shot taken with the camera high and looking down at the subject. High angles tend to diminish the subject and give viewers a sense of superiority. (The Visual Grammar of Motion Picture Photography)

High-Definition Television (HDTV)   A digital transmission system that allows many more times horizontal and vertical resolution that allows many times more resolution than standard definition televisions provide. Screen sizes can exceed six feet in width, with an aspect ratio similar to theatrical movie screens. (The Visual Grammar of Motion Picture Photography)

High-Pass Filter   An audio filter that diminishes the low frequencies where most wind and some equipment noises originate. (The Sound Track)

HMI Light   Short for Hydrargyrum Medium Arc-Length Iodide, HMI lights produce a soft, natural look with the color temperature of sunlight while using only about a fifth the energy of quartz lights. (Writing with Light)

Illustrative Video   Separate shots of video keyed to each sentence or paragraph of script, with little regard for continuity in subject matter or consecutiveness from one shot to the next. (How to Improve Your Storytelling Ability)

Impedance   A characteristic of microphones similar to electrical resistance. (The Sound Track)

Insert Shot   Close-up, essential detail about some part of the main action. (The Visual Grammar of Motion Picture Photography; Video Editing: The Invisible Art)

Internet   A global network of cables and computers encompassing thousands of smaller regional networks scattered throughout the world. *See also* "World Wide Web (WWW)." (Law and the Video Journalist)

Internet Reporting   Digital reporting via an organization's web site using web updates on breaking news stories, original video shot for web streaming, video provided by citizens with video phones, news scripts converted to web articles, anchor and reporter blogs, podcasts, video reports from traditional newscasts streamed to the web, and interview material not originally broadcast on air. (Law and the Digital Journalist)

Invasion of Privacy   Any act of intrusion, including trespass and publication of embarrassing facts, even if true, that violates an individual's reasonable expectation to privacy. (Law and the Digital Journalist)

Inverse-Square Law of Light   The law of physics stating that at twice the distance from a subject, artificial lights provide only one-fourth their original level of illumination. (Writing with Light)

Iris   An adjustable aperture inside the camera lens that can be regulated to control the amount of light entering the camera. (Shooting Television News: The Basics)

Jump Cut   An action that is seen to jump unnaturally into a new position, shape, or color on the screen. (The Visual Grammar of Motion Picture Photography; Video Editing: The Invisible Art)

Key   Words or graphics electronically inserted into the video scene. (Live Shots and Remotes)

Key Light   The primary or dominant light that illuminates a subject. (Writing with Light)

Kilohertz   A unit of frequency equal to 1,000 cycles per second (kHz). *See also* "Hertz." (The Sound Track)

Lavaliere Microphone   A miniature microphone that can be clipped to or hidden beneath the speaker's clothing. (The Sound Track; Live Shots and Remotes)

Law   The rules and principles of conduct enacted through legislation, and enforced by local, state, and federal authority, that dictate how the affairs of a community or society are to be conducted. (Law and the Digital Journalist)

Lead   The first shot in a news package. Its purpose is to telegraph the story to come instantly. (Telling the Visual Story)

Lead-In   The anchor copy that introduces the story and sets up the video package or prerecorded audio report in radio and television newscasts. To best serve audience understanding, the lead-in should instantly reveal the story rather than act merely as the introduction to a package still to come. The term *lead-in* also can refer to the sentence of copy that leads into a sound bite in a radio or television report. (Writing the Package)

Libel   The use of factual information, as opposed to opinion, that holds someone in hatred or contempt, subjects the person to ridicule, or otherwise lowers one's esteem for the individual. (Law and the Digital Journalist)

Lighting Ratio   The difference between the most brightly illuminated areas of a subject and the areas of least exposure. (Writing with Light)

Limited Invitation   A principle that holds that even in public places, such as restaurants and supermarkets, photography may be prohibited and the reporter's conduct limited to the primary activities of the business in question—in this example, dining or shopping. (Law and the Digital Journalist)

Long Lens   *See* Telephoto Lens.

Long Shot (LS)   A full view of a subject. (Telling the Visual Story; The Visual Grammar of Motion Picture Photography)

Low-Angle Shot   A shot taken with the camera low and looking up at the subject. This shot tends to make the subject more dominant and to reduce the viewer's sense of control or superiority. (The Visual Grammar of Motion Picture Photography)

Macro-Focusing   An adjusting lever permits the front lens element to be extended beyond the limit for normal focus in order to produce larger-than-life images. (Shooting Television News: The Basics)

Master Shot   A single camera is used to record a continuous take of the entire event from one location and generally at one focal-length lens setting. (The Visual Grammar of Motion Picture Photography)

Matched Action   The action of a subject in an edited sequence appears to flow smoothly and without interruption from one shot to the next. See also "Overlapping Action." (Telling the Visual Story; The Visual Grammar of Motion Picture Photography; Video Editing: The Invisible Art)

Maximum Depth of Field   The maximum or deepest range of depth of field, or what appears to be in focus in a scene, available in a given shot at a particular focus setting, focal length, and aperture setting. *See also* "Shallow Depth of Field." (Shooting Video: The Basics—Appendix A)

Medium Shot (MS)   Brings subject matter closer to the viewer than a long shot and begins to isolate it from the overall environment. (Telling the Visual Story; The Visual Grammar of Motion Picture Photography; Live Shots and Remotes)

Mike Flag   A small, four-sided box imprinted with the station logo and attached to handheld microphones. (The Sound Track)

Motivated Cutaway   A cutaway that contributes desirable or essential new information to the story. (The Visual Grammar of Motion Picture Photography)

Moving Shot   The camera swivels on a tripod or other fixed base to follow action. Different from a pan because the photographer's motivation is to follow action, rather than to show a static object in panorama. (The Visual Grammar of Motion Picture Photography)

Multidimensional Reporting   An attempt to heighten the viewer's sense of experience by addressing as many of the five senses as possible in a report, and by allowing viewers to see the reporter think, interpret, and react to the story. (Improving Performance in Field Reporting—Appendix B)

Multi-platform journalist   A person who works alone to report, write, shoot, and edit video reports and stories, whether for news, the web, or any other platform or field of employment. (Introduction, Video Journalism: Storytelling on Your Own). Also see Multimedia Journalist.

Multimedia Journalist   A person shoots, writes and edits stories alone, and also writes and produces content for the web, creates and updates blogs, assembles computer slide shows, "Tweets" on Twitter, and writes other content for social networking sites such as Facebook. (Video Journalism: Storytelling on Your Own)

Multi-platform reporter   A person who works alone to report, write, shoot, and edit video reports and stories, whether for news, the web, or any other platform or field of employment. (Introduction, Video Journalism: Storytelling on Your Own.) Also see: Multimedia Journalist.

Naked Live   A live television report that consists solely of a reporter talking on camera from a remote location, without supporting video or prerecorded interviews. *See also* "Blue Eye" and "Thumb Sucker." (Live Shots and Remotes)

Nats   Natural (nat) sounds from an environment that help communicate a sense of experience and often heighten the

listeners' or viewers' sense of realism. See also "Natural (Nat) Sound." (Live Shots and Remotes)

Natural (Nat) Sound   Natural sounds from an environment that often heighten the viewers' sense of realism. (Telling the Visual Story; The Sound Track; Live Shots and Remotes)

Negative-Action Shot   Action in the shot moves away from camera. (The Visual Grammar of Motion Picture Photography; Video Editing: The Invisible Art)

Nets   Panels or other devices used in artificial lighting to enrich or subdue particular areas of illumination within the scene. (Writing with Light)

Node   The optical center of a lens. (Shooting Television News: The Basics)

NPPA   National Press Photographers Association. (Preface; Journalistic Ethics)

Objective Camera   Action is portrayed as an observer on the sidelines would see it. *See also* "Subjective Camera." (The Visual Grammar of Motion Picture Photography)

Ohm   A measure of electrical resistance. (The Sound Track)

Omnidirectional   A microphone pickup pattern in which sound is picked up from all directions. (The Sound Track)

One-Person Band   A person who works alone to report, write, shoot, and edit video reports and stories, whether for news, the web, or any other platform or field of employment. (Introduction, Field Techniques of Shooting Video, Video Journalism: Storytelling on Your Own)

Open Shade   The quality of shade produced when an outdoor environment is protected from direct sunlight, but with nothing above the subject to obstruct secondary light from the sky itself. (Writing with Light)

Optical Center   The point inside the lens at which light rays first bend as they are brought to bear on the target during the focusing process. (Shooting Television News: The Basics)

Overlapping Action   Action that is contained in one shot to be edited also is present in the shot to which it will be joined. *See also* "Matched Action." (The Visual Grammar of Motion Picture Photography; Video Editing: The Invisible Art)

Package   An edited, self-contained video report of a news event or feature, complete with pictures, sound bites, voice-over narration, and natural sounds. (Telling the Visual Story; Writing the Package)

Pack Journalism   A high concentration of journalists from competing news organizations jammed into an area, each concerned primarily with his or her own interests. (Writing with Light)

Pan   The camera swivels on a tripod to show an overall scene in a single shot, or the handheld camera is moved in similar fashion. *See also* "Moving Shot." (The Visual Grammar of Motion Picture Photography)

Parallel Cutting   Intercutting between separate but developing actions. (Video Editing: The Invisible Art)

Perspective   The apparent sizes of photographed objects in relationship to one another as they appear at certain distances, in comparison with how the human eye would view the same scene from the same distance. (Shooting Television News: The Basics)

Phoner   A telephone interview either recorded or broadcast live as part of a radio or television report. (Live Shots and Remotes)

Photojournalist   An individual who uses or relies on the camera not merely to take pictures, but to tell stories. (Telling the Visual Story)

Pickup Shot   Any shot—such as a close-up or insert shot, reaction shot, point of view, or even a new camera angle—that emphasizes particular elements of action in the master shot. See also "Cut-In Shot." (The Visual Grammar of Motion Picture Photography)

PIO   See "Public Information Officer."

Point of View (POV) Shot   The view as seen through the subject's eyes. (The Visual Grammar of Motion Picture Photography; Video Editing: The Invisible Art)

Pool Coverage   An effort to minimize distraction by which information or television signals generated by one news agency are made available to all interested stations. (Law and the Digital Journalist)

Pop Cut   The visual "pop" or jump created when the zoom lens is used to shoot a long shot of a subject from a distance, followed immediately by a cut to a close-up from the same camera taken without having moved the camera off the original axis line. (Video Editing: The Invisible Art; Shooting Video in the Field)

Public Information Officer (PIO)   A police, fire, sheriff, or similar agency person who coordinates news coverage and access to news events, provides information, and helps arrange access to official sources during emergencies. (Live Shots and Remotes)

Rack Focus   Rotating the lens focus ring to shift the focus point from one subject to another while a shot is being recorded. (Shooting Television News: The Basics)

Radio frequency   The means through which audio and some video signals are transmitted. (The Sound Track)

Reaction Shot   A shot that shows a subject's reaction to an action in the previous shot. (The Visual Grammar of Motion Picture Photography; Video Editing: The Invisible Art)

Reader   A few well-written lines providing an overview of a story. (Video Script Formats)

Reestablishing Shot   A shot similar to the original establishing shot of an overall scene. Used to reintroduce locale or to allow the introduction of new action. (The Visual Grammar of Motion Picture Photography)

Remote   A news report originating live from a remote field location using a telephone, skype connection, portable radio transmitter, microwave relay facility, or satellite truck. (Live Shots and Remotes)

Reportorial Editing   The process of previsualizing the story, including the pictures, sounds, words, and other production elements that will be needed to give the story logical structure and continuity; a form of mind's-eye storyboard. (Telling the Visual Story)

Reveal Shot   See "Transition Shot." (The Visual Grammar of Motion Picture Photography)

Reverse-Angle Shot   A shot made by moving the camera so that it shoots back along the axis line as originally established in the first shot. (The Visual Grammar of Motion Picture Photography)

Room Tone   The ambient sound peculiar to each separate environment that is inserted during editing to prevent sound dropouts. (The Sound Track)

RTNDA   Radio-Television News Directors Association. (Journalistic Ethics)

Rule of Thirds   An approach to photographic composition in which the viewfinder is mentally divided into thirds both horizontally and vertically. Subjects are placed at points within the viewfinder where the lines can be imagined to intersect. (The Visual Grammar of Motion Picture Photography)

Scanner   A radio receiver that constantly monitors crosstalk on police, fire, aviation, Coast Guard, military, competitors, and similar noncommercial broadcast frequencies. Scanners help alert journalists to breaking news. (Live Shots and Remotes)

Screen Space   The space that surrounds subjects in the frame, including headroom, gaps between people, and the space into which subjects move. Improper use of screen space results in visual imbalance. (The Visual Grammar of Motion Picture Photography)

Sequence   A series of related shots of an activity in which continuing action flows smoothly from one shot to the next to create the illusion of an uninterrupted event. (Telling the Visual Story; The Visual Grammar of Motion Picture Photography)

Sequential Video   Video that produces a continuous, uninterrupted flow of action that tells a story and communicates a sense of experience. (How to Improve Your Storytelling Ability)

Shallow Depth of Field   Only a narrow area of depth within the scene appears to be in focus, as when a foreground object is reproduced in razor-crisp focus but the background is blurred. (Shooting Television News: The Basics)

Shield Law   A law that protects journalists from having to disclose the identities of confidential sources. (Law and the Digital Journalist)

Short Lighting   The lighting pattern that results when the fill light shines on the side of the subject's face closest to camera. (Writing with Light)

Shot   The single, continuous take of material that is recorded each time the camera is turned on until it is turned off. (The Visual Grammar of Motion Picture Photography)

Shotgun Microphone   A long, cylindrical microphone with a pickup pattern similar to a telephoto lens that picks up sound from as far away as thirty feet or more. (The Sound Track)

Situational Ethics   Deciding story coverage because of the good that will likely result. Situational ethics is sometimes used to justify unethical journalistic practices, and may help or harm the story subject and/or journalist. (Journalistic Ethics)

Slander   The defamation of a person made orally, as opposed to in writing. Generally, a broadcast organization would not be charged with slander but rather with libel (i.e., written defamation), especially whenever the broadcast originates from a written script or notes. (Law and the Digital Journalist)

Snap Zoom   A shot in which the photographer snaps the zoom lever, instantly zooming in or out to a different composition of an action. When the few frames of the snap zoom are eliminated during editing, two separate shots result. (The Visual Grammar of Motion Picture Photography)

SNG   Satellite news gathering.

Soft Focus   A scene, or an area within the scene, appears to be out of focus. (Shooting Television News: The Basics)

Solo journalist   A person who works alone to report, write, shoot, and edit video reports and stories, whether for news, the web, or any other platform or field of employment. (Introduction, Video Journalism: Storytelling on Your Own)

Solo video reporter   A person who works alone to report, write, shoot, and edit video reports and stories, whether for news, the web, or any other platform or field of employment. (Introduction, Video Journalism: Storytelling on Your Own)

SOT   Sound on tape, a standard reference to a sound bite. (Video Script Formats; Live Shots and Remotes)

Sound Bite   A short excerpt from an interview, public statement, or spontaneous comment that normally is aired as part of a broadcast news story. (Telling the Visual Story)

Specular Light   The effect created when direct light rays throw strong highlights and distinct shadows. (Writing with Light)

Split-Focus Presentation   The practice of a reporter dividing attention between the anchor and the audience (via camera) during on-set interaction with the anchor. (Improving Performance in Field Reporting—Appendix B)

Spot News   Hard news events, such as fires, explosions, airline crashes, hurricanes, and tornadoes, that break suddenly and without warning. A hallmark of many spot-news events is their unpredictability. (Telling the Visual Story; Writing the Package; How to Improve Your Storytelling Ability; Live Shots and Remotes)

Staging   The practice of asking people to do on camera what they normally don't do in real life, or directing people to engage in activities that are out of character. (The Visual Grammar of Motion Picture Photography; Shooting Video in the Field)

Standup   A reporter in the field delivers one or more sentences of dialogue while appearing on camera. (Telling the Visual Story; Writing the Package; Live Shots and Remotes; Improving Performance in Field Reporting—Appendix B)

Storyboard   A drawing, still photograph, or the reproduction of a single frame of video that represents one scene or sequence in a video story. Similar to cartoon panels, storyboards also can be hand-drawn, computer-generated, or reproduced as photographs from still slides or film. (Telling the Visual Story; Writing the Package)

Subjective Camera   Action is portrayed as the subject would see it. See also "Point of View Shot." (The Visual Grammar of Motion Picture Photography)

Subpoena   A court order to produce documents or other information, including on-air video, a reporter's notes, or perhaps even the names of sources. (Law and the Digital Journalist)

Talking Head   Any interview or sound bite; often, a tedious or boring interview or sound bite. (The Video Interview: Shooting the Quotation Marks; How to Improve Your Storytelling Ability)

Telephoto Lens   Lens greater than the focal length required to yield normal perspective. (Shooting Television News: The Basics)

Thumb Sucker   A live television report that consists solely of a reporter talking on camera from a remote location, without supporting video or prerecorded interviews. *See also* "Blue Eye" and "Naked Live." (Live Shots and Remotes)

Tilt Shot   The vertical equivalent of a pan shot in which the camera tilts up or down to reveal new action or subject matter. (The Visual Grammar of Motion Picture Photography)

Toss   The introduction and hand-off from studio anchor to a reporter live in the field. When the report ends, the reporter hands off or "tosses" back to the studio anchor. (Video Script Formats; Live Shots and Remotes)

Tracking Shot   Camera is moved physically through space to keep moving subjects in frame. Sometimes referred to as a "dolly shot." (The Visual Grammar of Motion Picture Photography)

Transition Shot   A shot that transfers the viewer's attention from the end of one sequence to the start of another (a close shot of a ship's whistle serves as the transition shot from scenes at a fish market along the wharf to shots of canning operations aboard a fishing ship, for example). Also called a "reveal shot." (The Visual Grammar of Motion Picture Photography; Video Editing: The Invisible Art)

Trespass   The illegal entry onto another's land, property, or premises. Also, the unlawful injury to a person, or to a person's rights or property. (Law and the Digital Journalist)

Trucking Shot   Camera moves through space past fixed objects. (The Visual Grammar of Motion Picture Photography)

T/Stop   A lens aperture setting somewhat equivalent to an f/stop, but which takes into account the various light-absorbing properties of the lens. (Shooting Television News: The Basics)

TV Cutoff   The phenomenon by which home television receivers, whether because of their design or faulty adjustment, clip off the edges of the transmitted video image. (The Visual Grammar of Motion Picture Photography)

Two Shot   A shot that shows two people in the frame. (The Visual Grammar of Motion Picture Photography; Live Shots and Remotes)

Umbrella Lighting   A soft, indirect form of light created by shining artificial light into a metallic-colored, heat-resistant umbrella. (Writing with Light)

Unidirectional   A microphone pickup pattern in which only sound in front of the mike is picked up. (The Sound Track)

VCR   Videocassette recorder. (Shooting Television News: The Basics)

Video journalist   A person who works alone to report, write, shoot, and edit video reports and stories, whether for news, the web, or any other platform or field of employment. (Introduction, Video Journalism: Storytelling on Your Own)

Video reporter   A person who works alone to report, write, shoot, and edit video reports and stories, whether for news, the web, or any other platform or field of employment. (Introduction, Video Journalism: Storytelling on Your Own)

Visual Essayist   A photojournalist, whether photographer or reporter, who incorporates all the writing instruments of television—words, camera, microphone, and edit console—to tell compelling visual stories. (Preface)

Visual Grammar   The rules that govern the visual reconstruction of events, including the raw material shot and recorded in the field and the process of editing the material for broadcast. (The Visual Grammar of Motion Picture Photography)

Visual storyteller   A person who works alone to report, write, shoot, and edit video reports and stories, whether for news, the web, or any other platform or field of employment. (Introduction, Video Journalism: Storytelling on Your Own)

Voice Over (VO)   Voice-over narration. The reporter's voice can be heard "over" the pictures on the screen. (Television Scripts Format)

Wallpaper Video   Pictures with little meaning but whose subject matter is close enough to illustrate the reporter's script. *See also* "Eyewash" and "Generic Video." (Introduction)

White Balance   The adjustment of camera circuitry to reproduce pure whites under the light source at hand; the absence of color "at white." (Shooting Television News: The Basics)

White Light   The quality that occurs when a subject is natural, unaffected, and emotionally transparent while on camera. (Shooting Video in the Field)

White Space   Pauses in voice-over narration that allow compelling pictures and sounds to involve the viewer more directly in the story. (Telling the Visual Story; Video Editing: The Invisible Art)

Wide-Angle Lens   A lens whose focal length produces a wider angle of view than a normal perspective lens. (Shooting Television News: The Basics)

Wild Sound   Natural sounds from an environment that help communicate a sense of experience and often heighten the listeners' or viewers' sense of realism. (Telling the Visual Story)

Windscreen   A foam or metallic mesh microphone shield that reduces wind noise. (The Sound Track)

Wipe   An optical effect in which one shot appears to be shoved off the screen by an incoming shot. (The Visual Grammar of Motion Picture Photography; Video Editing: The Invisible Art)

World Wide Web (WWW)   An information system that gives users on computer networks access to a large universe of documents and variety of media. *See also* "Internet," which refers to the global network of cables and computers that allow access to the WWW.

Zoom Shot   A shot produced from a fixed location with a continuously variable focal-length lens. When the lens is said to "zoom in," the subject appears to grow larger and move closer to the screen. When the lens is said to "zoom out," the subject appears to grow smaller and move away from the screen. (The Visual Grammar of Motion Picture Photography; Shooting Video in the Field)

Zoom Lens   A lens that provides for continuously variable focal-length settings from wide angle to telephoto, such as 12–120 mm or 25–250 mm. (Shooting Television News: The Basics)

CREDITS

INDEX